EPISTEMOLOGY

A contemporary introduction to the theory of knowledge

Robert Audi

London and New York

To Malou

First published in 1998
by Routledge
11 New Fetter Lane, London EC4P 4EE

Simultaneously published in the USA and Canada
by Routledge
29 West 35th Street, New York, NY 10001

© 1998 Robert Audi

Typeset in Aldus by RefineCatch Limited, Bungay, Suffolk

Printed and bound in Great Britain by
Clays Ltd, St Ives plc

British Library Cataloguing in Publication Data
A catalogue record for this book is available from the British Library

Library of Congress Cataloging-in-Publication Data
Audi, Robert
Epistemology: a contemporary introduction to the theory of
knowledge / Robert Audi.
(Routledge contemporary introductions to philosophy; 2)
Includes bibliographical references and index.
1. Knowledge, Theory of. I. Title. II. Series.
BD161.A783 1998
121—dc21 97–11598
CIP

ISBN 0–415–13042–5 (hbk)
0–415–13043–3 (pbk)

Contents

Part Three: The nature and scope of justification and knowledge   211

Chapter 8: The Analysis of Knowledge   213

Chapter 9: Scientific, moral, and religious knowledge   249

Chapter 10: Skepticism   281

Conclusion   317

Short annotated bibliography of books in epistemology   325

Index   335

Preface

This book is a wide-ranging introduction to epistemology, conceived as the theory of knowledge and justification. It presupposes no special background in philosophy and is meant to be fully understandable to any generally educated, careful reader, but for students it is most appropriately studied after completing at least one more general course in philosophy.

The main focus is the body of concepts, theories, and problems central in understanding knowledge and justification. Historically, justification – sometimes under such names as 'reason to believe', 'evidence', and 'warrant' – has been as important in epistemology as knowledge itself. This is surely so at present. In many parts of the book, justification and knowledge are discussed separately; but they are also interconnected at many points. The book is not historically organized, but it does discuss selected major positions in the history of philosophy, particularly some of those that have greatly influenced human thought. Moreover, even where major philosophers are not mentioned, I try to take their views into account. One of my primary aims is to facilitate the reading of those philosophers, especially their epistemological writings. It would take a very long book to discuss representative contemporary epistemologists or, in any detail, even a few historically important epistemologies, but a shorter one can provide many of the tools needed to understand them. Providing such tools is one of my main purposes.

The use of this book in the study of philosophy is not limited to courses or investigations in epistemology. Epistemological problems and theories are often interconnected with problems and theories in the philosophy of mind; nor are these two fields of philosophy easily separated (a point that may hold, if to a lesser extent, for any two central philosophical fields). There is, then, much discussion of the topics in the philosophy of mind that are crucial for epistemology, for instance the phenomenology of perception, the nature of belief, the role of imagery in memory and introspection, the variety of mental properties figuring in self-knowledge, the nature of inference, and the structure of a person's system of beliefs.

Parts of the book might serve as collateral reading not only in pursuing the philosophy of mind but also in the study of a number of philosophers often discussed in philosophy courses, especially Plato, Aristotle, Aquinas, Descartes, Leibniz, Locke, Berkeley, Hume, Kant, and Mill. The book might facilitate the study of moral philosophy, such as Kantian and utilitarian ethics, both discussed in some detail in Chapter 9; and it bears directly on topics in the epistemology of religion, some of which are also discussed in Chapter 9.

The writing is intended to be as simple and concrete as possible for a philosophically serious introduction that does not seek simplicity at the cost of falsehood. The territory surveyed, however, is extensive and rich. This means that the book cannot be traversed quickly without missing landmarks or failing to get a view of the larger segments and their place in the whole. Any one chapter can perhaps be read at a sitting, but experience has shown that even the shortest chapter covers too many concepts and positions for most readers to assimilate in a single reading and far more than most instructors can cover in any detail in a single session.

To aid concentration on the main points, and to keep the book from becoming more complicated, notes are limited, though parenthetical references are given in some places and there is also a short selected bibliography with thumbnail annotations. By and large, the notes are not needed for full comprehension and are intended mainly for professional philosophers and serious students. There are also some subsections that most readers can probably scan, or even skip, without significant loss in comprehending the *main* points of the relevant chapter. Technical terms are explained briefly when introduced and are avoided when they can be. Most of the major terms central in epistemology are defined or explicated, and boldfaced numbers in the index indicate main definitional passages. But some are indispensable: they are not mere words, but tools; and some of these terms express concepts valuable outside epistemology and even outside philosophy. The index, by its boldfaced page references to definitions, obviates a glossary.

It should also be stressed that this book is mainly concerned to introduce the *field* of epistemology rather than the *literature* of epistemology – an important but less basic task. It will, however, help non-professional readers prepare for a critical study of that literature, contemporary as well as classical. For that reason, too, some special vocabulary is introduced and a number of the notes refer to contemporary works.

The sequence of topics is designed to introduce the field in a natural progression: from the genesis of justification and knowledge (Part One), to their development and structure (Part Two), and thence to questions about what they are and how far they extend (Part Three). Even apart from its place in this ordering, each chapter addresses a major epistemological topic, and any subset of the chapters can be studied in any order provided some appropriate effort is made to supply the (generally few) essential points for which a later chapter depends on an earlier one.

For the most part this book *does* epistemology rather than talk about it or, especially, about its literature. In keeping with that focus, the ordering of chapters is intended to encourage *understanding* epistemology before discussing it in large-scale terms, for instance before considering what sort of epistemological theory, say normativist or naturalistic, best accounts for knowledge. My strategy is, in part, to discuss myriad cases of justification and knowledge before approaching analyses of what they are, or the skeptical case against our having them.

In one way, this approach differs markedly from that of many epistemological books. I leave the assessment of skepticism for the last chapter; early passages indicate that skeptical problems must be faced and, in some cases, how they are connected with the subject at hand or are otherwise important. Unlike some philosophers, I do not think extensive discussion of skepticism is the best way to motivate the study of epistemology. Granted, historically skepticism has been a major motivating force; but it is not the only one, and epistemological concepts hold independent interest. Moreover, in assessing skepticism I use many concepts and points developed in earlier chapters; to treat it early in the book, I would have to delay assessing it.

There is also a certain risk in posing skeptical problems at or near the outset: non-professional readers may tend to be distracted, even in discussing conceptual questions concerning, say, what knowledge *is*, by a desire to deal with skeptical arguments purporting to show that there is none. There may be no best or wholly neutral way to treat skepticism, but I believe my approach to it can be adapted to varying degrees of skeptical inclination. An instructor who prefers to begin with skepticism can do so by taking care to explain some of the ideas introduced earlier in the book. The first few sections of Chapter 10, largely meant to introduce and motivate skepticism, presuppose far less of the earlier chapters than the later, evaluative discussion; and most of the chapter is understandable on the basis of Part One, which is probably easier reading than Part Two.

My exposition of problems and positions is meant to be as nearly unbiased as I can make it, and where controversial interpretations are unavoidable I try to present them tentatively. In many places, however, I offer my own view. Given the scope of the book, I cannot provide a highly detailed explanation of each major position discussed, or argue at length for my own views. I make no pretense of treating anything conclusively. But in some cases – as with skepticism – I do not want to leave the reader wondering where I stand, or perhaps doubting that there is any solution to the problem at hand. I thus propose some tentative positions for critical discussion.

Acknowledgments

This book has profited from my reading of many articles and books by contemporary philosophers, and from many discussions I have had with them
and, of course, with my students. I cannot mention all of these philosophers,
and I am sure that my debt to those I will name – as well as to some I do not,
such as some whose journal papers I have read but have not picked up again,
and some I have heard at conferences – is incalculable. Over many years, I have
benefited greatly from discussions with William Alston, as well as from reading his works; and I thank him for detailed critical comments on parts of the
manuscript. Reading of books or articles (or both) by Roderick Chisholm,
Richard Foley, Paul Moser, Alvin Plantinga, Walter Sinnott-Armstrong, and
Ernest Sosa, and a number of discussions with them, have also substantially
helped me over many years. My colleagues at the University of Nebraska,
especially Albert Casullo, and several of my students have also helped me at
many points. I have learned greatly from the participants in the National
Endowment for the Humanities seminars and institutes I have directed. I also
benefited much from the papers given to the seminars or institutes by (among
others) Laurence BonJour, Fred Dretske, Alvin Goldman, Gilbert Harman,
Keith Lehrer, Ruth Marcus, and John Perry, with all of whom I have been
fruitfully discussing epistemological topics on one occasion or another for
many years.

In relation to some of the main problems treated in the book, I have learned
immensely from many other philosophers, including Frederick Adams, Robert
Almeder, David Armstrong, John A. Barker, Richard Brandt, Panayot Butch-
varov, Carol Caraway, the late Hector-Neri Castañeda, Wayne Davis, Michael
DePaul, Susan Feagin, Richard Feldman, Roderick Firth, Richard Fumerton,
Carl Ginet, Alan Goldman, Risto Hilpinen, Jaegwon Kim, John King-Farlow,
Peter Klein, Hilary Kornblith, Christopher Kulp, Jonathan Kvanvig, Brian
McLaughlin, George S. Pappas, John Pollock, Lawrence Powers, W. V. Quine,

William Rowe, Bruce Russell, Frederick Schmitt, Thomas Senor, Robert Shope, Donna Summerfield, Marshall Swain, William Throop, Raimo Tuomela, James Van Cleve, Thomas Vinci, Jonathan Vogel, and Nicholas Wolterstorff. In most cases I have not only read some epistemological work of theirs, but discussed one or another epistemological problem with them in detail.

Other philosophers whose comments or works have helped me with some part of the book include Anthony Brueckner, Stewart Cohen, Earl Conee, Dan Crawford, Jonathan Dancy, Timothy Day, Robert Fogelin, Elizabeth Fricker, Bernard Gert, Heather Gert, David Henderson, Terence Horgan, Dale Jacquette, Eric Kraemer, Noah Lemos, Kevin Possin, Dana Radcliffe, Nicholas Rescher, Stefan Sencerz, James Taylor, Paul Tidman, Mark Timmons, William Tolhurst, Mark Webb, Douglas Weber, Ümit Yalçin, and Patrick Yarnell.

I owe special thanks to the philosophers who generously commented in detail on all or most of some version of the manuscript: John Greco, Louis Pojman, and Matthias Steup. Their numerous remarks led to many improvements. Detailed helpful comments were also provided by readers for the Press, including Nicholas Everett, Frank Jackson, and Noah Lemos. All of the philosophers who commented on an earlier draft not only helped me eliminate errors, but also gave me constructive suggestions and critical remarks that evoked both clarification and other improvements. I am also grateful for permission to reuse much material that appears here in revised form from my *Belief, Justification, and Knowledge* (Wadsworth Publishing Co., 1988) and I thank the editor of *American Philosophical Quarterly* for allowing me to use material from 'The Place of Testimony in the Fabric of Knowledge and Justification' (vol. 34, 1997). For advice and help at several stages I thank Paul Moser, Editor of the series in which this book appears, and Adrian Driscoll and the staff at Routledge in London, including Moira Taylor and Sarah Hall, and Dennis Hodgson.

Robert Audi
February, 1997

Introduction

Before me is the tree-lined shore of a mountain lake. The trees seem to move slightly as I am carried by the cool blue waters surrounding me. A brisk wind chills my head. Suddenly, I hear a car passing. I open my eyes and realize that I have been dreaming. I have nodded off while reading. What is actually before me is the front lawn, the road, and, beyond that, a grassy green field. It has a line of trees at its far edge and is punctuated by a spruce on its left side and a maple on its right. Birds are singing. A warm breeze brings the smell of roses from a nearby trellis. I sit up, adjust the book in front of me, and reach for a tall glass of iced tea, still cold to the touch and flavored by fresh mint. I am alert now, the air is clear, the scene is quiet. My perceptions are quite distinct.

It is altogether natural to think that from perceptions like these we come to know a great deal – enough to guide us through many of the typical activities of human life. But we sometimes make mistakes about what we perceive, just as we sometimes misremember what we have done or infer false conclusions from what we believe. We may then think we know something when in fact we do not, as where we make errors through inattention or through being deceived by vivid dreams. It also seems possible that such vivid dreams as I have just described occur more often than we think.

Philosophers have given a great deal of thought to these matters, especially to the nature of perceiving and to what we can know – or mistakenly think we know – through perception or through other sources of knowledge, such as memory as a storehouse of what we have learned in the past, introspection as a way to know our inner lives, reflection as a way to acquire knowledge of abstract matters, or testimony as a source of knowledge originally acquired by others. In approaching these central topics in epistemology – which may be conceived as the theory of knowledge and justification – it is appropriate to begin with perception. In my opening recollection, what I described is of two main kinds. There was what I merely dreamt and what I *perceived*: what I saw, heard, smelled, felt, and tasted. In describing my experience, I also expressed some of what I *believed*: not what I merely dreamt to be so, which I did not believe, but rather that there was a green field before me, that there were bird songs in the air, that there was a smell of roses, that my glass was cold to the touch, and that the tea tasted of mint.

It seems altogether natural to believe these things given the kind of experi-ence I had, and I think I *justifiedly* believed them. I believed them not in the way I would if they resulted from my making a sheer guess, but with justification. By that I mean above all that the beliefs I refer to were *justified*. I count this a good thing; justified beliefs are reasonable ones to hold and indeed have a positive status from the point of view of representing a rational creature's outlook on the world.

Being justified, in the sense illustrated by my beliefs about what is clearly before me, is not a process. It is not, for instance, like being purified, which requires a process of purification. These beliefs are not justified because they have been through *a process of being justified*, as where one defends a controversial belief by giving reasons for it. They have not; the question whether they are justified has not even come up. No one has challenged them, or even asked me why I hold them. They are justified because there is something about them in virtue of which they are natural and appropriate for me as a normal rational person. Unlike believing something I might arrive at through a wild guess in charades, these beliefs are justified, and thereby appropriate for me, simply through their arising in the normal way they have from my clear perceptions. Roughly, they are justified in the sense that they are quite in order from the point of view of the standards for what I may reasonably believe. They are also a kind of belief that we tend to expect to be true.

In saying that I justifiedly believe there is a green field before me, I am implying something else, something that is quite different, though it sounds very similar, namely, that I am *justified in believing* there is a green field before me. To see the difference, notice that I could be justified *in* believing something without believing it at all, quite as one can be justified in doing something, such as buying a new toaster, without doing it. Thus, I might be justified in believing that I can do a certain difficult task, yet fail to believe this until someone helps me overcome my hesitation.

Being justified in believing something is a matter of having justification *for* believing it. This, in turn, is roughly a matter of having reason to believe it (and we sometimes speak of having *a* justification or *a* reason). Just as we can have reason to do things we do not do, we can have reason to believe things we do not believe. I can have reason to go to the library and forget to, and I can have reason to believe someone is making excuses for me but – because I have no inkling that I need any – fail to believe this. Our justification for believing is basic raw material for actual justified belief, which, in turn, is commonly a good raw material for knowledge.

The two justificational notions are intimately related: if one justifiedly believes something, one is also justified *in* believing it (hence has justification for believing it). But, as our example of the unnoticed excuses shows, the converse does not hold: not everything we are justified in believing is something we do believe. We have more justificational raw material than we use. There are indeed many things we are justified in believing which we do not actually believe, such as the proposition that normal people do not drink 100 gallons of water a day. Let us call the first kind of justification – justifiedly believing – *belief justification*, since it belongs to actual beliefs (it is also called *doxastic* justification, from the Greek *doxa*, translatable as 'belief'). Call the second kind – being justified in believing – *situational justification*, since it is based on the informational situation one is in. This situation includes not just what one perceives, but also one's background beliefs and knowledge at the time, such as the belief that people drink at most a few quarts of water a day.

In any ordinary situation in waking life, we have both a lot of general information stored in memory and much specific information presented in our perceptions. We do not need all this information, and our situational justification for believing something may or may not be accompanied by our having an actual justified belief that it is so. We tend to have situational justification for vastly more justified beliefs than we actually have – or need. In this way, nature is very generous. In forming beliefs, we can often draw on far more information than we normally need to use.

Without situational justification, such as the kind arising from seeing a green field, there would be no belief justification. I would not, for instance, justifiedly believe that there is a green field before me. We cannot have a justified belief without being in a *position* to have it. But without belief justification, we would have no beliefs of a kind we want and need, those with a positive status – being justified – that makes them appropriate for us to hold as rational creatures. Belief justification, then, is more than the situational kind it rests on.

Belief justification occurs when there is a certain kind of connection between what yields situational justification and the justified belief that benefits from it. The former occurs, we might say, when a belief is *grounded in*, and thus in a way supported by, something that gives one situational justification for that belief, such as seeing a green field. Seeing is of course perceiving; and perceiving is a basic source of knowledge – perhaps our most elemental source, at least in childhood. This is largely why perception is so large a topic in epistemology and such a natural subject with which to begin a book on knowledge and justification, as I do here.

Knowledge would not be possible without belief justification (or something very much like it). If I did not have the kind of justified belief I do – if, for instance, I were wearing dark sunglasses and could not tell the difference between a green field and a smoothly ploughed one that is really an earthen brown – then on the basis of what I now see, I would not know that there is a green field before me.

To see how knowledge fits into the picture so far sketched, consider two points. First, justified belief is important for knowledge because at least the typical things we know we also justifiedly believe. If I know someone is making excuses for me, say by the way she explains why I was late, I do not

just believe this but justifiedly believe it. Second, much of what we justifiedly believe we also know. Surely I could have maintained, regarding each
of the things I have said I justifiedly believed through perception, that I also
knew it. And do I not know these things – say that there is a lawn before me
and a car on the road beyond it – on the *same* basis on which I justifiedly
believe them, for instance on the basis of what I see and hear? This is very
plausible.

As closely associated as knowledge and justified belief are, there is a major
difference. If I know that something is so, then, of course, it is *true*, whereas I
can justifiedly believe something that is false. If a normally reliable friend
decided to trick me into believing something false, say that he has just lost my
car keys, I could justifiedly believe that he has lost them even if it were not
true. We may not assume, then, that everything we learn about justified belief
applies to knowledge. We should look at both concepts independently to discern their differences, and we should consider them together to appreciate
their relationship.

I said that I *saw* the green field and that my belief that there was a green
field before me arose from my seeing it. If the belief arose, in the normal way,
from my seeing the field (if I believed it is there simply because I saw it there),
then the belief was true, justified, and constituted knowledge. Again, however,
we can alter the example to bring out how knowledge and justification may
diverge: the belief might remain justified even if, unbeknownst to me, the
grass had been burned up since I last saw it, and there were now a perfect
artificial replica of it spread out there in grassy-looking strips of cloth (perhaps
the owners refuse to look at the ugly charred ground). Then, although I might
think I know the green field is there, I would only falsely believe I know
this. Such a bizarre happening is, to be sure, extremely improbable. But it is
certainly possible that a justified but false belief could arise in this way.

We can, moreover, be mistaken in just this way: deceived by our senses. One
might now wonder, as skeptics do, whether I *know* even that it is improbable
that I am now deceived by my senses. One might also wonder whether I am
even justified in my belief that no such mistake has occurred.

Suppose that I am in a public park in an unfamiliar city. I do not know or
even justifiedly believe that artificial grass has not been put in place of the
natural grass I take to be before me. (I may have heard of such substitutions
and may have no good reason to believe this has not happened, though I do not
consider the matter.) In that case, am I justified in believing that there is a
green field before me? Suppose that I am not. If I am not justified in believing
this, how can I be justified in believing what appear to be far less obvious
truths, such as that my house is secure against the elements, my car safe to
drive, and my food free of poisons? And how can I know the many things I
need to know in life, such as that my family and friends are trustworthy, that I
can control my behavior and can thus partly determine my future, and that the

world we live in at least approximates the structured reality portrayed by common sense and science?

These are difficult and important questions. They indicate how insecure and disordered human life would be if we could not suppose that we possess justified beliefs and knowledge. We stake our lives every day on what we take ourselves to know; it would be unsettling to revise this stance and retreat to the view that at best we have justification to believe. But if we had to give even this view up and to conclude, say, that what we believe is not even justified, we would face a crisis. Much later, in discussing skepticism, I want to explore such questions at some length. Until then I will assume the commonsense view that beliefs with a basis like that of my belief that there is a green field before me are not only justified but also constitute knowledge.

Once we proceed on this commonsense assumption, it is easy to see that there are many different kinds of circumstances in which beliefs arise in such a way that they are apparently both justified and constitute knowledge. In considering this variety of circumstances giving rise to justification and knowledge, we can explore how beliefs are related to perception, memory, consciousness, reason, and the testimony of others (the topics of Chapters 1 to 5, respectively).

As I look at the field before me, I *remember* carefully cutting a poison ivy vine from the trunk of the spruce. Surely, my *memory belief* that I cut off this vine is justified. I believe I also know that I did this. But here I confess to being less confident than I am of the justification of my perceptual belief, held in the radiant sunlight, that there is (now) a green field before me.

As our memories become less vivid, we tend to be correspondingly less sure that our beliefs apparently based on them are justified. Still, I distinctly recall cutting the vine. The stem was furry; it was bonded to the tree trunk; the cutting was difficult and slightly wounded the tree. By contrast, I have no belief about whether I did this in the summer or in the fall. I *entertain* the proposition that it was in the summer; I *consider* whether it is true; but all I can do is *suspend judgment* on it. I thus neither believe it nor disbelieve it, and I do not try to force myself to resolve the question and judge the proposition either way.

As I think about cutting the vine, it occurs to me that as I recall that task, I am vividly imaging it. Here, I seem to be looking into my own consciousness, thus engaging in a kind of *introspection*. I can still see, in my mind's eye, the furry vine clinging to the tree, the ax, the sappy wound along the trunk where the vine was severed from it. I have turned my attention inward to my own imagery. The object of my attention, my own imaging of the scene, seems internal and present to my consciousness, though *its* object is external and long gone by. But clearly, I believe that I am imaging the vine; and there is no apparent reason to doubt that I justifiedly believe this and know that it is so. This is a simple case, then, of self-knowledge.

The season has been dry, and it now occurs to me that the roses will not flourish without a good deal of water. But this I do not believe simply on the basis of perception. I learned it from repeated *observation*. But if some knowledge comes in this way from our own experience of its subject matter, much knowledge also originates with others. Thus, I might also have learned from *testimony* how much water roses need, as I learned from what a friend once told me where on the stem one should clip off dead roses. I needed perception to *learn* these things about roses, and I need memory to *retain* them. But they are generalizations, and they do not arise from perception in the direct and apparently simple way my visual beliefs do, or emerge from memory in the way my beliefs about past events I witnessed do. Yet do I not still justifiedly believe that the roses will not flourish without water for their roots? The commonsense view is that I both justifiedly believe and know that the roses will not flourish without water, and that I can know this either through generalizing from my own observations or from testimony, or both.

I now look back at the field and am struck by how perfectly rectangular it looks. If it is perfectly rectangular, then the angles at its four corners are all ninety degrees. Here I believe something different in kind from the things cited so far: that if the field is rectangular, then the angles at its four corners are all ninety degrees. This is a geometrical belief. I do not hold this belief on the same sort of basis I have for the other things I have mentioned believing. My conception of geometry as applied to ideal lines and surfaces seems to be the crucial basis here. On that basis, my belief seems to be firmly justified and to constitute knowledge.

I notice that the spruce is taller than the maple, and that the maple is taller than the crab apple tree on the lawn closer by. I now realize that the spruce is taller than the crab apple. My underlying belief here is that if one thing is taller than a second and the second taller than a third, then the first is taller than the third. And, perhaps even more than the geometrical belief, this abstract belief seems to arise simply from my grasp of the concepts in question, above all the concept of one thing's being taller than another.

The main examples just given represent what philosophers call perceptual, memorial, introspective, inductive, and a priori beliefs. My belief that the glass is cold to the touch is *perceptual*, being based as it is on tactual perception. My belief that I cut the poison ivy vine from the spruce is *memorial*, since it is stored in my memory and held because of that fact. My belief that I am imagining a green field is called *introspective* because it is conceived as based on "looking within" (the etymological meaning of 'introspection'). My belief that the roses will not grow well without abundant water is called *inductive* because it is formed (and held) on the basis of a generalization from similar experiences with trees. Those experiences, apparently through my beliefs recording them, "lead into" the generalization about roses, to follow the etymological meaning of 'induction'; for instance, I remember that in numerous cases roses have faded when dry and eventually conclude that they need abundant water. Finally, consider my belief that if the spruce is taller than the maple and the maple is taller than the crab apple, then the spruce is taller than the crab apple. A belief like this is called *a priori* (meaning, roughly, based on what is prior to observational experience) because it apparently arises not from experience of how things actually behave but simply from a rational grasp of the key concepts one needs in order to have the belief, such as the concept of one thing's being taller than another.

Each of the four basic kinds of belief I have described is grounded in the source from which it arises, and the nature of this grounding is explored in detail in the first four chapters, concerning perception, memory, introspective consciousness, and reason. These sources are commonly taken to provide raw materials for inductive generalizations, as where observations and memories about roses yield a basis for generalizing about their needs. Any of the beliefs we considered could instead have been grounded in testimony (the topic of Chapter 5), had I formed the beliefs on the basis of being given the same information by someone I trust. That person, however, would presumably have acquired it through one of these other sources (or ultimately through someone's having done so), and this makes testimony a different kind of ground. But it is, if less basic, unlimitedly broad. It can, for instance, justify a much wider range of propositions than perception can. We can credibly tell others virtually anything we know.

Our examples illustrate not only grounding of beliefs *in* a source, such as perception or introspection, but also *ways* in which they are grounded in these sources. There are at least three important kinds of grounding of beliefs in their sources – causal, justificational, and epistemic grounding – and all three are important for many major epistemological questions. Consider my belief that there is a green field before me. It is *causally grounded* in my experience of seeing the field because that experience produces or underlies the belief. It is *justificationally grounded* in that experience because the experience, or at least some element in the experience, justifies my holding the belief. And it is *epistemically grounded* in the experience because in virtue of that experience my belief constitutes knowledge that there is a green field before me ('epistemic' comes from the Greek *episteme* meaning, roughly, 'knowledge'). These three kinds of grounding very often coincide, and I will thus usually speak simply of a belief as *grounded* in a source, such as visual experience, when what grounds the belief does so in all three ways.

Causal, justificational, and epistemic grounding each go with a very common kind of question about belief.

Causal grounding goes with 'Why do you believe that?' An answer to this question, asked about my belief that there is a green field before me, would be that I see it. This is the normal kind of reply; but as far as mere causal production of beliefs goes, the answer could be brain manipulation or mere hypnotic suggestion. If, however, mere brain manipulation or hypnotic suggestion produces a belief, then the causal ground of the belief would not justify it. If, under hypnosis, I am told that someone is angry with me and as a result come to believe this, the belief is not thereby justified.

Justificational grounding goes with such questions as 'What is your justification for believing that?' or 'What justifies you in believing that?' ('Why do you believe that?' can be asked with this same justification-seeking force.) Again, I might answer that I see it. I might, however, have a justification (the situational kind) that, unlike seeing the truth in question, is not a *cause* of my believing it. My justification could be the testimony of a credible good friend, even in the case where, by a short circuit, brain manipulation does the causal work of producing my belief and leaves the testimony like a board that slides just beneath a roof beam but bears none of its weight. An element that provides justification for a belief may play no role in producing or supporting the belief, even if this element stands ready to play a supporting role if the belief is put under pressure by a challenge.

Epistemic grounding goes with 'How do you know that?' Once again, saying that I see it will commonly answer the question. Here, however, it may be that a correct answer must cite omething that is *also* a causal and justificational ground for the belief (a matter we return to in Chapter 8).

Clearly the same sorts of points can be made for the other five cases I have described: memorial beliefs are grounded in memory; introspective beliefs in introspection (or "consciousness"); inductively based beliefs in further, premise-beliefs that rest on experience; a priori beliefs in reason; and testimonially based beliefs in testimony.

There is a great deal more to be said about each of these sources of belief, justification, and knowledge and about what it is for them to ground what they do ground. The first five chapters will explore, and in some cases compare, the most basic sources of belief, justification, and knowledge. In the light of what we find out in those chapters, we can go on to discuss the development and structure of knowledge and justification (the task of Part Two). Much of what we believe does not come directly from perception, memory, introspection, or reflection of the kind appropriate to knowledge of such truths as those of elementary mathematics or those turning on simple relations, for instance the proposition that if the spruce is taller than the maple, then the maple is shorter than the spruce. We must explore how inference and other developmental processes expand our body of knowledge and justified beliefs (this is the task of Chapter 6). Moreover, once we think of a person as having the resulting complex body of knowledge and justified belief, we encounter the questions of what structure that large and intricate body has, and of how its structure is related to the amount and kind of knowledge and justification it contains. As we shall see in Chapter 7, these structural questions take us into the area where epistemology and the philosophy of mind overlap.

On the basis of what Part One shows about sources of knowledge and justification and what Part Two shows about their development and structure, we can fruitfully proceed to consider more explicitly what knowledge and justification are and what kinds of things can be known (the task of Part Three). It is true that if we had no sense at all of what they are, we could not find the kinds of examples of them needed to explore their sources and their development and structure. On the other hand, if we do not have before us a wide range of examples of justification and knowledge, we lack the data appropriate to seeking a philosophically illuminating analysis of them. It is in the light of the examples and conclusions of Parts One and Two that Chapter 8 clarifies the concept of knowledge, and to a lesser extent, that of justification, in some detail.

With a conception of knowledge laid out, it is possible to explore the apparent extent of knowledge and justification in three major territories – the scientific, the ethical, and the religious. In exploring these domains, Chapter 9 in effect applies some of the epistemological results of the earlier chapters. If, however, skepticism is in the end the correct position, then the commonsense assessment that the first nine chapters make regarding the extent of knowledge and justification must be revised. Whether it is correct is the focus of Chapter 10.

Along the way in all ten chapters, there is much to be learned about concepts that are important both in and outside epistemology, especially those of belief, causation, certainty, coherence, explanation, fallibility, illusion, inference, introspection, intuition, meaning, memory, reasoning, relativity, reliability, and truth. There are also numerous epistemological positions to be considered, sometimes in connection with historically influential philosophers. But the main focus will be on the major concepts and problems in the field, not on any particular philosopher or epistemological text. This may well be the best way to facilitate studying philosophers and epistemological texts; it will certainly simplify an already complex task.

Knowledge and justification are not only interesting in their own right as central epistemological topics; they also represent positive values in the life of every reasonable person. For all of us, there is much we want to know. We also care whether we are justified in what we believe – and whether others are justified in what they tell us. The study of epistemology can help in this quest, even if it often does so indirectly. Well-developed concepts of knowledge and justification can play the role of ideals in human life: positively, we can try to achieve knowledge and justification in relation to subjects that concern us; negatively, we can refrain from forming beliefs where we think we lack justification, and we can avoid claiming knowledge where we think we can at best hypothesize. If we learn enough about knowledge and justification conceived philosophically, we can better search for them in matters that concern us and can better avoid the dangerous pitfalls that come from confusing mere impressions with justification or mere opinion with knowledge. The more we know about the constitution of knowledge and justification, the better we can build them through our own inquiries, and the less easily we will fall into the pervasive temptation to take an imitation to be the real thing.

PART ONE

Sources of justification, knowledge, and truth

CHAPTER 1
Perception

1
Perception

As I look at the green field before me, I might believe not only that there is a green field there but also that I *see* one. And I do see one. I visually perceive it, just as I tactually perceive the glass in my hand. Both beliefs, the belief that there is a green field there, and the self-referential belief that *I* see one, are grounded, causally, justificationally, and epistemically, in my visual experience. They are produced by that experience, justified by it, and constitute knowledge in virtue of it.

The same sort of thing holds for the other senses. Consider touch. I not only believe, through touch (as well as sight) that there is a glass, I also feel its coldness. Both beliefs – that there is a glass and that it is cold – are grounded in my tactual experience. I could believe any of these things on the basis of someone's testimony. My beliefs would then have a quite different status. For instance, my belief that there is a glass would not be *perceptual*, but only a belief *about a perceptible*, that is, about a perceivable object, the kind of thing that can be seen, touched, heard, smelled, or tasted. Through testimony we have beliefs about perceptibles we have never seen or experienced in any way.

Our concern, then, is not with the hodgepodge of beliefs that are simply about perceptibles, but with perception and perceptual beliefs. Perceptual beliefs are not simply those that are about perceptibles; they are those grounded in perception. We classify perceptual beliefs by the nature of their roots, not the color of their foliage. Those roots may be visual, auditory, and so forth for each perceptual mode. But vision and visual beliefs are an excellent basis for discussing perception and perceptual beliefs, and I will concentrate on them and mention the other senses only occasionally.

Perception is a source of knowledge and justification mainly by virtue of yielding beliefs that constitute knowledge or are justified. But we cannot hope to understand perceptual knowledge and justification simply by exploring those beliefs by themselves. We must also understand what perception is and how it yields beliefs. We can then begin to understand how it yields knowledge and justification or – in some cases – fails to yield them.

The elements and basic kinds
of perception

There are apparently at least four elements in perception, all evident in our example: (1) the perceiver, me; (2) the object, the field; (3) the sensory experience, my visual experience of colors and shapes; and (4) the relation between the object and the subject, commonly taken to be a causal relation by which the object seems to produce the sensory experience in the perceiver. To see the field is apparently to have a certain sensory experience as a result of the impact of the field on our vision.

Some accounts of perception add to the four items on this list; others subtract from it. To understand perception we must consider both kinds of account and how these elements are to be conceived in relation to one another. First, however, it is essential to explore various examples of perception.

There are three quite different ways to speak of perception. Each corresponds to a different way of perceptually responding to experience. We often speak simply of what people perceive, for instance of what they see. We also speak of what they perceive the object to be, and we commonly talk of what they perceive about it. Visual perception is the readiest kind to illustrate this, so let us start there.

I see, hence perceive, the green field. Second, speaking in a less familiar way, I see it *to be* a rectangular field. Thus, I might say that I know it looks different from that hill, but from the air one can see it to be perfectly rectangular. Third, I see that it is rectangular. Perception is common to all three cases. Seeing, which is a paradigm case of perception, is central in all of them.

The first case is one of *simple perception*, perception taken by itself (here, visual perception). I simply see the field, and this experience is the visual parallel of hearing a bird (an auditory experience), touching a glass (a tactual experience), smelling roses (an olfactory experience), and tasting mint (a gustatory experience). If the first case is simply *perceiving of* some object, the second is a case of *perceiving to be*, since it is seeing something to be so: I do not just see the field, as when I drive by at high speed; I see it to be rectangular. The third case is one of *perceiving that*, since it is seeing that a particular thing is so, namely, that the field is rectangular. These cases represent three kinds, or *modes*, of perception. Perception of the simplest kind (or in the simplest mode), such as seeing, occurs in all three; but, especially because of their relation to knowledge and justified belief, they are significantly different. We can best understand these three kinds (or modes) of perception if we first focus on their relation to belief.

Perceptual belief

The latter two cases – perceiving that, and perceiving to be – are different from the first – perceiving of – in implying corresponding kinds of beliefs: seeing that the field is rectangular implies believing that it is, and seeing it to be a green field implies believing it to be a green one. If we consider how both kinds of beliefs – beliefs *that* and beliefs *of* (or *about*) – are related to perception, we can begin to understand how perception occurs in all three cases, the simple and the more complex. In the second and third examples of perception I gave, my visual perception issues in beliefs that are then grounded in it and can thereby constitute visual knowledge.[1]

In the first example, that of simple perception, my just seeing the field provides a basis for both kinds of beliefs. It does this even if, because my mind is entirely occupied with what I am hearing on the radio as I glance over the field, no belief about the field actually arises in me. The visual experience is in this instance like a foundation that has nothing built on it but is ready to support a structure. If, for instance, someone were to ask if the field has shrubbery in it, then given the lilacs prominent in one place, I might immediately form the belief that it does and reply affirmatively. This belief is visually grounded; it comes *from* my seeing the field though it did not initially come *with* it. When beliefs do arise from visual experiences, as is usual, what kinds of beliefs are they, and how are they specifically perceptual?

Many of my beliefs arising through perception correspond to perception *that*, say to seeing that something is so. I believe that the field is lighter green toward its borders where it gets less sunlight, that it is rectangular in shape, and that it is larger than the lawn. But I may also have various beliefs about it that are of the second kind: they correspond to perception *to be*, for instance to seeing something to be a certain color. Thus, I believe the field to be green, to be symmetrical, to be rectangular, and so on. The difference between these two kinds of belief is significant. As we shall shortly see, it corresponds first of all to two distinct ways in which we are related to the objects we perceive and, secondly, to two different ways of assessing the truth of what, on the basis of our perceptions, we believe.

The first kind of belief just described is *propositional*, since it is a case of believing a proposition – say, *that* the field is rectangular. The belief is thus true or false depending on whether the proposition that the field is rectangular is true or false. In holding the belief, moreover, in some way I think of what I see as a field which is rectangular: in believing that the field is rectangular, I conceive what I take to be rectangular *as* a field.

The second kind of belief might be called *objectual*: it is a belief regarding an object, say the field, with which the belief is actually connected. This is an object *of* (or about) which I believe something, say that it is rectangular. If I believe the field to be rectangular, there really is such an object, and I have a certain relation to it. A special feature of this relation is that there is no particular proposition I must believe about the field. To see that there is no particular proposition, notice that in holding this objectual belief I need not think of what I see *as* a field, for I might mistakenly take it to be (for instance) a lawn or a huge canvas or a grasslike artificial turf, yet still believe it to be rectangular. I might think of it just in terms of what I believe it to be and not in terms of what it obviously is. Thus, although there is *some* property I must take it to have – corresponding to what I believe it to be – there is no other particular way I must think of it. There is, then, no particular notion that must yield the subject of any proposition I believe: I do not have to believe that the field is green, that the grass is, or any such thing. Perception leaves us vast latitude as to what we learn from it. People differ markedly in the beliefs they form about the very same things they each clearly see.[2]

The concept of objectual perception, then, is very permissive about what propositions one believes about the object perceived. This is one reason why it leaves so much space for imagination and learning – a space often filled by the formation of propositional beliefs, each capturing a different aspect of what is perceived, say that the field is richly green, that it is windblown, and that it ends at a line of trees. Take a different example. After seeing a distant flare and coming to believe, of something blurry and far away, that it glowed, one might ask, 'What on Earth was it that glowed?' Before we can believe the proposition that a flare glowed, we may have to think about where we are, the movement and fading of the glow, and so forth. The objectual belief provides a guide by which we may arrive at propositional beliefs and propositional knowledge.

Perception, conception, and belief

The same kind of example can be used to illustrate how belief depends on our conceptual resources in a way that perception does not. Suppose I had grown up in the desert and somehow failed to acquire the concept of a field. I could certainly still see the green field, and from a purely visual point of view it might look the same to me as it does now. I could also still believe, regarding the field I see – and perhaps conceive as sand artificially covered with something green – that it is rectangular. But I could not believe that the *field* is rectangular. This propositional belief as it were portrays what I see *as* a field in a way that requires my having a concept of one. If I believe that the field is rectangular, I should be able to say that it is and to know what I am talking about. But if I had no concept of a field, then in saying this I would not know what I am talking about.[3]

Similarly, a two-year-old, say Susie, who has no notion of a tachistoscope, can, upon seeing one and hearing it work, believe it to be making noise; but she cannot believe specifically that the tachistoscope is making noise. Her propositional belief, if any, would be, say, that the thing on the table is making noise. Since, this is true, what she believes is true and she may know this truth, but she need not know much about the object this truth concerns: in a way, she does not know what it is she has this true belief *about*.

The general lesson here is important. A basic way we learn about objects is to find out truths about them in this elementary way: we get a handle on them through perception; we form objectual (and other) beliefs about them from different perspectives; and (often) we finally reach an adequate concept of what they are. From the properties I believe the flare in the distance to have, I finally figure out that it is a flare that has them. As this suggests, there is at least one respect in which our knowledge of (perceptible) properties is more basic than our knowledge of the substances that have them.

Unlike propositional beliefs, objectual beliefs have a significant degree of indefiniteness and so are best not viewed as true without qualification; they are accurate or inaccurate, depending on whether what one believes of the object (such as that it is rectangular) is or is not *true of* it. Recall Susie. If she attributes noise-making to the tachistoscope, she truly believes, *of* it, that it is making noise. She is, then, *right about it*. But this holds even if she has no specific concept of what it is that is making the noise. If we say unqualifiedly that her belief about it is true, we invite the question 'What belief?' and the expectation that the answer will specify a particular proposition. But we can be right about something without knowing or even having any notion of what kind of thing it is that we are right about. Knowledge is often partial in this way. Still, once we get such an epistemic handle on something we can usually use that to learn more about it.[4]

Corresponding to the two kinds of beliefs I have described are two ways of talking about perception. I see *that* the field is rectangular. This is (visual) *propositional perception*: perceiving that. I also see it *to be* rectangular. This is (visual) *objectual perception*: perceiving to be. The same distinction apparently applies to hearing and touch. Perhaps, for example, I can hear that a piano is out of tune by hearing its sour notes, as opposed to hearing the tuner say it needs tuning. As for taste and smell, we speak as if they yielded only simple perception: we talk of smelling mint in the iced tea, but not of smelling that it is minty or smelling it to be minty. Such talk is, however, quite intelligible on the model of seeing that something is so or seeing it to be so, and we may thus take the distinction between perceiving *that* and perceiving *to be* to apply in principle to all the senses.

It is useful to think of perceptual beliefs as *embedded* in the corresponding propositional or objectual perception, roughly in the sense that they are integrally tied to perceiving of that kind and derive their character and authority from their perceptual grounding. Thus, my belief that the field is rectangular is embedded in my seeing that it is, and Susie's believing the tachistoscope to be making noise is embedded in her hearing it to be doing so. In each case, without the belief, there would not be perception of that kind. These kinds of perception might therefore be called *cognitive*, since belief is a cognitive attitude: roughly the kind that has a proposition (something true or false) as its object.[5] The object of the belief that the field is rectangular is the specific proposition that the field is rectangular, which is true or false; and the object of believing the tachistoscope to be making noise is some proposition or other to the effect that it is making noise, which (though left unspecified by the ascription of the belief) is also true or false. In this respect, belief is unlike attitudes of approval or admiration or indignation, which are evaluated as, say, appropriate or inappropriate rather than true or false.[6]

Both propositional and objectual beliefs are grounded in simple perception: if I do not see a thing at all, I do not see *that* it has any particular property and I do not see it *to be* anything. Depending on whether perceptual beliefs are embedded in propositional or objectual perception, they may differ in the kind of knowledge they give us. Propositional perception yields knowledge both of *what* it is that we perceive and of some *property* of it, for instance of the field's being rectangular. Objectual perception may, in special cases, give us knowledge only of a property of what we perceive, say that it is green, when we do not know what it is or have any belief as to what it is.

In objectual perception, we are, to be sure, in a good position to come to know *something* or other about the object, say that it is a green expanse. Objectual perception may thus give us information not only about objects of which we have a definite conception, such as familiar things in a home, but also about utterly unfamiliar, unconceptualized objects or about objects of which we have only a very general conception, say 'that noisy thing'. This is important. We could not learn as readily from perception if it gave us information only about objects we conceive in the specific ways in which we conceive most of the familiar things we see, hear, touch, taste, and smell.[7]

Seeing and believing

Both propositional and objectual perceptual beliefs are quite commonly grounded in perception in a way that apparently connects us with the real, outside world and assures their truth. For instance, my visual belief that the field is rectangular is so grounded in my seeing the field that I truly see that it is rectangular; my tactually believing the glass to be cold is so grounded in my feeling it that I truly feel it to be cold.

Admittedly, I might visually (or tactually) believe that something is rectangular under conditions poor for judging it, as where I view a straight stick half submerged in water (it would look bent whether it is or not). My visually grounded belief might then be mistaken. But such a mistaken belief is not *embedded* in propositional perception that the stick is bent – something one does not see is so (or to be so) – since it is false. The belief is merely produced by some element in the simple perception of the stick: I see the stick in the water, and the operation of reflected light causes me to have the illusion of a bent stick. I thus do not see that the stick is bent: my genuine perception is of it, but not of its curvature. Seeing that curvature or seeing that it is bent would entail that it *is* bent, which is false. If the stick is not bent, I cannot see that it is.

As this suggests, there is something special about both perceiving *that* and perceiving *to be*. They are *veridical experiences*, i.e. they imply truth. If I see that the field is rectangular, or even just see it to be rectangular, then it truly is rectangular. Thus, when I simply see the rectangularity of the field, if I acquire the corresponding embedded perceptual beliefs – if I believe that it is rectangular when I see that it is, or believe it to be rectangular when I see it to be – then I am correct in so believing.

If perceiving *that* and perceiving *to be* imply (truly) believing something about the object perceived, does simple perception – perception *of* something – which is required for either of these more complex kinds of perception, also imply true belief? Very commonly, simple perception does imply truly believing something about the object perceived. If I hear a car go by, I commonly believe a car is passing. But could I not hear it, but be so occupied with my reading that I form no belief about it? Let us explore this.

Perception as a source of potential beliefs

As is suggested by the case of perception overshadowed by preoccupation with reading, there is reason to doubt that simple perceiving *must* produce any belief at all. This may seem to fly in the face of the adage that seeing is believing. But properly understood, that may apply just to propositional or objectual seeing. In those cases perception plainly does produce beliefs. Seeing that golfball-size hail is falling is believing it.[8]

In any event, how could I see the field and believe nothing regarding it? Must I not see it to be something or other, say, green? And if so, would I not believe, of it, *something* that is true of it, even if only that it is a green object some distance away? Consider a different example.

Imagine that we are talking excitedly and a bird flies quickly across my path. Could I see it, yet form no beliefs about it? There may be no decisive answer. For one thing, while there is much we *can* confidently say about seeing and believing, 'seeing' and 'believing' are, like most philosophically interesting terms, not precise. No standard dictionary definition or authoritative statement can be expected either to tell us precisely what they mean or, especially, to settle every question about when they do and do not apply.[9] Still, we should be wary of concluding that vagueness makes any significant philosophical question unanswerable. How, then, should we answer the question whether seeing entails believing?

A negative response might be supported as follows. Suppose I merely see the bird but pay no attention to it because I am utterly intent on what we are discussing. Why must I form any belief about the bird? Granted, if someone later asks if I saw a blue bird, I may assent, thereby indicating a belief that the bird *was* blue. But this belief is not perceptual: it is about a perceptible and indeed has visual content, but it is not grounded in seeing or any other mode of perception. Moreover, it may have been formed only when I recalled my visual experience of the bird. Recalling that experience in such a context may produce a belief even if my original experience did not. For plainly a recollected sensory experience can produce beliefs about the object that caused it, especially when I have reason to provide information about that object. Perhaps one notices something in one's recollected image of the bird, an image one merely recorded in the original experience, but formed no belief about.

It might be objected that genuinely seeing an object must produce beliefs. How else, one might ask, can perception guide our behavior, as it does where, on seeing a log in our path, we step over it? One answer is that not everything we see, including the bird which flies by as I concentrate on something else, demands a cognitive response. If I am cataloging local birds, the situation is different. But where an unobtrusive object I see – as opposed to one blocking my path – has no particular relation to what I am doing, perhaps my visual impressions of it are simply a *basis* for forming beliefs about it should the situation call for it, and it need not produce any belief if my concerns and the direction of my attention give the object no significance.

Despite the complexity of the relation between seeing and believing, clearly we may hold what is epistemologically most important here. If I can see a bird without believing anything about (or of) it, I still *can* see it to be something or other, and my perceptual circumstances are such that I might readily both come to believe something about it *and* see that to be true of it. Suppose that someone suddenly interrupts a conversation to say, 'Look at that bird!' If I see it, I am in a position to form some belief about it, if only that it is swift, though I need not actually form any belief about it, at least not consciously.

To see these points more concretely, imagine I am alone and see the bird in the distance for just a second, mistakenly taking it to be a speck of ash. If there is not too much color distortion, I may still both know and justifiedly believe it to be dark. Granted, I would misdescribe it, and I might falsely believe that it is a speck of ash. But I could still know something about it, and I might point the bird out under the misleading but true description, 'that dark thing out there'. It is that thing I point at; and I can see, know, and justifiedy believe that there is a dark thing there. My perception of the bird gives me a ready basis for this much knowledge and justification, even if the perception occurs in a way that does not cause me to believe (say) that there is a *bird* before me. Seeing *is* virtual believing, or at least potential believing. It is similar with the other senses, though some, such as smell, are in general less richly informative.[10]

The perceptual hierarchy

Our discussion seems to show that simple perceiving need not produce belief, and objectual perceiving need not always yield propositional perceiving. Still, the third kind of perception is clearly not possible without the first and, I think, the second as well: I cannot see *that* the bird is anything, for example dark, if I do not see it at all, and apparently I must also see it *to be* something, say a speck of blue. Thus, simple perceiving is fundamental: it is required for objectual and propositional perceiving, yet does not clearly entail either. If, for instance, you do not perceive in the simple mode, say see a blue speck, you do not perceive in the other two modes either, say see a speck to be blue or see that it is blue. And since objectual perceiving seems possible without propositional perceiving, but not conversely, the former seems more nearly fundamental than the latter.

We have, then, a perceptual hierarchy: propositional perceiving depends on objectual perceiving, which in turn depends on simple perceiving. Simple perceiving is basic, and it commonly yields, even if it need not always yield, objectual perceiving, which, in turn, commonly yields, even if it need not always yield, propositional perceiving. Simple perceiving, such as just seeing a green field, may apparently occur without either of the other two kinds, but seeing something *to be* anything at all, such as rectangular, requires seeing it; and seeing *that* it is something in particular, say green, requires both seeing it to be something and, of course, seeing it.

Thus, even if simple perception does not always produce at least one true belief, it characteristically does put us in a position to form any number of true beliefs. It gives us *access* to perceptual information, perhaps even *records* that information in some sense, whether or not we register the information conceptually by forming perceptual beliefs of either kind.

As this suggests, perception by its very nature is informational; it might even be understood as equivalent to a kind of receipt of information about the object perceived.[11] The point here is that not all perceptually given information is *propositional* or even conceptualized. This is why we do not receive or store all of it in the contents of our beliefs. Some of the information is imagistic. Indeed, if we think of all the senses as capable of images or their non-visual counterparts for the other senses – *percepts,* as they are sometimes called – it is in these sensory impressions they give us that the bulk of perceptual information apparently resides. Hence the idea that a picture is worth a thousand words – which is not to deny that, for some purposes, some words are worth a thousand pictures.

It is in part because perception is so richly informative that it normally gives us not only imagistic information but also situational justification: even if I could be so lost in conversation that I do not form any belief about the passing bird, I am, as I see it pass, normally justified in believing something about it, concerning its perceptible properties, for instance that it glides.[12] There may perhaps be nothing highly specific that I am justified in believing about it, say that it is a cardinal or that it has a wing span of ten inches, but if I really see it, as opposed to its merely causing in me a visual impression too indistinct to qualify me as seeing it, then there is something or other that I may justifiably believe about it.

When we have a clear perception of something, it is even easier to have perceptual justification for believing a proposition about it without actually believing it. Just by taking stock of the size and texture of the field in clear view before me, I am justified in believing that it has more than 289 blades of grass; but I do not ordinarily believe any such thing about grassy fields I look at. It was only when I sought a philosophical example about perception and belief, and then arbitrarily chose the proposition that the field has more that 289 blades of grass, that I came to believe this proposition. Again, I was justified in believing the proposition before I actually did believe it.

Seeing and seeing *as*

What is it that explains why seeing the bird or the field justifies me in believing something about what I see, that is, gives me situational justification for such a belief? And does the same thing explain why seeing something enables one to know various facts about it? One possible answer is that if I see something at all, say a bird, I see it *as* something, for instance black or large or swift, and I am justified in believing it to be what I see it as being. The idea is that all seeing and perhaps all perceiving is *aspectual perception.* We see things by seeing their properties or aspects, for instance their colors or their front sides, and we are justified in taking them to have the properties or aspects we see them as having.

Let us not go too fast. Consider two points. First, might not the sort of distinction we have observed between situational and belief justification apply to seeing itself? Specifically, might not my seeing the bird imply that I am only in a *position* to see it *as* something, and not that I *do* see it as something? After all, just because, when I do see something, I see it *by* seeing some property or aspect of it, we may not conclude that I see it as *having* this property or aspect. I might think of the property as belonging to something else, as I might see a person by observing her movements under her umbrella but take them to be those of her sister. Second, supposing that seeing the bird does imply seeing it *as* something, clearly this need not be something one is justified in believing it to be (and perhaps it need not be something one *does* believe it to be). Charles might erroneously see a plainly black bird as blue, simply because he so loves birds of blue color and so dislikes black birds that (as he himself knows) his vision plays tricks on him when he is bird-watching. He might then not be justified in believing that the bird is blue.

Suppose for the sake of argument that seeing implies seeing *as* and that typically seeing as implies at least objectually believing something or other about the thing seen. Still, seeing an object as having a certain property – say, a stick in the water as bent – does not entail that it has the property. Nor does it always give one situational justification for believing it to have that property.

Seeing *as* and perceptual grounds of justification

Whether or not seeing always implies seeing *as*, it is clear that seeing something normally puts one in a position to form at least one justified belief about it. Suppose I see the bird so briefly and distractedly that I do not see it as anything in particular; still, my visual impression of it has some feature or other by which I am justified in believing something of the bird, if only that it is a moving thing. Even Charles would be justified in believing something like this. His tendency to see black birds as blue is irrelevant to his perception of movement and does not affect his justification for believing moving objects to be in motion.

Suppose, however, that for hours Charles had been hallucinating all manner of unreal things, and he knows this. Then he might not be justified in taking the bird he sees to be *anything* real, even though it is real. For as a rational person in this position he should see that if his belief is true, it may well be true only in the way a lucky guess is. Thus, the best conclusion here is – and this is an important justification principle concerning perception – that *normally*, seeing an object gives one situational justification for believing something or other about it. More broadly, *the evidence of the senses* – including above all the sensory experiences characteristic of perception – normally provides justification for beliefs with content appropriate to that evidence. If your experience is of a green expanse, you are justified in believing there is something green before you; if it is of something cool in your hand, you are justified in believing there is something cool in your hand; and so on.

One might also say something slightly different, in a terminology that is from some points of view preferable: seeing an object gives one *prima facie* justification for believing something or other about it, where prima facie justification is roughly justification that prevails unless defeated, for instance by such factors as a strong justification for believing something to the contrary. If I see a green field, I have a justification for believing it to be green, but I may not be justified, overall, in believing this if credible friends give me compelling reason to believe that despite appearances the field is entirely covered by blue grass, or that I am not seeing a field at all but hallucinating.[13]

If seeing is typical of perception in (normally) putting us in a position to form at least one justified belief about the object seen, then perception in general normally gives us at least situational justification. This is roughly justification *for* forming a belief of the proposition for which we have the justification. As our examples show, however, it does not follow that every perceptual belief *is* justified. Far from it. Some perceptual beliefs, like perceptual beliefs that are evidentially outweighed by similar beliefs grounded in hallucinations, are not. As with the biased bird-watcher, belief can be grounded in perception under conditions that prevent its being justified by that grounding.

Nevertheless, there is a simple principle of justification we can see to be plausible despite all these complexities: when a visual belief arises in such a way that one believes something in virtue of either seeing *that* it is so or seeing it *to be* so, normally the belief is justified (and it is always prima facie justified). If I see that the field is rectangular and, in virtue of seeing that it is rectangular, believe that it is, then (normally) I justifiedly believe that it is. Call this *the visual principle*, since it applies to cases of belief based on seeing that what is believed is true (or seeing it to be true).

I say *normally* (and that the justification is prima facie) because even here one's justification can be *defeated*. Thus, Charles might see that a bird is blue and believe on this basis that it is, yet realize that all morning he has been seeing black birds as dark blue and thus mistaking the black ones for the blue ones. Until he verifies his first impression, then, he does not justifiedly believe that the bird is blue, even though it in fact is. (We could say that he has some justification for believing this, yet better justification for not believing it; but to simplify matters I am ignoring degrees of justification.) He does indeed see a bird and may justifiedly believe that, but his belief that the bird is black is not justified.

Suppose, on the other hand, that Charles has no idea that he has been hallucinating. Then, even when he does hallucinate a blue bird he may be justified in believing that there is one before him. This suggests a related principle of justification, one applicable to visual experience whether it is a case of seeing or merely of visual hallucination: when, on the basis of an apparently normal visual experience (such as the sort we have in seeing a bird nearby), one believes something of the kind the experience seems to show (for instance that the bird is blue), normally this belief is justified. Call this the *visual experience principle*, since it applies to cases in which one has a belief based on visual experience even if not an experience of actually seeing (the veridical kind). The visual principle takes us from seeing to justification; the visual experience principle takes us from visual experience – conceived as apparent seeing – to justification.

Similar principles can be formulated for all of the other senses, though the formulations will not be as natural. If, for example, you hear a note to be flat and on that basis believe that it is flat, normally your belief is justified. It is grounded in a veridical perception in which you have discriminated the flatness you believe the note has. And suppose, by contrast, that in what clearly seem to be everyday circumstances you have an utterly normal-seeming auditory hallucination of a flat note. If that experience makes it seem clear that you are hearing a flat note, then if you believe on the basis of the experience that this is a flat note, normally your belief would be justified. In your situation, you have no reason to suspect hallucination, and the justification of your belief that the note is flat piggybacks, as it were, on the principle that normally applies to veridical beliefs.[14]

Seeing as a ground of perceptual knowledge

Some of what holds for the justification of perceptual beliefs also applies to perceptual knowledge. Seeing the green field, for instance, normally yields knowledge about the field as well as justified belief about it. This suggests another visual principle, which might be called an *epistemic principle*, since it states a condition for the visual generation of *knowledge*: at least normally, if I see that a thing (such as a field) has a property (say is rectangular), I (visually) know that it has it. A parallel principle holds for objectual seeing: at least normally, if I see something to have a property (say to be rectangular), I know it to have the property.

There are, however, special circumstances that explain why these epistemic principles may have to be restricted to "normal" cases. Perhaps I can see that something is so, believe on that basis that it is, and yet not know that it is. Charles's case *seems* to show this. For if, in the kind of circumstances he is in, he often takes a black bird to be blue, then even if he sees that a certain blue bird is blue and, on that basis, believes it is blue, he apparently does not know that it is.[15] He might as well have been wrong, one wants to say; he is just lucky that this time his belief is true and he was not hallucinating. Since he has no reason to think he has been hallucinating, and does not realize he has been, one cannot fault him for holding the belief that the bird is blue or regard the belief as inappropriate to his situation. Still, knowledge apparently needs better grounding than is provided by his blameless good fortune. This kind of case has led some philosophers to maintain that when we know that something is so, our being right is not *accidental*.

There is an important difference here between knowledge and justification. Take knowledge first. If Charles is making errors like this, then even if he has no idea that he is and no reason to suspect he is, he does not know that the bird he believes to be blue is blue. But even if he has no idea that he is making errors, or any reason to suspect he is, he may still justifiedly believe that the bird is blue. The main difference may be this: he can have a true belief which does not constitute knowledge because there is something wrong for which he is in no way criticizable (his errors might arise from a handicap which he has no reason to suspect, such as a sudden color blindness); but he cannot have a true yet unjustified belief without being in some way criticizable. The standards for knowledge, one might say, permit fewer unsuspected weaknesses in discriminating the truth than those for justification, if the standards for knowledge permit any at all.

This difference between knowledge and justification must be reflected in the kinds of principles that indicate how justification, as opposed to knowledge, is generated. Justification principles need not imply that the relevant basis of a belief's justification assures its truth; but since a false belief cannot be knowledge, epistemic principles (knowledge principles) cannot capture elements that generate knowledge unless they rule out factors that may produce a false belief (or at least factors that have a significant chance of producing one). A ground of knowledge must, in *some* way, suffice for the truth of the proposition known; a ground of justification must in some way *count toward* the truth of the proposition one is justified in believing, but need not rule out its falsehood.

On the basis of what we see, hear, feel, smell, and taste, we have a great many beliefs, propositional and objectual. We have seen no reason to doubt that these perceptual beliefs are commonly justified or that, quite often, they are true and constitute knowledge. But to see that perception is a basis of justification and knowledge is to go only part way toward understanding what perception, justification, and knowledge are. Here the main question is what constitutes perception, philosophically speaking. Until we have a good understanding of what it is, we cannot see in detail how perception grounds belief, justification, and knowledge. These problems cannot be fully resolved in this book, but we can achieve partial resolutions. I want to discuss (further) what perception is first and, later, to illustrate in new ways how it grounds what it does. Let us start by considering some of the major theories of the nature of perception. Again, I concentrate on vision, and I want to discuss mainly simple perceiving, the fundamental kind.

Some commonsense views of perception

One natural thing to say about what it is for me to see the green field is appealingly brief: I simply see it, at least in that I see its facing surface. It is near and squarely before me. I need no light to penetrate a haze or a telescope to magnify my view. I simply see the field, and it is as it appears. This sort of view thought to represent untutored common sense has been called *naive realism*: it says roughly that perception is simply a matter of the five senses telling us about real things, and it presupposes that no philosophical account of how they do this is needed.

The view is naive because it ignores problems of a kind to be described in a moment; it is a form of realism because it takes the objects of perception to be real things external to the perceiver, the sorts of things that are "out there" to be seen whether anyone sees them or not.

A more thoughtful commonsense view retains the realism without the naivety. It is quite commonsensical, for instance, to say that I see the field *because* it is before my open eyes and stimulates my vision, thereby *appearing* to me as a green, rectangular shape. Stimulating my vision is a causal relation: the field, by reflecting light, causes me to have the visual experience that is part of my seeing that very field. Moreover, the field apparently must cause my visual experience if I am to *see* it. Since the more thoughtful commonsense view specifies that the object of perception must be a real external thing, we might call it a *perceptual realism*. Most – but not all – theories of perception incorporate this kind of realism.

To understand why perception must have a causal element of this sort, suppose I am looking at the field and, without my noticing, someone instant-aneously drops a perfect picture of the field right in front of me. If the picture is shaped and textured correctly, my visual experience might not change. The scene might appear to me just as it did, yet I no longer *see* the field. Instead, I see a picture of it. (I do see the field *in* the picture, but that is secondary seeing and not the kind I am talking about.) The reason I do not now see the field is roughly that it has no (causal) effect on my visual experience.

Perception as a causal relation and its four main elements

Examples like this suggest that *perception is a kind of causal relation* between whatever is perceived and its perceiver. This is a plausible and very important point, though it does not tell us precisely what perception is. I call any theory of perception which incorporates the point *a causal theory of perception*. Most theories of perception are causal.

We can now better understand the four elements I have described as among those crucial in perception: the perceiver, the object perceived, the sensory experience in which the object appears to the perceiver, and the causal relation between the object and the perceiver, by virtue of which the object produces that experience. Thus, if I see the field, there is a distinctive way, presumably through light transmission to my eyes, in which the field produces in me the visual sensory experience of a green, rectangular shape characteristic of my seeing it. If a picture of the field produces an exactly similar visual experience in the same way, it is the picture I see, not the field. Similarly, if I hear a piano piece, there is a special way in which it causes me to have the auditory sensations of chords and melody and harmony that go with it.

It is difficult, though fortunately not necessary for a general understanding of perception, to specify precisely what these ways – these causal paths from the object to the perceiver – are. Some of the details are the business of the psychology and neurophysiology of perception. Others are determinable by philosophical inquiry. Philosophical reflection shows us, for instance, that not just any causal chain is the right sort for perception. Suppose the piano sounds cause a special machine to produce in me both temporary deafness and a faithful auditory hallucination of the piece. Then I do not *hear* it, though my sensory experience, the auditory experience I live through in my own consciousness, is just what it would be if I did hear it. Nor do I hear it if, though the sound waves reach my brain and cause me to believe a piano is playing just the piece in question, I have no auditory experience. Even a highly informed inner silence is not musical. Different theories of perception tend, as we shall see, to give strikingly different accounts of how these four elements (or some of them) figure in perception.

Illusion and hallucination

We can make significant progress by pursuing the question of why naive realism is naive. Suppose there is a gray haze that makes the green field look gray. Or suppose the book I am holding appears, from a certain angle, as if its cover were a parallelogram rather than a (right) rectangle, or feels warm only because my hand is cold. These are *perceptual illusions*. They illustrate the point that things are not always as they seem. The book's cover is neither parallelogrammic nor warm.

Now imagine that the field burns up. I sorely miss its rich green and the spruce and maple, and on waking from a slumber in my chair I have a *hallucination* in which my visual experience is just as it would be if I were seeing the field as it originally was. Here the grass I seem to see is not there at all. The point here is not that *something* I see is not as it seems (as in the case of illusion) but that there seems to be something where there is nothing. With illusion, as illustrated by a partly submerged stick's looking bent, experience distorts what is there; with hallucination, something seems to be there that apparently is not there at all.

Illusions and hallucinations are possible for the other senses too. When they occur, we do not just see (or hear, taste, smell, or touch) the object. Either we do not see it as it is or (perhaps) do not see anything at all. So even if naive realism is right in its implication that some things are as they appear, not everything we perceive is as it appears to be.

One way to deal with illusion and hallucination is to stress how they show the need to distinguish appearance from reality. In a visual illusion, one sees something, but it does not appear as it really is, say rectangular. In a hallucination, if anything appears to one, it is in reality even less what it appears to be than is the object of an illusion, or is not what it appears to be at all: instead of a blue spruce tree's appearing blue to me, for instance, perhaps the conical section of space where it stood appears "bespruced." The sense in which the space appears blue to me is roughly that I *see it as* blue.

The theory
of appearing

The sort of account of perception just sketched as an improvement over naive realism has been called *the theory of appearing*: it says roughly that perceiving an object, such as a book, is simply its appearing to one to have one or more properties, such as being rectangular. Thus, one perceives it – in this case, sees it – *as* rectangular. The theory can also provide the basis of an account of sensory experience, including not just the kind one has in actually perceiving something but also the sort one has in hallucination as opposed to normal perception: that, too, the theory takes to be a case of something's appearing to one to have a set of properties; the object that appears is simply a different kind: it is hallucinatory.[16]

The theory of appearing is initially quite plausible. For one thing, it incorporates much reflective common sense. It includes, for instance, the view that if one sees something, then it appears to one in some way, say as a red barn or as a red spot in a field or at least as a visually experienced rectangular patch. The theory also does justice to the view that things are not always as they appear. Moreover, it can explain both illusion and, with some imaginative development, hallucination.

The theory of appearing says nothing, however, about the need for a causal relation between the object and its perceiver. If, consistently with its commonsense motivation, one stipulated that the crucial relation of appearing to the perceiver to have a property – say, to be rectangular – is or implies a causal relation, one would then have a different theory (of a kind to be discussed shortly).

In addition to the question of how the theory can do justice to the causal element in perception, it faces a problem in accounting for hallucinations in which apparently there is no object to appear to the person at all. I could, after all, hallucinate a green field when I see nothing physical at all, say because it is pitch dark or my eyes are closed. In such an *empty hallucination* – one that occurs despite my perceiving nothing – what is it that appears green to me?

There is a plausible answer, but it is associated with a quite different theory of perception. Let us explore that contrasting view.

Sense-datum theories
of perception

Once we think seriously about illusion and hallucination, we begin to question not only naive realism but also any kind of *direct realism*, any view which, like the theory of appearing, says that we see (or otherwise perceive) external objects directly, rather than *through* seeing (or at least visually experiencing) something else. After all, not only do light rays come between us and what we see, there are also events in the brain crucial for seeing. Perhaps these or other intermediaries in perception produce or indicate an intermediate, interior object, presumably a mental object, in the perceptual process.

Hallucination illustrates most readily how such an intermediary may seem essential to understanding perception. Imagine that when I vividly hallucinate the field just as it would be if it were before me, my visual experience – roughly, what I am aware of in my visual consciousness – is exactly like the experience I have when I see the field. Does it not then seem that the difference between ordinary seeing and visual hallucination is simply in what *causes* the visual experience, rather than in what I directly see? When I see the field, *it* causes my visual experience. When I hallucinate it, something else (such as my deep desire to have it back) causes my visual experience. But apparently what I directly see, that is, the immediate object of my visual experience, is the same in both cases. This point presumably explains why my visual experience – what occupies my visual consciousness – is the same whether I am hallucinating the field or really seeing it. If it were not the same, we could not say things like 'It was exactly as if I were seeing the tree in normal light'.

The argument from hallucination

We might develop these ideas by considering an argument from hallucination, consisting of two connected arguments as parts. The first constituent argument attempts to show a parallel between hallucination and ordinary perception:

1   A perfectly faithful (visual) hallucination of a field is intrinsically indistinguishable from an ordinary experience of seeing that field, that is, not distinguishable from it just in itself as a visual experience, as opposed to being distinguishable

through verifying one's visual impression by touching the
things around one.

Hence,

2   What is *directly* seen, the immediate object of one's visual
    experience, is the same sort of (non-physical) thing in a perfect
    hallucination of a field as in an ordinary experience of seeing a
    field.

But – and we now come to the second constituent argument, which builds on
(2) as its first premise – clearly,

3   What is directly seen in a hallucination of a field is not a field
    (or any other physical thing).

Indeed, no field is seen at all in an hallucinatory visual experience, so (3) seems
plainly true. Hence, putting (1)–(3) together, we may infer that

4   What is directly seen in an ordinary experience of seeing a field
    is not a field.

The overall idea is that when we ordinarily see an everyday perceptible object
such as a field, we see it through seeing something else *directly*: something
not seen *by* seeing anything else. What we see directly – call it a sense-datum
– might be an image. One may prefer (as some philosophers do) to say that
we do not *see* such things but are only visually acquainted with them. To
simplify let us just bear this alternative in mind, but use the more natural
term 'see'.

Just what is directly seen when one sees a field, then, and how is the field
*in*directly seen? Why not say that what is *directly* seen is a two-dimensional
object (or perhaps even a three-dimensional item) consisting of the colors and
shapes one sees in the hallucinatory experience? After all, nothing, not even
(physical) light, intervenes between me and them. There is no "space" for
intermediaries. Hence, no intermediaries can misrepresent these special
objects. These objects are apparently internal to me: as traditionally conceived,
they could exist even if I were a disembodied mind in an otherwise empty
world. The only space they need is in my mind. Yet I do see the field *by* seeing
them; hence, I see it indirectly.

The idea that experiencing sense-data is required for perception is nicely
expressed in Emily Dickinson's poem 'I Heard a Fly Buzz When I Died'. In the
final moment of her terminal experience,

There interposed a fly,
With blue, uncertain stumbling buzz,
Between the light and me;
And then the windows failed, and then
I could not see to see.

The external light from the window blocks her eyesight, but this leaves inner seeing – portrayed here as a condition for ordinary seeing – still possible. Until the end, she can see *to* see. It is sense-data that are conceived as the direct objects of such inner sight.

A sense-datum theory does not require us to give up holding a causal theory of perception: the field causes the colors and shapes to arise in my visual consciousness in a way that fully accords with the view that perception is a causal relation between something external and the perceiver. Perception is simply a *mediated*, hence indirect, causal relation between external objects I perceive and me: the object produces the mediating colors and shapes that appear in my visual field, and, through seeing them, I see it.

The theory I am describing is a version of a *sense-datum theory of perception*. Such theories are so called because they account for perception by appeal to a view of what is directly given *in* sense experience, hence is a *datum* (a given) for such experience – the sort of thing one is visually aware of in hallucinating a field. This sense-datum thesis (unlike the phenomenalist sense-datum view to be discussed shortly) is a realist view; but its realism, by contrast with that of naive realism and the theory of appearing, is indirect.[17]

Sense-datum theory as an indirect, representative realism

A sense-datum theory might be called a *representative realism* because it conceives perception as a relation in which sense-data represent perceived external (hence real) objects to us. On some conceptions of sense-data, they are copies of those objects: shape for shape, color for color, sound for sound. John Locke held a view of this kind (and in 1689 published it in *An Essay Concerning Human Understanding*, especially Books II and IV), though for him sense-data are copies ('resemblances') only of the *primary qualities* – solidity, extension (in space), shape, and mobility – not of the *secondary qualities*, above all colors, sounds, smells, and tastes. Our question is whether any sense-datum version of representationalism is sound, and we need not pursue the interesting question of how these two kinds of qualities differ.

Sense-datum theories have had brilliant defenders down to the present age.

The theory has also had powerful opponents. To appreciate it better, let us first consider how it takes perception to be indirect. Sense-datum theorists might offer several reasons to explain why we do not ordinarily notice the indirectness of perception (I speak generally here, not solely of Locke's version of the theory). Here are two important ones.

First, normally what we directly see, say colors and shapes, roughly corresponds to the physical objects we indirectly see by means of what we see directly. It is only when there is an illusion or hallucination that we are forced to notice a discrepancy between what we directly see and the object commonly said to be seen, such as a book.

Second, the beliefs we form on the basis of perception are formed spontaneously and not based on any process requiring us to consider sense-data. Above all, we do not normally *infer* what we believe about external objects from what we believe about the colors and shapes we directly see. This is why it is easy to think we "just see" things, directly. Perceiving is not inferential, and for that reason (perhaps among others) it is not *epistemically indirect*, in the sense that knowledge of external objects or belief about them is based on knowledge of sense-data, or belief about them. I know that the field is green through *having* green sense-data, not through *inference from* propositions about them.[18]

Perception is not, then, inferentially indirect. It is, so far as inference goes, direct; but it is nonetheless causally and objectually indirect. The perceived object is presented to us via another object, though not by way of a *premise*. Let me describe a bit differently how the sense-datum view conceives the indirectness of perception.

Perception is causally indirect because perceived physical objects cause sensory experience, say of colors and shapes, *by* causing the occurrence of sense-data, with which we are directly (and presumably non-causally) acquainted in perceptual experience. Perception is objectually indirect because we perceive external things, such as fields, *through* our acquaintance with other objects, namely, sense-data. Roughly, we perceive external things through perceptual acquaintance with internal things.

By contrast, we normally do not use information about sense-data to arrive at perceptual beliefs inferentially, say by an inference from my directly seeing a grassy, green rectangular expanse to the conclusion that a green field is before me. Ordinarily, when I look around I form beliefs about the external environment and none at all about my sensory experience. That experience causes my perceptual beliefs, but what they are *about* is the external things I perceive. It is when the colors and shapes do not correspond to the external object, as where a rectangular book appears as a parallelogram, that it seems we can understand our experience only if we suppose that the direct objects of sensory experience are internal and need not match their external, indirect objects.

Appraisal of the sense-datum approach

Let us focus first of all squarely on the argument from hallucination, whose conclusion suggests that what is directly seen in visual perception of external objects is a set of sense-data. Suppose I do have a hallucination that is intrinsically just like the normal experience of seeing a field. Does it follow that what is directly seen in the hallucination is the same sort of thing as what is directly seen in the normal experience? There are at least two problems that confront the sense-datum theory here.

First, why must anything be seen at all in a hallucination? Imagine that you see me hallucinate the burned-up field. I might get up, still half asleep, and cry out, 'It's back!', pointing to the area. You might conclude that I *think* I see the field again. My own initial reaction to realizing I had hallucinated the field might be that, hallucination or no, I *saw* it. But I might just as easily slump back in my chair and mumble that I wish I had seen it.

We could compromise and agree that I saw the hallucinated field (vividly) *in my mind's eye*. But suppose I did see it in my mind's eye, and again suppose that the hallucination is intrinsically just like the ordinary seeing. Does it follow that what I directly see in the ordinary experience is the same as what I see in the hallucination, namely, something in my mind's eye? It does not. The notion of seeing in one's mind's eye is metaphorical, and such seeing need not imply that there is any real thing seen, in or outside the mind. However vividly I may, in my mind's eye, see myself standing atop a giant pyramid in Toronto, there is no pyramid there, nor need there be any pyramidal object in my mind.

There is a second reason for resisting the conclusion that something must be directly seen in hallucinations. Recall that my seeing a green field is apparently a causal relation between a sensory experience in me and the field that produces the experience. If this view is correct, why should the possibility that a hallucination can mimic my seeing the field tell us anything about what is directly seen when one sees that field? It is not as if we had to assume that only an *object* can produce the relevant sensory experience, and must then conclude that it is an internal perceptual object, since there is no other candidate. Many effects can have more than one cause, and the sense-datum theorist has no argument to show that only an internal perceptual *object*, as opposed, say, to an abnormality in the visual cortex, can cause the hallucinatory experience.

Moreover, from the similarity of the internal, experiential elements in the hallucination and the genuine perception, one might as well conclude that since the ordinary experience is one of seeing only an external rather than an internal object, the hallucinatory experience is different only in the absence of the external object. Rather than add to the components that seem needed to account for the ordinary experience, we subtract one that seems needed to account for the hallucination. This yields a more economical theory of perception.

An analogy may help. Compare trying to infer facts about how we see an original painting from facts about how we see it in a cinematic picture of it. From the indirectness of the latter seeing, it certainly does not follow that ordinary seeing of the painting is indirect. And even if a cinematic viewing can be so realistic that it perfectly mimics an ordinary viewing, it does not follow that cinematic, two-dimensional objects are components in ordinary seeing. Similarly, no matter how like ordinary experiences hallucinations can seem, it does not follow that the former have all the internal elements (roughly, mental or mind-dependent elements) of the latter.

It may help to consider a different analogy. Two perfect ball-bearings can be intrinsically indistinguishable, having the same diameter and constitution, yet still differ significantly, one being on my left and one on my right. Their intrinsic properties can thus be identical, while their *relations* (to me) differ: one is left of me, the other right of me; hence they *do* differ in their relational properties. Similarly, the hallucination of a field and the ordinary visual experience of a field can be intrinsically indistinguishable, yet differ in their relations to me or to other things. One of them, the visual experience of a field, may be an element in a perceptual relation to the field, and the experience we call hallucination, which is not based on perceiving the external object hallucinated, may not be an element in any perceptual relation to the field, but only a process I undergo (an element simply "in" me on the plausible assumption that it is mental).

To account for the difference between the two kinds of experience, we might say this: the visual experience, it seems, represents an external thing to me; the hallucinatory experience, though intrinsically just like the visual one, does not, but as it were only pretends to represent an external thing. Thus, for all the argument from hallucination shows, the ordinary experience of seeing might be a relation to an object such as a green field, namely the relation of directly seeing, while the hallucinatory experience of a green field is not a relation to that field, such as being an internal copy of it, or even a relation to any other object, such as a perceiver.

The points just made about the argument from hallucination indicate that it is not sound. Its first premise, (1), does not entail the conclusion drawn from it, (2). Nonetheless, the argument poses serious problems for alternative theories. What explanatory account of hallucinations and illusions besides the sense-datum account might we adopt? To see what some of the alternatives are, it is best to begin with illusion rather than hallucination.

Recall the book viewed from an angle. A sense-datum theory will say we directly see a parallelogrammic shape and indirectly see the book. The theory of appearing, however, can also explain this: it reminds us that things need not be what they appear to be and says simply that the book can appear parallelogrammic even if it is rectangular.

One could also combine the causal element in the sense-datum approach with the direct realism of the theory of appearing and move to a third theory,

one that says the book causes us to see it directly, rather than through producing sense-data in us, yet (because of our angle of vision) we see it as if it
were parallelogrammic. To avoid suggesting that anything in one's experience
need be parallelogrammic, one could take this to mean that the book visually
appears parallelogrammically to us. Here the adverb 'parallelogrammically'
describes a *way* in which we visually experience the book; it does not imply
that there is an object that appears to us and *is* parallelogrammic.[19] Let us
explore this idea in relation to the theory associated with it.

Adverbial theories
of perception

It should now be clear why we need not grant (what sense-datum theorists
sometimes seem to assume about perception) that in order for an object to
appear a given way to us there must *be* something we see that *is* that way, for
instance a parallelogrammic sense-datum. Moreover, it is not only the theory
of appearing that makes use of this point. Suppose that one says simply that
the book appears parallelogrammically, using this adverb to designate the way
it appears, or (speaking from the perceiver's point of view) *how* one visually
experiences it: parallelogrammically. To say it appears parallelogrammically is
roughly to say it appears in the way a parallelogram does, as opposed to the
way a rectangle does.

   If this adverbial interpretation of such statements as 'I see a parallelogram'
seems artificial, consider an ordinary analogy. If I say I have a fever, no one
could plausibly insist that there is an object, a fever, which I have. 'I have a
fever' is a way of saying I am feverish, i.e., my body is above a certain temperature. What our language seems to treat as a statement of a relation to an
object, a fever, is really an ascription of a property: having a temperature above
a certain level. Just as 'having a fever' can be a term that ascribes a certain
temperature, 'seeing a parallelogram' (in illusional and hallucinatory cases)
can be a term for ascribing a certain visual experience. Indeed, the adverbial
approach to perception is above all distinctive in the way it represents the
sensory experiences widely agreed to be essential in perception.

   On the basis of this move, one can construct what is called *the adverbial
theory of perception*. Unlike the theory of appearing, which takes perception
to be an unanalyzable relation in which things appear to us as having one or
more properties, an adverbial theory conceives perception as an analyzable
way of experiencing things. In what may be its most plausible form, it says
roughly that to perceive an object is for that object (in a certain way) to
produce in one a sensory experience of it: to cause one's experiencing it in a
certain qualitative way, say to see a stick as straight (or, given the illusion

induced by partial submersion, as bent). Both theories are, however, direct realist views, though they reject the idea that we "just see" things, as naive realism holds. Other similarities (and some differences) between the two theories will soon be apparent.[20]

The adverbial theorist stresses that we see (or otherwise perceive) things in a particular qualitative way and that they thus appear to us in that way. Often they appear as they are; sometimes they do not. In each case they are seen directly, not through intermediaries. Even if I do not see the book as rectangular, I do see *it*: it is seen directly, yet appears parallelogrammically.

So far, so good, perhaps. But what about hallucinations? Here the adverbial theory again differs from the theory of appearing. Unlike the latter, it denies that all sensory experience is *of* some object. The importance of this denial is not immediately apparent, perhaps because we suppose that usually a person visually hallucinating does see *something*. Consider Shakespeare's Macbeth, distraught by his murder of Duncan, hallucinating a dagger that seems to him to hover in mid-air:

> Is this a dagger which I see before me,
> The handle toward my hand? Come, let me clutch thee.
> I have thee not, and yet I see thee still.
> Art thou not, fatal vision, sensible
> To feeling as to sight? or art thou but
> A dagger of the mind, a false creation,
> Proceeding from the heat-oppressed brain?
> I see thee yet, in a form as palpable
> As this [sword] which I now draw.

(Act II, scene i)

Presumably Macbeth sees something, say the wall behind "the dagger" or at least a chunk of space where it hovers. An adverbial theorist might thus posit an object where the "dagger" seems located, if only the space for Macbeth to experience "daggerly." Somehow this object might be thought to play a role in causing him to have daggerish visual sensations, just as, for the theory of appearing, the space before him, despite being transparent, might somehow appear to him to be a dagger. Indeed, in this case what the adverbial theorist calls experiencing "daggerly" might be roughly equivalent to what the theory of appearing calls having something appear to one to be a dagger.

Supposing we accept this adverbialist account, what happens if it is pitch dark and Macbeth's hallucination is therefore *empty*, in the sense that there is nothing he sees, and hence nothing to serve as an object distorted into an apparent dagger? Then, whereas the theory of appearing may have to posit something like a sense-datum (or other special kind of object) to serve as what appears to be a dagger, the adverbial theory can take a different line and deny that there is *any* kind of object appearing to him. It may posit some quite different account of his "bedaggered" visual experience, such as a psychological account appealing to the influence of drugs or of his "heat-oppressed brain."

Is it really plausible to hold, with the adverbial theory, that in this instance Macbeth saw nothing at all? Can we really explain how the normal and hallucinatory experiences are intrinsically alike without assuming they have the same direct objects? In the light of the special case of empty hallucination, then, the sense-datum theory may seem the most plausible of the three. It provides an object of Macbeth's visual experience in utter darkness, whereas the adverbial theory posits no objects at all to appear to one in empty hallucinations. Moreover, the sense-datum view postulates the same sort of direct object for ordinary perception, illusion, and hallucination, whereas the theory of appearing does not offer a uniform account of their direct objects and must explain why entities like sense-data do not occur in normal perception as well as in empty hallucination.

Perhaps, however, the hallucination problem seems more threatening than it should to the adverbial theory because hallucinations are felt to be *perceptual* experiences and hence expected to be *of* some object. But as we have seen, although hallucinatory experiences can be intrinsically indistinguishable from perceptual ones, all that can be assumed is that they are *sensory experiences*. Hallucinatory experiences, on the adverbial view, are simply not cases of perceiving, at least not in a sense requiring that any object appear to one. Thus, nothing at all need appear to one in hallucinations, though it may *appear to the subject* that something is there. The hallucinator may then be described as having a visual sensory experience, but – since nothing is perceived – not a normal perceptual experience.

Adverbial and sense-datum theories of sensory experience

A perceptual experience is always sensory, and normally a sensory experience of the sort we have in perceiving is genuinely perceptual. But a kind of short-circuit can cause the sense-receptors to produce sensory experience that is not a normal perceptual experience (or even part of one). It is important to consider the debate between adverbial and sense-datum theories in relation to sensory experience. Both theories take such experience to be essential to perception; both offer accounts of sensory experience as well as of perception; and some in each camp make take the former as a more basic concern.

The most natural thing for adverbial theorists to say about hallucinatory experience is that it is not genuinely perceptual, but only sensory. They might, however, say instead that where a perceptual experience is hallucinatory, it is not a case of *seeing* (except perhaps in the mind's eye, or perhaps in the sense that it is seeing colors and shapes conceived abstractly as properties and not as belonging to sense-datum objects). The former description accords better with how seeing is normally understood.

The theory suggested by these responses to the hallucination problem might be called *the adverbial theory of sensory experience.* It says that having a sensory experience, such as a hallucination of a green field, is experiencing in a certain *way*, for example visually experiencing "green-fieldly." Our commonsense assumption is that hallucination is not usual (for normal people) and that most such vivid sensory experiences are genuinely perceptual. They are of, and thus caused by, the external object apparently perceived. But some sensory experiences are neither genuinely perceptual nor externally caused. People having them are in a vision-like state, and what is going on in their visual cortex may be the same sort of process that occurs when they see things; yet they are not seeing, and their visual experience typically has an internal cause, such as an abnormal emotion.

May we, then, regard sense-datum theories of perception as refuted by the points just made in criticism of the argument from hallucination and on behalf of the suggested adverbial theory and the theory of appearing? Certainly not. We have at most seen how one major argument for a sense-datum theory of perception fails and how alternative theories of perception can account for the apparently central elements in perception: the perceiver, the (ordinary) object perceived, the sensory experience, and the causal relation between the second and third.

Indeed, supposing that the argument from hallucination fails to show that sense-data are elements in normal everyday perception, sense-data might still be needed to account for non-perceptual sensory experience (sometimes loosely called perceptual experience because it is characteristic of that). In this limited role, one might posit a *sense-datum theory of non-perceptual sensory experience.* On this view, such experience is simply direct acquaintance with sense-data. This view may seem preferable to an adverbial theory of sensory experience. For one thing, there is something unsatisfying about the idea that even in a visual hallucination so vivid that, if one did not suspect error, one would stake one's life on the presence of the hallucinated object, one sees nothing, except either metaphorically in one's mind's eye, or in a sense of 'see' which does not require that any object be seen. Still, perhaps there is such a sense of 'see', or perhaps one can experience colors and shapes in a visual way without seeing anything.

There is another aspect of the controversy. It concerns the *metaphysics* associated with adverbial and sense-datum theories of any kind, specifically, the sorts of things they require us to take as fundamental realities. In this respect, the adverbial theories of perception and sensory experience have a definite advantage over the counterpart sense-datum theories: the former do not posit a *kind* of object we would not otherwise have to regard as real. From the adverbial perspective, the objects that perception and sensory experience involve are simply perceivers and what they perceive. These are quite familiar entities which we must recognize and deal with anyway.

Sense-data are quite different from ordinary (presumably physical) objects of perception. Sense-data are either mental or at least depend for their existence on the mind of the subject. Yet they are unlike some mental phenomena in that no good case can be made for their being really brain phenomena, since they have properties, for instance green color and perfect rectangularity, not normally found in the brain.[21]

Moreover, there are difficulties in the way of fully understanding sense-data in any terms. Is there, for instance, even a reasonable way of counting them? Suppose my image of the green field gradually gets greener. Is this a sense-datum changing or a new one replacing an old one? There seems to be no way to tell. If there is no way to tell, how can we ever be sure we learn more about a sense-datum than what initially appears to us in experiencing it: how can one distinguish learning something more about *it* from learning about something new?[22]

Problems like these also affect the theory of appearing insofar as it must posit sense-data or similar entities to account for hallucinations. To be sure, such problems can beset our understanding of ordinary objects as well. Can we always distinguish a mountain with two peaks from two mountains, or one snarled barberry bush from two? But apparently these problems are less serious, if only because there is no question that there are *some* things of the physical kind in question. The corresponding problems may in the end be soluble for sense-data, but they at least give us some reason to prefer a theory that does not force us to regard sense-data as the only objects, or as even among the objects, we are directly aware of when we see, hear, touch, taste, and smell.

Phenomenalism

If some philosophers have thought that perception can be understood without appeal to sense-data, others have conceived it as understandable in terms of sense-data alone as its objects. This view has the advantage of being, in at least one way, simpler than the adverbial and sense-datum theories. But the view is motivated by other considerations as well.

A sense-datum version of phenomenalism

Think about the book you see. It is a perceptible object. Suppose we may conceive a real perceptible object as a perceptible object that is as it is independently of what we think it to be. Still, real perceptible objects, such as tables and chairs and books, are also plausibly conceived to be, by their very nature, *knowable*. Indeed, it is doubtful that real objects of this sort could be unknowable, or even unknowable through the senses if lighting and other perceptual conditions are good. Now suppose we add to these ideas the assumption that our only genuine, certain knowledge of perceptibles is restricted to what directly appears to us and would be as it is even if we should be hallucinating. And what more does appear to us besides the colors and shapes of perceptible objects? Further, how do we know that this book, for example, could even exist without someone's perceiving its color and other sensory properties? Certainly we cannot *observe* the book existing unperceived. If you observe it, you perceive it.

Moreover, if you imagine subtracting the book's sensory properties one by one – its color, shape, weight, and so on – what is left of it? This is not like peeling an apple, leaving its substance. It is like stripping layer after layer from an onion until nothing remains. Might we not conclude, then, that the book is not only *known by* its properties, as the other theories of perception also hold, but simply *is* a stable collection of sensory properties, a collection of visual, tactual, and other sense-data which in some sense recur in our experience, confronting us each time we have the sense-data corresponding to, say, a certain bookcase in our home? Similarly, might it not be that to see the book is simply to be visually acquainted with such a stable collection of sense-data?

George Berkeley argued from a variety of angles that this is indeed what a perceptible object is. This view (which Berkeley developed in detail in his *Treatise Concerning the Principles of Human Knowledge*, published in 1710) is a version of what is often called *phenomenalism*, since it constructs external objects out of phenomena, which, in this use of the term, are equivalent to sense-data. The view is also considered a kind of *idealism*, since it construes physical objects as ideal, in the sense of being composed of ideas rather than material stuff that would exist even if there were no minds and no ideas.[23]

Adverbial phenomenalism

Phenomenalism as just described is focused on the nature of perceptible objects but implies a related view of perception. In the sense-datum version of phenomenalism we have been examining, the associated account of perception retains a sense-datum theory of sensory experience, but not a sense-datum theory of perception. The latter view posits external objects as causes of the sense-data experienced in ordinary perception, whereas sense-datum phenomenalism says physical objects *are* collections of sense-data.

Using the adverbial theory of sensory experience, one might also formulate an *adverbial phenomenalism*, which constructs physical objects out of sensory experience alone and says that to see (for instance) a green field is to experience "green-fieldly" in a certain vivid and stable way. To see such a thing is to have a visual experience that predictably occurs under certain conditions, say when one has the related experiences of walking out on the porch and looking ahead.

On this phenomenalist view, perception can occur without even sense-data; it requires only perceivers and their properties. Sense-datum versions of phenomenalism, however, have been more often discussed by philosophers, and I will concentrate on them.

Whereas the sense-datum theory is an indirect realism, phenomenalism is a *direct irrealism*: it says that perceptual objects are directly perceived, but it denies that they are real in the sense that they are mind-independent and can exist apart from perceivers. This is not to say they are not perceptually real – real items in sensory experience. The point is that they are not metaphysically real: things that are "out there," which are the sorts of things we think of as such that they would exist even if there were no perceivers.

Phenomenalism does not, then, deny that physical objects exist in the sense that they are both stable elements of our experience and governed by causal laws, such as those of physics. Nor does it deny that there can be hallucinations, as where certain sense-data, like those constituting Macbeth's hallucinatory dagger, are too unstable to compose a physical object, or are perceivable only in one mode, such as vision, when they should have tactile elements as well, such as a cool, smooth surface. What phenomenalism denies is that physical objects are real in the classical sense, implying that their existence is independent of experience.

One naturally wonders why things would not go in and out of existence depending on whether they are experienced, and why, when they do exist, they obey the laws of physics, which certainly do not seem to depend on our minds. Berkeley did not neglect to consider what happens to things when we cease to perceive them, as where we leave a book in an empty room. His answer has been nicely put in a limerick:

> There was a young man who said "God
> Must think it exceedingly odd
> If he finds that this tree
> Continues to be
> When there's no one about in the quad."

Reply:

> Dear Sir:
> Your astonishment's odd:
> I am always about in the quad
> And that's why the tree

> Will continue to be,
> Since observed by Yours faithfully, God.

If the very existence of external objects is sustained by divine perception, it is not difficult to see how their behavior could obey laws of nature that are divinely ordained. A phenomenalist need not be a theist, however, to offer an account of the stability of external objects and their lawful behavior. John Stuart Mill, writing in the same epistemological tradition as Berkeley but without any appeal to God, called external objects "permanent possibilities of sensation." To say that the book is in the room when no one is in there to perceive it is to say that there is a certain enduring possibility of the sensations one would have if one perceived such a book. If one enters the room and looks in the appropriate direction, that possibility should be realized. By contrast, if one merely hallucinated there would be no reason to expect this. A phenomenalist can, however, be more radical and take objects not to have any kind of existence when unperceived. They are born and die with the experiences in which they appear.

Appraisal of phenomenalism

Unlike the sense-datum theory of perception, phenomenalism is only occasionally defended by contemporary philosophers. But it has had major influence. Moreover, compared with the sense-datum theory, it is more economical and in that way simpler. Instead of perceivers, sense-data, and external objects, it posits, as the things figuring in perception and sensory experience, just perceivers and sense-data. Indeed, adverbial phenomenalism does not even posit sense-data, though it does appeal to a special kind of property, that of experiencing in a certain way, for instance blue-bookly.

As a theory of perception, then, phenomenalism has fewer objects to analyze and interrelate than do the other theories we have discussed. In addition, it appears to bridge the most important gap between sensory experience and perception of objects: since the objects are internal and directly experienced, it seems natural to say that they must be as they appear to be – we see all there is of them, or at least of the surface facing us. On the other hand, for the external objects of common sense, whose reality is independent of perceivers, (non-theistic) phenomenalism must substitute something like permanent possibilities of experience. Thus, the bare-bones appearance of the theory is illusory. Even that metaphor is misleading; for even our bodies are also collections of sense-data; even the flesh itself is not too solid to melt into the sensations of its perceivers.

It is tempting to reject phenomenalism as preposterous. But if we flatly reject it, we learn nothing from it. Let me pose just one objection from which we learn something important about the relation between sense experience and external objects. The theory says that a book, for instance, is – or at least that its presence implies – one's having or potentially having a suitably stable collection of sense-data, and that seeing it is being visually acquainted with them. If this is a correct analysis of what seeing a book is, then there is a combination of sense-data, sensory items like colors and shapes in one's visual field, such that if, under appropriate conditions, these elements occur in me, then it follows that I see a book. But surely there is no such combination of sense-data. No matter how vividly and stably I (or anyone) may experience the colors and shapes appropriate to a book, it does not follow that anyone sees one. For it is still possible that I am just hallucinating one or seeing something else *as* a book.[24]

This kind of hallucination remains possible even if I have supporting tactual experiences, such as the smooth feel of paper. For even the sense of touch can be stimulated in this way without one's touching a book. Thus, seeing a book is not *just* having appropriate booklike experiences, even if it is *partly* this, and even though, as phenomenalists hold, there is no experienceable difference between a sufficiently stable combination of booklike sense-data and an independently real material book. Still, if seeing a book is not equivalent to any such collection of sensory experiences, phenomenalism fails as an account of the perception of ordinary objects. If there are objects for which it holds, they are not the kind we have in mind in seeking an account of perception.

Perception and the senses

I want to conclude this chapter by indicating some remaining problems about perception. I have already suggested that adverbial theories, sense-datum theories, and the theory of appearing provide plausible accounts of perception, though I consider some version of the first kind prima facie best and I leave open that some theory different from all of them may be better than any. I have also suggested that at times perceptually grounded beliefs fail to be justified, and that, even when justified and true, they can fail to constitute knowledge. There are two further kinds of problems we should explore. One kind concerns observation, the other the relation of perception to the five senses.

Indirect seeing and delayed perception

Observing something in a mirror can count as seeing it. Indeed, it illustrates the sort of thing ordinarily considered seeing something indirectly, as opposed to seeing it by virtue of seeing sense-data. We can also speak of seeing through telescopes and other instruments of observation, again indirectly. But what if the object is microscopic and colorless, yet appears to us through our lens as gray? Perhaps we see it, but not quite as it is.

If we see a microscopic object at all, however, there must be some respect in which what we see it by is faithful to it or at least represents it by some relation of causal dependence – sometimes called *functional dependence*, since perceptual experience seems to vary as a function of certain changes in the object, as where a bird's moving leftward is reflected in a movement of the image. But what we see a thing *by*, such as color and shape, need not be faithful in all respects. A green field can look black at night; we are nonetheless seeing it, and we can see something move in the field even if its color *and* shape are distorted.

How much correspondence between an object and our sensory impressions representing it to us is required in order for us to see it (or hear it, touch it, and so on)? There may be no answer to this question that is both precise and highly general. The cases vary greatly, and many must be examined in their own terms.

Observation of faraway objects poses further problems. Consider seeing the nearest star in the night sky. It is commonly taken to be about four light years away. Presumably we see it (if at all) only as it *was*. For the sense-datum theory, we have a sense-datum produced by it as it was; on the adverbial view, we are sensing "starly" in the way we would have if we had received the relevant visual stimuli at the time the star produced them. If, however, we see it only as it was, do we literally see it at all or just its traces?

Suppose that unbeknownst to us the star exploded two years ago. Is it not odd to say we now see it at all, as opposed to traces of it (as it was)? The latter view is preferable, on the ground that if we unqualifiedly see something now, it exists now. This point is compatible with the view that even though we may see a thing that exists now only *as* it was, we still literally see it now.

Similar points hold for ordinary seeing, since there is still some temporal gap, and for hearing. But if I can see the field only as it was a fraction of a second ago, can I still know that it is now green? I think so, provided there is no reason to believe its color has suddenly changed (but this is something to be reconsidered in the light of our discussion of skepticism in Chapter 10). The same is not clear for the star: may we know by sight alone that it exists now, when it would take about four years for us to realize that the light that had been emitted is no more? This seems doubtful, but it may depend on how likely it is that a star of the kind in question might have burned out during the period in question. If we knew that such stars last billions of years and that this one is only a few million years old, we might plausibly think we know it still exists. It is plain, however, that understanding perception and perceptual knowledge in these sorts of cases is not easy.

Sight and light

We normally regard seeing as intimately connected with light. But must seeing involve light? To approach this question, suppose you could step into a pitch-dark room and have the experiences you would have if it were fully lighted. The room would thus *look* to you just as it would if fully lighted, and you could find any unobscured object by looking around for it. Would this not show that you can see in the dark? If so, then the presence of light is not essential to seeing.

However, the case does not establish quite this much. For seeing is a causal relation, and for all I have said you are just vividly hallucinating precisely the right things rather than seeing them. But suppose you are not hallucinating. Indeed, if someone puts a coin in a box or covers your eyes, you no longer feel that you see the coin. In this case it could be that somehow the coin affects your eyes through a mechanism other than light transmission, yet requiring an unobstructed path between the object seen and your eyes. *Now* it begins to seem that you are seeing. You are responding visually to stimuli that causally affect your eyes. Yet their doing so does not depend on the presence of light.

Vision and the eyes

In an ominous couplet in Shakespeare's *Othello*, Desdemona's father warns Othello:

> Look to her, Moor, if thou hast eyes to see;
> She has deceived her father and may thee.

It would not have occurred to him to question whether there is any way (literally) to see without eyes (figuratively, Othello cannot see well at all, which is his downfall). But philosophers must sometimes ask whether what seems patently obvious is in fact true. Let us, then, go a step further than treating light as inessential to seeing.

Suppose Emma has lost her eyes in an accident, but a camera is later connected to her brain in the way her eyes were. When she points it in a given direction in good light, she has just the visual sensations, say of color and shape, that she would have had by looking with her eyes. Might this not be seeing? Indeed, do we not think of the camera as *functioning* like the eye? If, under the right causal conditions, she gets the right sorts of sensations through her eyes *or* a functional equivalent of them, she is seeing.

But are even "eyes" (or organs functioning like eyes) necessary for seeing? What if someone who lacks "eyes" could get visual sensations matching the objects in the room by strange radiations they emit? Suppose, for instance, that the sensations are stopped by enclosing the coin in cardboard, and that moving it away from the person results in the person's visual impression's representing a decrease in its size. If no part of the body (other than the brain) is required for the visual impression of the coin, there is no organ plausibly considered a functional equivalent of eyes, but might we not have seeing?

If what is crucial for seeing an object is its producing visual sensations suitably corresponding to it, presumably the case is one of seeing. If seeing requires the use of an eye or equivalent organ, then it is not – unless the brain itself is a visual organ after all. It is clear enough that the person would have knowledge of what we might call visual properties, above all colors and shapes. One might call that visual knowledge. But visual knowledge of this kind could be held not to be grounded in seeing, nor acquired through use of any sense organs. For these reasons, it may seem somewhat doubtful whether it must be a kind of *perceptual* knowledge. But a case can surely be made for the visual sensation conception of seeing, as against the organ-of-sight conception.

This case, however, may be challenged: can there be "blind sight," seeing in the absence of visual sensations? For people with blind sight, it is apparently possible to navigate among obstacles as if they saw them, while they honestly report having no visual sensations. Could this be seeing? We automatically tend to understand such behavior in terms of seeing, and there is thus an inclination to say that they are seeing. The inclination is even stronger if light's reaching the eyes is necessary for the person to avoid the obstacles. But if the subject has no visual sensation, it is not clear that we must say this, and I doubt that it would be so. The most we must say is that the person seems to *know* where the obstacles are. Knowing through some causal process by which objects produce true beliefs about them is not necessarily perception, and certainly need not be seeing.[25]

It may seem that blind sight is genuine seeing because it produces knowledge of visual propositions. But knowledge of visual properties is possible without vision, for instance by something like sonar. Moreover, even dependence on light does not establish that the process in question is visual: the light might somehow stimulate non-visual mechanisms that convey information about the objects emitting it. Similar questions arise for the importance of sensations to perception in the other sensory modes, for instance of auditory sensations in hearing. There, too, we find hard questions for which competing answers are plausible.

It is difficult, then, to provide an overall philosophical account of just what seeing, or perception in general, is; and while all the theories we have discussed can help in answering the questions just posed, none does so in such a simple and decisive way as to leave all its competitors without some plausibility. Still, in exploring those theories we have seen many important points about perception. It is a kind of causal relation. Even its least complex and apparently most basic mode, simple perceiving, requires, in addition to the perceiver, both an object of perception and a sensory experience that in some way corresponds to that object and records, if only imagistically, an indefinite and possibly quite extensive amount of information about the object. Partly on the basis of this information, perception tends to produce beliefs about the perceived object. It implies that the perceiver at least normally has justification for certain beliefs about the object, and it normally produces both justified beliefs about that object and knowledge of it.

Perception may be illusory, as where something appears to have a property it does not have, such as acute angles where it really has right angles. Perception – or sensory experience that seems to the subject just like it – may also be hallucinatory, as in the case of Macbeth's dagger. When it is, the question arises whether there must be interior objects, sense-data, with which the subject is directly acquainted. But both illusions and hallucinations can apparently be accounted for without positing sense-data, and thus without adding a further kind of element to the four that seem central in perception – the perceiver, the object perceived, the sensory experience, and the causal relation between the object and perceiver in virtue of which that experience is produced – or reducing perceptual objects to sense-data. Illusion and hallucination can also be accounted for, I think, without denying that perceptual experience – the prime source of the evidence of the senses – normally yields justified belief and knowledge about the world outside the perceiver. So far, we have seen no reason to doubt that perception is a rich and basic source of both knowledge and justification.

Notes

1 Perceiving *of*, perceiving *to be*, and perceiving *that* may also be called perception of, perception to be, and perception that, respectively; but the second expression is not common, and in that case, at least, the -ing forms usually better express what is intended.

2 A related way to see the difference between objectual and propositional beliefs is this. If I believe something to have a property, say a British Airways plane to be a Boeing 747, then this same belief can be ascribed to me using any correct description of that plane, say as the most traveled plane in the British Airways fleet: to say I believe BA's most traveled plane to be a 747 is to ascribe the same belief to me. This holds even if I do not believe it meets that description – and it can hold even where I cannot understand the description, as a child who believes a tachistoscope to be making noise cannot understand 'tachistoscope'. By contrast, if I have a propositional belief, say that the United Airlines plane on the runway is the most traveled in its fleet, this ascription cannot be truly made using just any correct description of that plane, say the plane on which a baby was delivered on Christmas Day, 1995. I may have no inkling of that fact – or think it holds for a British Airways plane.

A rough way to put part of the point here is to say that propositional beliefs about things are about them *under a description or name* and objectual beliefs about things are not (even if the believer could describe them in terms of a property they are believed to have, such as being noisy). It is in part because we need not conceptualize things – as by thinking of them under a description – in order to have objectual beliefs about them that those beliefs are apparently more basic than propositional ones.

3 In terminology common in epistemology, objectual belief is *de re* – of the thing – whereas propositional belief is *de dicto* – of the proposition; and I am making a similar distinction between objectual and propositional perception. The objectual cases, unlike the propositional ones, require no particular concept of the thing in question. To be sure, those who do have the concept of a field and know that I believe it to be rectangular may say, 'He believes the field is rectangular', meaning that I believe it *to be* rectangular. English idiom is often permissive in this way, and nothing need turn on the difference in everyday life. Moreover, some philosophers have held that a thing, such as a field, can be a constituent in a proposition, and this might provide a basis for saying that the two belief ascriptions may be properly interchangeable. I am here ignoring that controversial and uncommon conception of a proposition.

4 I want to leave open here that Susie could, at least for a moment, believe of a tachistoscope that it is making noise, yet not believe any proposition about it: she *attributes* noise-making to it, yet does not conceptualize it in the way required for having a propositional belief about it, the kind of belief expressed in a complete declarative sentence such as 'The thing on the table is making noise'. She would then have no propositional belief about the instrument, the kind of belief that should unqualifiedly be called true (or false), such as that the tachistoscope is making noise. On this approach, what I am calling objectual belief is better called property attribution.

5 Specifically, these are *doxastic* attitudes (from the Greek *doxa*, for 'belief'). A fear can be propositional and thereby cognitive, but it need not entail believing the proposition feared. Some might consider objectual awareness, say awareness of perfect symmetry, cognitive, at least when the person has the concept of relevant property. By contrast, desires, the paradigm *conative* attitudes, are not generally taken to have propositional objects (e.g. 'to swim' in 'my desire to swim' does not express a truth or falsehood).

6 Perceptions that embody beliefs in the ways illustrated are also called *epistemic*, since the embedded belief is commonly considered to constitute knowledge. Their connection with knowledge is pursued in this chapter and others.

7 The distinction between simple and propositional perceiving and others drawn in this chapter are not always observed. At one point W. V. Quine says, "think of '*x* perceives *y*' rather in the image of '*x* perceives that *p*'. We say 'Tom perceives the bowl' because in emphasizing Tom's situation we fancy ourselves volunteering the observation sentence 'Bowl' rather than 'Surface of a bowl', 'Front half of a bowl', 'Bowl and background', and so on. When we ask 'What did he perceive?' we are content with an answer of the form 'He perceived that *p*'." See *Pursuit of Truth*, revised edn. (Cambridge, Mass.: Harvard University Press, 1992), p. 65. Notice that since seeing that (say) there is a bowl in front of one obviously entails seeing a bowl, it is no surprise that we are content with a report of the propositional perception even if we wanted to know only what object was seen. It does not follow that simple seeing *is* or even entails propositional seeing. It is also worth noting that Quine is apparently thinking of seeing here; for the other four senses, there is less plausibility in maintaining what he does.

8 The adage could not be taken to refer to simple seeing, for what we simply see, say a glass or leaf or field, is not the sort of thing that can be believed (to be true or false). To be sure, seeing something, especially something as striking as golfball-size hail, produces a *disposition to believe* certain propositions, say that this is a dangerous storm. But, by what seems an economy of nature, there are many things we are disposed to believe but do not. I

have defended these points in detail in 'Dispositional Beliefs and Dispositions to Believe', *Nous* 28 (1994), 419–34.

9 This applies even to full-scale philosophical dictionaries written by teams of experts, though such a work can provide concise statements of much valuable information. See, for example, the entries on blind sight and perception in Robert Audi (ed.) *The Cambridge Dictionary of Philosophy* (Cambridge and New York: Cambridge University Press, 1995).

10 In the light of what has been said in this chapter so far we can accommodate much of what is plausible in the common view that, as D. M. Armstrong puts it, perception "is an acquiring of knowledge or belief about our physical environment (including our own body). It is a flow of information. In some cases it may be something less than the acquiring of knowledge or belief, as in the cases where perceptions are entirely discounted or where their content has been confidently anticipated." See *Belief, Truth and Knowledge* (Cambridge: Cambridge University Press, 1973), p. 22. First, I can agree that perception entails acquisition of information; the point is that *not all our information is possessed as the content of a belief*. Second, Armstrong himself notes an important way in which perception might fail to produce belief: it is "discounted," as, for example, where one is sure one is hallucinating and so resolutely refuses to accept any of the relevant propositions.

11 This is the kind of view developed in detail by Fred Dretske. See esp. *Knowledge and the Flow of Information* (Cambridge, Mass.: MIT Press, 1981).

12 The notion of normality here is not statistical; it implies that what is not normal is calls for explanation. In the world as we know it, exceptions to the normality generalizations I proposed seem at least quite rare; but the point is not that statistical one but to bring out that the very concepts in question, such as those of seeing and knowing, have a connection in virtue of which explanation is called for if what is normally the case does not occur.

13 In speaking of justification that prevails and of overall justification, I have in mind the kind appropriate to a rational person's believing the proposition in question, construed as roughly the kind such that, when we believe a true proposition with that kind of justification then (apart from the kinds of case discussed in Chapter 8 that show how justified true beliefs *need not* constitute knowledge), we know it.

14 There are complexities I cannot go into, such as how one's competence figures. I am imagining here someone competent to tell whether a note is flat (hence not virtually tone deaf): in general, if one is not competent to tell whether a kind of thing has a property or not, an experience in which it seems to have it may not justify one in believing it does. There is also the question of *what* the belief is about when the "object" is hallucinatory, a problem discussed shortly. Still other problems raised by this justification principle are discussed in Chapter 8 in connection with the controversy between internalism and externalism.

15 If, as is arguable, seeing that it is blue entails knowing that it is, then he does *not* see that it is, though he sees its blue color. But this entailment claim is far from self-evident.

16 The theory of appearing has not been widely defended, but a detailed sympathetic treatment is given in William P. Alston's 'Back to the Theory of Appearing' (in preparation).

17 For a contemporary study and defense of a sense-datum theory see Howard Robinson, *Perception* (London and New York: Routledge, 1994).

18 The view that ordinary perceptual belief is non-inferential is controversial and – for various senses of inferences – has been widely discussed by both philosophers and psychologists. Not *all* sense-datum views, moreover, take perceptual belief to be non-inferential. For a discussion of perception that brings to bear both psychological and philosophical literature see John Heil, *Perception and Cognition* (Berkeley and Los Angeles: University of California Press, 1983), esp. ch. 2.

19 Granted, the book does not appear to us *to be* parallelogrammic if we realize its shape cannot be judged from how it visually appears at an angle, but that is a different point. It concerns

what shape we *take* it to have, not what shape visually appears in our consciousness antecedently to our taking it to be of any particular kind.

20 For a detailed and influential discussion of the adverbial theory, with criticism of the sense-datum view, see R. M. Chisholm, *Perceiving* (Ithaca, NY: Cornell University Press, 1957).

21 This is a very important point. One major materialist theory of the mind–body relation – the identity theory – says that mental phenomena are identical with brain states or processes. But this theory fails if sense-data exist as mental entities and have properties, such as being green and rectangular, that no brain process has. Identity theorists thus generally oppose the sense-datum theory. See, for example, J. J. C. Smart's influential paper, 'Sensations and Brain Processes', *Philosophical Review* 68 (1959), 141–56.

22 These and other problems are brought against the sense-datum theory by Winston H. F. Barnes in 'The Myth of Sense-Data', *Proceedings of the Aristotelian Society* 45 (1944–5).

23 For a detailed twentieth-century defense of phenomenalism, see Book II of C. I. Lewis's *An Analysis of Knowledge and Valuation* (La Salle, Ill.: Open Court, 1946) and R. M. Chisholm's widely known criticism of this defense in 'The Problem of Empiricism', *Journal of Philosophy* 45 (1948).

24 Berkeley might hold that if *God* has booklike sense-data, it does follow that there really is a book. A case can be made for this, but one might also argue that as an all-powerful being God could bring it about that there is a distinction between his creating a physical object and having the corresponding sense-data.

25 A subject who really *does* have visual impressions could also misreport. The possibility of such misreporting about one's own consciousness is discussed in Chapter 3.

CHAPTER 2
Memory

2
Memory

I believe that in the past I have pruned the flowering crab apple tree that stands in the center of the lawn. This belief is apparently grounded in my memory. When I look at the tree and notice its shape, it often occurs to me that I have pruned it, and when it does I have a sense of already believing the proposition that I have pruned the tree. This proposition does not seem to be either a discovery or a result of inference or a bit of wishful thinking, but rather something I have had in mind before and now believe with some conviction.

On the basis of all these facts about my belief that I have pruned this tree, I think that the belief is both justified and constitutes knowledge. Indeed, I cannot help thinking I know that I have pruned the tree. In particular, the belief that I have seems to me to be grounded in memory, in the way that what I am sure I genuinely *remember* is grounded there. Consider remembering one's having just read the preceding part of this page. If one has just done so, there is likely to be a clear sense of having done it; I do not, for instance, simply have a dreamlike recollection, nor am I concluding what I seem to remember from something else, as one might conclude that one had pruned a tree from its distinctive shape.

What, in general terms, is memory? Is it anything beyond a capacity we think of as a storehouse of what we have experienced and learned in the past? And what is it to remember something? Remembering is the chief "function" of memory. Is it exercising, or being able to exercise, the capacity of memory, or is there – as with perceptual knowledge by contrast with mere perceptual belief – a special kind of success that goes with remembering something as opposed to simply believing it from memory?

In pursuing these questions, it will be useful at many points to compare memory with perception. Both are crucial for knowledge of what is external to the mind: the latter gives us a view of what is outside of us in the present, the former of what is outside of the present altogether. Moreover, memory builds on perception; it preserves important information acquired through the senses. It also preserves information about one's own mental life. But how does it do this? Must it, for instance, operate by storing images or can it preserve bare facts? Before we can adequately see how memory is connected with knowledge and justification, we must first understand what it is and something about how it works.

Memory and
the past

We can learn some basic points about memory and remembering by clearing away some tempting mistakes. We cannot say simply that memory is a capacity for knowledge or belief about the past. If I have not lost my memory, I have that capacity, but one could have and even exercise the capacity without exhibiting memory of anything in the past. Consider the events of World War II. I can know a good deal about them through reading about them, but I have no memory of them. I witnessed none of them, and I do not remember them. To be sure, I may remember a *description* of them and thereby say – perhaps recalling a history class – that I remember (for instance) the invasion of Normandy. This could be called remembering the events *indirectly*. But it is not remembering them in the direct and primary sense that concerns us.

Far from all knowledge of the past being a kind of remembering, then, we commonly know propositions about the past on a basis other than remembering it. Consider again the knowledge of the past obtained while reading about it; this knowledge is not an instance of remembering the past but a kind of knowledge of the past acquired through present testimony about it. Similarly, I can gain knowledge about the past from your present description of what you did yesterday. This knowledge may not be *retained*, hence need not be memorial. It may never get into the storehouse: I could possess some of the detailed knowledge you give me, say that you were carrying a camera, for just a moment and immediately lose it after I have acquired it, just as one forgets a phone number needed only for a moment. In these instances, I have knowledge of the past, but only for too brief a time to qualify as remembering the propositions I momentarily knew.

The same example shows that beliefs about the past, such as those I acquire about your activities, do not necessarily represent memory. For they need not be retained and so are not *memory beliefs*, that is, beliefs grounded in memory. They are grounded in testimony and are forgotten before being memorially stored.

Moreover, even when one does memorially retain beliefs about the past, they need not amount to *remembering* something. Retained beliefs about the past can be sheer fabrications unconnected with memory capacities. Imagine, for instance, that although I have not seen you for a year, for some reason I groundlessly form the belief that precisely a month ago you were wearing the same belt I see you wearing now. This belief, even when retained, would not be memorial; it comes not from memory but from undisciplined imagination. Retaining a conviction grounded in fantasy does not upgrade it into a memorial belief.

One might think that beliefs about the past, when they *are* memorial, and not merely retained, represent remembering. But this need not be so, because they may be false, whereas everything we genuinely remember to be the case is true. If, for instance, I remember that Thomas Reid discussed John Locke's ideas about memory, then he in fact did. To see that even a memory belief need not represent genuine remembering, suppose my memory plays a trick on me and I misremember an actual event, falsely thinking I planted a green spruce when it was really a blue one I planted on the occasion in question. I would then have a memory belief (one tracing back in a normal way to an event it is about) that is mistaken, even though its close relatives in my memory are true. Still, I cannot remember planting a green spruce that time if in fact I did not. A falsehood is not elevated into a case of remembering simply because it is retained in a memory belief. Unlike memory beliefs, the things we remember to be true invariably are true.

A further point is that even if beliefs about the past are true, they may be utterly baseless and true only by lucky accident. Suppose that my memorially retained belief that you wore that belt just happens to be true because by chance you did select the same belt for both occasions. This belief still does not represent *remembering* that you did. I have merely retained my luckily true impression that you did. A retained belief of this sort is stored in memory, but only properly grounded true beliefs stored there constitute remembering.[1] Remembering, then, will be of special interest for epistemology, conceived as the theory of knowledge and justification.

The causal basis
of memory beliefs

One might think that just as perceptual beliefs are caused by an object perceived, memory beliefs are caused by a past event remembered. Some memory beliefs are caused in this way, and we will soon see that causal connections to the past are essential for genuine remembering. But even if it should be true that all memory beliefs are produced at least partly by events in the past, past events are not the only *objects* of memory or the only things it "stores." We remember, and thereby retain and believe, general truths, such as mathematical theorems. These mathematical propositions are certainly not past events (propositions are not events of any kind); *learning* them is a past event for most of us, but that is a quite different point. Nor are the propositions past objects of some other sort, or even about the past; but many truths of mathematics are clearly among the objects of remembering – the things we remember.

Moreover, even if every memorial belief is at least partly caused by a past event, the converse does not hold. A belief at least partly caused by a past event need not be memorial. This point applies even if the belief is true. Suppose that my unknowingly taking a non-poisonous drug causes me to feel strangely ill an hour later, and my feeling ill then causes me to believe I have been poisoned. Then, indirectly, the past event of taking medication causes me to believe that I have been poisoned. But this belief is not memorial: it is in no way grounded in my capacity for remembering; I arrive at it by inference to what I think best explains my illness, and I might as well have believed something similar about the present, say to the effect that I am now being poisoned. Even if my suspicious belief that I was poisoned is true – say because I was poisoned by something *else* that I did not even know I had ingested – I may have no memories connected with the belief, such as a memory of someone's sprinkling an unfamiliar powder into my soup. Thus, the belief's being caused by the past event of my taking the drug need not make it a memory belief, even if the belief is true. My memory has played no role in supporting the *content* of the belief. The belief lacks a ground appropriate for suitably connecting it with the past event it represents.

An analogy with perception may help. Consider a belief caused by a flash that I do not see, but merely feel as a momentary heat. This belief need not be a visual belief, even if it is a true belief with visual content, say that a camera flashed near my hand. A belief caused by something visible is not thereby a visual belief, just as a belief caused by a past event – something memorable – is not thereby a memory belief. Since a belief caused by a past event need not be memorial, it would be a mistake to think that a memory belief simply is a belief at least partly caused by a past event.[2]

The analogy between memory and perception is limited, but it does get us on the right track. For surely a belief about the past is memorial *only* if it has some causal connection to a past event, just as a belief is perceptual (say, visual) only if there is some causal connection between it and the perceiver. Even a belief that arises from testimony and not from first-hand observation and is then stored in memory is *traceable* to the past event of one's acquiring it. A thing cannot normally be stored in memory unless it at least once entered that storehouse. Since memory beliefs can concern any subject matter, including future events or mathematical truths, we can see that such beliefs need not be *about* any particular event even if their existence does *trace* to one.

Could one, however, have an *innate* belief? If so, this could be about the past but not connected with a past event, perhaps because the belief is possessed at the time one came into being and does not in any way trace to a remembered experience. It would not enter the storehouse of memory, because it is part of one's initial equipment. To be sure, perhaps an innate belief could be memorial in roughly the ordinary way if in some previous incarnation there is an appropriate event to which it traces, something of the kind that produces a memory.[3] Otherwise, it is merely a retained belief, say retained from birth as part of one's native endowment, rather than a belief entering one's memory through, say, observation or testimony.

Just as it hard to specify how an object must affect a person to be perceived, it is hard to specify just what kind of causal connection to the past is necessary for a memorial belief. This will become clearer as we explore memory, but fortunately many points can be made about memory without a detailed account of the kind of causal connection in question.

Theories of memory

If we model theories of memory on the three major kinds of theories of perception discussed in Chapter 1, there is much we can discover both about the kinds of causal relations required for remembering and about how memory grounds justification and knowledge. Broadly speaking, the three kinds are direct realism (including the adverbial theory and the theory of appearing as well as naive realism), representative realism, and phenomenalism. Each has an analogue in the theory of memory.

Three modes of memory

In constructing theories of memory, there are at least three different but closely related notions we must keep track of: *memory*, *remembering*, and *recalling*. We remember, and recall – roughly, call back to mind – in virtue of the power of our memory. There are things we remember, such as isolated facts, that we may never have occasion to recall. But they remain in the storehouse of memory ready to be retrieved should they be needed. Our memory, then, is a general capacity: the better it is, the more and better we remember and recall.

Like the capacity of perception, however, memory, as the capacity *for* remembering and recalling, can produce impressions that are illusory or, in a way, hallucinatory. There are, then, three things to be accounted for by a theory of memory: first, remembering of events, things, and propositions; second, recalling those items; and third, memory as the capacity in virtue of which remembering and recalling occur.

In developing the memorial counterparts of the three main kinds of theories of perception, I will concentrate mainly on remembering, particularly on the simple remembering *of* events, for instance of my pruning the tree, as opposed to remembering *that* I pruned it (propositional remembering) or remembering the pruning *to be* hard (objectual remembering). I assume that, like simple perception of something, simple remembering of an event, such as a bird's flying by, does not entail having a belief about it, as opposed to being disposed to form beliefs about it if the occasion warrants. But let us concentrate on cases in which one does have such a belief. These cases are crucial for understanding memorial knowledge.

The direct realist view

The memorial counterpart of naive realism in the theory of perception is the view that when we remember an event, we just plain remember it and it is as it seems to us to be. This might be taken to mean that the event is directly presented to us by our memory, as if it were *present* in memory, just as a cat might be present before us. The difference is that the event is not literally taken to be occurring, as a cat one sees is literally before one. Like all the major accounts of memory, this one is best construed as a causal view: as assuming that some causal chain links us to the remembered event. If, for example, I remember seeing Bill a year ago, then it must be in part *because* I did see him that I believe (or am disposed to believe) that I did, and not, say, because I dreamt that I did.

As a direct realist view, this position also maintains that our memorial belief is not produced by any intermediary with which we are acquainted, such as an image. To say that would imply a counterpart of the sense-datum theory. We would have an *in*direct realism: just as we perceive through sense-data presenting the outside world to us, we remember by virtue of memory's presenting the past to us.

At this point, however, naive realism about memory must be revised. To begin with, not just any causal connection to the past will do, as we saw with the poisoning case. The causal chain linking a memory belief to a remembered event must be in a sense *unbroken*. To see why, consider the effect of a broken chain. Imagine that you saw me prune the apple tree and you remember my doing so. The pruning is then the main causal ground of your memory belief, as it is of mine, and we both remember my pruning it. But suppose I forget the event and thus no longer believe I pruned the tree, then later come to believe, solely on the basis of your testimony, that I pruned it. There is still a causal chain from my present belief back to the pruning; for the pruning produced your belief, which in a way produced your testimony, which in turn produced my present belief. But the memorial chain in me was broken by my forgetting. I do not remember my pruning; I simply know, from your testimony, that I did it. *After* your testimony, when I have retained the knowledge you gave me, we might say that I now remember *that* I pruned the tree but no longer remember *pruning it*. Propositional memory *about* an event, even an action of one's own, does not entail event memory *of* it.

Thus, when a break in the chain of events running from a past event to my true belief about that event, say of the pruning, prevents my remembering the event, I may still have knowledge of the pruning; but I do not *remember* it. My knowledge of the event no more represents remembering than my knowledge based solely on your testimony that there is a radiant sunset visible from the front porch represents my seeing it, when I am inside reading.

Some form of the realist view of remembering seems correct, then, insofar as it requires an unbroken causal chain. But as stated so far the view is deficient in some of the ways that naive realism about perception is. For one thing, memory is subject to illusion. I might remember an event, such as meeting you, but not quite as it was, just as you might see white paper in yellow light, and thus not see it as white but as yellow. Here I do not simply remember; I remember incorrectly, for example in remembering the meeting as taking place in New York when it was in fact in Chicago. Second, there is the memorial counterpart of hallucination: I may have a vivid image of mailing a letter, and might believe I remember doing so, yet be quite mistaken. We must, then, account for memorial illusion and similar problems.

The representative theory of memory

The territory may begin to look familiar, particularly if we recall the sense-datum theory of perception, which posits sensory objects that, as intermediaries between external things and the mind, represent the former to the latter. For instance, we might suppose that there are memory images, and that they are genuine objects which figure in remembering rather as sense-data are thought to figure in perceiving. These images might even *be* sense-data if they are vivid enough, but normally they are more like the images of fantasy. It might be like this: seeing the apple tree as I prune it produces sensory images in me (whether these are sense-data or not); my memorial images of the tree might be conceived as a kind of *residue of perception*.[4]

Perhaps, then, we may properly be said to remember an event when we have at least one true belief about it suitably grounded in a memorial image of it, that is, an image of it which derives, by a suitable unbroken chain, from our experience of the event and represents it correctly in at least some way. The better the representation of the event, the better our memory of it. Call this view of the memory of events *the representative theory of memory*. It takes such memory to be a representational faculty that works through images that in some sense picture the things they represent to us.

Like the sense-datum theory of perception, the representative theory of memory is an indirect realism. It construes our remembering as mediated by memory images (though not as based on inference from facts about such images); it is *through* images that we are acquainted with the past. The view is also like the sense-datum theory in readily accounting for memorial illusion and similar problems. To remember incorrectly, as opposed to simply having a false belief about the past with no basis in memory, is to be acquainted with a memory image that, despite its being sufficiently faithful to the remembered event to ground one's remembering it, has some aspect which produces a false belief about the event, say that it was in New York rather than in Chicago.

The counterpart of hallucination is also treated as one would expect from a study of the sense-datum theory. Memorial hallucination occurs when one has an image that is intrinsically like a memorial one, but not linked to a past event by a suitable causal chain, just as, in perceptual hallucinations, the sense-data are not produced by the object (or are produced by it in an abnormal way).

Unfortunately, the representative theory of memory has many of the difficulties of the sense-datum theory and some of its own. Consider the similar difficulties first, particularly in relation to remembering.

Remembering an event surely does not require acquaintance with an image of it. It is not impossible for me to reel off, from memory, some details of a conversation I heard a week ago, even if I have no images, even auditory ones, of the conversation or what it concerned. Moreover, misremembering an event does not require acquaintance with something, such as an image, which actually *has* the property one mistakenly remembers the event as having had, as a sense-datum representing a book viewed from a certain angle is supposed to have (say) the property of being parallelogrammic. I can misremember meeting you by remembering the meeting as being in New York, when it was actually in Chicago, even if the correct aspect of my memory is not accompanied by an image that is of our actual meeting in Chicago. I may simply remember the occasion with its animated conversation, yet have the false impression that it was in New York. That false impression does not require, for instance, my imaging the waters of Lake Michigan visible from our Chicago restaurant.

Memorial thinking – an episode of thinking about one or more remembered objects or events – may also be possible without objects to serve as images of the past. In retrospective imagination, might I not vividly experience our meeting even if I am acquainted with no object that represents it for me in the way that, in hallucinations, sense-data are supposed to represent physical objects? Granted, I cannot *recall* – in the sense of bringing back into my consciousness – the color of your sweater, but I might surely remember what you said and the hoarseness of your voice owing to the flu, and I might remember what color your sweater was even if I cannot bring the color itself to mind (perhaps you said that the pale blue matched your jacket, and it is by that remark that I remember what the color was without imaging it). I can apparently imagine past events without having direct acquaintance with memorial pictures of them, just as I can apparently hallucinate an object without having direct acquaintance with a sense-datum representation of it.

A further difficulty for the representative theory arises when we consider a disanalogy between remembering and perceiving. I can remember our meeting now and describe it to someone from memory even if I have *no* images or image-like experiences at all, whereas I apparently cannot see a tree if I have no visual sensations, such as the impressions of foliage that make up an image of a tree. Remembering, even of events that one has perceived, is neither a sensory process nor necessarily an *imaginational* one (even if it often is, especially in some people, such as those who are highly "visual"). So there need not be, in every case of remembering, even the *makings* of a representative theory to which images are crucial.

The phenomenalist conception of memory

The kinds of difficulties we have seen in relation to the representative theory of memory suggest that the memorial counterpart of phenomenalism may also suffer irreparable difficulties. Above all, a phenomenalist account of memory relies on images or imaging or something like them at least as heavily as does the representative theory, and images do not seem either necessary or sufficient for our remembering events. Let us explore this.

On the most plausible phenomenalist account of memory, remembering an event is understood in terms of the imaginational content of present experience. To remember an event is (roughly) to have a suitable collection of images representing it, on the basis of which, in a certain way, one believes (or is disposed to believe) something about that event. But this will not do. Remembering an event simply does not require a collection of images analogous to the sense-data from which phenomenalists try to construct physical objects (or even a collection of imaging experiences such as an adverbial phenomenalist might posit).

Images of the kind posited to account for remembering are not only not necessary for remembering, as our examples show; they are not sufficient for it either. Just as no collection of sense-data is such that its existence implies perception of an external object, no collection of images (even apparently memorial images) is such that, in having a belief about the past grounded on those images, one must be remembering something. No matter how vivid my images of talking with you beneath the skyscrapers of Wall Street, I may not remember our talking there, and my belief that we did talk there (or anywhere) may be mistaken.

The adverbial conception of memory

If these difficulties are as serious as they seem, then if, in search of a better account of memory, we are to change course and construct a plausible alternative theory of remembering, we must take account of them. First, such a theory will not claim that remembering is direct in one of the ways perception is. Plainly, memory is not *temporally direct*, since past events are not temporally present, whereas we can see a thing's properties at the same time that it has them.[5] By contrast, any plausible account of remembering, such as a properly developed adverbial theory of it, will take remembering to be (as perceiving apparently is) *epistemically direct*. Memory beliefs, as we have seen, are not inferential. It is not on the basis of any premise that I believe (or know) that I have pruned that crab apple tree. My belief is grounded in memory as a preserver of beliefs and other elements, not in other beliefs giving me premises to support the belief.[6]

Moreover, such a theory must not say that (actively) remembering an event, such as pruning a tree, is memorially imaging in a way suitably caused by that past event, as perceiving an object is sensory stimulation suitably caused by the thing perceived. For no such imaging need occur (though it commonly does in what I am calling active remembering). One can describe a past event to others, and in doing so actively remember it, even if one is imaging nothing but the faces one sees.

Positively, the adverbial view of memory, applied to remembering events, should be expressed as something like this. First, *actively* (*occurrently*) *remembering* an event is realizing a memorial capacity concerning it, where this capacity is linked to the event by an unbroken causal chain. Just as in observing a cat walk by one is realizing a perceptual capacity, in describing a play from memory one is realizing a memorial one. The typical realizations – the things that constitute experiencing in a memorial way – are imaging processes concerning the event, and expressions or formations of beliefs about it; but there may be other realizations, such as recognizing a picture of the event. Second, *passively* (*dispositionally*) *remembering* an event is having this capacity in an unrealized state, as where, though I can (and have a disposition to) recall the pruning if I want to, my mind is wholly on other things. Something would have to call the pruning to mind for me to remember it actively.

To see the difference between the dispositional and the occurrent in another context, consider elasticity. It is a dispositional property, whereas stretching is an occurrent property that manifests the disposition (this distinction is further discussed in Chapter 3). Recalling an event can be to remembering it much as a thing's stretching is to its elasticity. Just as stretching manifests the disposition of elasticity, recalling is a case of actively remembering that manifests the dispositional memory that retains the thing recalled.

Propositional remembering – remembering *that* – can be construed similarly. On the adverbial view imagined here, to remember that an event occurred is a memorial *way* of truly believing that it did, roughly, to have one or more true beliefs about it which are suitably linked by an unbroken chain to past experience and represent the event as having a certain character, say as happening in bright sunlight. These beliefs constitute knowledge that is preserved in memory. On this view, then, remembering that something is so is knowledge *from memory*, rather as seeing that the cat is walking by is knowledge through perception.

Most of what we propositionally remember is dispositional, roughly, recorded in dispositional beliefs. When these beliefs are called up in active propositional remembering, as where I describe how I pruned the apple tree, one is experiencing in a memorial *way*. This does not require being acquainted with imagistic memorial objects. One may, but need not, image memorially, as where one actually calls up the remembered experience and focuses on its features in one's imagination.

Moreover, whether one images a remembered event or not, the event need not be entirely *as* one remembers it. Here event memory differs from propositional memory; the former, like seeing *as*, can misrepresent the thing in question, whereas remembering that something is so, like seeing that it is, entails its being so. One can remember a meeting as being in the wrong city, thus remember it in the wrong way geographically, just as one can see a rectangular book as parallelogrammic and so see it in the wrong way visually. In neither case does one have to be fooled. With memory as with perception, illusion does not always produce false belief. Typically, if I remember something as having a certain quality, say a conversation as being rushed, I believe it was like that; but I can remember it *as* such, yet know from independent evidence (such as having often transacted the painstaking business in question) that it was not rushed. If, however, one really remembers some object or event, then one is right about at least some aspect of it, or is at least in a position to form some true beliefs about it on considering the matter. This is parallel to the point that if one really sees something, one is at least in a position to see it to be something or other.

Remembering, recalling, and imaging

So far, the adverbial view seems superior to its competitors in relation to the crucial notions to be accounted for, such as remembering and recalling. Will this direct realist view stand scrutiny? Here is one nagging doubt. When I am remembering an event, especially a perceived one like a ship's docking as opposed to an imperceptible one like thinking about knowledge, I typically *do* have some related image. I refer, of course, to active remembering, as opposed to my stored remembering of events that are now far from my mind but which I *could* actively recall if the subject came up. The first kind of remembering is occurrent, since it is in part a matter of something's occurring in me. The second kind is dispositional, since it is a matter of my being disposed (roughly, tending) to remember a thing actively (occurrently) *provided that* something, such as a question about the event, activates my memory. Thus, although yesterday's concert may be far from my mind while I write a letter, if someone asks how I liked the Chopin, then my dispositional memory may be activated; and, as I recall it, thereby occurrently remembering it, I may say I thought it inspiring.

It is occurrent remembering that is analogous to perception and is my main concern now; and it is occurrent remembering that is closely associated with imaging. Does occurrent remembering require some sort of imagery after all, even if not images as sense-datum objects?

Here is a natural way to answer. Consider one of your memories of an event, for instance meeting someone for the first time. Do this in such a way that you take yourself to be actively remembering that event. Second, ask yourself whether you are now imaging. When I do this, I image. Here, remembering involves imaging. But notice what has happened: I have called up a memory and inspected the results of my effort. Perhaps I am imaging because of the *way* I evoked the remembering, or because I scrutinized the process of my calling up the meeting. Self-conscious evocation of the past and scrutiny of the results may yield findings unrepresentative of remembering in general.

This procedure of evoking memories of the past, then – selecting them by recalling past phenomena – is defective as a way of determining whether remembering requires imaging. But the procedure does show something. For suppose that what I have done is to *recall* a past event. Perhaps recalling, which is calling back to mind, often by a lengthy search of one's memory, *does* require imaging provided it is a recalling *of* an imageable event, such as pruning a tree, as opposed to, say, a theorem. There is some reason to think this is so. If no imaging of our luncheon comes into my consciousness, how can I have recalled it? Sometimes, moreover, we say that we cannot recall someone, meaning not that we do not know full well who the person is, but that we cannot image the person. There, recalling seems to imply some sort of imaging.

Even if recalling should imply imaging, however, remembering does not. Why, then, does that idea persist? For one thing, when we collect specimen memories in order to examine remembering, we often do it by recalling things. If so, it should be no surprise that the specimen memories involve recalling something. If, in trying to determine the shades of beech leaves, I collect specimens only from the nearby copper beeches, it is no surprise that I may think beeches in general have copper-colored leaves.

A deeper point is that what we cannot recall we often *believe* we cannot remember. On the adverbial view, this is natural; for an inability to remember is a lack of a memorial capacity, and, understandably, we may think we lack that capacity when, under normal conditions, we cannot exercise it in an expectable way – such as recalling an event we have been taking ourselves to remember. But imaging is only *one* exercise of memorial capacity, important though it is; and just as we can be capable of climbing a mountain, but not necessarily by every route to the top, we may have the capacity constituted by remembering something but be unable to exercise the capacity in every way it can be exercised. Hence, inability to image does not imply that one does not remember the thing in question. We can see, then, both why there is a tendency to think that remembering requires imaging and why we should not accept this view. Let us explore this further.

If imaging seems more important for remembering than so far granted, consider another case. Suppose I can neither recall nor image Jane. I can still remember her; for *on seeing her*, I might recognize her and might remember, and even recall, our last meeting. This would suggest that my memory simply needed to be "jogged." In adverbial terms, before I see her again I can dispositionally know her in a certain memorial way – I can objectually remember her – even though I cannot imagistically experience her in that memorial way – namely, recall her.

I choose the example of remembering a person because it is easy to show that one does remember someone by creating the right occasion. Recalling her is an indication of my remembering her but may not be possible despite my remembering her; recognizing her when I meet her is a proof of the pudding. We cannot draw this contrast with past *events*, since they cannot be literally brought back. But even here, there is indirect recognition, as where one recognizes a ship's docking in Helsinki harbor upon seeing a picture of the event. It is doubtful, then, that the relation between recalling and remembering is different with events.

It is important to see that the way I am now considering the relation between recalling and remembering is direct and non-introspective. I am exploring what is possible and what it would show. Now it is possible for me to have no image of pruning the crab apple tree, yet give an account of the pruning that is both remarkably accurate *and* grounded by a suitable causal chain in the original experience of the pruning. If this occurs without my having received any information about the event from anyone else, it is an excellent reason to think I remember the event.

To be sure, our *beliefs* about what events we remember may depend on what we can recall, which, in turn, may be largely dependent on what we can image. But what events we *do* remember is a matter of how our memorial capacities are grounded in the past and not of what kind of evidence we can get, imagistically or otherwise, concerning that grounding.

In exercising my capacity to remember events, then, I need not rely on my images or even on my ability to image, though in fact retention of images doubtless aids remembering. The representative theory of memory therefore seems mistaken, and some memorial analogue of direct realism regarding perception is apparently preferable. The suggested adverbial view of remembering is a good position from which to work; but I leave some important questions about memory unexplored, and it would be premature to present that view as clearly correct.

The epistemological centrality of memory

We can now see some points about memory as a source of belief, knowledge, and justification. Let us start with beliefs, the least complex of the three cases. Memory is a source of beliefs in the way a storehouse is a source of what has been put there, but it is not a source of beliefs in the way perception is. Obviously our memory, as a mental capacity, is a source of beliefs in the sense that it *preserves* them and enables us to *call them up*. It also enables us to *draw on our beliefs to supply premises* in reasoning. This occurs when we solve mathematical problems using memorized theorems. But we may also rely on presupposed premises that guide us without having to be recalled.

When our memory beliefs are of propositions we remember to be true, they constitute knowledge. If you remember that we met, you know that we did. Similarly, if you remember me, you know me (at least in the sense of knowing who I am, which is not to say you can recognize me in person). So memory, when it is a source of what is remembered, commonly yields both knowledge *that* and knowledge *of*. The analogy to perception is significant here too.

Is memory also a source of justification? Surely what justifies the great majority of my justified beliefs about the past is my memory. For instance, my belief that I twice pruned the crab apple tree is justified because of the way that belief is preserved in my memory. It has, for example, a special kind of familiarity, confidence, and connection with other things I seem to remember. Moreover, it appears that if I remember that I met you, I am justified in believing I met you. It thus seems that where memory yields genuine remembering it also yields justification. Certainly this commonly holds.

Remembering, knowing, and being justified

Perhaps, however, I could remember that I met you, yet *fail* to be justified in my belief because (in fun) you convince me, by good arguments and by enlisting the corroboration of plausible cohorts, that I am confusing you with someone else. Still, if my belief remains properly grounded in my actual memory of having met you (perhaps because the memory is so clear that the belief is almost unshakable), I may nonetheless genuinely remember that I met you.

Despite this point, if your arguments are good enough, I may properly reproach myself for still holding the belief that I met you, and my belief may perhaps cease to be justified. Its justification would be defeated by your arguments and by my own credible self-reproaches based on seeing their plausibility.

If this case is possible, it has an important implication. If, as I have suggested, remembering that something is so entails knowing it is so, then the case as described implies that knowing that something is so does *not* imply justifiedly believing it. (In Chapter 8, I return to the relation between knowledge and justification, but it is important here to see that the domain of memory provides a challenge to understanding that relation.[7])

Furthermore, if the case is possible and one *can* remember that something is so, yet fail to be justified in one's believing that it is so, then we might question whether memory yields any justified beliefs after all. Fortunately, the example by no means rules this out. Quite apart from cases of genuine remembering, memory often yields justified belief. If I have a vivid and confident belief that I met Jane, and this belief seems to me to arise from a memory of the occasion, I may, simply on that basis, be justified in the belief. Surely this is, after all, just the sort of belief that usually does represent remembering; in any case, I have no reason to question its credentials. Memory can justify a belief even where that belief does not constitute knowledge or rest on actual remembering. If, for instance, I do not in fact remember meeting Jane, perhaps the only reason why I do not is that it was her identical twin, of whose existence I had no idea, whom I met. That excusable ignorance may prevent my knowing that I met Jane, but it does not preclude my justifiedly believing that I did.

Memorial justification and memorial knowledge

A justification principle suggested by these reflections is this: normally, if one has a clear and confident memory belief that one experienced a given thing, then the belief is justified. Similarly, we might call such beliefs prima facie justified.[8] A memory belief is one grounded in memory; this is typically a kind of belief which represents the event or proposition in question as familiar in a certain way. Commonly, if one considered the matter, the belief would seem to one to arise from one's memory; but the notion cannot be defined by that normal property of such beliefs, and it is not easily defined at all.[9]

A still broader principle may perhaps be true: normally, clear and confident memory beliefs with any subject matter are justified provided they do not conflict with other beliefs one holds. (Again, we might call such beliefs prima facie justified.) With both principles the degree of justification may not be great, particularly if there is no corroboration, such as apparently recalling a sequence of events related to the belief. My belief that I met someone at a restaurant tends to be better justified if I apparently remember related events, such as a friend's recently mentioning our meeting that person there, than if it is isolated from other apparent memory beliefs that confirm it.

Both these and similar principles help to describe how memory is plausibly conceived as a source of justification. This is certainly how it is standardly conceived. Imagine someone saying "I have a clear and confident memory that we met at the Café Rouge, but this gives me no justification whatever for thinking so." We can understand someone's holding that there is *better* justification for not believing this – say, because of known memory failure – but that would show only that the justification is defeated, not that there is none whatever to be defeated.

Memory as a preservative and generative source

There is a very important difference between the way in which memory is a source of knowledge and the way in which it is a source of justification. To see this, we must take account of several points. Memory is a *preservative* capacity with respect to both belief and knowledge. First, when you initially come to believe something, you do not (yet) remember it. Second, you cannot remember something unless you *previously* knew or at least believed it, for instance perceptually.

Thus, memory *retains* belief and knowledge. It does not generate them, except in the sense that, by *using* what you have in memory, you can acquire beliefs and knowledge through inference (or perhaps through other processes that themselves yield belief and knowledge). I may, for instance, infer much from propositions I remember, or I may arrive at greater knowledge of a movie I saw by calling up images of various scenes. Here it is thought processes – inferential and recollective – that, partly on the basis of retained material, produce belief and knowledge.

To say that memory is not a generative source of knowledge is not to deny that memory is sufficiently connected with knowledge to figure in an epistemic principle. It is plausible to say that normally, a *true* memory belief, supported by a vivid, steady experience of recall that is in turn corroborated by other memory experiences, represents knowledge. But if this principle is correct, it is *because* such beliefs are of a kind that ordinarily constitute knowledge originally, say when one learned through perception the truth that the crab apple tree has recently been pruned, and continued therefore to have grounds, preserved by one's memory, for holding this belief.

Memory is not, then, a *basic source* of belief or knowledge, a source that generates them other than through dependence on some different source of them. It is, however, a basic source of justification. We can be justified in believing something either on the basis of remembering that it is so, or of our having a clear and confident memorial belief that it is. If we genuinely remember that it is so, it is so, and we know that it is. Justification for believing the proposition, by contrast, is possible even if that proposition is false.

This justifying capacity of memory often operates even where we have no associated images. But in accounting for what justifies memorial beliefs, images do have a significant if restricted role. We are better justified in a memorial belief supported by imagery, especially vivid imagery, than in memorial beliefs not thus supported (other things being equal). Perhaps the reason is that we have at least some justification for believing that there is less likelihood of error if both imagery and beliefs point in the same direction, say to my having met you two years ago. But we need not ascertain the basis of the point to see that it holds.

For all the analogy between memory and perception, then, there are important differences. If both are essential to our justification for believing at least a huge proportion of what we believe, perception is more fundamental in a way that is crucial to the development of our outlook on the world. It supplies memory with much of its raw material, whereas memory, though it guides us in seeking what to observe and, in that way, often determines *what* we perceive, does not supply raw materials to perception: it manufactures no perceptibles. It does, to be sure, supply raw materials for introspection and thought: we would have vastly less to look in on or think about if we did not remember sights and sounds, conversations and embraces, ideas and plans.

Both memory and perception, however, are to be causally conceived, and both are, in different ways, sources of belief, justification, and knowledge, propositional as well as objectual. But perception is a basic source of all three: it can produce them without dependence on another belief-producing capacity, such as reasoning. Memory, being a capacity for the preservation, and not the creation, of belief and knowledge, is not a basic source of them. Still, without it, perceptual knowledge could not be amassed and used to help us build theories of the world or of human experience, or even to make local maps to guide daily living. We would not even have a sense of who we are, since each moment would be dead to us by the next. Beyond this, memory is a basic source of justification. That is a vitally important epistemological point. And as we shall see, the role of memory in our knowledge in general is also of enormous epistemological importance.

Notes

1 We might call merely retained beliefs *weakly* grounded in memory, but I reserve the terms 'memory belief' and 'memorial belief' for beliefs grounded in the normal way illustrated by remembering what I come to believe from testimony.

2 The point that how beliefs are caused, and what their content is, may not indicate how they

are grounded (where grounding is the notion crucial to determining whether the belief is justified or represents knowledge) is even wider than so far suggested. A noise too faint for me to hear may cause Tom to jump, which in turn causes me to believe that he is startled; my belief that he is startled is thus (indirectly) caused by the noise, but it is not auditory. It is in no way grounded in my hearing.

3 In both Western philosophy – for example, in Plato and Descartes – and Eastern philosophy, innate ideas have played a significant part. In recent times there has been much skepticism about whether they – as opposed to innate dispositions to form ideas – are even possible. I cannot discuss this issue here, but I see no reason not to leave the matter open for the sake of argument. In any case, the possibility of "innate" beliefs seems implicit in something less controversial: that in principle a person could be created as a perfect copy of another, and so would have at least some beliefs at the moment of "birth."

4 John Locke, for example, in his *Essay Concerning Human Understanding*, speaks of perception as "the inlet of all the materials of" knowledge (Book II, ch. IX, section 15) and says, comparing perception and memory, that "when my eyes are shut or windows fast, I can at pleasure recall to my mind the ideas of light, or the sun, which *former sensation had lodged in my memory* . . . there is a manifest difference between the ideas laid up in my memory . . . and those [of perception] which force themselves upon me . . . there is nobody who doth not perceive the difference in himself between contemplating the sun, as he hath the idea of it in his memory, and actually looking upon it: Of which two, his perception is so distinct, that few of his ideas are more distinguishable from one another" (Book IV, ch. XI, section 5; italics added).

5 Or virtually the same time: the time-lag argument discussed in Chapter 1 indicates that if light transmission is essential to seeing there will be a tiny gap between the time at which something we see has a property we are visually caused to believe it has and the time at which we see it as having, or believe it to have, that property. We also noted, however, that light transmission does not seem *absolutely* essential for seeing.

6 I am assuming that simple inferences do not require the use of memory; but even if they do, once a belief is formed inferentially, it can be inferentially *held* only insofar as it is supported by the premise beliefs. Then memory may well be what preserves the *inferential structure* represented by believing something on the bases of premises, but the belief of this is itself only preserved by memory without being genuinely memorial. Not every way that memory preserves a belief renders the belief memorial, and one would explain why one holds this belief not by saying 'I remember . . . ' but by citing one's premises.

7 I develop this case, defend the conclusion tentatively stated here, and discuss other matters considered in this chapter, in 'Memorial Justification', *Philosophical Topics* 23, 1 (1995), 31–45. For a different position on some of the relevant issues see Carl Ginet, *Knowledge, Perception, and Memory* (Dordrecht: D. Reidel, 1975).

8 It is natural to wonder whether the degree of justification normally belonging to such memory beliefs is as great as that normally belonging to perceptual beliefs. Perhaps not, and one could add 'to some degree' in the normality formulation. But it still appears that the kind of justification is such that it is generally reasonable to believe the propositions in question and that when they are true we commonly can know them on the basis of the relevant kind of justifier.

9 The paper just cited and some of the literature it refers to consider this difficult question; fortunately, it is not one that requires here any more than the sketch of an answer given.

CHAPTER 3
Consciousness

Two basic kinds of mental properties

Introspection and inward vision

Some theories of introspective consciousness

Realism about the objects of introspection
An adverbial view of introspected objects
The analogy between introspection and ordinary perception
Introspective beliefs, beliefs about introspectables, and fallibility

Consciousness and privileged access

Infallibility, omniscience, and privileged access
Difficulties for the thesis of privileged access
The possibility of scientific grounds for rejecting privileged access

Introspective consciousness as a source of justification and knowledge

The range of introspective knowledge and justification
The defeasibility of introspective justification
Consciousness as a basic source

Consciousness

So far, I have talked mainly about beliefs regarding things outside myself: the green field before me, the smell of roses in the air, the cold glass in my hand. But there is much that we believe about what is internal to us. I believe that I am *thinking* about self-knowledge, that I am *imaging* cool blue waters, and that I *believe* I am a conscientious citizen. In holding these three beliefs, I am attributing rather different sorts of properties to myself: thinking, imaging, and believing. What sorts of properties – or at least phenomena – are they, and how do our beliefs about them give us justification and knowledge? For instance, are some of these self-directed beliefs the products of a kind of *inner perception*? This seems a natural view. If there is some truth in it, then exploring the analogy between perception and self-consciousness might help to explain how such beliefs are justified or constitute knowledge.

Our most important kind of self-knowledge is not about our bodies but about our minds – for instance about what we believe, want, feel, and take ourselves to remember. It will help to start by describing the three kinds of mental properties illustrated by thinking, imaging, and believing. Since they are all broadly mental, this is a task in the philosophy of mind. But epistemology cannot proceed without considerable reflection on mental phenomena: thinking, inferring, and believing, for instance, are central in both branches of philosophy; and if we are to understand self-knowledge, we need a good sense of what kinds of properties characterize us. We might begin with the two kinds that, for our purposes, yield the most basic division.

Two basic kinds of mental properties

Thinking is a kind of *process* and involves a sequence of events, events naturally said to be in the mind. Thinking in human beings has a beginning, a middle, and an end; it is constituted by mental events, such as considering a proposition one believes; and these events are ordered at least in time, often in subject matter, and sometimes in logic.

Simply *having* an image, in the minimal way one does when there is a static, changeless picture in the mind's eye, is (I assume) being in a certain (mental) *state*. Unlike something that changes, such a state does not absolutely require the occurrence of any events. *Imaging* can be a process of calling up a succession of images or, as when one of them is held changeless in the imagination, static. I could image something for a time without any change whatever in my imaging, and without the occurrence of any mental event that might be part of the imaging. (The same holds even if having an image is standing in a relation to, say, a sense-datum.)

Believing could also be called a mental state, but this terminology can be misleading in suggesting that having a belief is a state of mind, where that implies a global mental condition like worry or excitement. Unlike images and aroused emotions like jubilation, beliefs do not tend to crowd one another out. Beliefs differ from images in at least two further ways. First, beliefs need not be in consciousness. I have many which, unlike my belief that I am now writing, I cannot call to mind without making some effort. Second, believing need not in any sense be "pictorial." Consider a belief present in consciousness, in the way my belief that the rain has stopped is. This belief is present because I have called it to my attention; I might have had it without attending to it or even the fact it records.

Even a belief present in consciousness in this way *and* about something as readily picturable as the Statue of Liberty need not involve anything pictorial in the way my imaging must. Suppose I believe that the Statue of Liberty has a majestic beauty standing high in the Bay of New York. Without picturing anything, I can entertain this proposition, and in that way have this belief present in my consciousness. By contrast, imaging cool blue waters requires picturing a blue surface.

To be sure, when we *call up* this belief about the statue, we tend to picture that structure. But I could later get the proposition in mind, as where I am listing some majestically beautiful landmarks deserving preservation, without picturing anything. I could even retain the belief if I had forgotten what the statue looked like and simply remembered my aesthetic judgment of it.

It will help in sorting things out if we observe a distinction that has already come up but needs more development. Let us call mental properties like beliefs *dispositional* and mental processes like thinking *occurrent*. The latter are constituted by mental events and are occurrences: they take place in the way events do and may be said to happen or to go on. The former are not occurrences and may not be said to happen, take place, or go on.

The basic contrast is this. To have a dispositional property or (perhaps not quite equivalently) to be in a dispositional state is to be disposed – roughly, to tend – to do or undergo something under certain conditions, but not necessarily to be actually doing or undergoing or experiencing something or changing in any way. Thus, my believing that I am a conscientious citizen is, in part, my being disposed to say that I am one, under conditions that *elicit* that sort of verbal manifestation of my belief, such as your asking me whether I intend to vote. Yet I can have this belief without doing or undergoing anything connected with it, just as sugar can be soluble in water while it is still in a solid, unaltered lump. I can have the belief even in dreamless sleep. By contrast, to have an occurrent property *is* to be doing, undergoing, or experiencing something, as sugar undergoes the process of dissolving. Thus, if you are thinking about mental phenomena you are doing something, even if you are in an armchair; and if you are imaging a flowering crab apple tree, you are experiencing something, at least in the sense that your imaging the tree is now present in your consciousness, as a feature of your experience.

Having a static image, however, as opposed to *calling up* an image, is not a process as, for example, silently talking to oneself is. Occurrent mental properties, then, must be subdivided. To mark a difference between them, we might call occurrent mental properties like thinking *experiential process properties* and occurrent mental properties like having a static image in mind *experiential state properties*.[1] Clearly, both differ from dispositional properties. All three kinds of mental properties turn out to be important for understanding the epistemological role of introspection.[2]

Introspection and inward vision

If we take a cue from the etymology of 'introspection', which derives from the Latin *introspicere*, meaning 'to look within', we might construe introspection as attending to one's own consciousness and, when one's mind is not blank, thereby achieving a kind of inner seeing. I might introspect my images, for instance, and conclude that my image of the spruce indicates that the spruce is taller than the maple.

It is not only in consciously introspecting that one can vividly image. In *King Lear* there is a scene in which Edgar wants to convince Gloucester, who has lost his sight, that he is at the top of a cliff. Edgar's description is so vivid that the deception succeeds:

> How fearful and dizzy 'tis to cast one's eye so low!
> The crows and choughs that wing the midway air
> Show scarce so gross as beetles. Halfway down
> Hangs one that gathers samphire, dreadful trade!
> Methinks he seems no bigger than his head.

The fishermen that walk upon the beach
Appear like mice, and yond tall anchoring bark . . .
Almost too small for sight.

(Act IV, scene vi)

What Gloucester sees in his mind's eye is so vivid that he believes he is at the
edge of a precipice. His visual consciousness is filled with images from Edgar's
portrait.

If introspective consciousness does produce inner seeing and other sensuous
imagery (such as, commonly, sound), we can try to understand it by drawing
on what we know about perception. For instance, we can explore introspectional counterparts of some theories of perception and sensory experience. But
one limitation of that procedure is apparent the moment we reflect on the
dispositional mental properties, for instance believing, wanting, or having a
fear of cancer. We do not see such properties in any sensory way, as we may be
thought to see (in our mind's eye) an image of cool blue waters. Wants are not
seen, not even in our mind's eye.

The analogy to vision might, however, still hold for introspection regarding
occurrent mental properties. If it does, it presumably applies only to the mental state properties, like imaging. For surely thinking is not seen. It need not
even be heard in the mind's ear. I may hear my silent recitation of Shelley's
'Ozymandias', but thinking *need* not occur in inner speech, certainly not
speech of that narrative, punctuated sort.

Perhaps it is only pictorial mental properties that we see through inner
vision; and perhaps it is only *sensory* properties, such as inner recitations,
tactual imagings (say, of the coldness of a glass), and the like that seem accessible to inner analogues of perception: hearing in the mind's ear, touching in the
tactual imagination, and so on. It is doubtful, then, that we can go very far
conceiving introspection as simply producing inward seeing. Still, it is worth
exploring how the analogy to seeing holds up for the one important case of
pictorial properties.

Some theories of
introspective consciousness

Suppose that introspecting such things as images of cool blue waters does
produce a kind of inner seeing. Are we to understand this seeing on realist
lines, so that there must be some real object, such as a sense-datum, that is
seen by the introspective eye?

Realism about the objects of introspection

One might think that the sense-datum view simply cannot be extended in this way to introspection. This is at least a natural assumption about self-understanding. For on the introspectional counterpart of the sense-datum view, seeing (in one's mind's eye) an image of cool blue waters would require something like *another* image, one that represents the first one in the way sense-data represent a physical object seen by virtue of the perceiver's acquaintance with them. Call it a *second-order image*, since it is an image of an image.

What would second-order images be like? If I try to have an image of my image of cool blue waters, I either get that very image all over again, or I have an image of something else, or I get something that is not an image at all, such as a *thought* of my original image. But this point does not show that there could not be a second-order image. Perhaps there could be second-order images that are less vivid than the originals they picture, just as my imaginational image of cool blue waters is less vivid than the sensory image I have in actually seeing those waters.

Perhaps. But a defender of an adverbial account of sensory experience might argue that even when perceptual imaging is later "copied" in retrospective imagination, there is really just *one* kind of imaging process, and it occurs more vividly in perception than in imagination. Thus, imaging blue waters is simply imaginationally, rather than perceptually, sensing in the way one does upon seeing blue waters – in short, sensing blue-waterly, as we might adverbially express it. Since the adverbial view conceives imaging as a way of experiencing rather than as a relation to an object, there is *no* image as an object to be copied.

An adverbial view of introspected objects

On the suggested adverbial view, then, there is no need for second-order images to represent first-order (ordinary) mental images to us, and the less vivid imagings which might seem to represent mental images are best construed as less vivid occurrences of the original imaging process. This point does not show that there *cannot* be second-order images, but the adverbial view reduces the inclination to think that there are in fact any by suggesting a plausible alternative account of the facts that originally seemed to demand second-order images for their explanation. Chief among these facts is that in recalling an image, one may have a less vivid image which apparently stands to the former as an imaginational image of a scene stands to the sensory image of that scene from which the imaginational image seems to have been copied. The adverbial account of sensory (and other) experience might explain this by interpreting the recalled image, say of blue waters, as *recollectively* sensing blue-waterly, where this is like visually sensing blue-waterly, but less vivid.

Given these and other points, it seems doubtful whether any realist theory of the introspection of images – one that takes them to be objects existing in their own right, or at least having their own properties – can justify a strong analogy between that kind of introspection and ordinary viewing. For it is by no means clear that there is *any* object introspected to serve as the counterpart of an object of ordinary vision. For the adverbial approach to experience, although realism about the (physical) objects of perception is a highly plausible view, realism about the objects of introspection is not. The idea is roughly that mental properties, such as imaging, can adequately represent physical objects in our mental life; inner objects should not be postulated for this task.

The anti-realism of this view should not be exaggerated. To conclude that mental images are not objects having their own properties, and in that sense are not real, would not commit us to denying that *imaging* is real. Imaging processes are surely real properties of persons, even though they are apparently not relations between persons and objects of immediate, inner perception. This is not to say that introspection has no object in the sense of something it is *of* (or about), such as imaging blue waters. But on the adverbial view of introspection, this kind of object is determined by the *content* of the introspection – what it is about – and is not a thing with its own properties, such as colors and shapes, sounds and movements, depths and textures.[3]

The analogy between introspection and ordinary perception

The adverbial view in question may seem unable to do justice to the apparently causal character of introspection. There is surely some causal explanation of our being acquainted with, say, imaging blue waters rather than imaging the Statue of Liberty when we monitor a daydream of a rural summer holiday. Perhaps such introspective consciousness differs from seeing mainly in what causes the relevant imaging. How might this difference be explained?

Suppose the adverbial account of introspection is true. Introspection may still be like simple perception in two ways. First, introspective viewing may imply some kind of causal relation between what is introspected in it, say an imaging, and the introspective consciousness of that state or process. Second, such viewing may imply a causal relation between the object of introspective knowledge – for instance one's imaging blue waters – and the beliefs constituting this knowledge.

In explaining the analogy between introspection and perception, I want to concentrate mainly on introspective beliefs as compared with perceptual beliefs; we can then understand how introspection, and indeed consciousness in general, can ground justification and knowledge. A major question here is how we can tell whether, in introspecting something, as when we concentrate on our own imaging, the beliefs we thereby form about what we are concentrating on are produced by that very thing, or by some aspect of it, such as its imagined blue color. It is only to the extent that they are that we should expect introspection to ground justification and knowledge in the broadly causal way that perception does. Many considerations are relevant here, but let me cite just two sorts.

First of all, it is surely *because* I am imaging cool blue waters that, when I introspectively consider what I am conscious of, I believe that I am imaging them (and am conscious of my imaging them). It is natural and apparently reasonable to take this 'because' to express a causal relation. If the cause is not some inner object seen (as the sense-datum theory would maintain), it is presumably the state or process of imaging. This is, in any event, how the adverbial theory of sensory experience would view the causal relations here. Similarly, if I introspectively believe that I am thinking about introspection, I believe this because I *am* thinking about it: the thinking process itself is what causes me to believe that it is occurring. In both cases the introspective beliefs are produced by inner processes, and indeed in a way that makes it plausible to consider them to be true. Some inner processes are *like* seeing an object in still other ways, but these processes can all be understood without presupposing that there really are special inner objects analogous to perceptible objects like trees and seen by the introspective eye.

A second point is this. Suppose my believing that I am imaging cool blue waters is not caused by my imaging them. The belief is then *not* introspective at all. It is *about* what is introspectable, but it is not grounded in introspection, any more than a belief merely about a perceptible, such as the rich red in a painting in a faraway museum, is a perceptual belief. Here, then, is another important similarity between introspection and perception.

Introspective beliefs, beliefs about introspectables, and fallibility

It may seem that the case described – believing one is imaging something when in fact one is not – is impossible. But suppose I have been asked to image cool blue waters, yet I hate the water and anyway have a lot on my mind. Still, if I want to be cooperative, then even though my mind is mainly on my problems, I may call up an image. However, since I am not concentrating on calling up the image, the image that I actually get might be only of a blue surface, not of blue waters. I might now inattentively assume (and thereby come to believe) that I have called up the requested image of cool blue waters. This belief is produced by a combination of my calling up the wrong image, which I do not attentively introspect at all, and by non-imaginational factors such as my desire to cooperate. I might even retain the belief for at least some moments after I cease to image at all. In that case, it is not only not true; it is not even introspective.

This example suggests that even a true belief about one's conscious states or processes would not be introspective without being causally connected with them. It would be about these introspectable elements but not grounded in "seeing" them in the way required for being an introspective belief. Other examples support the same point. Imagine that my task is to think about introspection for a solid hour. I monitor myself and, on the basis of introspection, conclude from time to time that I am thinking about introspection. As I reflect on my topic, I continue to believe that I am thinking about introspection. Now when I truly believe this simply because I have repeatedly confirmed it and am confident of steady concentration, and *not* because I am still monitoring myself introspectively, my belief, though perfectly true, is not introspective.

The best explanation of this point seems, again, to be that my belief is not caused (in the right way, at least) by the thinking that should be its ground. It is a retained belief about my ongoing mental activity; it is not produced by that activity as a focus of my introspective attention. The language appropriate to perception is appropriate here too: my belief that I am thinking about introspection is a propositional belief *that* I am now doing so, but it is not an objectual belief, regarding my present thinking, to the effect that it is about introspection. It is not grounded in my *present* thinking at all, any more than my belief about the rich red in a painting in a distant museum is grounded in seeing it.

The overall conclusion we come to here is that, although there may be no objects such as sense-data or imaginational copies of them which we introspect, the process by which introspection leads to introspective beliefs, and thereby to knowledge and justified beliefs about one's own mind, is nevertheless causal. Like perception of the outside world and (though in a different way) recalling events of the past, it produces something like a sensory impression and, at least typically, beliefs about what seems to be revealed to one by that impression. The causes of introspective beliefs, however, are apparently processes and events in the mind. They are not, or need not be, objects that reside therein.

Consciousness and privileged access

In the light of what has been said, let us suppose that introspective consciousness is a causal process, though with limited similarities to seeing. Still, if it is a causal process, then we should raise some of the same epistemological questions about it that we raised about perception. For instance, is introspection subject to counterparts of illusion and hallucination? And if it is, how might it still be a source of justification and knowledge? Let us start with the question of how anything like illusion or hallucination might occur in consciousness.

Infallibility, omniscience, and privileged access

One might think that the inner domain, which is the subject of introspective beliefs, is a realm about which one cannot make mistakes. If it is, one might conclude that neither illusion nor hallucination regarding this domain is possible. Indeed, David Hume maintained that since the contents of the mind are known by "consciousness" (by which he meant something at least much like introspection), they must appear in every respect what they are, and be what they appear.[4]

Hume's statement suggests two far-reaching claims about self-knowledge. One claim – that the contents of the mind must be what they appear to one to be – expresses the idea that introspective consciousness can give us beliefs that cannot be mistaken. The other claim – that these contents must appear to be what they are – expresses the idea that introspective consciousness is so richly aware of the (introspectable) contents of the mind that it guarantees us knowledge of them. These ideas need refinement before we can reasonably appraise them.

The first claim suggests a thesis of *infallibility* (impossibility of error): one cannot be mistaken in a belief to the effect that one is now in an occurrent mental state (such as imaging) or that one is undergoing a mental process (such as thinking) or that one is experiencing something (such as pain). The infallibility thesis rests largely on the idea that we are in such a strong position regarding occurrent mental phenomena that we cannot err in thinking they are going on inside us.

The second claim suggests a thesis of *omniscience* (all-knowingness) with respect to the current contents of consciousness: if one is in an occurrent mental state, undergoing a mental process, or experiencing something, one cannot fail to know that one is. The omniscience thesis rests largely on the idea that occurrent mental phenomena are so prominent in consciousness that one cannot help knowing of their occurrence.

Together, these two theses constitute the *strong doctrine of privileged access*. The first says that our access to what is (mentally) occurring in us is so good that our beliefs about its present make-up are infallible; there is no risk of error. The second says that our access to it is so good that we cannot fail to know what (mentally) occurs in us; there is no risk of ignorance. It is because no one else is in such a good position to know about our mental life, and because we ourselves are not in such a good position to know about the external world, that it is natural to speak here of *privileged* access. The strong doctrine of privileged access is associated not only with Hume but, even more, with René Descartes, who is widely taken to maintain it in his famous *Meditations on First Philosophy* (1641), especially in Meditation Two.

Suppose for the sake of argument that both the infallibility and omniscience theses are true. Would that rule out inward counterparts of illusion and hallucination? Not necessarily. For having illusions and hallucinations does *not* imply having false beliefs or being ignorant of anything. Looking from a sharp angle in a line from corner to corner, you can see a book as having the shape of a parallelogram without believing that it has that shape; and I can hallucinate a spruce tree like one that has burned to the ground without believing it is before me. In both cases, we may know the facts.

Suppose, on the other hand, that there are *no* inner objects, such as blue, watery images, to appear to us to have properties they do not possess, such as wavy surfaces. If not, then illusions of the kind we have in perception, in which an object appears to have properties it actually lacks, cannot occur, since there is no object to appear to us. Nor can a hallucination of, say, an image of blue waters be *of* such an object and true or false *to* it. Suppose, however, that there are inner objects that we see when we image. What would be the difference between hallucinating an image of, for instance, a loved one, and just *having* that image? A sense-datum theorist might say that the hallucinatory image would be less vivid or unstable than a real one. But it is still an image of the same thing and might also be just like a normal image in vividness and other respects. It would be wrong to say, then, that a hallucinatory image is simply a less vivid or unstable version of a normal image, and the difficulty of explaining the difference between hallucinatory and real images is an additional reason to avoid (as the adverbial view does) positing mental images as objects.[5]

Difficulties for the thesis of privileged access

It might be, however, that quite apart from illusion or hallucination, we can have false beliefs, or suffer some degree of ignorance, about our mental life. I think this is clear for *some* mental phenomena, such as dispositions like believing, wanting, and fearing. We can mistakenly believe that we do not have a certain ignoble desire (say, to make a fool of a pretentious boss), particularly if it is important to our self-image that we see ourselves as having only righteous desires. For the same reasons, we can fail to know that we *do* have the desire. One can also discover a fear which, previously, one quite honestly disavowed because it was at odds with one's sense of oneself as courageous.[6]

Dispositions, however, should not be conceived as *occurring* in us, and in any case it is the occurrent mental phenomena to which philosophers have tended to think we have the kind of privileged access expressed in the theses of infallibility and omniscience. Can we be mistaken, or at least ignorant, about our occurrent mental states or processes?

Consider first the possibility of mistake. Could one believe one is thinking about the nature of introspection when one is only daydreaming about the images and feelings one might introspect? It would seem so, provided one does not attend closely to what is occurring within oneself. This would be a bit like thinking one is watching someone else observing a game but becoming pre-occupied with the game itself and ceasing to pay attention to its observer. But suppose the infallibility thesis is restricted to beliefs based on *attentive* introspection, where this implies "looking" closely at the relevant aspect of one's consciousness. Call this the *restricted infallibility view*; it says only that attentive introspective beliefs are true.

If I carefully consider the proposition that I am thinking about introspec-tion, and I believe it on the basis of attentive introspection (that is, on the basis of my carefully focusing on the relevant aspect of my consciousness), could this belief be mistaken? This seems doubtful. But is it impossible? Suppose I desperately want to believe that I am doing such thinking. Could this not lead me to take my daydreaming to be such thinking and even to have an attentive introspective belief that I am doing such thinking? It seems so. Similarly, I could believe, on the basis of attentive but imperfect introspection, that I am imaging an octagon and then, concentrating harder and counting sides, discover that the figure has only seven.

If it is possible to be mistaken in believing that one is now in an occurrent mental state (such as thinking), then the omniscience thesis of privileged access should also be abandoned along with the infallibility view. This holds even if the omniscience thesis, too, is restricted, as it should be, to cases of carefully attending to (introspective) consciousness. The easiest way to see why falli-bility cuts against omniscience is to note how omniscience would tend to guarantee *in*fallibility and so would be cast in doubt if the latter is. Let me explain.

Given the extensive self-knowledge implied by omniscience, if I am day-dreaming rather than thinking about the nature of introspection, then I must know that I am daydreaming. But then I will presumably not be so foolish as *also* to believe that I am thinking about introspection – something plainly different from daydreaming. Since I would know as well that I am occupied with, say, a series of images that portray me as swimming in cool blue waters, it is even less likely that I will believe I am thinking about introspection. It appears, then, that if I know every truth about – am omniscient about – my consciousness, then I presumably cannot believe any falsehood about it and so am infallible about it as well.[7]

It is at best unlikely (though perhaps not impossible) that these two things – knowing every truth about one's consciousness and nonetheless believing some falsehood about it – occur together, leaving one omniscient regarding one's own consciousness, yet inconsistent and fallible about it. One would know every truth about it yet would also somehow believe falsehoods incompatible with those truths. This being at best improbable, if I am fallible I am at least very likely not omniscient. Now recall our daydreaming example. It casts doubt even on the restricted thesis of omniscience. In that example, while I am in fact daydreaming, I would presumably not know that I am. If I do know that I am daydreaming, I would believe this, and then it is very doubtful that I would *also* believe I am thinking about introspection.

These points suggest that, contrary to the thesis of omniscience, I can fail to know certain things about my consciousness even when I am attending to it; but they do not imply that the omniscience side of the privileged access view is wildly mistaken, in that I might be ignorant of *every* truth about my day-dreaming. Far from it. Since I (objectually) believe it to be thinking about introspection, I presumably at least know my daydreaming to involve words or colors or shapes. But I would still not know that I am daydreaming and thus would not be omniscient regarding the mental processes occurring in me.

The possibility of scientific grounds for rejecting privileged access

It may help to point out that there could someday be a source of significant evidence against even the strong doctrines of privileged access. For it could turn out that every occurrent mental phenomenon is uniquely correlated with some distinct brain process. Then someone could devise a "cerebroscope" for viewing the brain and could read off the contents of consciousness from the cerebroscopic data. What would guarantee that our introspective beliefs must match what the machine says about our mental lives? And what would a mismatch show?

Imagine that we could discover cerebroscopically a unique neural pattern for, say, believing on the basis of attentive introspection that one is imaging cool blue waters, at the same time as we discover the pattern for imaging a field of blue-green grass. It would be natural here to suppose the subject is mistaking the grassy image (or imaging process) for a watery one. Might we not regard the sophisticated equipment as more likely to be right than the subject?

There is a problem with this reasoning. How could one *establish* the unique correlations except by relying on the accuracy of people's introspective beliefs? Would it not be necessary to start by *asking* people what they are, say, imaging, to assume that they are correct, and only *then* record the associated brain state? And if learning the correlations would depend on the accuracy of introspective reports, how could the correlations show such reports to be mistaken?

A possible reply is this. First, let us grant for the sake of argument that learning the correlations would depend on the accuracy of introspective reports. Still, neuroscientists would not have had to rely on the accuracy of precisely the introspective belief being shown to be mistaken, and perhaps not even on the accuracy of highly similar beliefs. In any event, once they have constructed their instrument, they might no longer consult introspection to use it. They might throw away the very ladder they have climbed up on.

Imagine, however, that they did have to rely on just the sorts of belief we are examining, together with evidence regarding these beliefs' reliability which we already have independently of the cerebroscope. Would this imply that the cerebroscope could not provide powerful evidence against introspective beliefs?

Consider an analogy. We might use a mercury thermometer to construct a gas thermometer. We might calibrate a container of gas with a piston that rises and falls as the gas is heated and cooled. The new temperature readings might correlate perfectly with mercury readings in many instances: in measuring water temperature, wood temperature, and other cases. The gas thermometer might then be used for the same jobs as the mercury thermometer *and* might gauge temperatures that the mercury thermometer cannot measure, say because they are above the boiling point of mercury. Could we not use a gas thermometer to correct a mercury thermometer in some cases, or perhaps to correct all mercury thermometers in restricted ways? We could. This seems so even if we had originally taken the mercury thermometer to be infallible in measuring temperature, perhaps because we mistakenly thought of its readings as partly definitive of what temperature *is*. We would rebuild the ladder we have climbed up on.

Similar points might hold for beliefs about what is now occurring in one. If the analogy does extend this far – if the gas thermometer is to the mercury thermometer rather as the cerebroscope is to sincere testimony about one's current mental life – then even the restricted omniscience view fares no better than the restricted infallibility view. For even when one is attentive to what is occurring internally, a cerebroscope could indicate that one does not believe (hence does not know) that a certain thing is occurring, such as a frightening image which one thinks one has put out of mind.

Introspective consciousness as a source of justification and knowledge

It is important not to overextend our criticism of various claims of privileged access. After all, even the restricted infallibility and omniscience views are very strong claims of privileged access. They can be given up along with the strong theses of privileged access quite consistently with holding that our access to what is occurring in us is very privileged indeed. Let us explore the extent of this privilege.

The range of introspective knowledge and justification

Nothing I have said undermines a qualified epistemic principle: that our attentively formed introspective beliefs about what is now occurring in us are *normally* true and constitute knowledge. The difficulty of finding grounds for thinking they even *could* be false provides some reason to consider them at least very likely to be correct. Similarly, when we are attentive to what is occurring in us, then if something (knowable) *is* occurring, such as a certain melody in the mind's ear, *normally* we know that it is occurring, or at least we are in a position to know this simply by attentively forming the belief that the melody is going through our mind. At least this qualified epistemic principle holds for the domain of our conscious life.

Granted, our "access" to our dispositional properties is not as good as our access to what is occurring in us. We need not be conscious of the former properties, whereas the very existence of one's imaging (or of an image if there are such objects) *consists in* its place in consciousness. Beliefs and other mental dispositions need not even enter consciousness, or ever be a subject of our thoughts or concerns. Some of them may indeed be "repressed," so that we normally cannot easily become aware of them.[8]

Nevertheless – and here is a justification principle applicable to the mental domain – our beliefs to the effect that we are now in a dispositional mental state, for instance want, fear, intend, or believe something, are normally justified. We might also say that such beliefs, though defeasibly justified, are prima facie justified, so that they are justified overall unless some defeating factor, such as an abnormal psychological interference, occurs. Moreover, normally, when we have a want (or fear, intention, belief, or similar disposition), we are in a position to know (and justifiedly believe) this. We can, then, usually know this if we need to. (We very commonly do *not* know it, however; for such things may not enter consciousness at all, and there is often no reason to take any notice of them or form any beliefs about them.)

There are a great many issues and details I have not mentioned; but if what I have said is correct, we can now generalize about introspection (roughly, consciousness turned toward one's own mind) in relation to belief, justification, and knowledge, and summarize our main epistemological conclusions. Plainly, many beliefs arise from introspection, and the points that have emerged suggest an epistemic principle which, though far weaker than the infallibility thesis, is far-reaching: normally, beliefs grounded in attentive introspection are true and constitute knowledge. A second epistemic principle, though far weaker than the omniscience thesis, is that normally, if I attentively focus introspectively on something going on in me, I know that it is going on, under at least some description: I may not know that I am humming the slow movement of Beethoven's *Pathétique Sonata*, but I do know I am humming a melodic piano piece.

The corresponding justification principles suggested by our discussion seem at least equally plausible: normally, beliefs grounded in attentive introspection are justified; and normally, if I attentively focus on something going on in me, I am justified in believing that it is going on in me. To be sure, some are better justified than others, and even some that are not attentive are justified. All of them are plausibly regarded as prima facie justified.

There are many possible principles regarding our justification and knowledge about ourselves, and there are many possible qualifications of the four just stated. But those four principles are sufficient to suggest the power of introspection as a source of justification and knowledge. The examples I used to argue that introspection is fallible do not show that the apparently false introspective beliefs were *unjustified* or that true ones are not knowledge. A false belief, particularly if it is of a kind usually justified, can still be justified; and a true belief of a kind that can sometimes be false may itself constitute knowledge.[9]

The defeasibility of introspective justification

These points about the degree of privileged access we apparently do have may create a danger of overestimating the strength of introspective justification. From our examples, it might be thought that attentive introspection, even if not absolutely infallible, generates a kind of justification that at least cannot be defeated. Even if I am somehow mistaken about whether I am imaging blue waters, if I believe this on the basis of introspection, it would seem that I am *in the right*, even if objectively I am *not right*.

How could I fail to be justified in believing that I am imaging cool blue waters, if my belief is grounded in attentive introspection? If the question seems rhetorical, this may be because one thinks there simply is nothing else I should have done besides attending and hence no possible defeaters of my justification by appeal to the results of some other kind of ground for belief. Let us explore this.

Granting that I could not fail to be justified *unless* I could have good reason to believe I may be mistaken, still, perhaps I could fail to be justified if I had sufficient evidence for believing I am mistaken, such as repeated cerebroscopic results indicating that I have been mistaken in many quite similar cases. It is far from obvious that I could not have sufficient evidence of this sort. It seems wisest, then, to conclude that although introspective justification tends to be very strong, it remains prima facie rather than absolute and can be defeated by counter-evidence.

In any case, plainly beliefs grounded in attentive introspection, such as my belief that I am now imaging blue waters, are normally justified to a very high degree. Moreover – and here we have still another justification principle – normally, my simply being engaged in attentive introspection also yields situational justification for beliefs about what I am attending to, even where it does not in fact yield any such beliefs. If I somehow "notice" my imaging blue waters yet do not form the belief that I am doing so, I am nonetheless (prima facie) justified *in* believing that I am, just as, if I see a bird fly past and take no notice of it, I am still justified in believing it flew past. The analogy to perception seems sound here, and that is one reason why introspection is considered a kind of inner observation and (unless it somehow yields no content) a kind of inner perception.

Consciousness as a basic source

If we now ask whether consciousness, including especially introspective consciousness, is a *basic* source of belief, justification, and knowledge, the answer should be evident. It is. In this, as in many other respects, it is like perception. But it may well be that the degree of justification which consciousness (including introspection) generates is greater than the degree generated by perceptual experience, other things being equal. The special strength of justification on the part of beliefs about elements in consciousness has led some philosophers to think that these beliefs are a kind of foundation for knowledge and for the justification of all other beliefs (and Descartes is often thought to have so regarded introspectively grounded beliefs or knowledge). Whether knowledge and justification need a kind of foundation and whether, if they do, these beliefs are the best candidates to serve as that foundation – better than, say, perceptual and memory beliefs – are the major questions pursued in Chapter 7.

There seems to be a further epistemologically significant difference between perception and consciousness, especially as manifested in introspection, as sources of knowledge (and justification). We can by and large introspect *at will* – roughly, just by (sufficiently) wanting to – though we may also do it quite spontaneously; and there is no limit to how many things we can come to know by introspecting, if only because we can, without limit, call up images and construct thoughts. But we cannot perceive at will; and what we can know through perception is limited by what there is outside us to perceive and by external conditions of observation, just as what we can know through remembering or recalling is limited by what has actually happened (or what propositions are true) and by the conditions of belief or image retention crucial for remembering or recalling.[10]

Introspective consciousness, then, is unlike perception and memory in enabling us to acquire a considerable amount of knowledge whether external circumstances cooperate or not. Whatever one can "observe" in one's own mind is a possible subject of study, and it appears that many of the beliefs we attentively form concerning our mental lives tend to constitute genuine knowledge. Very roughly, introspective consciousness is a substantially *active* faculty; perception and memory are largely *reactive* faculties. Granting that some content – like sensations of pain – comes into consciousness uninvited, we can very freely *call to mind* both propositional and imagistic content. But sensory content, such as perceptual images, enters our mind only when our senses are *taken*, by our own observational efforts or by contingencies of experience, to it. In the inner world, by sharp contrast with the external world, there is far more at our beck and call. This is perhaps another reason why introspectively grounded beliefs have sometimes seemed to be such good material to serve as foundations for knowledge and justification.

There is a trade-off, however. Through perception, we acquire (primarily) justified beliefs and knowledge about the external world; without these, we would be unlikely to survive. Through introspection, we acquire (primarily) justified beliefs and knowledge only about the internal world; with only this, our knowledge and justification would be sadly limited to our own minds. This is not to underplay the importance of the internal world: without good access to it we would have little if any self-knowledge and, for that reason, probably at best shallow knowledge of others.

Self-knowledge is also important as a back-up when questions arise about one's justification or knowledge regarding external objects. Confronted with a strange object, one may carefully consider the stability, coherence, and variations of one's perceptual experiences of it in order to rule out hallucination. Told that one merely imagined a car's passing, one may try to recall it and then scrutinize both the vividness of one's imagery and one's confidence that the belief comes from memory rather than merely imagination. Without the kind of self-knowledge possible here, we would have less knowledge about the external world. Both perceptual and introspective knowledge are vital, and both, as we shall soon see, can be extended, by good reasoning from the raw materials they supply, far beyond their beginnings in our experience.

Notes

1 To be sure, images can be possessed memorially, as is my image of the Statue of Liberty when I do not have it in mind; and 'imaging' can designate a process, as when I call up the series of images corresponding to looking at the statue from the Brooklyn Heights Promenade and glancing northward to Lower Manhattan, thence to the Brooklyn Bridge, and up the East River beyond the bridge.
2 Both kinds of properties are experiential, in that they represent features of experience. Both,

then, might be considered *phenomenal*, but sometimes the term 'phenomenal property' is restricted to the sensory kind that characterizes either the five senses or "inner sense," by which pain and pleasurable sensations are felt.

3 Such contentual objects are often called *intentional objects*, largely the ground that, like lofty deeds we intend to perform but do not do, they need not exist.

4 See David Hume, *A Treatise of Human Nature* (first published in 1739–40), Part IV, Section II), ed. by L. A. Selby-Bigge (Oxford: Oxford University Press, 1888).

5 One might still distinguish between genuine and hallucinatory images by insisting that in order to be a genuine image *of* (say) a loved one, an image *must* be caused by, say, seeing that very person. This view has an odd consequence, however. Through hearing a detailed description I could have an accurate image of Maj that is in a sense *of* her, since it matches her sufficiently well, even if I have never seen her; but this would be a hallucinatory image, on the causal conception just stated. There are certainly different kinds of images and various ways in which they can mislead, but the analogy between perception and introspective consciousness does not extend in any simple way to the possibility of inner illusions and hallucinations, and there is no need to pursue the matter in more detail here. For a detailed non-technical discussion of mental imagery see Alastair Hannay, *Mental Images: A Defence* (London: George Allen & Unwin, 1971) and my critical examination of this book in 'The Ontological Status of Mental Images', *Inquiry* 21 (1978), 348–61.

6 Some of these cases seem to occur in *self-deception*, a phenomenon that raises profound questions for both epistemology and the philosophy of mind. For a comprehensive collection of papers on it (including one offering my own account), see Brian P. McLaughlin and Amelie O. Rorty (eds), *Perspectives on Self-Deception* (Berkeley and Los Angeles: University of California Press, 1988).

7 The thesis of omniscience might be restricted to *introspectable* truths, as opposed to such truths as that there are 1,001 berries visible on the blackberry bush I am imaging, which I could know only on the basis of memory (and arithmetic) as well as introspection. The infallibility thesis might also be plausibly restricted in a similar way. This point bears on the connection between the two theses but should not affect the argumentation in the text.

8 Repression need not be exactly the kind of thing Sigmund Freud described, requiring psychoanalysis or very special techniques to come to consciousness. There are various kinds and degrees of repression; the point here is simply that *having* a belief (or other dispositional state) is possible even if it is repressed. One might, for example, still act in the way expected of a believer of the relevant proposition.

9 For reasons to be considered in Chapter 10, skeptics tend to deny this.

10 There is less disanalogy in the negative cases: we cannot always cease at will to concentrate introspectively on our mental life, as illustrated by preoccupying pains; and we cannot cease perceiving at will without, for example, closing our eyes or turning off a radio. This blocks the path of observation, just as an aspirin might block the path of pain.

CHAPTER 4
Reason

Self-evident truths of reason

The classical view of the truths of reason

Analytic propositions
Necessary propositions
The analytic, the a priori, and the synthetic
The empirical
Analytic truth, concept acquisition, and necessity

The empiricist view of the truths of reason

Rationalism and empiricism
Empiricism and the genesis and confirmation of arithmetic beliefs
Empiricism and logical and analytic truths

The conventionalist view of the truths of reason

Truth by definition and truth by virtue of meaning
Knowledge through definitions versus truth by definition
Conventions as grounds for interpretation

Some difficulties and strengths of the classical view

Vagueness
Meaning change and falsification
The possibility of empirical necessary truth
Reason, experience, and apriori justification
Loose and strict senses of 'a priori justification' and 'a priori knowledge'
The power of reason and the possibility of indefeasible justification

Reason

I see the green field and I believe that it is there before me. I look away, and I believe that I am now imaging it. I remember its shape, and I believe that it is rectangular. These are beliefs grounded in my experience: perceptual, introspective, and memorial. But I also believe something quite different about what I see: that *if* the spruce to my left is taller than the maple to my right, then the maple is shorter than the spruce.

On what basis does one believe this obvious truth? Do we even need to see the trees to know it? Certainly it is on the basis of perception that I believe *each* of the two comparative propositions; it is easy to see, for instance, that the spruce is taller than the maple. But I do not believe on the basis of perception that *if* the spruce is taller than the maple then the maple is shorter than the spruce. As a rational being I apparently just grasp this truth and thereby believe it.

The kind of apparently elementary use of reason this example illustrates seems basic for both knowledge and justification. But there are other kinds of examples to be considered, and there is continuing debate about the nature and grounds of the knowledge and justification we have regarding the simple, obvious truths that we seem to know just in virtue of the kind of understanding of them any rational being might be expected to have. A good way to seek an understanding of the epistemological role of reason is to begin with a notion that seems central for the most basic kind of knowledge and justification reason gives us. This notion has been widely taken to be that of self-evidence.

Self-evident truths
of reason

Such truths as the luminous one that if the spruce is taller than the maple, then the maple is shorter than the spruce, have been said to be evident to reason, conceived as a mental capacity of understanding. They are presumably called *self-evident* because they are thought to be evidently true taken by themselves, with no need for supporting evidence. Similarly (but not quite equivalently), they are often thought to be obvious in themselves, in the sense that if one comprehendingly considers them, one can quite *thereby* see their truth: one needs no premises or explanation or reflection to make them evident. Simply upon attentively coming to understand them, one normally sees their truth and thereby knows it.

In the light of such points, we might more specifically characterize self-evident propositions as those truths such that (1) if one (adequately) understands them, then by virtue of that understanding one is justified *in* believing them, and (2) if one believes them on the basis of (adequately) understanding them, then one thereby knows them.[1] (1) says roughly that understanding them suffices for being situationally justified in believing them; it provides a justification *for* belief. (2) says in effect that this understanding can ground knowledge: the understanding is sufficient to render a belief based on it knowledge. (2) implies, then, that self-evident propositions are true. This implication is appropriate, since the self-evident is standardly regarded as true. It is not implied, however, that the justification one gains from understanding them is indefeasible (i.e., so secure that it cannot be defeated) rather than prima facie, but this kind of justification is plausibly considered as strong as any justification there can be.

There is an analogy to perception here. Just as one may see something without forming any particular beliefs about it, one may comprehendingly (understandingly) consider a plainly true proposition without coming to believe it; and just as one's seeing a bird fly past gives one justification for believing it did whether or not one forms this belief, understanding the proposition that if the spruce is taller than the maple, the maple is shorter than the spruce, gives one (situational) justification for believing this whether one does or not. When it comes to concepts, there seems to be a further analogy to perception: a hierarchy analogous to the perceptual one. There is understanding a concept, such as *being taller than*; there is objectually believing it to apply to a pair of things, such as the spruce and the maple, whether one has any specific concept of the relation or not; and there is propositionally believing that it does, where one conceives the trees as, say, the spruce and the maple and believes that the spruce is taller.[2]

With self-evident propositions like the straightforward proposition that if the spruce is taller than the maple, then the maple is shorter than the spruce, one need not consult one's experience of the kind of thing described, or even ponder the propositions in question, in order to grasp – roughly, to understand – them. And when one does come to understand them and focuses on them in the light of that understanding, one thereby normally comes to believe and know that they are true.[3]

There are many truths which, in the way just illustrated, we readily grasp and thereby immediately believe. That is, we believe them immediately in the sense that we see their truth without having to infer them from anything else. The point is not the temporal one that we grasp them instantly, though we may. What is crucial is that our belief exhibits *epistemic immediacy*: it is not based on inference or on a further, evidential belief. If it were, it would be epistemically mediate: mediated by (and thereby at least partly grounded in) the set of premises from which we infer (or through which we believe) the proposition, as my belief that Socrates is mortal is mediated by the two propositions which are part of the basis of my believing this: that he is a human being, and that all human beings are mortal.[4]

The proposition that Socrates is mortal is in another way unlike the proposition that if the spruce is taller than the maple, then the maple is shorter than the spruce. It is not self-evident. There are at least two ways to explain this. First, Socrates and mortality are not intrinsically connected, as are one thing's being taller than a second and the second's being shorter than the first. Second (and speaking more generally), it takes more than a simple use of reason to know that Socrates is mortal. One apparently needs information not contained in the proposition one considers. Even thinking of him as a human being does not absolutely preclude every route to his immortality. But a simple use of reason seems to assure us that the spruce's being taller than the maple precludes the maple's not being shorter than the spruce.

This kind of point concerning propositions like the one about the two trees has led philosophers to consider them to be *truths of reason* – roughly, truths knowable through the use of reason as opposed to sense experience. The same kind of point has led philosophers to regard them as also *necessarily true* (necessary, for short): as such that their falsehood is absolutely precluded; there are simply no circumstances in which they are false. If a proposition is not necessary *and* its negation is also not necessary, it is called *contingent*, since its truth or falsity is contingent on (dependent on) circumstances. How might we understand the justification of our beliefs of such self-evident and apparently necessary propositions and other truths of reason? And how do we know them?

The classical view of
the truths of reason

The best-known answers to these questions, and probably the only ones we might call the *classical* answers, derive largely from Immanuel Kant, though there are similar ideas in earlier philosophers. He discussed both the truth of the kinds of propositions in question and how we know them.[5]

What Kant said is complex and difficult to interpret precisely, and I am simply going to lay out a version of the classical account which may correspond only roughly to Kant's views. Moreover, although I am interested mainly in our justification and knowledge regarding the truths of reason, I will also talk about the basis of these truths themselves where that is useful in discussing how we know or justifiedly believe them.

Analytic propositions

Take the proposition that all vixens are female. I easily grasp its truth, and I immediately believe it: I depend on no premises or evidence. There was a time when 'vixen' was not in my vocabulary. I might then have looked at the sentence 'All vixens are female' and not known what proposition it expressed, much less seen the particular truth (true proposition) it does express. But this point does not show that I do not immediately believe that truth once I *do* (comprehendingly) consider it. It shows only that encountering a sentence expressing a truth does not enable one to consider that truth unless one *understands* the sentence.

We can see, moreover, that when we do consider the truth that all vixens are female, we do not (or at least need not) know it on the basis of beliefs about the sentence 'All vixens are female'. For we can consider that same truth by using some other sentence to express it (say in Spanish), and perhaps without using a sentence at all.[6] If, however, we think about what constitutes the basis of the truth of the proposition, we may discover something which in turn helps to explain why we so readily understand and believe it.

To get a sense of the basis of this truth, consider what a vixen is. It is a female fox. Indeed, the concept of a vixen may be analyzed in terms of being female and being a fox. So, in saying that a vixen – any arbitrarily chosen one – is a female fox, one could be giving an elementary analysis of the concept of a vixen. Now suppose that (like Kant) we think of an analysis of a concept as indicating what the concept contains (or, in a certain way, includes). We can now say that the concept of being female is part of the concept of a vixen, and that being female is thus an element in being a vixen.[7]

In the light of all this, we might call the truth that all vixens are female an *analytic proposition*. In one major conception Kant presented, this is a proposition such that what it predicates of its subject can be analyzed out of the concept of that subject. Here the subject is vixens (or any given vixen), and the predicate is *being female*, which is part of, and so analyzable out of, the concept of a vixen. The same sort of thing holds for the propositions that all bachelors are unmarried, that all triangles have three angles, that all sound arguments have true premises and true conclusions, and so on. Analytic propositions are usually considered clear cases of the self-evident.[8]

Necessary propositions

This way of looking at our example helps to explain something else that is true of the proposition that all vixens are female: it *cannot* be false and, in that sense, is necessary (a necessary truth). To see this point, try to conceive of a non-female vixen. Since the concept of a vixen is analyzable as (and hence equivalent to) that of a female fox, one is in effect trying to conceive of a *non*-female female fox. This would be something that is and is not female. We would have a contradiction. Hence, there cannot be such a thing, on pain of contradiction. It is thus absolutely impossible that there be a non-female vixen. By contrast, it is possible that there is, and also that there is not, a 200-pound vixen.

Because the falsity of analytic propositions entails a contradiction in this way, they are often thought to be – and are sometimes even *defined* as – those that are true on pain of contradiction. That is, their falsity entails a contradiction, and hence they can be false only if a contradiction is true. That is absolutely impossible. Analytic propositions are therefore regarded as truths that hold in *any* possible situation and hence are necessary (though other kinds of truths may also be considered necessary).

Now if analytic propositions are true by virtue of the sort of conceptual containment relation we have been exploring, might we not know each one we do know in virtue of grasping the containment relation basic to it, in the sense of having an adequate understanding of that relation? In considering the proposition that all vixens are female, one in some way grasps the containment relation between the concept of a vixen and that of being female. Intellectually – *intuitively*, in one widely used terminology – one sees the relation and thereby sees and (non-inferentially) knows the truth it underlies.

It might be objected that the correct account is instead this. One quickly or subconsciously reasons: the concept of a vixen is analyzable as that of a female fox; *being female* is contained in that analysis; hence all vixens are female. A defender of the classical view would reply that this second-order reasoning indicates how one might *show* that one knows that all vixens are female, but it does not indicate *how* one *knows* it, at least not if one just grasps its truth in the normal way.

The classical account can grant that one perhaps *could* come to know the proposition in that indirect way. But one need not come to know it in that way; and normally, if one did not *already* know that vixens are female foxes, one would not even be in a position to know (on one's own) the sophisticated truth that the *concept* of a vixen is analyzable as that of a female fox. Believing that all vixens are female, in virtue of grasping the crucial containment relation between the concept of a vixen and that of a female, does not require coming to know it in that sophisticated way.

The analytic, the a priori, and the synthetic

We can now see how the classical account of the truths of reason might apply to apparently non-analytic truths that are directly and intuitively grasped.

Think about the proposition that nothing is both red and green all over at one time. Is this analytic? Can we analyze *being non-red* out of the concept of being green, or *being non-green* out of the concept of being red, so that in saying that something is red and green all over at once someone could be shown to be implying that it is (wholly) red and non-red, or green and non-green? This is doubtful. For one thing, it is not clear that we can analyze the concept of being red (or the concept of being green) at *all* in the relevant sense of 'analyze'. Still, in the classical view, we can know through the use of reason the necessary truth that nothing is red and green all over at once.

We *can* scientifically clarify what being red is by appeal to facts about light. But on the classical view, such clarification helps us to understand certain facts about red *things* (and perhaps about the property of being red), rather than telling us what the *concept* of a red thing is equivalent to, as we are told that the concept of a vixen is equivalent to that of a female fox. Compare analyzing the concept of a vixen with making discoveries about vixens scientifically. One could discover empirically that they have a unique tracking system, but not that they are male. Although the cases are similar in that one also could not *discover* empirically that what is red all over is not also green all over at the same time, they differ in that being non-green is not analyzable out of the concept of being red.[9]

On the classical view, we cannot identify anything as a vixen – say, for experimental purposes – except under the assumption that it is female. Thus, the possibility of discovering anything inconsistent with its being female is ruled out from the start. If our experimental subject is *selected* by its having a specified property, we cannot find out experimentally that *it* (as opposed to something else it may turn into) lacks that property. This does not make analytic truths more important than scientific truths. The former are simply of a different kind: they are not of the right kind to be open to scientific verification or falsification, and in part for this reason they also do not compete with scientific truths.

There may be another way to argue (against the classical view) that the proposition that nothing is red and green all over at once is analytic. Could one not indirectly analyze the concept of being red as equivalent to the concept of having a color other than green and blue and yellow, and so on, where we list all the remaining colors? This claim may seem right, because it *seems* self-evidently true that red is the only color filling that bill. But the claim is doubtful. For one thing, it is questionable whether a determinate list of all the other colors is even possible. More important, even if it is, the concept of being red is not a *negative* concept of this sort. There is, in addition, an important disanalogy: one could have the concept of being red (have an understanding of it) without even having all of these other color concepts, whereas one could not have the concept of a vixen without having the concepts of a fox and a female.

Moreover, proponents of the classical view would stress here (what is independently plausible) that an analysis does not merely provide a *conceptual equivalent*, that is, one which (necessarily) applies to the same things to which the concept being analyzed does, as the concept of being not-not-red applies to everything the concept of being red does. An analysis of a concept (as we shall see in Chapter 8 in exploring analyses of the concept of knowledge) must meet at least two further conditions. First, it must exhibit a suitable subset of the elements that constitute the concept; second, it must do so in such a way that one's seeing that they constitute it can (to some significant degree) yield *understanding* of the concept. The concept of being red is surely not constituted by the complex and mainly negative property of being a color that is not green, not blue, and so on; and one could not understand what it is for something to be red simply in terms of understanding that long and perhaps indefinite list.

Indeed, one could presumably understand the list of other colors quite well even if one had never seen or imagined redness, and one had *no* perceptual, imaginational, or other concept of redness at all. It is arguable, in fact, that the concept is *simple* in the sense that, unlike that of a vixen, it is not analyzable into elements of any kind.

It appears, then, that the concept of being red is not analyzable into elements of any sort and that the proposition that nothing is red and green all over at once is not analytic. However, we can still rationally grasp, that nothing is red and green all over at once. Truths that meet this rational graspability condition – roughly a knowability through conceptual understanding condition – have been called *a priori propositions* (propositions knowable 'from the first'), because they have been thought to be such that they can be known a priori, in a very strict sense of this phrase: known simply through reason as directed toward them and toward the concepts occurring in them, at least if reason is used extensively enough and with sufficient care. Propositions that are a priori in this strict, knowability sense are also plausibly considered self-evident.[10]

By contrast with analytic propositions, however, the kind of a priori proposition exemplified by the proposition that nothing is red and green all over at once seems to assert something beyond what analysis of the relevant concepts can show. For this reason, propositions of this kind are also called *synthetic propositions*, though these are typically defined negatively, simply as *non-analytic*. Positively conceived, they typically bring together or "synthesize" concepts and properties, even if in a negative way (as by linking redness with colors other than green – by including it among these other colors). Synthetic propositions do not or need not, even in part, analyze concepts.

It is noteworthy that although analytic propositions are characterized roughly in terms of how they are *true* – by virtue of conceptual containment (or, on a related account, on pain of contradiction) – a priori propositions are characterized in terms of *how they are* known, or can be known: through the operation of reason.[11] (This allows that they can *also* be known through experience, say through testimony, at least if the testifier's knowledge is, directly or indirectly, grounded in the operation of reason.) On this basis, the latter are also negatively characterized as knowable "independently of experience," where this phrase above all designates no need for evidential dependence on experiential grounds, such as those of perception. But even if this negative characterization of a priori propositions is correct so far as it goes, understanding them through it will require understanding the kinds of positive characteristics I am stressing. Let us pursue these further.

If we take knowability through the use of reason as a rough indication of what constitutes the a priori in general, then it includes certain propositions that are not self-evident: those *not* themselves knowable simply through reason as directed toward them and toward the concepts occurring in them, but self-evidently following from (entailed by) such (self-evident) propositions. This is a case of what is *a priori in the broad sense.* Consider the proposition that either nothing is red and green all over at once or I am flying to the Moon. This self-evidently follows from the proposition about red and green, which (apparently) is self-evident. It self-evidently follows because it is self-evident that *if* nothing is red and green all over at once, then either that is true or I am flying to the Moon. Still, even though this self-evidently follows from something that is self-evident, one knows it inferentially, on the basis of knowing that simpler proposition. One cannot know it just from understanding it, as with a self-evident proposition, but only through seeing that if nothing is both red and green at once, then either that proposition is true or I am flying to the Moon. This conditional (if–then) proposition is self-evident; hence, it is an utterly secure ladder on which to climb from knowledge that nothing is red and green all over at once to knowledge that either this is so or I am flying to the moon. That is a priori in the broad sense.

We could say, then, that for the kind of classical view in question, the self-evident is the base of the a priori: a priori propositions are those that are either self-evident (i.e., a priori in the narrow sense) or, though not themselves self-evident, self-evidently follow from at least one proposition that is (hence are a priori in the broad sense). The general notion of an a priori proposition, applicable to both cases, is roughly the notion of a truth that either is a self-evident proposition or is self-evidently entailed by one.[12] Knowledge of propositions a priori in the broad sense, unlike knowledge of those a priori in the narrow sense, depends on knowledge of some self-evident proposition as a ground. But neither kind of knowledge depends on knowledge of any empirical proposition, and in that sense both kinds are "independent of experience."[13] Suppose, however, that a proposition is neither self-evident nor self-evidently entailed by a self-evident proposition, but *is* provable by self-evident steps (perhaps many) from a self-evident proposition. This proposition might or might not be knowable without reliance on memory, depending on the mental capacity of the rational being in question. Nonetheless, since it can be known through such a rigorous proof, it may be called a priori in the broad sense (though some in the classical tradition might not include it).

It is because a priori propositions are understood in relation to how they can be known that the notion of the a priori is commonly considered epistemological. The notion of the analytic is more often taken to be of a different kind, say conceptual, since analytic truths are conceived as grounded in a simple containment relation of concepts.[14] It should perhaps not be surprising, then, that the categories of the analytic and the a priori are not identical. In both cases, however, proponents of the classical view have taken the relevant propositions to be necessary: this is commonly thought to be obvious for the analytic ones, which are true "on pain of contradiction," but it has seemed reasonable to classical theorists to hold that even synthetic a priori propositions must be necessary. The thought is apparently that if their truth were contingent and so depended on what holds in some possible situations but not others, one could not know it just on the basis of understanding the proposition itself. This is plausible, and I shall tentatively assume it.

The empirical

A huge variety of truths are not a priori. That the spruce is taller than the maple is one of them. These non-a priori truths are called *empirical* (or *a posteriori*) *truths*. This means, roughly, that the propositions in question can be known only *empirically*, that is, are knowable (assuming they are knowable) only on the basis of experience, as opposed to reason – above all on the basis of perceptual or introspective experience (in the ways described in Chapters 1 and 3). Saying simply that a proposition is empirical (or a posteriori) leaves open whether it is true: there are empirical falsehoods, such as that it is not the case that the spruce is taller than the maple, as well as empirical truths. (In this the term 'empirical proposition' is unlike 'a priori proposition', which is not normally used to refer to falsehoods, but my main examples of empirical propositions will be truths.)

For the classical view, empirical propositions as well as a priori propositions are crucial for our lives. Indeed, the former include every truth known perceptually, such as those known through observing the colors and shapes of things around us, and all truths known scientifically, such as generalizations linking the temperatures and the volumes of gases. A certain range of a priori propositions, such as those of logic and pure mathematics, are presupposed by common sense and science. Empirical propositions are also required to guide us in dealing with the world, but the classical view sees them as open to disconfirmation through experience in a way that a priori propositions are not.

Analytic truth, concept acquisition, and necessity

Analytic truths, as well as certain synthetic ones, are called a priori because analytic truths are knowable through the use of reason. But analytic truths appear to be knowable – or at least are showable – through a different use of reason than is appropriate to the synthetic a priori truths. It may be that I know that nothing is red and green all over at once by virtue of simply grasping, as a rational creature, a kind of incompatibility between the concept of being red (at a time and place) and the concept of being green. But I apparently do not know it by virtue of grasping a *containment* relation between being red (or green) and anything else. If this does not illustrate two different uses of reason, it at least indicates a different kind of application of reason to different kinds of relations of concepts.

Since my knowledge of the proposition that nothing is red and green all over at once is not based on grasping a containment relation, it differs from my knowledge of the analytic truth that all vixens are female. Yet in both cases the relation between the concepts involved in the truth seems to be the basis of that truth. In both, moreover, I apparently know the truth through rationally *understanding* that relation: analytic containment in one case, mutual exclusion in the other.

These points do not imply that experience is irrelevant to knowledge of the a priori. On the classical view, I do need experience to *acquire* the concepts in question, for instance to acquire color concepts or the concept of a fox. But once I have the needed concepts, it is my grasp of their relations, and not whatever experience I needed to acquire the concepts, which is the *basis* of my knowledge of analytic and other a priori truths.

In part because of these similarities, as well as because the falsity of a priori propositions seems absolutely inconceivable, the classical view takes synthetic a priori truths as well as analytic truths to be necessary. They cannot be false, even though in the synthetic cases it seems not to be strictly contradictory to deny one. For instance, claiming that something is red and green all over is not contradictory in the sense that it entails that some proposition – say, that the object in question has a definite color – is and is not true. Still, on the classical view it is absolutely impossible that something *be* red and green all over at once. We need only reflect on the relevant concepts (above all, the color concepts) to realize that nothing is red and green all over at once; for being red self-evidently excludes being green.

It is also commonly held by philosophers in the classical tradition that all necessary propositions are a priori. One rationale for this might be that necessity is grounded in relations of concepts and these are the same in all possible situations. A mind that could adequately survey all possible situations (like the divine mind as often conceived) could thus know the truth of all necessarily true propositions. Since this survey method would be possible without analyzing one concept out of another, the grounding of necessity in conceptual relations would also explain how there can be synthetic necessary truths. And for the classical view, these, being necessary, are also a priori.

Summarizing, then, the classical view says that all necessary propositions are a priori and vice versa, but it maintains that analytic propositions are a subclass of a priori ones, since some a priori propositions are synthetic rather than analytic. The view tends to conceive the truth of all a priori propositions as grounded in relations of concepts, but it accounts for these propositions differently: for necessary propositions in terms of the *circumstances* of their truth (the absolute impossibility of their falsehood), for analytic ones in terms of *how* they are true (typically, by virtue of containment relations), and for a priori propositions in terms of how their truth is *known* (through understanding).

The empiricist view of the truths of reason

The classical view of the nature of what I am calling a priori truths – also called truths of reason – and of our knowledge of them has been vigorously challenged. To appreciate the epistemological significance of reason as a source of justification and knowledge, and of truths of reason themselves, we must consider some alternative accounts of these truths.

John Stuart Mill held that ultimately there are only empirical truths and that our knowledge of them is based on experience, for instance on perception.[15] We might call this sort of view *empiricism about the (apparent) truths of reason*. The name suits the view, since the position construes apparently a priori truths as empirical, though it need not deny that reason as a capacity distinct from perception has *some* role in giving us justification and knowledge. Reason may, for example, be crucial in extending our knowledge by enabling us to prove geometrical theorems from axioms. But the sort of view I want to explore (without following Mill in particular) denies that reason grounds justification or knowledge in the non-empirical, a priori way described by the classical theory.

Rationalism and empiricism

Before we consider Mill's thesis in detail, we should contrast it, from the most general epistemological point of view, with Kant's to get a better sense of what is at stake in the controversy between rationalism and empiricism. Kant's position on the truths of reason might be called rationalist, Mill's empiricist. These terms are used too variously to make precise definition wise. Very roughly, however, *rationalism* in epistemology takes reason to be far more important in grounding our knowledge than empiricism allows, and rationalists virtually always assert or imply that, in addition to knowledge of analytic truths, there is knowledge of synthetic a priori truths. Very roughly, *empiricism* in epistemology takes experience to be the basis of all of our knowledge except possibly that of analytic propositions, understood as including purely logical truths, such as the truth that if all whales are mammals and no fish are mammals, then no whales are fish. (For both empiricists and rationalists, analytic propositions are typically taken to include logical truths.[16])

One might wonder why some empiricists grant that purely logical truths may be a priori. The central point (though an empiricist might not put it this way) may be seen if we use the terminology of the classical theory: even if such logical propositions are not true by virtue of containment relations, they are in an important respect like those that are. Their negations entail contradictions, for instance that some whales are and are not mammals. They are therefore paradigms of truths of reason; for the use of logic alone, which is perhaps the purest use of reason, can show that they can be false only if a contradiction is true – which is absolutely impossible if anything is impossible. This is another reason why, as noted above, analytic propositions are sometimes given a broader characterization than I have proposed and are taken to be those whose negations entail a contradiction.[17]

Some empiricists do not allow that any knowledge, even of so-called analytic propositions, is genuinely a priori. A *radical empiricist*, like Mill, takes *all* knowledge to be grounded in experience. A *radical rationalist* (which Kant was not) takes all knowledge to be grounded in reason, for instance to be intuitively grounded in a grasp of self-evident propositions or deductively based on inference from a priori truths that are intuited.[18]

Empiricism and the genesis and confirmation of arithmetic beliefs

Empiricism about what are called the truths of reason is most plausible for the apparently synthetic a priori ones, so let us sketch it with reference to an apparently synthetic kind of a priori proposition that has been much in dispute. Mathematical truths, particularly truths of simple arithmetic, are often regarded as synthetic a priori. Consider the proposition that $7 + 5 = 12$ (Kant's example, also found in Plato's *Theaetetus*). It is easy to say that one just knows this, as one knows that nothing is red and green all over at once. But how does one know it?

Here we cannot readily find a good analogy for the simple exclusion relation we apparently grasp in the case of red and green. Could it be that from experience with objects, say with counting apples, then combining two sets of them, and recounting, we learn our first arithmetic truths and then use reason to formulate general rules, such as those for calculating larger sums?

Viewed in this way, arithmetic develops rather as a scientific theory is often thought to, with observations crucial at the base, generalizations formulated to account for them, and broader principles postulated to link all the observations and generalizations together. And do we not first learn to add by counting physical things, or by counting on our fingers?

To be sure, we perhaps cannot imagine how the number 7 added to the number 5 could fail to equal the number 12. But the world *could* go haywire so that when (for instance) five apples and seven oranges are physically combined, the result of counting the new set is *always* eleven. If that happened, would we not begin to think that arithmetic must be revised, just as Einstein's work showed that the physics of the incomparable Sir Isaac Newton needed revision? Perhaps the crucial epistemological consideration is what overall account of our experience is most reasonable; and if the best overall account should require rejecting a proposition now considered a priori and necessary, so be it.

From the standpoint of the classical view, several critical responses can be made here. One concerns the distinction between two related but quite different things: the *genesis* of one's beliefs – what produces them – and their *justification*, in the sense of what justifies them. A second point concerns the question whether arithmetical propositions can be tested observationally. The third focuses on the possibility of taking account of what looks like evidence against arithmetical truths, so that even if one's final epistemological standard is meeting the demands of the best overall account of experience, these truths can be preserved in *any* adequate account. Consider these ideas in turn.

First, granting for the sake of argument that our arithmetic beliefs arise from physical counting, is the experience that produces them what *justifies* them? The genesis of a belief – what produces it – is often different from what justifies it. The testimony of someone I realize is unreliable might, when I am off guard, produce my belief that different brands of aspirin do not, as aspirin, differ chemically. My belief would at that point be unjustified; but it might become justified later when I learn that aspirin is simply acetylsalicylic acid. Moreover, regardless of what produces our arithmetic beliefs initially, when they are justified in the *way* my belief that $7 + 5 = 12$ now is, it does not appear that experience is what justifies them. For my part, I do not see precisely how the truth of the proposition might be grounded in the behavior of objects when they are combined; and I would not try to justify it, as opposed to *illustrating* it, by citing such behavior.

This brings us to the second point: it is far from clear that the proposition that $7 + 5 = 12$ is *testable*, say by examining how objects combine, though it is *exemplifiable* in that way. The empiricist might reply that this by no means shows that the proposition is, as the classical view insists, necessarily true rather than contingent and empirical. Indeed, it does not. But let us look closely at the idea that it could be tested, and could thereby be disconfirmed by our discovering that when sets of five objects are combined with sets of seven, we then find just eleven.

This brings us to a third response. How might one deal with repeated and systematic counter-evidence? Classical theorists will argue that it is possible for the world to alter in such a way that this combination procedure results in one item's disappearing, or in our failing to see it, or in our misremembering how many items entered the mix before our re-counting. They will also argue that this would be a better interpretation of the strange cases described than saying that it has turned out to be false that $7 + 5 = 12$. Thus, instead of saying that an arithmetical principle has been falsified, we would say that the world no longer exemplifies it.

One consideration favoring the classical view is that it is at best difficult to understand how the purely arithmetical principle could be false. The number 7 plus the number 5 equals the number 12, regardless of how apples and oranges behave. The arithmetic statement is apparently not *about* apples and oranges, though (so far as we know) their behavior exemplifies it. For the classical view, at least, it is about *numbers*, which, unlike the arabic or roman or other *numerals* we use to express them linguistically, are abstract and non-physical.

Notice something else. In order to gather purportedly significant counter-evidence to the arithmetic proposition in question, one would have to rely, as already noted, not only on memory and perception (both highly fallible sources) but also on simple arithmetic: one would have to count disconfirming cases. A single apparent instance, say, of seven and five things not adding up to twelve, would not be significant, and one must keep track of how many anomalies there are, relative to confirmatory instances where the expected sum is counted out. Even if one appealed, not to apparent counter-instances to the principle, but to a well-confirmed *theory* to argue that it could be false that $7 + 5 = 12$, one would need to count one's confirmatory data regarding that theory (not to mention other ways in which theory confirmation relies on arithmetic). One would, then, have to rely on some arithmetic propositions, such as that $1 + 1 + 1$ disconfirmations $= 3$ (a significant number) in order to mount an effective challenge to the (necessary) truth that $7 + 5 = 12$. Given the interconnections among arithmetic propositions, it is not clear that one could consistently (or at least with any plausibility) maintain the needed disconfirmatory propositions while denying that $7 + 5 = 12$. There may be a way around this difficulty, but even finding it would leave one far from a strong case for the contingent or empirical status of arithmetic truths.[19]

None of these points requires us to deny that there *is* a similar arithmetic proposition about apples and oranges, namely, that when we *count* five of the first and *place* them next to the result of counting seven of the second, we *can count* twelve all told. This proposition may easily be confused with its pure mathematical counterpart. The former is clearly contingent and empirical, but its being so does not show that the purely arithmetic proposition is also.

By contrast with the classical view, radical empiricism denies that there *are* abstract entities and so, believing that mathematical propositions are about something concrete, radical empiricists naturally view them as generalizations about the behavior of physical objects. We need not accept the empiricist view to grant that if physical things did not exemplify the proposition that $7 + 5 = 12$, the proposition would be of far less *value* to us even if necessarily true. If the physical world went haywire, it could turn out to be false that when seven apples are placed together with five more and the total collection is counted, the count yields twelve. This chaotic situation would falsify the *physical* principle already contrasted with the arithmetic one in question. But the physical principle is not, and does not even follow from, the purely mathematical proposition we are discussing.

Empiricism and logical and analytic truths

The empiricist view of the a priori can also be applied to analytic propositions and even to self-evident logical truths, and it may indeed be more plausible in that case. Suppose that through scientific investigation we discover that vixens have certain characteristics we think of as male, such as certain hormones. Imagine that gradually these discoveries mount up so that the female foxes in our laboratory begin to seem better classified as male than as female. Could not a time come when we begin to doubt that vixens are female after all?

And what about the logical principle of the excluded middle, which says that every proposition is either true or false? Consider the proposition that Tom is bald. Must this proposition be either true or false no matter what the quantity or distribution of hair on his head? Surely it is an appropriate counter-example to the principle of the excluded middle.

The classical view can offer its own account of these examples. For one thing, particularly over a long time, we can begin to use a term in a sense different from the one it now has. Thus, the discoveries about vixens could result in our someday using 'vixen' to mean not 'female fox', but 'fox with female external sexual characteristics and of the anatomical kind K' (where K is the kind we have in our laboratory). Then, when we utter such words as 'Vixens are not really female', we are not denying the analytic proposition now expressed by 'All vixens are female'. We have confirmed something else, rather than disconfirming this.

In this way, then, our experience might result in our someday no longer assertively uttering 'Vixens are female' to say anything that we believe. This certainly does not show that experience might falsify the proposition we *now* assert when we assertively utter that. Given what we now mean by 'vixen', in saying that all vixens are female we do not rule out that *those* "vixens" in the lab could turn out to have internal biological and chemical characteristics in the light of which *they* ultimately need not be considered female.

Regarding the principle of the excluded middle, I would stress that Aristotle plausibly argued against it, and some contemporary logicians do, too. The main reasons for doubting it, moreover, do not depend on empiricism. Let us explore some of them.

Consider again the vague statement that Tom (who has lost much of his hair) is bald. It may certainly be argued that this need not be either true or false. It is not as if 'bald' meant, say, 'having fewer than 500 hairs on the top of one's head'. It does not. And if it did, the term 'top' would still be vague and would cause the same trouble: it would be unclear in what *area* we must find hair. If the middle possibility – neither truth nor falsity – is to be ruled out here, it must be by a better argument. The principle of the excluded middle, though often used to suggest that even logical truths are not necessarily true, is controversial among rationalists and empiricists alike. The principle is surely a poor example to support the empiricist case against the necessity of logical truths.

When, by contrast, standard examples of simple logical truths are used, the effect seems very different. Consider the proposition that if Ann is coming by bus or she is coming by plane, and if she is not coming by bus, then she is coming by plane (which exemplifies the general logical truth that if at least one of two propositions is the case and the first is not, then the second is). Is there any plausibility in the view that this might be false? I find none; and while nothing said here proves that the empiricist account of the a priori is mistaken, it appears less plausible than the classical account.

The conventionalist view
of the truths of reason

There is another important approach to understanding the truths of reason and our justification and knowledge regarding them. It builds on the undeniable connections between how we use our language – specifically, our linguistic conventions – and our knowledge of truths expressible in that language.

Truth by definition and truth by virtue of meaning

To see how this approach goes, suppose that analytic propositions may be said to be *true by definition*. On the assumption that the truth or falsity of definitions turns on linguistic conventions, one can now make moves parallel to the classical ones that are expressed in terms of concepts. Thus, 'vixen' is definable as meaning (the same thing as) 'female fox'; 'female' is part of the phrase; hence, by grasping a definition (even if we do not call it to mind) we can *see* how the proposition that all vixens are female is true. The predicate, 'is female', expresses part of the meaning of the subject, 'vixen', just as the concept of being female is part of the concept of a vixen. Thus, according to conventionalism, by *appeal* to the definition of 'vixen' as having the same meaning as 'female fox', we can *show* that the proposition that all vixens are female expresses an analytic truth.

Granted, in the case of synthetic truths of reason, for instance that nothing is red and green all over at once, we cannot make the same moves. But we can still speak of truth by virtue of *meaning*, in the limited sense that it seems to be a matter of the meanings of, say, the terms 'red' and 'green', that if one of the terms applies to something at a time and place, the other does not. Why else would someone who sincerely denies that nothing can be red and green all over at once seem to exhibit an inadequate understanding of at least one crucial term used in expressing that proposition?

What terms mean is a matter of convention. It depends entirely on agreement, usually tacit agreement, among the users of the relevant language, concerning the proper application of the term. We could have used 'vixen' differently, and we in fact would have done so if the history of our language happened to differ in a certain way with respect to that term. Moreover, even now we could decide to use 'vixen' differently.

The suggested account of the truths of reason – *conventionalism* – grounds them in conventions, especially definitional conventions, regarding meaning; and it conceives our knowledge of them as based on our knowing those conventions. Since knowledge of conventions is reasonably taken to be empirical knowledge based on suitable observations of linguistic behavior, conventionalism (on this interpretation) turns out to be a kind of empiricism regarding the truths of reason, and it has been held by some philosophers in the empiricist tradition.

Knowledge through definitions versus truth by definition

Some of the points made by conventionalism are quite plausible. In grasping the definition of 'vixen' as meaning the same thing as 'female fox', perhaps we can see that all vixens are female; and by appeal to the definition perhaps we can show that this truth holds. But do these points really undercut the classical view? If the points hold, that may well be because of something *non-*linguistic: perhaps, in grasping the definition we understand the *concepts* involved and thereby see a containment relation between the concept of a vixen and that of being female.

Furthermore, it seems possible to grasp the relevant conceptual relations, and thereby already know the analytic truth, even if one does not know any such definition. Perhaps it could be like this. One is able to *construct* such a definition on the basis of the analytic truths one knows, such as that all vixens are female and that all female foxes are vixens. The definition would reflect what is already true in virtue of how the concepts in question are related; the concepts are not themselves created by or grounded in linguistic conventions. The knowledge of analytic truths would then be the basis of the definitional knowledge, not the other way around. Understanding the relations between the concepts expressed by the words in question would be the basis for judging the relevant definitions of those words; it would not be through a knowledge of the truth of those definitions that one understands the conceptual relations or knows the analytic truth. Hence, knowledge of analytic truths apparently does not depend on knowledge of conventions.

Conventionalism also fails to give a good account of what grounds the *truth* of analytic propositions. It is not *because* 'vixen' means the same thing as 'female fox' that all vixens are female. For, as we saw in assessing the empiricist view, this analytic truth does not depend on what 'vixen' means. This truth holds whether there is such a word or not. It could be expressed in some other language or by other English terms. It could be so expressed even if the word 'vixen' never existed, or if, although 'vixen' had always meant the same thing as 'female fox', *both* terms had meant something else, for example 'wily creature'. In that case, 'All vixens are female' would still have expressed an analytic truth, but not the one it now does. It would have meant what we now mean by 'All wily creatures are wily creatures'.

Moreover, although one can come to know that all vixens are female *through* understanding definitions of terms that express this truth, one cannot know it wholly on the *basis* of the truth of those definitions. A route to a foundation is not itself a foundation.[20] To know that all vixens are female by virtue of knowing that, say, 'vixen' has the same meaning as 'female fox', I need a bridge between knowledge of linguistic convention and knowledge of vixens. Consider one thing such a bridge requires. I must be justified in believing a general principle something like this: that a proposition expressed by a subject–predicate sentence such as 'All vixens are female' is true if its predicate – here 'female' – expresses something contained in the concept designated by its subject term, here 'vixen'. But this bridge principle is a good candidate for an analytic truth. If it is analytic, then apparently one can know an analytic truth by knowing conventions only if one *assumes* some other analytic truth.

Moreover, to know, in the light of this bridge principle, that all vixens are female, I must take the relevant sentence, 'All vixens are female', to be the kind of thing the principle applies to, that is, to be a sentence with a predicate that expresses something contained in the concept designated by its subject. I am in effect using logic to discern something about a particular sentence by bringing that sentence under a generalization about sentences. But how can conventionalism account for my knowledge (or justified belief) of the logical truths I thereby depend on, such as that if all sentences of a certain kind express truths, and this sentence is of that kind, then it expresses a truth?

I cannot respond by doing the same thing all over again with this logical truth; for that would presuppose logic in the same way, and the procedure would have to be repeated. The problem would arise yet again. No finite number of steps would explain my justification, and an infinite number would not be possible for me, even if it would help. We could thus never account for knowledge of a given logical truth without presupposing knowledge of one. Since conventionalism presupposes (at least) logical truths of reason, in order even to begin to account for analytic ones, it cannot show – and provides no good reason to believe – that either every truth of reason, or all knowledge of such truths, is grounded in convention.

Conventions as grounds for interpretation

These criticisms should not be allowed to obscure a correct conventionalist point. The meaning of 'vixen' *is* crucial for what proposition is expressed by the sentence 'All vixens are female', that is, for what one is asserting when (in the normal way) one uses this sentence to make an assertion. Thus, if 'vixen' came to mean the same as 'wily creature', that sentence would express a falsehood, since there are plenty of wily males. But from the fact that change in what our terms mean can result in our saying different things in uttering the same words, nothing at all follows regarding whether *what* we say in using these words is necessarily true, or true at all. Those matters depend on what it *is* that we say.

There are, however, insights underlying conventionalism: truths of reason are associated with meanings; they can be known when meanings are adequately understood; and they can be shown through pointing out relations of meanings. Moreover, without conventions, our "words" could not be said to have meanings: strictly speaking, we would have no words and could not plausibly call anything true by virtue of (verbal) meaning.

Important as these points about conventions are, they do not support the conventionalist view that the truths of reason themselves, or even our justification or knowledge regarding those a priori propositions, are *based* on what words mean or on our conventions for using them. For all that these points establish, our understanding of word meanings (including sentence meanings) is simply a route to our grasping of concepts and shows what it does about the truths of reason only because of that fact.

Some difficulties and strengths
of the classical view

Of the accounts just considered, then, the classical view of the truths of reason and our knowledge of them apparently stands up best. But there are other accounts and many variants on the ones discussed here. Moreover, I have sketched only the main lines of the classical view and only some of the challenges to it. There are still other difficulties for it.

Vagueness

Recall the problem of vagueness. Perhaps the concept of being red, as well as the term 'red', is vague. Is it, then, an a priori truth that nothing is red and (any shade of) orange all over? And how can we tell?

One answer is that although words are by and large vague, concepts are not, and what *is* red (i.e., what instantiates the concept of redness) is never orange even though we have no non-arbitrary way of precisely specifying the limits of colors. Thus, we might confront a sentence, say 'That painting has a patch that is at once red and orange', which we cannot assess until we see whether it implies the necessary falsehood that the patch is two different colors all over at once or, because of the vagueness of its terms, expresses the possible truth that the patch has a single color that can be considered red just as appropriately as orange.

This answer is only the beginning of a solution to the problem of how to deal with vagueness and is less plausible for highly complex concepts such as that of a work of art. The more vague our terms, the harder it is to discern what propositions are expressed by sentences using those terms, and thus the harder it is to decide whether these sentences express truths of reason. None of this implies, however, that there are not some clear cases of synthetic a priori truths.

Meaning change and falsification

A related problem for the classical view emerges when we consider the close connection (which some regard as an equivalence) between what a term means and the concept it expresses. With this connection in mind, notice too that meaning can change gradually, as where we discover things about vixens a little at a time and thereby almost imperceptibly come to mean something different by 'vixen'. A point may then come at which it is unclear whether the term 'vixen' expresses the concept it now does or not and, correspondingly, whether what is then expressed by 'All vixens are female' is analytic or not.

This unclarity about what concept 'vixen' expresses does *not* give us reason to doubt, regarding the proposition which that sentence now expresses, that it is analytic; but it does show that it may be difficult to decide whether or not an utterance or sentence we have before us expresses an analytic proposition. That difficulty may drastically limit the usefulness of the notion of the analytic in understanding philosophical and other problems.

It might be argued, moreover, that on reflection the distinction between meaning change (semantic change) of the kind illustrated and falsification of the proposition we started with simply does not hold. This point is especially likely to be pressed by those who think that the basic epistemological standard, the fundamental standard for judging whether a belief is justified or constitutes knowledge, is what is required for an overall account of our experience. This broad standard is compatible both with many versions of empiricism and with some versions of rationalism.

Compare the following states of affairs: (1) scientists' discovering that despite appearances vixens have such significant male characteristics that they are *not* really female – an outcome the classical theory says is impossible – and (2) scientists' making discoveries about vixens so startling that we come to use 'vixen' in a new sense, one such that, while scientists deny that "vixens" in this new sense are always female, what they are thereby saying provides no reason to doubt that what we *now* mean by 'All vixens are female' is true. Is there really a clear difference between (1) and (2) – roughly, between falsification of the belief we held and a change in the meaning of the terms we used to express it?[21]

Classical theorists take (2) to be possible and tend to hold that it is only because possibilities like (2) are not clearly distinguished from (1) that (1) *seems* possible. They regard the difference between (1) and (2) as clear enough to sustain their view and tend to conclude that what may seem to be a falsification of an analytic proposition is really only a change in meaning that leads us to substitute for an analytic truth what looks like a proposition inconsistent with it, yet is actually compatible with it. Other philosophers think that the difference is not clear at all and that future discoveries really can weigh against what the classical view calls analytic propositions.[22]

It is difficult to doubt, however, that there are *some* truths of reason, such as elementary logical principles, and such simple analytic propositions as that all vixens are female, which are both a priori and necessarily true. Whether some truths of reason are also synthetic is more controversial, but it looks as if some of them are. Whether, if some of them are, those synthetic truths are also necessary is also very controversial. I see no good reason to deny that they are necessary, but there may be no clearly decisive argument to show this.

If synthetic truths of reason are necessary, perhaps one must simply see that this is so by reflecting on the examples. In any case, our capacity of reason, our rational *intuition*, as it is sometimes (perhaps misleadingly) called, is a source of beliefs of simple truths of reason, such as the self-evident truth that if the spruce is taller than the maple, then the latter is shorter than the former. We can know the *truth* of these intuitively, even if more is required to know their *status* as, say, necessary or contingent, a priori or empirical. Moreover, reason, applied in our contemplating or reflecting on certain a priori truths, can yield both situational justification – hence justification for holding beliefs of them – and actual justified beliefs of them. Clearly, reason can also yield knowledge of them.

The possibility of empirical necessary truth

It is one thing to say, with the classical view, that every a priori truth is necessary; the thesis that every necessary truth is a priori is less plausible. Consider the truth that sugar is soluble in water. Ordinarily this is thought to be a law of nature and as such something that must (of necessity) hold. Yet it is apparently not a priori: one could adequately understand it without thereby being justified in believing it; nor does it seem to follow self-evidently from anything self-evident. Indeed, it seems to be the kind of truth that can be represent an empirical discovery. Proponents of the classical view would maintain that the necessity in question is not "logical" in the sense of absolutely precluding falsehood, but *nomic* (from the Greek *nomos*, for law), in roughly the sense characterizing laws of the natural world as opposed to every possible world or situation.

It does appear that one can clearly conceive of a lump of sugar's failing to dissolve in water, whereas one cannot clearly conceive of something that is (in overall shape) both round and square (if this is conceivable at all). But perhaps once the idea of solubility in water is properly qualified (in ways sketched in Chapter 9), there may no longer seem to be any more than a difference of degree between the two cases. I am inclined to doubt that the difference is only one of degree, but let us leave the matter open and proceed to cases that pose a greater challenge to the classical view.

The truth that gold is malleable is arguably more basic to what gold is than solubility in water is to what sugar is. Is it even possible for something to be gold without being malleable? Compare the question whether a vixen could turn out to be male. This also seems impossible, but one difference is that whereas there are good ways of identifying specimens of gold without selecting them in part on the basis of malleability, there are no comparable ways of identifying vixens without selecting them in part on the basis of being female. Still, even classical theorists will grant that taking the proposition that gold is malleable to be necessary does not commit one to considering it analytic, as is the proposition that all vixens are female. Critics of the classical view will maintain that it is surely not obvious that a specimen of gold could turn out to lack malleability, yet it is equally far from obvious that adequately understanding the proposition that gold is malleable is sufficient to justify it.

If we move to a theoretical identification statement, such as that water is H_2O, it seems even less likely that we have a proposition that is contingent rather than absolutely necessary, yet it also appears that the proposition is not a priori. But what of "heavy water," which has a different formula? Is this not really water, or is water not necessarily H_2O? The issue cannot easily be settled. In any case, a different kind of example may more strongly support this conclusion that some necessary truths are empirical. This time we turn to the domain of biology.

As the identity of human beings is normally understood, who they are is essentially tied to their parents. It is simply not possible that I might have had (biologically) different parents. Anyone otherwise like me but born of different parents is only a fortuitously identical twin. Here, then, is an empirical proposition that is apparently necessary as well.

Notice, however, that the proposition that I have the parents I do is singular and existential, implying the existence of the particular thing it concerns (me), whereas all the clear cases of necessary truth we have considered are general and non-existential. To say that nothing is both round and square, for instance, does not entail that there is anything round or square: it says roughly that anything which is round is non-square, and it would be true even if all the round and square things in the universe had been destroyed (and presumably even if there never had been any except perhaps in the mind of someone contemplating creating them). What a proponent of the classical view might say of the parentage case is that the proposition that I have the parents I do is an *essential truth* – one attributing to a thing a property absolutely essential to it, roughly in the sense that it could not exist without it – but not a necessary truth. The idea is roughly this: a necessary truth holds in any possible world or situation; an essential truth holds only in those possible worlds or situations in which what it is about exists.[23]

One trouble with this view is that we could talk of water and H_2O in a world without them, as we can of what is round or square. Perhaps the best the classical view can do here is, first, to distinguish between two kinds of necessary truth, those applicable to entities that must exist, such as (arguably) numbers, and those applicable to entities that need not exist, and second, to argue that the former are a priori. The idea might be that necessary truths are grounded in the nature of things, and that the nature of the kinds of things that must exist is knowable through the use of reason. The nature of water must be discovered by scientific inquiry; that of the abstract property of roundness is apparent to adequate reflection.

The idea that necessary truths are grounded in the nature of (the relevant) things has some plausibility. At best, however, it does not in any obvious way apply to purely formal necessary truths, such as that if some As are Bs, then some Bs are As, where 'A' and 'B' are variables and stand for nothing in particular. There is, moreover, a further objection to extending the idea to imply the apriority of all necessary truths. A theorem might follow from a necessarily true proposition and thereby be a necessary truth, yet not be a priori because there is no way to know it simply through adequately understanding it or its self-evident entailment by something that is self-evident. It cannot be simply assumed that every such theorem is entailed by a *self-evident* proposition, or that some proof of it must proceed by self-evident steps from a self-evident proposition. Moroever, the only possible proof could be long and complicated; this would put the theorem a long inferential distance from the axioms. Granted, such a theorem would still be *provable* from what is self-evident. But simply being provable does not entail being a priori.

It appears, then, that there can be necessary truths knowable only through the work of empirical investigation or of arduous mathematical proof of a kind that cannot ground a priori knowledge. The latter, to be sure, might be both provable and knowable just on the basis of *a* use of reason – though knowledge based on a long proof also seems to depend on memory. Not just any use of reason, however, qualifies knowledge reached through it as a priori. From the falsity of the classical thesis that every necessary truth is a priori, it does not follow, of course, that the classical view is mistaken in positing synthetic a priori knowledge or in claiming that every a priori proposition is necessary (see Figure 1).

Reason, experience, and a priori justification

Reason – conceived roughly as our mental capacity of understanding, especially in conceptual reflection or in inference – is, furthermore, a basic source of belief, justification, and knowledge. Like introspective consciousness and unlike perception and memory, it is an *active* capacity, in that we can, within limits, employ it successfully at will. I can, simply because I want to, reflect on logical and mathematical propositions. But although I can look around me just because I want to, whether I perceive anything depends on there being something there: trees and roses and books are not available to the eye in the same unfailing way that numbers are available to thought. Through reflection on the huge range of objects of thought, we can acquire a vast amount of justified belief and significant knowledge.

To maintain that there is a priori knowledge and justification does not commit one to denying that reason has a genetic dependence on experience.

Figure 1   The a priori, the analytic, and the necessary

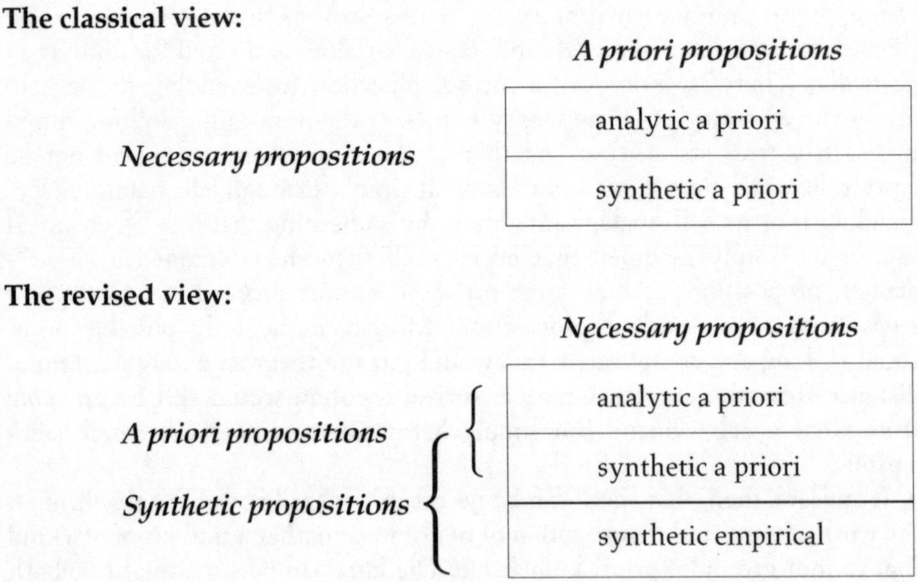

The classical view:

A priori propositions

Necessary propositions

| analytic a priori |
| synthetic a priori |

The revised view:

Necessary propositions

A priori propositions $\left\{\vphantom{\begin{array}{c}a\\b\end{array}}\right.$

Synthetic propositions $\left\{\vphantom{\begin{array}{c}a\\b\\c\end{array}}\right.$

| analytic a priori |
| synthetic a priori |
| synthetic empirical |

Reason yields no knowledge or justified belief until experience, whether perceptual, reflective, or introspective, acquaints us with (or develops in us) concepts sufficient for grasping a priori propositions. But despite this genetic dependence of reason on experience, in one way reason may be an even firmer basis of justification and knowledge than experience. If experience is the ground from which reason grows, it is not the sole determinant of the range or power of reason. The view from the top of the tree may be more comprehensive than the view on the ground.

The following plausible justification principle is a partial indication of the justificatory power of reason: normally, if one believes a proposition solely on the basis of understanding it – in an *a priori way*, as we might call it – this belief is justified.[24] Similarly, there is a plausible epistemic principle to the effect that normally, if one believes a *true* proposition in this way, one knows that it is true. The first says roughly that a belief held in an a priori way is normally justified (to some degree); the second says roughly that true beliefs thus held normally constitute knowledge. Believing in this a priori way is appropriate to (and typical for) beliefs of a priori propositions (though they may often be believed on the basis of testimony), but it does not entail that the object of belief is a priori (or a necessary truth or necessary falsehood).

It may also be true that normally, if one believes a proposition solely on the basis of one or more premises that self-evidently entail it and are believed in the a priori way just described, this belief is justified. Again, such a proposition need not be a priori, but this principle is highly appropriate to what is a priori in the broad sense (not self-evident but self-evidently entailed by something that is, or provable by self-evident steps from a self-evident proposition). What the principle expresses is the idea that normally self-evident entailment carries the kind of justification that is based solely on understanding across a self-evident entailment: normally, if you believe a proposition on the basis of believing, with this kind of justification, a second one which self-evidently entails the former, then your belief of the former is also justified.

If these principles seem too permissive, note that we do not normally believe propositions in this a priori way unless they are a priori and thus *can* be known on the basis of understanding them. We normally have no tendency whatever to believe, solely on the basis of understanding them, propositions about the state of the weather or of the objects in our environment or of the well-being or plans of others. Philosophers commonly say of such propositions that we cannot "determine a priori" (or tell or know a priori) whether they are true, and here 'a priori' designates an a priori way of believing rather than the status of the propositions in question. Compare how much we believe on the basis of perception, memory, and introspection; not only is this far more than is normally believed on the basis of conceptual understanding, it is also quite different in the kind of grounding of the resulting beliefs.[25]

Loose and strict senses of 'a priori justification' and 'a priori knowledge'

So far, I have been speaking of knowledge and justification arising from believing in an a priori *way*. This is not necessarily a priori knowledge or a priori justification, just as not everything perceptually believed is perceptual knowledge or perceptually justified. When such knowledge or justification is not strictly speaking a priori, one might still call it a priori knowledge or a priori justification in the loose sense. Let us consider justification first.

Consider the proposition that people tend to feel offended when they are insulted. This is vague, but not too vague to make it clear that it is not an a priori truth (it seems empirically true or false). Still, imagine someone who thinks that insulting self-evidently entails being offensive and that feeling offended is necessarily appropriate to what is offensive. Such a person might argue that, on the basis of understanding it, we can believe the proposition that people tend to feel offended when insulted, and that we may, on this basis, be justified in believing that. If one might be so justified, then we might speak of a priori justification in the loose sense. We may also say that the belief itself is a priori in the loose sense, since it is grounded in an a priori way. And just as a perceptual belief can be justified and false (as where one first sees a straight stick half submerged in water and thinks it is bent), this belief can be also.

Another case of a priori justification in the loose sense can occur when, although one believes a proposition that *is* a priori, one believes it on the basis of an inadequate understanding of it. One might, for instance, overlook a subtlety or confuse one notion with a similar one, such as believing a proposition and being disposed to believe it. Suppose that, on the basis of my understanding of it, I believe a mathematical theorem that is a priori in the broad sense. Suppose further that this understanding, although inadequate, is reasonable (say because it represents a reasonable though subtly misguided interpretation of the theorem). Then my belief may be justified. This is a second case of a belief held in an a priori *way* and exhibiting a priori justification in the loose sense. Here the proposition is a priori, but the justification, though based on understanding is defectively grounded. In the other case of a priori justification in the loose sense, the belief is also held in an a priori way, but the proposition is not a priori.

If a belief that is a priori justified in the loose sense constitutes knowledge and is based on understanding the relevant proposition(s), we might speak of a priori knowledge in the loose sense. But since both our examples of such justification exhibit a defective (though reasonable) understanding in the basis of the justification, they are not plausibly considered instances of knowledge. If one believes something (wholly) on a basis embodying conceptual error, this belief is not plausibly taken to constitute knowledge. (This seems so even if the conceptual error is justified.)

Suppose, however, that I believe a mathematical theorem on the twofold basis of a self-evident axiom (which I adequately understand) and the justified true belief that the theorem is entailed by the axiom (we may assume the belief to be grounded wholly in my mathematical knowledge and understanding). Suppose further that the theorem is clearly entailed, but not *self-evidently*, because adequately understanding the conditional proposition that if the axiom holds, then the theorem does is not sufficient to justify believing this conditional. To see the truth of this proposition, I must note several intermediate steps from the axiom to the theorem, so that I do not see its truth (or the entailment it expresses) on the basis of adequately understanding the proposition. Still, I may know the theorem. This is surely an a priori way of knowing it, and we may speak of a priori knowledge in the loose sense here. But my knowledge of the proposition is not a priori, in the strict sense; for the theorem is not a priori, even in the indirect sense. By valid deduction, I can prove it using the a priori procedures illustrated, but such provability of a proposition is not sufficient for its being self-evident or even knowable a priori in the strict sense of that phrase.

By contrast, a priori knowledge in the strict sense is not only more than true belief held in an a priori way, it is also more than knowledge of an a priori proposition. Again, the analogy to perception is helpful. Just as perceptual knowledge is knowledge based on perception and thus more than knowledge about a perceptible, a priori knowledge is knowledge based on understanding and thus more than knowledge of an a priori proposition. I could know a simple logical truth on the basis of testimony, even if it can be known on the basis of understanding alone. This would be knowledge of an a priori proposition that is not even a priori knowledge in the loose sense.

To achieve a more specific characterization of a priori knowledge we do well to begin with a crucial constituent of it – *a priori justification*. In the strict sense (the sense that mainly concerns us), this is justification based directly or indirectly on understanding a self-evident proposition (the justification will be only situational if the person in question does not believe the proposition). A priori justification (in the strict sense) thus divides into two kinds, depending on whether it is directly or indirectly based on understanding some self-evident proposition. A priori justification for believing a proposition is based directly on such understanding where the justification depends only on understanding that proposition itself. This is a priori justification in the strict and narrow sense. A priori justification for believing a proposition is based indirectly on such understanding where the justification depends on understanding a self-evident entailment of that proposition by some self-evident proposition. This is a priori justification in the strict but broad sense.[26]

If this outline is correct, then *a priori knowledge*, in the strict sense, might be plausibly taken to be knowledge that is based, directly or indirectly, in the sense just indicated, on understanding one or more self-evident propositions. There is, then, in addition to a division between a priori justification and a priori knowledge in the strict and loose senses, a division between direct and indirect (non-inferential and inferential) a priori justification and a priori knowledge in both senses[27] (see Figure 2).

The power of reason and the possibility of indefeasible justification

We have seen that, and perhaps to some extent how, the justificatory and epistemic power of reason enables it to ground a priori knowledge and a priori justified beliefs of a priori propositions. We have also seen its power to provide such knowledge and justification, in a loose sense of 'a priori knowledge' and 'a priori justification' for propositions that are not a priori. These senses are especially appropriate for propositions that are provable from what is a priori. Is the power of reason such that it provides for something that even introspective experience apparently does not – indefeasible justification? It will help to focus on a concrete example.

There may be truths of reason that are so simple and luminously self-evident that they *cannot* be unjustifiably believed, at least at a time when one comprehendingly considers them. Could one comprehendingly consider, yet unjustifiably believe, that if Shakespeare is identical with the author of *Hamlet*, then the author of *Hamlet* is identical with Shakespeare? This is doubtful. One could believe it partly on the basis of a bad argument; if so, there is

Figure 2 Outline of a four-dimensional conception of the a priori.

PROPOSITIONS:

A priori in the narrow sense: self-evident; roughly, adequate understanding is a sufficient ground for justification; belief based on such understanding constitutes knowledge. (This basic case is *direct self-evidence*.)

A priori in the broad sense: not self-evident but either (a) *indirectly self-evident*, i.e., not self-evident but self-evidently entailed by a self-evident proposition, or (b) *ultimately self-evident*, i.e., not self-evident but provable by self-evident steps from a self-evident proposition.

JUSTIFICATION:

A priori in the strict sense: (a) based on an adequate understanding of a self-evident proposition, or (b) indirectly based on such an understanding via a self-evident entailment of the proposition in question by a self-evident proposition.

A priori in the loose sense: not a priori in the strict sense but based on *an* understanding of the proposition in question (the proposition itself need not be a priori or true).

KNOWLEDGE:

A priori in the strict sense: knowledge (a) of an a priori proposition that is directly or indirectly self-evident, and (b) constituted by a belief that is a priori justified in the strict sense.

A priori in the loose sense: knowledge (a) of a proposition that is not directly or indirectly self-evident but is provable by self-evident steps from some self-evident proposition, and (b) constituted by belief based on understanding such a proof.

BELIEF:

A priori in the narrow sense: (a) held in an a priori way; roughly, based on an understanding (possibly an inadequate understanding) of the proposition in question, and (b) of a non-empirical proposition (i.e., either it or its negation is a priori).

A priori in the broad sense: (a) held in an a priori way but (b) of an empirical proposition.

something unjustified in the *way* one believes it. But if one believes it, one has some understanding of it, and if one understands something this simple to the extent required for believing it, it is at best difficult to see how one could fail to have an understanding of it adequate to yield justification for believing it, at least at a time when one comprehendingly considers it. Perhaps, then, such a belief would be – or at least could be – indefeasibly justified.

If there are propositions like this, then there can apparently be indefeasible justification: justification so secure that those possessing it cannot be unjustified in believing the proposition in question, even if they believe it in part on the basis of a bad argument. But not all a priori justification should be considered indefeasible. Witness how justification for believing even a simple logical theorem can be defeated by the discovery of mistakes in one's proof. Moreover, perhaps not all presumptively indefeasible justification need be a priori: consider my justification for believing that I exist, a proposition that is neither a priori nor necessary but is arguably such that I cannot unjustifiably believe it.

If there is no indefeasible justification, however (something I want to leave open here), at least our understanding of simple self-evident truths of reason gives us both very secure justification for believing those truths and, when we do believe them on the basis of adequately understanding them, knowledge of them.

In summarizing some apparently warranted conclusions regarding the truths of reason, we might focus on how much seems plausible in the classical view that the a priori is coextensive with the necessary but includes the analytic as a subcategory: that any proposition that is a priori is necessary and conversely, but not every a priori proposition is analytic. Apparently, it is true that not all propositions knowable on the basis of adequately understanding them are analytic: we have seen good reason to think that not everything a priori is analytic. The classical view seems correct in this. It seems mistaken, however, in the idea that every necessary proposition is a priori, though probably not in the plausible idea that every a priori proposition is necessary.

More positively, in addition to our having a priori knowledge of self-evident propositions, on the basis of such knowledge we may know many truths that are a priori in a broad sense: not themselves self-evident but self-evidently entailed by, or provable by self-evident steps from some proposition that is. Many of our beliefs, most clearly certain logical and mathematical ones, are grounded in understanding in the indicated way. Reason, then, as manifested in our capacity for understanding, is one of the basic sources of belief, justification, and knowledge; and, in a way that the other three sources we have explored do not, it enables us to know truths that hold not only in the world of our experience but in any circumstances whatever.

Notes

1 *Adequacy* of understanding of a proposition cannot be merely partial, and it is more than simply getting the general sense of a sentence expressing it, as where one can analyze the grammar of the sentence, indicate something of what it means through examples, and perhaps translate it into another language one knows well. Adequacy here implies not only seeing what the proposition says but also being able to apply it to (and withhold its application from) an appropriately wide range of cases. This matter is treated in some detail in my 'Intuitionism, Pluralism, and the Foundations of Ethics', in Walter Sinnott-Armstrong and Mark Timmons, (eds) *Moral Knowledge?* (Oxford and New York: Oxford University Press, 1996). Note also that there is no appeal here to understanding the *necessity* of the propositions (though the characterization lends itself to taking them to be necessary). In this respect the notion – and that of the a priori given below, which applies to self-evident propositions as described here – are simpler and more moderate than the traditional one common in much of the literature. See, for example Laurence BonJour, 'Toward a Moderate Rationalism', *Philosophical Topics* 23, 1 (1995), 47–78, esp. section 3.

2 This analogy is meant to leave open what concepts are and what it is to understand one. As will later be apparent, philosophers differ in their understanding of the truths of reason in part because of their understanding of the nature of concepts.

3 One reason for the normality qualification is to make room for the possibility that one can consider and adequately understand a proposition yet fail to come to believe it. Brain manipulation might cause such failure. We should also make room for the possibility that, especially with more complex self-evident propositions – say that if *p* entails *q* and *q* entails *r* and *r* entails *s*, and *s* is not true, then *p* is false – it may take a person time to form the belief.

4 *Temporal immediacy*, unlike epistemic immediacy, is a property not primarily of beliefs as such but of their formation. A belief is temporally immediate when its formation occurs "without delay" upon considering the proposition in question. One could also say that propositions are temporally immediate in a derivative sense when they are so obvious that one normally believes them immediately on considering them. Many self-evident propositions are like this. But when I consider some self-evident propositions, such as that if there never have been siblings, then there never have been first cousins, it may or may not take me a moment to see their truth. Still, when one does see such a truth, the belief one forms will (at least normally) be epistemically immediate, not inferential. So, this proposition and my coming to believe it may or may not be temporally immediate. By contrast, the proposition that I am now seeing print *is* temporally immediate (for me) but is not self-evident. It is evident not in itself but *through* what I see.

5 Kant's most detailed presentation of his views on these matters is in his *Critique of Pure Reason* (first published in 1781), but a short presentation is provided in the Preamble to his *Prolegomena to Any Future Metaphysics* (1783).

6 There has long been controversy about whether such thought is possible without using language, or at least having a language. Donald Davidson is among those to argue for a strong dependence of thought on language. See, for example his *Inquiries into Truth and Interpretation* (Oxford: Oxford University Press, 1984). Relevant critical discussion of Davidson is provided by Ruth Barcan Marcus in 'Some Revisionary Puzzles About Belief and Believing', *Philosophy and Phenomenological Research* supplement to vol. 50 (1990), 133–53, which brings out serious problems for the view that beliefs must have sentence-like objects. There is no need to take a stand on this issue for my main purposes in this book.

7 *One* way to conceive this is as follows: if the concept of *F* is part of the concept of *G*, then having the property (of) *F* is entailed by having the property (of) *G*.

8 This is plausible if (1) the correct analysis of a key concept in an analytic proposition, say that of a vixen, is discernible, without reliance on anything beyond understanding that concept, to anyone with an (adequate) understanding of the proposition, and (2) given a correct analysis of that concept, it is appropriately evident that the analytic proposition is true. However, some analytic propositions are not understandable in this way; some might be *provable* only by a lengthy process from one that is (a notion discussed on page 102). Further, it is by no means clear that every analytic proposition is self-evident in the very common sense that implies a fairly high degree of obviousness. If, as seems plausible, the self-evidence of a proposition simply implies that *some* kind of adequate understanding is sufficient for justification for believing it, then we might plausibly distinguish between the immediately and the mediately self-evident and allow that the latter propositions may be understandable (to normal persons) only on the basis of considerable reflection.

9 There are philosophers who regard colors as subjective in a way that might seem to under-mine the example here. I do not see that taking the proposition that nothing is red and green all over at once to be necessary, synthetic, and a priori entails any particular analysis of color properties, and I doubt that the example fails. If the example should depend on a mistaken realist account of color and for that reason fail, anti-realism about shape properties is less plausible, and the proposition that nothing is round and square might serve as well. For accounts of the status of color see C. L. Hardin, *Color for Philosophers, Unweaving the Rainbow* (Indianapolis: Hackett, 1988), and Edward Wilson Averill, 'The Relational Nature of Color', *Philosophical Review* 101 (1992), 551–88. For a detailed discussion of color proper-ties, with application to the apparently synthetic a priori proposition that nothing is red and green all over at once and with a defense of the view that color properties supervene on (and so are determined by) dispositional properties of physical objects, see Colin McGinn, 'Another Look at Color', *Journal of Philosophy* XCIII, 2 (1996), 537–53.

10 This allows that such propositions can *also* be known empirically, say through testimony, though there are restrictions (discussed in Chapter 5) on how this may occur. The character-ization suggests that an a priori proposition is knowable non-inferentially even if only on the basis of considerable reflection, but the exact mode of the appropriate reflection is not something that need be settled here. A full account of this conception of the a priori would explicate the kind of possibility of knowledge in question; it is presumably not mere logical possibility in the sense that no contradiction is formally entailed by the occurrence of the relevant knowledge, but a conceptual possibility, roughly in the sense that such knowledge is provided for by the concept of the relevant kind of knowledge: the kind grounded in under-standing propositions of the sort in question. My preference is to characterize the a priori in terms of self-evident propositions and leave open what kind of possibility there has to be of the sort of understanding that grounds justification for believing those propositions. For a valuable treatment of possibility and necessity arguing that such modal notions are irreducible, see Scott A. Shalkowski, 'Conventions, Cognitivism and Necessity', *American Philosophical Quarterly* 33 (1986), 375–92.

11 Kant's Section 2b of his Preamble to the *Prolegomena to any Future Metaphysics* (trans. by Lewis White Beck, New York: Liberal Arts Press, 1950) opens with 'The Common Principle of All Analytical Judgments is the Law of [non]Contradiction' and almost immediately continues: "For the predicate of an affirmative analytical judgment is already contained in the concept of the subject, of which it cannot be denied without contradiction."

12 In a broader usage, a falsehood can be called an a priori proposition provided it is an a priori *truth* that it is false. This less common usage raises no special problems but presents a terminological complication I ignore in the text.

13 There is a subtlety here that needs comment: imagine that a self-evident axiom, *A*, self-evidently entails a theorem, *t*, which in turn self-evidently entails a second theorem, *t'*. Self-evident entailment (as opposed to entailment in general) is not *transitive*: *A* can self-evidently entail *t* and *t* can self-evidently entail *t' without A*'s self-evidently entailing *t'*. Here one could understand the conditional proposition that if *A*, then *t'*, quite adequately without thereby having justification for believing it. One might need the intermediate step, *t*, to achieve that justification, and it need not be discerned simply in adequately understanding the conditional itself. This possible limitation does not preclude there being *some* kind of understanding of that conditional and related concepts, such as a perfectly omniscient being might have, in virtue of which the proposition that if *A*, then *t'*, can be seen to be true. This shows that there is a related notion – self-evidence *for a particular person* (or mind) – which must be distinguished from self-evidence in its basic, non-relativized form, making reference only to anyone's understanding. Still, even if what is self-evident for God might not be self-evident for us, some propositions are unqualifiedly self-evident. The case also shows that not every proposition *provable* by individually self-evident steps from a self-evident premise may be assumed to be a priori in the (moderately) broad sense of being self-evidently entailed by a self-evident proposition; for (as just explained) such a proposition might not be self-evidently entailed by a self-evident proposition.

14 There is much difference in judgment about how to classify the analytic. It might be considered a semantic concept by those who think of it as truth by virtue of the *meanings* of the relevant terms. It might be regarded as ontological by those who think such truths are basic to the structure of reality. For epistemology the notion of the a priori is the more important of the two. For an immensely influential paper arguing that neither notion is clear see W. V. Quine, 'Two Dogmas of Empiricism', in his *From a Logical Point of View* (Cambridge, Mass.: Harvard University Press, 1953). Among the widely noted replies is H. P Grice and P. F. Strawson, 'In Defense of a Dogma', *Philosophical Review* 55 (1956), 114–58.

15 See especially J. S. Mill, *A System of Logic* (first published in 1843), particularly Book II, ch. 5–7. For a much more sophisticated critique of a priorism in mathematics and an empiricist account of mathematical truths, see Philip Kitcher, *Mathematical Knowledge* (New York and Oxford: Oxford University Press, 1984).

16 Granting it is at best not obvious how logical truths are knowable by any analysis that reveals containment relations, their negations can be clearly seen to entail contradictions.

17 How broad this is depends on the notion of entailment used. I have in mind a notion for which the negation of a proposition entails a contradiction provided the use of formal logic, supplemented only by (correct) definitions, renders a contradiction deducible.

18 Someone might think all truth is a priori on the ground that it is true a priori that (1) God exists, (2) a certain universe specifiable in every detail is the best of all possible universes, and (3) God creates the best of these universes. Then, with sufficient intellectual power, one could (arguably) reason one's way to any truth. Gottfried Wilhelm Leibniz (1646–1716) has been read as holding a view close to this (but there are reasons to doubt that he did, including considerations about divine freedom).

19 That $1 + 1 + 1 = 3$ might be held to be more intuitive than the proposition that $7 + 5 = 12$. But, first, in practice we might need to rely on less intuitive or much more complicated arithmetic to get a good case for the possible falsehood of the original proposition; second and more important, the simpler proposition that $1 + 1 + 1 = 3$ will also do as a case of a necessary mathematical truth.

20 At least in his classic 'Two Dogmas of Empiricism', in his *From a Logical Point of View* (Cambridge, Mass.: Harvard University Press, 1961), W. V. Quine sometimes talks as if he thinks that a knowledge of synonymy (sameness of meaning) of words is necessary for any

possible knowledge of analytic propositions. See, for example, section 4, on semantical rules. One important comment is that "definition turned out to be a will-o-the-wisp, and synonymy turned out to be best understood only by dint of a prior appeal to analyticity." In the overall context, the suggestion may be that only an independent conception of synonymy would clarify analyticity.

21 Cf. W. V. Quine's remark that "truth in general depends on both language and extra-linguistic fact. The statement 'Brutus killed Caesar' would be false if the world had been different in certain ways, but it would also be false if the word 'killed' happened rather to have had the sense of 'begat'" (*op. cit.*, section 4). Compare saying that the *sentence* 'Brutus killed Caesar' would have expressed a different, and false, proposition (which is what defenders of the classical view would likely say).

22 For a valuable discussion of the notion of the analytic in relation to the conceptual, see M. Giaquinto, 'Non-Analytic Conceptual Knowledge', *Mind* 105, 418 (1996), 249–68. One of his major conclusions bears on the status of such cases as the proposition that all vixens are female: "What the liberated position [Quine's, freed of behaviorism] maintains is that any belief may be rationally rejected in the light of future findings; what it has to accommodate is that some beliefs may be rationally retained even when their customary linguistic expressions become unacceptable. These [positions] are not inconsistent" (p. 266).

23 The terminology of possible worlds traces especially to Gottfried Wilhelm Leibniz and has been influentially discussed in relation to a number of the issues concerning necessity and the a priori by Saul Kripke in *Naming and Necessity* (Cambridge, Mass.: Harvard University Press, 1980). Kripke offers a different kind of example of empirical necessities: true identity statements formed using proper names, as in 'Hesperus is identical with Phosphorous' (both being names of Venus). He also argues, using the example of the standard meter stick in Paris, that an a priori truth, say that the length of the standard meter stick in Paris at time *t* is 1 meter, may not be necessary. This is a highly controversial example (more often attacked than defended), which I cannot take time to discuss here. For detailed criticism, see Albert Casullo, 'Kripke on the A Priori and the Necessary', *Analysis* 37 (1977), 152–9. Casullo also usefully distinguishes knowledge of the *truth value* (truth or falsity) of a proposition from knowledge of its *modal status* (its being necessarily true or false, or contingently true or false), and argues that the classical view could be mistaken in holding that the truth value of necessary propositions is always knowable a priori yet correct in holding that their modal status is knowable a priori.

24 Two comments are appropriate here. First, it might be appropriate to widen the characterization to allow beliefs based *at least predominantly* on understanding the proposition in question (which requires understanding the concepts figuring in the proposition); but since the understanding is not required to be adequate, the formulation is already permissive compared with the characterization crucial for the a priori as such. Second, to avoid a complex discussion not needed here, I shall not generally qualify 'based on' and similar terms. The main points in question will hold if it is taken as equivalent to 'essentially based on'. Third, although the relevant beliefs might be thought to be *always* prima facie justified, there is at least one difficulty with this: perhaps there could be an abnormal case of a kind that prevents *any* justification from arising. This is not obviously possible, since if understanding is a sufficient basis for the belief, that might arguably carry some degree of justification. In any case, the normality formulation is significantly strong.

25 The quantitative comparison may be challenged by those who think we have infinite sets of mathematical beliefs (e.g. that 2 is even, 4 is even, and so on) and of beliefs based on others by trivial operations, such as forming new beliefs by adding an 'or', as where, given my belief that I am seated I form, as I just did, the belief that either I am seated or I am flying to the Moon. That this conception of belief is mistaken will be argued in Chapter 7, which also

notes relevant literature. In any case, the contrast I am drawing here would be adequately strong even without its quantitative dimension.

26 This implies that even if one justifiedly believed, and knew, an a priori proposition on the basis of a self-evident axiom, but *not* on the basis of a self-evident entailment of the former by the latter (say, by a chain of non-self-evident inferences instead), the justification and knowledge would still not be a priori in the strict sense – though they might be very close to it. A terminological point may be helpful here: one could define the broad senses of the relevant terms as *including* the narrow ones. Thus, the a priori in the broad sense is either the directly *or* the indirectly *or* the ultimately self-evident. For my purposes this may be less clear.

27 Four comments are needed here. First, for one's justification to be a priori, at least in the strict sense, it must not depend (epistemically) on memory. Thus, suppose there are too many self-evident premises for me to hold in mind at the same time as I understand some conclusion's following from them. Or, suppose there are so many self-evident steps linking a single self-evident premise to a conclusion that I cannot hold them all in mind in a way that assures understanding a self-evident entailment of that conclusion by the premise. Then *my* justification for believing this conclusion is not a priori (though I may be able to prove the conclusion). Second, and related to this, so long as there can be a mind sufficiently capacious to understand the entire set without dependence on memory, a priori justification for *someone's* believing it is possible. Third, although there is both direct and indirect a priori knowledge in the strict sense, there *may* be only indirect a priori knowledge (as opposed to justification) in the loose sense; this is because defective understanding may be required for the *non*-inferential cases of a priori justification, in a way that prevents the relevant belief from being knowledge. Fourth, as in this book generally, I regard the justification referred to as defeasible (a notion considered in this chapter and again in Chapter 8) unless otherwise specified.

CHAPTER 5
Testimony

Formal and informal testimony

The psychology of testimony

The inferentialist view of testimony
The direct source view of testimony

The epistemology of testimony

Knowledge and justification as products of testimony
The epistemic dependence of testimony

The indispensability of testimonial grounds

Conceptual versus propositional learning
Testimony as a primeval source of knowledge and justification
Non-testimonial support for testimonially grounded beliefs

5

Testimony

If our only sources of knowledge and justified belief were perception, consciousness, memory, and reason, we would be at best impoverished. We do not even learn to speak or think without the help of others, and much of what we know depends on what they tell us. Children in their first few years of life depend almost entirely on others to learn about the world. In talking about our dependence, for knowledge and justification, on what other people say to us, philosophers have commonly spoken of our reliance on their testimony. If perception, memory, consciousness, and reason are our primary individual sources of knowledge and justification, testimony is our primary social source of them. There are various kinds of testimony, however, and there are many questions about how one or another kind yields knowledge or justification.

Formal and informal testimony

The word 'testimony' commonly evokes images of the courtroom, where formal testimony is given. Someone sworn in testifies, offering information that is supposed to represent what the person knows or believes. Often such testimony recounts what was witnessed first-hand, but our testimony can be an expression of what we believe about something we did not witness, such as the implications of a scientific theory or the potentials of human character.[1]

Formal testimony is not the basic kind (if indeed there is any basic kind) and, as suggested already, is not necessarily *witnessing*. To see that it is not the basic kind, notice that if we could not rely on what people say outside of court, there would be no point in having courtroom testimony or other formal kinds. Formal testimony differs from the informal kind in the conditions under which it is given, but not necessarily in credibility. Testimony of the wider kind – roughly, saying something in an apparent attempt to convey (correct) information – is what plays the large role in our lives that raises the question of the importance of testimony for knowledge and justification.

Even for the informal giving of information, for instance in telling someone where one was last night, 'testimony' is too heavy a word. We could speak of 'informing', but this is also too narrow, both in suggesting a prepared message (as in 'Yesterday she informed me of her plan to attend') and in (normally) implying that what is conveyed is true. We might regard all testimony as a kind of saying, but not all saying – even apart from what is said in fiction – is testimony. Someone who says, 'Ah, what a magnificent tree!' is expressing a sense of the magnificence of the tree, but not giving testimony that it is magnificent, as where an arborist cites features of shape and color in supporting a claim that the tree is magnificent and worth the high cost of pruning and feeding.

It can help to speak of *attesting*. This covers both formally testifying that something is so and simply saying, in the relevant informational way, that it is so, for instance in telling someone the time. It also captures the idea of saying something *to* someone. Testimony is always given to one or more persons (to oneself, perhaps, in the limiting case), actual or hypothetical, as where a diarist describing atrocities for posterity does not know whether anyone will read the testimony. In any event, what we must understand here is the role of testimony of all these kinds – roughly, of people's telling us things – in accounting for our knowledge and justification. I want to begin with how testimony yields belief. The psychology of testimony is both intrinsically interesting and epistemologically important.

The psychology
of testimony

If we begin thinking about testimony by focusing on formal cases, we might conclude that as a source of belief, testimony is quite unlike perception in that testimony produces in us only inferential beliefs of what is said, whereas perception produces non-inferential beliefs about what is perceived. The idea that beliefs based on testimony arise by inference from one or more premises is probably a natural result of concentration on formal testimony. When I hear courtroom testimony, I appraise the witness, place the testimony in the context of the trial and my general knowledge, and accept what is said only if, on the basis of this broad perspective, it seems true. I do not just believe what I hear, as I may just believe that a bat flew by if I see one zigzag across the evening sky. Rather, given the premises that (for example) the witness seems credible and that the statement in question – say that the accused dined in a certain restaurant on New Year's Eve – fits what I know about the case, I may thereby come to believe this statement. Let us assess the idea that testimonially based beliefs in general arise in this way.

The inferentialist view of testimony

If this inferentialist picture of testimony is correct, then testimony seems a less direct source of belief than perception: it yields belief only through both the testimony itself and one or more premises that support the proposition attested to or the attester's credibility. If that is so, testimony is also not as direct a source of knowledge or justification; for one would know, or be justified in believing, what is attested only if one knows, or is at least justified in believing, one's premise(s). One could not know simply *from* testimony, but only from premises *about* it as well.

There is a danger of going too fast here. There is another, probably more plausible, account that can also explain the psychological role of background beliefs. On this account, beliefs about the credibility of the attester and beliefs pertinent to the attested proposition play a mainly filtering role: they prevent our believing testimony that does not "pass," for instance because it seems insincere; but if no such difficulty strikes us, we "just believe" (non-inferentially) what is attested. These filtering beliefs are like a trapdoor that shuts only if triggered; its normal position is open, but it stays in readiness to block what should not enter.[2] The open position is a kind of *trust*. The absence or laxity of filtering beliefs yields credulity; excessively rigorous ones yield skepticism.

It could very well turn out that, in different circumstances, each of these accounts – the inferentialist account and the filtered, non-inferential belief account – applies. The psychological possibilities here are numerous. Fortunately, we need not describe them all. It is enough to see that belief based on testimony *need* not be inferential, say grounded in a further belief that the attester has spoken plausibly.

In the case of informal testimony – the most common kind – the beliefs it produces in the hearer are typically not inferential. Certainly when trusted friends speak to us on matters we have no reason to think are beyond their competence, we normally "just believe" what they tell us. Indeed, if I am sufficiently credulous, or simply very trusting of people's word, then normally, when people tell me something, my belief system stands ready to be stocked. I will hesitate only if (for instance) a would-be new belief conflicts with one or more beliefs already in my inventory. If you look vigorous and tell me you once swam the English Channel, I may readily believe you, whereas in the absence of special evidence I would not believe someone claiming to have climbed Mount Everest without a rope. For on the basis of my relevant background beliefs about climbing, I take that feat to be almost impossible.

These points about how testimony produces belief need expansion. Just as it is misleading to try to build an account of the psychology of testimony from the formal cases, it is a mistake to take a *static* view of how testimony produces belief. Our beliefs and even our belief-forming processes may change in the course of our receiving testimony. I meet someone on a plane. She tells me about a conference in which a speaker I know lost his temper. Initially, I suspend judgment about whether he did so, since the incident is of a rare kind and I do not know her. Then, as she describes the conference further, other details begin to fit together very well, and she notes information I already know, such as who was there. Soon I am listening in an accepting attitude, forming beliefs of each thing she says as fast as she proceeds. At the end, I find that I *now* believe that the speaker did in fact lose his temper.

Even at the beginning, I need not have inferred that I should suspend judgment on the initially unlikely statement about the speaker; suspended judgment may be a non-inferential response to the constraints set by my independent beliefs. Moreover, her testimony is *blocked*, but not *overridden*, by my antecedent beliefs and impressions. They prevent my believing what she attests to; they do not overturn a testimonially grounded belief I formed and then gave up because of what I already believed or came to believe, as where I discover it is inconsistent with apparent facts. As her narrative progresses, the constraints set by my independent beliefs may relax, and, regarding each statement she makes, I may form beliefs not only non-inferentially, but even spontaneously, in the sense that any constraints that might have operated do not come in. Her statements no longer have to be tested by passing through the gaze of my critical scrutiny, nor are any filtered out by the more nearly automatic checking the mind routinely does when people offer information.

The most difficult thing to explain here is why, at the end, I believe the proposition that, at the beginning, was an object of suspended judgment. One possibility is an unconscious inference, say from the general credibility of her account to the conclusion that this proposition, as an essential part of it, is true. But perhaps the cognitive *influence* of my standing beliefs, such as a newly formed belief that she is credible, need not proceed through an *inference* from them. Another possible explanation is more moderate: even apart from my forming beliefs about her credibility, her eventually becoming, in my eyes, a quite credible person, can in some fairly direct way produce in me a general disposition to believe her. This disposition is strengthened as she speaks with an evident credibility; and at the end it overcomes the resistance to belief which was exercised earlier by my constraining beliefs. On the subject she is addressing, I have come to trust her.

The direct source view of testimony

There are still other possibilities that support the conclusion that the inferentialist view of testimony is too narrow. Perhaps people (or some of us) have a credibility scale on which attesters acquire – commonly without our conscious attention to the matter – a place that can change, also without our conscious attention. This is an interesting empirical hypothesis that I cannot pursue, but all that is crucial here is that we see how beliefs based on testimony – testimonially grounded beliefs – can be *constrained by* other beliefs without being inferentially *based on* them and how beliefs based on testimony can be formed *later* than the attestation that is their ultimate source. Perception, too, can produce belief after it has begun or, with the help of memory, even after it has ceased. One may look at a shape for a long time before believing that it is a tree stump and not a stroller who stopped to gaze at the night sky. This same belief could also arise much later, from vividly recalling the image a day later when one is questioned about the scene. The connection in virtue of which a belief is based on a source need not be direct or simultaneous or a result of inference from premises.

Is the analogy with perception sufficient to warrant concluding that, like perception, testimony is a basic source of belief, in the sense, roughly, that it can produce belief without the cooperation of another source of belief? Consider perception. If I see a tree, this can produce in me a belief that there is a tree before me without my having a potentially belief-producing experience of any other sort, such as a separate consciousness of an image of a tree.[3] But I cannot form a testimonially grounded belief unless I *hear* (or otherwise perceive) the testimony. Perception is crucial for the formation of testimonially grounded beliefs in a way that no other belief source is crucial for the formation of perceptual beliefs.[4]

Granted, perception does not produce belief without appropriate background conditions, nor does its being a basic source of belief imply that antecedent beliefs are irrelevant. If I firmly believe I am hallucinating the Moon, then even if I actually see it I may withhold judgment on whether it is out. A basic source does not derive its generative power from another source, but it need not operate in complete independence of other sources or their outputs. It can produce belief without the help of another source, but it may also cooperate with other sources in producing it, and they may suppress some of its would-be products or undermine the justification of some of the beliefs it does produce.

Since testimonially grounded beliefs need not be inferential, and so need not be based on a belief that the attester is sincere or even on a belief that someone is speaking to one (though one must be at least disposed to believe this), one may be puzzled by the point that testimony is not a basic source of belief. The puzzlement may arise from failing to see that perception itself can be a basic requirement for the formation of belief based on testimony, even if perceptual *belief* is not a requirement. I may have to be *disposed* to believe someone has said that the speaker lost his temper to acquire a belief of this based on testimony; but that seems to be only because I must have perceived this being said, not because I must have formed the belief that it was said, just as perception of a sentence in a convincing article one is reading can produce belief of what it says without one's forming the belief that the sentence says that. There is surely no reason to think the mind must keep such semantic double books. It is my perception of what is said, typically my hearing or reading it, that is required for formation of a testimonially grounded belief of the proposition attested to.

The positive point here is that testimony can be a source of *basic beliefs*, in the sense of beliefs not based on other beliefs. The beliefs it evokes need not be based on premises at all, much less on premises grounded in another belief source. The kind of non-inferential belief that testimony commonly produces can also be basic knowledge *if* it meets the conditions for non-inferential knowledge (and so is not based on premises). It can certainly be basic *for* a person in the everyday sense of being central in the person's life. A major epistemological point that the case of testimony shows nicely here is that a basic belief – roughly, one basic in the order of one's beliefs, and so not premise-dependent – need not come from a basic source of belief – roughly, one basic in the order of cognitive sources and so not source-dependent. A belief that is not based on, and in that sense does not depend on, another belief may come from a source of beliefs that does depend on another source of them.

The epistemology of testimony

In the light of what has emerged about how testimony produces belief, we are now in a good position to ask the further question of how testimony yields knowledge and justification and whether it ever yields basic knowledge or basic justification in the way perception and reflection, for instance, apparently do. The case of knowledge is in some ways easier to deal with than that of justification, and I want to start with knowledge. As with perceptual knowledge and justification, testimonially based knowledge and justification turn out to differ.

Knowledge and justification as products of testimony

Testimony can give knowledge to its hearers only under certain conditions. If I do not know that the speaker at yesterday's conference lost his temper, then you cannot come to know it on the basis of my attesting to it.[5] This is obvious if I am mistaken and he in fact did *not* lose his temper. But suppose I make a lucky guess and am right. Then I give you correct, conjectured information which I do not know; but you are also lucky to be correct and also do not know that he lost his temper. It is a fluke that I get it right; it is even more of a fluke that you get it right, since in your case there are, in addition to the chance I have taken of making a mistake, the other liabilities you escape: of my having distorted the truth, of your having misheard me, of your adding a false detail to what you take from my testimony, and so forth.

There is a more common defect in testimony that prevents its producing knowledge in the hearer. Imagine that I do not guess at, but incautiously accept, the proposition that the speaker lost his temper, from someone I know often lies about others. Again, I lack knowledge that he lost his temper, even if this time the proposition is true; and again, you cannot know it on the basis of my testimony, which is now ill-grounded in another way. What I do not have, I cannot give you.

The case with justification is quite different. Even if I am not justified in believing that the speaker lost his temper, I can be credible to you in such a way that you *can* become justified in believing this on the basis of my attesting it to you. To see this, consider the two facets of *testimonial credibility*: the *sincerity* dimension, concerning the attester's honesty, and the *competence* dimension, concerning the attester's having experience or knowledge sufficient to make it at least likely that if the attester forms a belief of the proposition in question or of closely related ones, then they are true. Surely you can justifiedly regard me as credible on the topic of whether the speaker lost his temper if you have good reason to believe that I am honest, possess normal acuity and memory, and was present and reasonably attentive on the occasion.

It may now seem that there is a further asymmetry: I cannot give you testimonially grounded knowledge that something is so without having knowledge that it is so, yet I *can* give you justification without having it. But this conclusion is not warranted. In the case of my credible but false testimony that gives you justification for believing what I attest to, *I* do not give you justification for believing what I say – that the speaker lost his temper – without having *that* justification (as I do not). Rather, the way I attest to the proposition, together with your background justification regarding me and the circumstances, gives you this justification, independently of whether I have it. This is not my giving you justification in the way one gives knowledge. Testimonially based knowledge is received by *transmission* and so is not at all independent of whether the attester knows the truth of the proposition in question – call it *p*. It is natural to say that in the first case you would gain knowledge *through* my testimony, whereas in the second you would gain justification *from* my testimony, but not through it. Testimony that *p* can convey the attester's knowledge that *p*; it can *produce* in the hearer *a* justification for believing *p*, but it does not convey the attester's justification for believing it – the attester need not even have such justification. My testimony that *p*, then, is not my giving you justification in the way one gives knowledge. Such knowledge is testimonially passed on by *transmission*.

This contrast between conveying knowledge and providing justification helps to explain the original asymmetry: if I do not know that a proposition is true, my attesting to it cannot transmit to you testimonially grounded knowledge that it is so (I have no knowledge to give here); but even if I am not justified in believing it, my attesting to it can provide you with justification for believing it, through providing the main materials for your becoming justified in believing it.[6] One might claim that this is still not testimonially grounded justification, but I think it can be, in the clearest sense in which there is such a thing. To see this compare testimony with memory.

The contrast between how testimony produces knowledge and how it produces justification in the recipient is reminiscent of a contrast applicable to memory (drawn in Chapter 3). Just as we cannot know that p from memory unless we have *come* to know it in another way, say through perception, we cannot know that p on the basis of testimony unless the attester (or someone from whom the attester comes to know it) has come to know it (at least in part) in another way; whereas we can become justified in believing p through memory impressions, whether or not p is true or known,[7] and we can become justified in believing p on the basis of testimony, whether or not the attester has true belief or knowledge of it or even justification for it.

With testimonially grounded knowledge, as with memorial knowledge, there must apparently be a certain kind of unbroken chain from the belief constituting that knowledge to a source of the knowledge in some other mode, such as perception; but with testimonially grounded justification, as with memorial justification, what is essential is apparently a matter of the present epistemic situation of the subject or recipient, such as the contents of apparently memorial consciousness and the content and justifiedness of background beliefs. Memory and testimony can both generate justification (though in different ways); but they are not generative with respect to knowledge: characteristically, the former preserves knowledge, the latter transmits it.[8]

There is another way in which justification and knowledge apparently differ in their relation to testimony. Suppose I *am* justified in believing p, but you have no justification of your own for believing p or for taking me to be credible on the topic. To vary the conference example, imagine that in passing, and without giving evidence, I say that three speakers lost their tempers, and your background information neither disconfirms nor supports this claim or my credibility in the matter. Here justification follows your lights rather than mine: my would-be contribution to justifying you in believing p is undermined by your lack of justification for thinking my testimony is credible or for believing p on some other basis. Receptivity to justification sometimes requires already having some measure of it: for believing the attester credible or for believing p, or for both.

Knowledge seems somewhat different on this score: to know something through my attesting to it in expression of my own knowledge, you do not have to know that I am credible; it is surely enough that you have some reason to believe I am and no reason to doubt it. It is probably enough that you presuppose it and have no reason to doubt it. Surely you can know that it is nine o'clock on the basis of my knowing this and telling it to you, even if you simply find me a normal-seeming person with a normal-looking watch and take me to be credible.[9] And why indeed must you meet any more than a negative condition: not having any reason to doubt my credibility? After all, we are talking about a case where I know that it is nine o'clock, attest to this *from* my knowledge of it, and thereby produce your (true) belief that it is nine.

A natural objection to this credible-unless-otherwise-indicated view of testimony as a ground for knowledge is that in our example one's evidence is so scanty that one would at best have only some reason to believe it is nine o'clock. But is this true? Granted, one's having some reason to believe the proposition may be all one can *show* from one's evidence or from what one feels certain of. Still, on the assumption that I in fact do know the time and sincerely tell it to you, it would seem that you can thereby know the proposition I have attested to you. That appears to hold even where you simply have no reason to doubt my credibility.[10]

These points suggest both a justification principle and an epistemic principle applicable to testimony. First, we might say that at least normally, a belief based on testimony is thereby justified (that is, justified on the basis of the testimony) provided the believer has overall justification for taking the attester to be credible regarding the proposition in question. Second, we might say that at least normally, a belief based on testimony thereby constitutes knowledge provided that the attester knows the proposition in question and the believer has no reason to doubt either this proposition or the attester's credibility regarding it.[11]

The epistemic dependence of testimony

Whatever we say about the exact conditions under which testimony can ground knowledge or justification in its recipient, we have so far found no reason to doubt that under *some* conditions testimony can be a source of both knowledge and justified belief on the part of someone believing what is attested. It has seemed so far, however, that it cannot be a basic source of knowledge, since one cannot know something on the basis of testimony unless the attester knows it. Testimony transmits knowledge but does not, as such, generate it. It may of course generate knowledge *incidentally*, as where, by attesting in a surprised tone that it is 4 a.m., I give a fellow insomniac knowledge that I am awake. This knowledge is grounded not on the testimony but on the mere hearing of it, and that kind of knowledge could as easily have been conveyed without testimony, by my sitting down nearby and opening a book.

Testimony, like inference, can exist in indefinitely long chains. An attester might know the proposition in question on the basis of a third person's testimony, and the third might know it on the basis of testimony by a fourth, rather than from a generative source such as perception. But how far can this go, with each attester informed by a prior one? There is surely some limit or other in each situation, as opposed to an infinite regress (difficulties with infinite regresses will be pursued in Chapter 7). That brings us to a second respect in which testimony cannot be a basic source of knowledge. Surely if no one knew anything in a non-testimonial mode, no one would know anything on the basis of testimony either. More specifically, testimonial knowledge seems ultimately to depend on knowledge grounded in one of the other sources we have considered: perception, memory, consciousness, and reason. To enable others to know something by attesting to it, I must know it myself; and my knowledge must ultimately depend at least in part on non-testimonially based knowledge, such as knowledge grounded in seeing that the clock says five.

One might try to reinforce this view as follows. Even if someone had attested to a proposition before me, I would have to *perceive* this and to know some supporting proposition, say, that someone had credibly said it is five o'clock. Once the point is put this way, however, it is evident that it cannot stand without qualification. The required kind of perceiving does not entail forming a belief of this sort, perhaps not even the specific perceptual belief that someone said it is five o'clock. The case shows, then, only that testimony is *operationally dependent* on perception, not that it is *inferentially dependent* on perceptual belief. It requires perceptual raw materials, but not beliefs of premises about those materials.[12]

If, as seems to be the case, testimonial knowledge and justification are not dependent on premises that support the testimonially grounded belief – say, premises confirming the credibility of the attester – this explains how such a belief can be basic. Testimony as a source of knowledge and justification need not be basic relative to other sources of knowledge and justification in order for beliefs grounded in it to be basic in the order of beliefs.

A different but related point is that, although testimonially based beliefs can be basic, the *attester's* knowledge that is the basis of the hearer's (potentially basic) knowledge cannot ultimately be grounded in testimony. Knowledge that is directly and wholly based on testimony for the recipient cannot be *ultimately* based wholly on testimony for the giver: the first would have no "right" to transfer it to the second, just as I would have no right to give someone what I had merely borrowed from someone else, who had merely borrowed it from a third person, and so on to infinity.

The point that testimonially grounded beliefs can be non-inferential and in that way not dependent on premises is important. But the operational dependence of testimony has both epistemological and conceptual significance. For if one did not have perceptual *grounds* for knowledge, or at least for justified belief, that someone has attested to the proposition in question, one could not know it on the basis of the testimony. This is an epistemic dependence not paralleled in the case of perception.[13] It shows that even if testimonially grounded knowledge need not inferentially depend on *having* knowledge grounded in another mode, it does epistemically depend on having grounds, from another mode, grounds *for* knowledge in that other mode. Testimonially grounded knowledge thus depends on – and in this sense presupposes – the availability, or one might say the potential cooperation, of another source of knowledge, even if such knowledge does not require the actual operation of that source in yielding beliefs of the premises it stands ready to supply.

The case with justification is similar on this point. I cannot acquire justification for believing something on the basis of testimony unless I have justification for believing that the testifier is credible, as well as for certain other propositions, such as that I heard the testimony correctly. This justification cannot come entirely from testimony. Jane may assure me about Bert, but what if I am not justified in taking Jane to be credible? Other grounds of justification, such as perception or memory, must at least tacitly cooperate. But their cooperation can be justificational without being inferential: they need not produce in me beliefs of premises from which I infer that the attester is credible; they simply give me a justification that I could appeal to in framing such premises if I needed them.

It may help to describe one of my overall conclusions – that testimony is not a basic source of knowledge or justification – as reflecting a disparity between the superficially simple psychology of testimony and its even more complex epistemology. Often, when we hear people attesting to various things, we just believe these things, non-inferentially and even unreservedly. But this natural psychological process yields knowledge and justification only when certain epistemic conditions are met: there must be grounds, apparently from one of the four basic sources, *for* knowledge and justification, even if there need be no knowledge or justified beliefs of the propositions warranted *by* these grounds. In the case of testimonially grounded knowledge, there must be knowledge, even if not necessarily justification, on the part of the attester, whereas in the case of testimonially grounded justification there must be justification, even if not knowledge, on the part of the recipient. The first requirement concerns the attester's epistemic situation with respect to the proposition attested to; the second concerns the recipient's epistemic situation with respect to the attester, or the proposition, or both.[14]

The indispensability of testimonial grounds

The epistemic dependence of testimony on other sources of belief must be squared with the plain fact that tiny children learn from what others tell them even before they are properly said to have grounds for knowledge or justification of the kinds in question. Consider teaching a child color words. After a time, the child has learned that the sofa, say, is red. But the tiny child has no concept of credibility or other notions important in gaining justification from testimony and, initially, insufficient experience to be justified in believing that its adult teachers are credible. On the view developed here, however, this point is quite compatible with the child's acquiring *knowledge*.

Conceptual versus propositional learning

The first thing to note in explaining this compatibility is that there are at least at least two ways to learn from testimony: one can learn (in the sense of coming to know) the content attested to, and one can learn something shown by the testimony itself. The first case is learning *that*, i.e., that something is so. The second is learning *of* or *about* something (and may extend to learning how to do something). A tiny child just learning the basic colors is not, primarily, learning *that* (say) the sofa is red, but, above all, becoming aware of redness as the color of the sofa.

In introducing the word 'red' to the child, then, the parent is only incidentally attesting to the proposition that the sofa is red. The point is to pair the word with an instance of what it stands for, with the aim of teaching the child that word (or, say, what the color red is), and the child can learn the main lesson without conceptualizing the sofa as such at all (something required for propositionally believing that the sofa is red). The former case – the *propositional testimony* – may result in propositional knowledge; we would thus have *propositional learning*. The parental introduction of vocabulary – *demonstrative testimony* – may result in *conceptual learning*.

It is important to see that the success conditions for the introductory function of language apparently require that for the most part the attestations are at least approximately true. A child cannot learn 'red' unless, in teaching the child English, a goodly proportion of the samples to which 'red' is applied are red.[15] This does not of course show that most testimony is true, but it does imply that *if* communication is occurring when testimony is given, then one may reasonably assume that both attester and recipient have at some point benefited from a background in which a substantial proportion of attestations of a certain sort were true. How else can children be plausibly thought to have learned the language in which the communication occurs? This in turn supports the reasonableness of taking testimony to be normally credible.[16]

At the time concepts are initially grasped in childhood, it does not seem necessary that (propositional) belief and knowledge are acquired in every case. Conditions sufficient for conceptual learning do not seem automatically sufficient for propositional learning. Belief and knowledge are commonly acquired at the time that concepts are initially grasped. Conditions for mere conceptual learning are not, however, self-evidently sufficient for propositional learning.[17] Testimony easily produces both together, but if it cannot produce the former without the latter, it can produce the latter without the former. It can be concept-producing, belief-producing, or both. The former case seems to be the more primitive, and the conditions for its possibility should not be taken as adequate for the possibility of the latter.

It is very difficult to say when a child begins to form beliefs, as opposed to mimicking its elders by saying things that, in adults, would express beliefs. Let us suppose both that belief-formation comes very early in life and that many of the first beliefs formed are based on what adults tell the child is the case. The child's defenseless credulity is a precondition for learning. Must this pose a problem for the epistemology of testimony suggested here? Again, it will help to consider knowledge and justification separately.

Testimony as a primeval source of knowledge and justification

Very early in their lives we speak of babies and children as knowing things. One might object that this kind of talk is simply projective: *we* would know in their situation if we behaved in the relevant way, so why not say the child does? This is a defensible line of response, but let us suppose for the sake of argument that at least by the time children begin to talk they do know certain things. After all, we may surely speak of their learning – that the milk spills when tipped, that the stove is hot, and so on – and learning (in general) implies knowledge. At about the same time, children begin to learn on the basis of testimony, for instance that steaming tea is hot and that when the doorbell rings, someone is outside.

If, as seems a reasonable assumption, gaining testimonially grounded knowledge requires only having no reason for doubt about the credibility of the attester, then the view proposed above encounters no difficulty. If a tiny child perhaps *can* have no reason for doubt, at least the child has none; nor need there *be* any reason, since much testimony is highly credible.

Suppose, however, that a stronger requirement must be met: that the child must have (possibly in a preconceptual way) some ground for taking the speaker to be credible, for instance a series of experiences repeatedly corresponding to what the speaker says. It is not clear that we could not sketch a case of having such a correlational ground that would be elementary enough to fit the rudimentary character of the child's knowledge. I doubt, however, that such a ground is required for testimonially based knowledge.

With justification, there may be greater difficulty in dealing with the case of tiny children. But the first thing to notice is that we do not use the vocabulary of justification, as compared with that of knowledge, for as conceptually undeveloped creatures. For a child to be justified in believing the proposition that the sofa is red, the child would have to be capable not only of having a ground for believing this but, correspondingly, of failing to have one and yet believing this proposition anyway, thereby being *un*justified. It is arguable that by the time we may properly speak of children in this two-sided way (which is perhaps soon after they can speak), they do have a sense of the track record of adults in giving them information that bears out in their experience. If parents say it is cold outside, it is; and so forth. Children will not, of course, *use* the notion of credibility; but they will be able to understand related concepts, such as those needed for understanding that Mommy is right about things and baby brother must be corrected.

Another possibility is that very early in life children acquire a sense that they themselves generally give information only when they have gotten it themselves, say through perception or sensation, as where they see that it is snowing outside or they feel hungry. For misinformation we commonly and sometimes sternly correct children, whereas we patiently instill habits of correct reporting. This correlational sense that children apparently develop, it might be argued, provides a kind of analogical justification for taking others to be providing, when they give testimony, information *they* have obtained. A related and compatible hypothesis is that children have a rudimentary understanding of others in terms of what apparently explains their observed behavior. And what would explain Mommy's saying that it is snowing outside as well as her having seen that it is?

None of this is to say just when knowledge or justification enters the scene in human development, whether through the basic sources or through testimony. These are psychological questions; a philosophical theory need only leave room for plausible answers to them. The theory outlined here suggests that knowledge may arise before justification, but it does not entail even that. Moreover, it has at least this much harmony with the most familiar data about human development: the more natural it is, and the less figurative it seems, to speak of growing children as acquiring knowledge and justification based on testimony, the easier it is to find some elementary way in which they can satisfy the epistemic and justificational conditions set out above, such as making discriminations that enable them to assess what they are told and gaining some sense of the track record of those around them who offer information.

To say that testimony is not a basic source of justification or knowledge is not to imply that it is any less important in normal human life than a basic source. A source of knowledge and justification can be indispensable in life even if it is not basic. It may be that no normal human being would know anything apart from dependence on receiving testimony.[18] If there is no innate knowledge, and if one knows nothing before learning a language (something I here assume for the sake of argument but wish to leave open), then unless one could acquire linguistic competence without the help of others, they would be essential in one's coming to know anything at all. Certainly, if one tried to imagine what would be left if one gave up all the knowledge and beliefs one acquired on the basis of testimony, one would be quite unable to accomplish the sorting in the first place. But even beginning the task of trying to put aside what one knows in the indicated way suggests that one would at best be thrust back to a primitive stage of learning.

Non-testimonial support for testimonially grounded beliefs

If one ponders David Hume's view of testimony as capable of grounding knowledge only on the basis of a kind of legitimation by other sources, one may want to know to what extent testimonial knowledge and justification, even taken item by item, can be backed up by other kinds. For Hume, our "assurance" in any matter depending on testimony "is derived from no other principle than our observation of the veracity of human testimony, and of the usual conformity of facts to the reports of witnesses."[19]

Let us ask whether, for every proposition one justifiedly believes (wholly) on the basis of testimony, one has a justification from other sources. Since these other sources would include what one justifiedly believes on the basis of memory, they could plainly contribute propositions originally based on testimony that is independent of the testimony needing support. Much of what we have stored in memory we came to believe through what others have told us in person or in writing. If what was testimonially learned and is memorially preserved may justify believing a proposition someone attests to, it may be that I do have some degree of independently grounded justification for everything I justifiedly believe on the basis of testimony. Many of my beliefs about conditions under which people are credible, for instance, are preserved in my memory; thus, even if I have no evidence regarding p I may have reason to think the attester's saying it is some reason to believe it. Some of these memorially justified beliefs, however, would not be justified unless I had been at some point justified in believing something on the basis of testimony, as where I accept one person's testimony in checking on another's. There may be a kind of circularity here, but it might be argued that since memory is a basic source of justification, and testimony itself is a source of non-inferential justification, at least there need be no vicious circularity in supporting some testimony by appealing to memorially justified beliefs originally justified on the basis of other testimony.

To illustrate some of these points about justifying a belief based on testimony, take a case regarding a country I do not know first-hand. Consider a radio news program announcing an earthquake in Indonesia. I have – though I may never have articulated it – a sense of the track record of the network in question and of the geological situation in Indonesia, a sense of how often errors of that kind are made, and so forth. One could always say that this is a very weak justification, especially since I rely on some beliefs acquired through testimony (though that testimony may be independent of the credibility of the network in question). Certainly such a justification is far from conclusive. But there is still no good reason to think it must be inadequate.

It may be natural to ask whether one can fashion a *global* justification of the entire set of the propositions one believes, or originally believed, on the basis of testimony. There are at least two questions one could be asking here. If the reference is to all the propositions one believes conjoined together – to the long proposition consisting of the first *and* the second *and* the third item, etc. – then one cannot even imagine contemplating such a monstrosity, much less justifying it. If the reference is to the set of one's testimonially grounded beliefs considered in the abstract, it is still not clear how to conceive justifying it. If, however, we do not allow some testimonially grounded beliefs to justify others and we try to suspend judgment on all such beliefs we hold (assuming such massive suspension of judgment is even possible), I do not see that this corporate global justification project would work.[20]

It is doubtful that we can always avoid relying on testimony, at least indirectly, in appraising testimony. Even one's sense of an attester's track record, for instance, often depends on what one believes on the basis of testimony. Think of how one news source serves as a check on another: in each case, testimony from one source is tentatively assumed and checked against testimony from another.

There seems not to be any general procedure by which one can produce a global justification for the proposition that the whole set of one's testimonially grounded beliefs (or even a major proportion of its elements) is justified. But that project of global justification is not one we need attempt, and the epistemology of testimony I have sketched implies on this matter at most that justified testimonially grounded beliefs are *individually* justifiable for the believer in terms of the basic sources of belief.[21] With testimonially grounded knowledge, not even this seems required; the conditions by which knowledge is testimonially transmitted seem not to depend on justification in the same way: although testimony may be defeated by justified beliefs to the contrary, in the absence of such beliefs the recipient acquires it. If this were not so, it would be at best difficult to explain how children learn language in the way they do.

Testimony is a pervasive and natural source of beliefs. Many of these beliefs are justified or constitute knowledge. They may even constitute basic knowledge or basic belief, both in the sense that they are not grounded in premises and in the sense that they play a pivotal role in the life of the believer. We might thus say that testimonially based beliefs are psychologically, epistemically, and existentially basic. But they are epistemically basic only in the sense that they are not inferentially dependent on knowledge or justified belief of prior premises. They are epistemically dependent, in a way perceptual beliefs are not, on one's having grounds for knowledge or justification, and they are psychologically dependent on one's having some ground – such as hearing someone speak – in another, non-testimonial experiential mode. Testimonially based beliefs are, then, source-dependent though not necessarily premise-dependent. As a source of knowledge and justification, testimony depends both epistemically and psychologically on other sources. This is entirely consistent, however, with its playing an incalculably important role in the normal development of our justification and knowledge.

Notes

1 For a wide-ranging, historically informative account of what constitutes testimony and numerous epistemological problems surrounding it see C. A. J. Coady, *Testimony* (Oxford: The Clarendon Press, 1992).

2 Thomas Reid spoke eloquently on this topic; he said, for example, "The wise author of nature hath implanted in the human mind a propensity to rely upon human testimony before we can give a reason for doing so. This, indeed, puts our judgment almost entirely in the hands of those who are about us in the first period of life." See *Essay on the Intellectual Powers of Man* in *Thomas Reid's Inquiry and Essays*, ed. by Ronald Beanblossom and Keith Lehrer (Indianapolis: Hackett, 1983), p. 281.

3 Granted, I must have (and so must memorially retain), a concept of a tree; but this merely conceptual memorial state is not a potential source of belief (which is not to deny that it can play any other kind of causal role in belief-formation).

4 Three points may help here. First, telepathic or otherwise strange reception of testimony may, at least for our purposes, be construed as some kind of perception. Second, granting that one cannot form perceptual beliefs without having whatever additional beliefs may be needed to possess the concepts required to understand what is believed perceptually – for instance the concept of a star-gazing stroller in my example earlier – this does not imply the kind of dependence on any other belief source exhibited by that of testimony upon perception. One can perceive, though not interpret, such a stroller without having these concepts; one cannot even receive testimony, and so cannot begin to interpret or learn from it, without perceiving it. Third, supposing perception cannot occur without some manifestation in consciousness (which is itself a source of beliefs), here consciousness is an element in perception in a way that perception by an audience is plainly not an element in testimony.

5 You might come to know it on the basis of something *about* my testimony: perhaps, for example, I give it nervously and you know that the nervousness is an after-effect of my being shaken by the fit of temper, which I have since half forgotten and attest to conjectur-ally. This would be a case of belief merely *caused* by testimony but not *based* on it (not an easy distinction to define in much detail). One requirement for a belief to be based on testimony is the believer's holding the proposition because it was attested to, as opposed, for example, to how or from what motive it was attested to.

6 The qualifier 'testimonially grounded' is crucial: suppose I attest, in a baritone voice, that I have a baritone voice, but do not know this because I falsely believe I have a tenor voice; then you come to know, *from* my testimony, but not on the basis of it (its content), that the proposition to which I attest is true. The same point holds for justification in place of knowledge. One might also say that you come to know it *through* my testimony in a weak sense of 'through' not implying that the content of what I attest is crucial.

It is also possible that the content, but not *my attesting it*, is essential, as where I present an argument you know I barely understand, and you come to know its conclusion, not because I attest to it or to the premises, but on the basis of yourself realizing, by bringing to bear your background knowledge, that they are true and entail the conclusion. This would be knowledge based on the *content* of testimony, but it would not be what we call 'testimoni-ally grounded knowledge'.

7 I develop and defend this contrast in 'Memorial Justification', *Philosophical Topics* 23 (1996).

8 I leave open whether knowledge transmitted by testimony can be as *well-grounded* as that of the attester (though I am inclined to think it can be, say where the attester is "absolutely" reliable, a property that in principle could perhaps belong to memory in some cases). By contrast, so far as knowledge goes, "a testimonial chain is no stronger than its weakest link," as Alvin Plantinga puts it in *Warrant and Proper Function* (Oxford and New York: Oxford University Press, 1993), p. 84. He is speaking of warrant, roughly what makes true belief knowledge; and if, as I am inclined to think, the points holds there too, then justification contrasts with warrant on this score as it does with knowledge.

9 If this is so, it may show something else: on the assumption that you cannot know a proposition on the basis of premises you do not also know, this case would show that your testimony-based knowledge is not inferential, since the would-be credibility premise is not known but only permissibly assumed.

10 One possibility raised here is that of knowledge without justification. This will be considered in some detail in Chapter 8.

11 These principles are formulated cautiously in several ways: for instance, they allow for abnormal circumstances to provide exceptions; they are compatible with but do not require that the testimonially based belief be inferential; they allow that the resulting justification not be strong but only "adequate" for what might be called reasonable belief; they allow, but do not entail (what I think plausible but leave open) that the testimonially based belief *always* acquires prima facie justification from the testimony; and they permit the recipient to have justification or knowledge of the proposition in question from some *other* source as well. The epistemic principle might well be broadened by specifying that the recipient has no *overall* reason for doubt, but I offer that as a suggestion without adopting it.

12 Here I differ from Elizabeth Fricker, who holds that the recipient must perceptually believe "that the speaker has made an assertion with a particular content . . . capable of being knowledge . . . I have been convinced by John McDowell's contention that hearers' percep-tions of speakers' utterances are . . . a case of perceptual knowledge." See 'The Epistemology of Testimony', *Proceedings of the Aristotelian Society* 61 (1987), p. 70. The reference to McDowell is to 'Anti-realism and the Epistemology of Understanding', in H. Parret and J. Bouveresse (eds) *Philosophical Subjects* (Oxford: The Clarendon Press, 1980).

13 John Greco (in correspondence) has raised the question why consciousness is not to perception as perception is to testimony. The beginning of an answer may be that (sensory) consciousness is a constituent in perception, whereas perception is not a constituent in testimony. Perceptual justification depends on *having* consciousness of the perceptual object which the justification concerns, but not on a separate exercise of consciousness, whereas testimonially based justification does not depend on perception regarding what the justification concerns – the proposition attested to – and does depend on an exercise of perception separate from the testimony.

14 The epistemology of testimony suggested here may be more stringent than that of Thomas Reid. For an interpretation and defense of the apparently Reidian view that testimonially grounded beliefs need not depend even for their justification on other sources of justification see Mark Owen Webb, 'Why I know About as Much as You: A Reply to Hardwig', *Journal of Philosophy* 90 (1993), 260–70.

15 Strictly, they need only look red, as where white objects are flooded by red light; and arguably, one could even teach 'red' by producing only hallucinations of the color.

16 It can be connected with arguments such as we find in Donald Davidson's work for the conclusion that most of our beliefs must be true, but it does not imply that stronger conclusion. For discussion of this and other Davidsonian hypotheses see Coady, *op. cit.*, esp. chapter 9.

17 It is difficult to see how one could, through testimony, produce conceptual learning without producing some belief. Could a child become acquainted with what redness is in connection with being told the sofa is red, yet not acquire a belief of some sort, for example objectually believing the sofa to be red? There is no need to settle this matter here; nor can I pursue related questions concerning conceptualization in higher animals.

18 One reason this point is restricted to normal human beings is that it seems possible for a human being to be created, as a full-blown adult, artificially, in which case much knowledge of abstract propositions and perhaps of other sorts, such as knowledge of the perceptible external environment in which the person is made, can occur before any testimony enters the picture. The story of Adam and Eve is a theological version of creation at the adult stage. There are also evolutionary conceptions of how knowledge first arises in human history, but these genetic questions would take us too far from our main questions.

19 *An Enquiry Concerning Human Understanding*, ed. by L. A. Selby-Bigge (Oxford: Oxford University Press, 1902), section 88.

20 We would certainly not be able to appeal to any significant segment of scientific knowledge, for there we are heavily dependent on testimony, written and oral. A plausible case that this dependence is even greater than it seems is made by John Hardwig in 'Epistemic Dependence', *Journal of Philosophy* LXXXII (1985), 693–708.

21 For supporting considerations favoring the possibility of the local justification and opposing that of a global one, see Elizabeth Fricker, 'Telling and Trusting: Reductionism and Anti-Reductionism in the Epistemology of Testimony': C. A. J. Coady's *Testimony: A Philosophical Study*, *Mind* 104 (1995), 393–411.

PART TWO

The structure and growth of justification and knowledge

CHAPTER 6
Inference and the extension of knowledge

Inference and the extension of knowledge

As I sit reading, I hear knocking. I wonder whether someone is at the door. I then hear extended, very rapid knocking. It now occurs to me that it is a pecking sound, and I realize that there is a woodpecker nearby. This way of coming to believe something differs from the way I came to believe there was a knocking in the first place. That belief was perceptual; it arose from my hearing the knocking. My belief that there is a woodpecker nearby is not perceptual. It arises not from, for instance, seeing the bird but from a further belief, namely my belief that the rapid knocking sounds like the pecking of a woodpecker. I hear the rapid knocking, recognize its character, and come to believe that it sounds like the pecking of a woodpecker. On the basis of this belief, I naturally conclude that there is a woodpecker nearby.

Some beliefs, then, arise from other beliefs and are based on them, rather than directly on the sources described in the first part of this book: perceptual, memorial, introspective, rational, and testimonial. This occurs with abstract matters as well as concerning perceptibles. Mathematical proof is a familiar example; on the basis of knowledge of an axiom, we may infer a theorem. An inference – which we may think of as a kind of *reasoning* – may also proceed by way of something abstract to something quite concrete. Studying a speech, one may determine that it is largely copied from someone else's article; given the abstract general point that so representing someone else's work as one's own is plagiarism, one reluctantly concludes that the speech is an instance of that. If we had only the beliefs arising from perception, memory, introspection, reflection, and testimony, we could not – by ourselves, at least – build theories to explain our experience or our own view of the world. It is largely because we can inferentially build on what we already believe (or assume) that there is no limit to the richness and complexity of the ideas and theories we can construct.

The nature of the inferential processes in which one belief is formed on the basis of other beliefs is a major question in the philosophy of mind and the psychology of cognition. The way those processes can extend justification and knowledge is a major question in epistemology. Not just any inference that begins with truth ends with it; some embody poor reasoning. We can best pursue the second, epistemological question – how inference extends knowledge and justification – by starting with the first, concerning what inferential belief is.

The process, content, and structure of inference

What sort of process is it by which my belief that there is a woodpecker arises from my belief that there is a knocking which sounds like its pecking? One clue is the naturalness of saying that on the *basis* of my belief that the knocking sounds like such a woodpecker's pecking, I *conclude* that there is a woodpecker nearby. I *infer* that there is one nearby from what I believe about the knocking: that it sounds like the pecking of a woodpecker. In inferring this, I conclude something on the basis of something else I believe.

What I conclude – the conclusion I draw – I in some sense derive from something else I believe. The concluding and the beliefs are mental. But neither what I conclude, nor what I believe from which I conclude it, is mental: these things are *contents* of my beliefs, as they might be of yours; they are not properties of anyone's mind, as beliefs themselves are. Such contents of beliefs – also called *objects* of beliefs – are commonly thought to be propositions (or statements, hypotheses, or something else that is not mental).[1]

Two senses of 'inference'

There are, then, two sorts of things involved when I draw a conclusion. One is the mental process of my concluding it on the basis of one or more beliefs of mine, as where I conclude that Alberto has been bitten by a deer tick on the basis of my belief (just acquired) that he has lime disease and my background belief that this is caused by such tick bites. The other element in my drawing a conclusion is the set of two or more propositions which are my conclusion and my ground for it. Call the first item the *inferential process*; it is a mental episode of reasoning. Call the second its *inferential content*; it is abstract and not a process. It indicates what is inferred from what, and it does this in a way that shows how my inferring that there is a woodpecker nearby is drawing the *same* inference as you would make if you inferred this from the proposition that there is knocking which sounds like that of a woodpecker. Our inferrings are two different processes, one in me and one in you. But their content is the same. Sometimes 'inference' is used for the content of the process. I want to talk about inference in both of these senses: as a process and as a structure consisting of propositions.

If inferring is a process corresponding to a conclusion and one or more premises for it, should we then suppose that in drawing my inference I *said* to myself something like, 'Those knocks sound like a woodpecker's; hence, there is a woodpecker nearby'? This might apply to someone just learning to recognize woodpecker knocking, but not to me. I do not need to concentrate on the proposition that there are those sounds, much less to say to myself something like 'hence there is a woodpecker'. I quickly realize, through hearing the sounds – and remembering what sort of sound a woodpecker makes – that they are its sounds; and on the basis of believing this proposition, I draw my conclusion without signposting my doing so by a silent 'hence'.

Reasoned belief and belief for a reason

My drawing of the inference is something I do; it is a kind of *reasoning*. But it is not necessarily self-conscious, as when one engages in reasoning with the aim of proving a theorem from a set of axioms. We need not introspect or even be focally conscious of our reasoning. We may instead simply draw our conclusion when our ground for it registers in our consciousness in an appropriate way. Thus, in response to wondering what I hear, I categorize the sounds as a pecking, and I then infer that there is a woodpecker. My resulting belief that there is one is, then, arrived at by reasoning and may on that ground be called a *reasoned belief*.

Compare this with a case in which, as I am reading on an unusually still morning, a vehicle backfires. I go on reading without thinking about the noise, though I do have the thought that someone drove by. Have I *inferred*, while reading, that someone drove by, say on the basis of believing that I heard a vehicle backfire? Surely I *need* not have. I am not like someone who must think about whether the sound had certain qualities and, only after determining that it does, concludes that a vehicle passed. Being familiar with backfires, I might simply have recognized the sound as a backfire and, on the basis of my belief that it is from a vehicle, automatically formed the belief that someone drove by. The former belief expresses my reason for holding the latter, which is thus a *belief for a reason*. It is not also a reasoned belief, however, because it is not grounded in a process of reasoning. A reasoned belief is always *held* for a reason – one expressed by the premise(s) of the reasoning, but a belief (held) for a reason need not be a reasoned belief – one arrived at by reasoning.[2]

This contrast between a belief for a reason and a reasoned belief may lead to the objection that I did not even form the belief that a vehicle backfired but only automatically believed, upon hearing the noise, that a vehicle passed. This is a possible case, and it lies at the other end of the spectrum from the case in which one cautiously forms the belief that the noise is a backfire, and then self-consciously infers that a vehicle passed. But my case is intermediate: I am neither so familiar with backfiring vehicles that I "just hear" vehicles pass when I hear those sounds, nor so unfamiliar with backfires that I must go through a process of inferring that conclusion when I hear the sounds.

People differ in the background knowledge and belief they bring to their experiences, and this in turn influences how those experiences produce new beliefs in them, say directly versus inferentially. Thus, in the very same situation, one person's inference may be another's perception. What one person believes only inferentially another believes perceptually: what the first must, for instance, arrive at by steps from one or more items of information to a conclusion from them, the other grasps as a whole, as a percept. Both cases may occur almost instantaneously; their difference is easily missed. It is in part the failure to distinguish the cases that apparently leads some people to think that perceptual belief as such is inferential.

In seeing the difference between reasoned belief and (non-reasoned) belief for a reason, it may help to notice that the *contexts* of the backfire and woodpecker noises differ significantly. The backfire is a kind of noise that can make it obvious that someone is driving by, whereas the pecking, far from coinciding with a flutter of wings that clearly mark the presence of a bird, is an isolated stream of sounds in the quiet of the afternoon, and it can be associated with many sources, natural and mechanical. Certainly there is an event of *belief formation* when I hear the bang and come to believe that someone is driving by. The point is that such a belief need not be reasoned: one need not form it by drawing an inference.

The contrast just drawn between a reasoned belief and a belief for a reason must not be allowed to obscure something important that is shared by the two kinds of belief formation. In both cases, I believe one thing on the basis of another thing I believe; for instance, I believe that someone drove by on the basis of believing that a vehicle backfired. In both instances, then, there is an inferential (roughly, argumental) *structure* corresponding to my beliefs. It consists of a proposition we might think of as a conclusion and at least one we might think of as a premise on which the conclusion is based. This similarity helps to explain why there is an inclination to regard my coming to believe that someone drove by as somehow inferential.[3]

The basing relation: direct and indirect belief

There is a way to describe our two examples that helps to remind us of both their similarities and their differences. Call my reasoned belief that there is a woodpecker nearby *episodically inferential*, since (at the time in question) it arises from a process or episode of inferring, of explicitly drawing a conclusion from something one believes. Call my belief that someone drove by *structurally inferential*, since, as a belief for a reason, it is *based on* another belief in

156 STRUCTURE OF JUSTIFICATION AND KNOWLEDGE

much the *way* one belief is based on a second when the first does arise from the second by inference. Being so based implies (among other things) that my holding the second belief, the basis (or premise) belief, is at least part of what explains why I hold the first. Yet my belief that someone drove by is not episodically inferential, because it arises, not from my drawing an inference, but in an automatic way not requiring a process of reasoning. Episodically inferential beliefs – those that are reasoned – are beliefs for a reason, but not every case of the latter is a case of the former.

In both instances there is an inferential structure (which is no doubt reflected in the brain) corresponding to my beliefs: I believe the conclusion *because* I believe the premise(s), even though the beliefs are related by an inferential episode in one case and by an automatic process of belief formation in the other. In the first case, I do something – I infer a conclusion. In the second, something *happens* in me – a belief arises on the basis of one or more other beliefs I hold. The resulting structure is much the same; hence, both beliefs are structurally inferential, though a belief that is episodically inferential at the time it is formed will become structurally inferential when it is retained after the inference is drawn if, as is common, it remains based on the reason expressed by the premise(s). The difference is that the two beliefs arise in different ways. Only the belief that there is a woodpecker nearby is (at the time it is formed) episodically inferential.[4]

Another way to see how a belief can be inferentially based on a second without being episodically inferential is to consider a case – a kind especially important in understanding knowledge and justification – in which one *first* believes something perceptually and then the belief comes to be based on a premise. Suppose I see someone I take to be Alasdair. I do not get a good look, but believe in any case that I saw Alasdair. When a friend says that she has just met Alasdair's wife at the train station, I now believe (in part) on the *basis* of her information that I saw him. But I need not have at any point inferred this from her information. It can become a structurally inferential basis of my belief without my *using* it as a premise by drawing an inference. It is like an additional pillar placed beneath a porch after it is built: the pillar adds support but otherwise leaves the porch as it is. The addition of this support can justify the belief it supports, and one may now have justified belief or even knowledge where one previously believed the proposition unjustifiedly.

To bring out what the two kinds of inferential belief have in common I call them *indirect*. For in each case I believe one thing on the basis of, and so in a sense *through*, believing another thing. Indirect beliefs are mediated by other beliefs, whether through inference or not. We are talking, of course, about particular beliefs held by specific people at particular times. People differ in their inferential patterns, and these may change over time. As with backfires, one could become so familiar with woodpecker knocks that when one hears them, one just believes (non-inferentially) that they are occurring, rather as, on seeing green grass in good light, I may just believe, perceptually, that there is grass before me.

Such effects of increased familiarity show that one person's indirect belief may be another's direct belief, just as one person's conclusion may be another's premise. Similarly, my conclusion at one time can later become a basic premise, or vice versa: a proposition I believe indirectly at one time I may believe directly at another, as where I forget the premise I originally had, but I retain the proposition in memory.

There is a wide-ranging point illustrated here that is important for epistemology, psychology, and the philosophy of mind: we cannot in general specify propositions which can be believed only in one way, or determine whether a belief is inferential by considering just the proposition believed.[5] To be sure, it would be *abnormal* to believe (wholly) indirectly that if some dogs are pets, then some pets are dogs – in part because one could not easily find a good premise to constitute a basis for this – or to believe (by sight) directly that there are seventeen cats eating scraps of beef in the backyard, since normally one would have to arrive at this on the basis of counting.[6] But strange cases like these are possible.

Inference and the growth of knowledge

The examples I have given represent one way in which we learn through using our senses in combination with our rational powers. Through making inferences and through forming beliefs that are structurally inferential, we acquire not only new beliefs, but new justified beliefs and new knowledge. Indeed, a great many of our justified beliefs and knowledge arise in this way. The woodpecker case illustrates how this process works. In a single moment I come to believe, among other things, that no one is at the door and that there is a woodpecker nearby. I also acquire situational justification for these beliefs, justifiedly hold them, and know the truths which, in holding them, I believe.

Much of life is like this: through the joint work of perception and our rational powers, particularly our inferential capacities, we acquire new beliefs, our justification is extended, and we gain new knowledge. We also forget, cease to be justified in believing certain things when we acquire evidence to the contrary, and sometimes infer conclusions we are not entitled to infer. But let us first concentrate on the way belief, justification, and knowledge develop.

Confirmatory versus generative inferences

Inference is typically a source of new beliefs. But as we have seen, it need not be. Recall the backfire, and suppose I am so familiar with such sounds that no categorization of them is necessary for me to recognize them. Then I may well *directly* – i.e., non-inferentially – believe that a vehicle backfired. But now imagine that, realizing firecrackers have lately been set off nearby in honor of Guy Fawkes Night, I wonder whether the sound might have been the blast of a firecracker. I recall the sound, remember that it had a muffled, not a popping, quality, and infer from its having that quality that it was indeed a backfire. Here I infer something I already believe. It is as if one had arrived at a place without noticing one's route and, wanting to be sure one is where one thinks one is, considers by what route one could have arrived there. Finding a plausible route can confirm one's sense that all is well, whether or not it is the route one in fact took.

My inference, then, is not a *source* of new belief, though it does in a way *alter* my belief that the sound was a backfire; the belief now becomes inferential. This is not a change in its content, but in its basis. The inference does not produce a new belief but instead adds to my belief system a new ground for something I already believe. It is *confirmatory*, but not, as in typical cases, *generative*. Like an inference drawn in doing certain logic book exercises, it is not a belief-forming inference; but unlike many such cases (which often concern fictitious people or places), it has a conclusion that is already believed.

Inference as a dependent source of justification and knowledge

Even when inference is not generative and hence is not a source of belief, it may still be a source of both justification and knowledge. Again, suppose I know that lately there have been firecrackers exploding nearby. I now might *not* know, or be justified in believing, that there was a vehicle backfire, until I recall the quality of the sound, rule out its being that of a firecracker, and infer in this light that a vehicle backfired. I might thus have neither justification for believing a vehicle backfired, nor knowledge that it did, until I draw the inference. Similarly, scientists who believe a hypothesis might not come to know it until, through investigating and ruling out certain alternatives, they reason their way to it, thereby inferring it, from new premises.

On the other hand, suppose I am not justified, and indeed am *un*justified, in believing that the muffled sound in question represents a backfire. My situation might be this: in my whole life I have heard only one backfire; I have, however, heard many firecrackers with that sort of sound; and my belief that this sound represents a backfire is based on testimony from someone I think is usually unreliable. Here I do not become justified, inferentially or testimonially, in believing that there was a vehicle backfire. For a crucial premise of my inference – that this kind of noise represents a backfire – is one I am unjustified in believing. The same would hold if I had been unjustified in believing my other premise: that there was a muffled sound.

Now imagine a different case, this time regarding knowledge. Suppose I *am* justified in believing my premise that the muffled sound represents a backfire, since my previous experience adequately justifies my believing this. But suppose that, through no fault of my own, I have somehow failed to discover that there are common firecrackers which sound precisely the same. Then, although I am still correct in believing my conclusion – that there is a backfire – I am mistaken in believing, and so do not *know*, my *premise* that this muffled sound *represents* a vehicle backfire. For it might just as well indicate a firecracker. Thus, I infer a true conclusion, but using a premise which, though I justifiedly believe it, is false. This example shows something important (which will be considered from a different point of view in Chapter 8): that I may be justified (and even correct) in believing that there was a vehicle backfire, yet not *know* that. My would-be knowledge is defeated by my false premise, though my justification is not.

This last case is not typical. Perhaps more often than not, inference on the part of rational persons is a source of beliefs that are both justified and constitute knowledge. If inference is often a source of justification and of knowledge, is it a *basic* source? Our example suggests that it is not. If, for instance, I am not justified in believing my premises that there was a muffled sound, and that such a sound represents a backfire, then my inferring that there was a backfire does not yield justification for my believing this conclusion, and I do not justifiedly believe it. Apparently my inference justifies me in believing my conclusion only if I am justified in believing its premise (or premises).

Inference as an extender of justification and knowledge

Points like this suggest that inference is not a basic source of justification or knowledge, but rather *transmits* and thereby *extends* them, in appropriate circumstances, from one of more premises to the conclusion inferred from them. We can extend our justification and knowledge by inference, but it appears that if we have none to start with, inference, unlike, say, perception, can give us none: even careful and amply justified inferences – roughly, inferences one is justified in drawing *given* the assumption of the truth of the premise(s) – do not *create* justification or knowledge where there is none to start with, because one neither knows nor has justification for one's premise(s).[7]

Our examples show two kinds of inferential extension of knowledge and justification. The first is acquisition of new knowledge and new justified beliefs; the second is increase in our justification for believing something we already hold or a buttressing of our knowledge of it, as where we infer it from a newly discovered premise.

There is a third kind of extension of justification and knowledge that can be a variant of either one. Consider a belief that arises from or is supported by inference from two or more *independent* sets of premises, such as evidence presented by two independent observers. One may be better justified in believing (or may better know) what the witnesses jointly attest to than one is in believing that on the basis of the evidence of any one of them alone. Moreover, our experience often leads to inferential extension of all three sorts without our making any particular effort to draw inferences. For the formation of structurally inferential beliefs, and even of many episodically inferential beliefs, occurs quite often and very naturally, as a timber can be silently and unobtrusively placed beneath a porch in a way that supports it.

Source conditions and
transmission conditions

If inference is not a basic source of justification and knowledge, but transmits it, it must meet two kinds of conditions. One kind concerns the premise(s) of the inference – its pillars, so to speak – the other concerns the relation of the premise(s) to the conclusion – how well those evidential pillars support what is built on them, for instance whether or not they express strong evidence for believing it. Let us take these in turn.

First, there are *source conditions*, as our examples show: one needs justification or knowledge in the first place. To see what the second kind of condition is, suppose I do know that the muffled sound I hear represents a vehicle backfire and I infer that a *truck* backfired. But imagine that I really cannot tell the difference between car and truck backfires. Then I do not know, in virtue of my inference, that a truck backfired. I started with knowledge, but it was not transmitted to my belief of my conclusion, since I drew a conclusion from it which it did not warrant. There was, we might say, no justificatory path from my premises to my conclusion.

There are, then, *transmission conditions*, as well as source conditions, that an inference must satisfy in order to yield knowledge of its conclusion. Chapters 1 through to 5 in effect deal with source conditions in some detail, for example with how perception yields non-inferential knowledge that can provide premises for inference. Thus, I say little about source conditions here and concentrate on transmission conditions.

Deductive and inductive inference

We can best understand transmission conditions if, as is common in discussions of logic, we divide inferences into two categories, deductive and inductive. The usual basis of this division is an interpretation of the character of the inferential structure underlying the process of inference, or at least a choice of the kind of standard appropriate for assessing that structure. We can simplify matters by calling these structures *arguments*, even though they need not represent anyone's actually arguing for something or *with* anyone.

In this abstract sense of 'argument', an argument is discernible even where, simply to assure myself that I was correct in believing that there was a vehicle backfire rather than a firecracker blast, I inferred – *reasoned*, to put it in terms appropriate to the context of evaluation from the point of view of justification – from reconsidering the kind of noise I heard, that there was in fact a backfire. I relied on the argument from propositions about the character of the noise to the conclusion that a backfire occurred, even though I was not trying to convince anyone, even myself, of anything. Instead, I was trying to justify something I believed. I did this by tapping a justified source and transmitting its justification to my belief that a vehicle backfired. A natural interpretation of the case is this: I reasoned from the premises that (1) the noise represented a backfire and (2) if it did represent that, then there was a backfire, to the conclusion that (3) there was a backfire.

My argument here, and hence my reasoning – from its premises to its conclusion, is (deductively) *valid*; that is, it is absolutely impossible for its premises, (1) and (2), to be true and its conclusion, (3), false. For short, the premises of a valid argument (logically) *entail* its conclusion. It is of course not in general impossible for the *premises* of valid deductive arguments to be false, and many of these premises are. But it is absolutely impossible that the premises are true *and* the conclusion false.[8]

In the most careful terminology, 'valid' applies only to deductive reasoning; and we might think of deductive reasoning as the sort that "aims" at validity, in the sense that it is of a kind best evaluated as valid or invalid. Thus, even though the argument from hallucination (discussed in Chapter 1) is invalid, the philosophical reasoning that employs it seems meant to be valid and is appropriately assessed as deductive.

By contrast, much reasoning that is not valid simply does not seem meant to be deductive in the first place. Suppose, for instance, that my reasoning had run: (A) the noise sounds like that of a backfire; (B) the likeliest explanation of the noise is that a vehicle backfired; so, probably, (C) a vehicle backfired. As the word 'probably' signals, I do not take my reasoning to be valid or to be deductive at all: I simply take its premises to provide some reason to believe its conclusion. Even if I had not used 'probably', it would be inappropriate to consider this reasoning deductive. For it is obvious that even the likeliest explanation *need* not be true or even considered true; it would thus be a mistake to regard such reasoning – or the person using it – as trying to produce valid reasoning.

We *could* call such probabilistic reasoning "inductively valid," meaning roughly that relative to its premises there is a high probability that its conclusion is true (where high probability is usually taken to be such that it is reasonable to accept a proposition having it); but to avoid confusion I simply term reasoning of that sort 'inductively good' (or 'inductively strong'). Moreover, it is reasoning processes and not abstract structures that I call deductive or inductive. I do not take arguments, as abstract structures, to be intrinsically of either kind, though we *speak* of them as deductive or inductive so far as they seem best assessed by deductive or inductive standards. (The intentions of those presenting them are one among many other factors determining the appropriate standards.)

I want to stress in passing that we should not conceive deductive and inductive reasoning as they have often been characterized. Deductive reasoning has been described as "going" from the general to the particular, say from (a) all human beings are mortal and (b) Socrates is a human being to (c) Socrates is mortal. But our deductive backfire case, embodying the valid argument from (1) and (2) to (3), is different; it is about only particular things. Even in the classical example about Socrates, one premise is particular, in the sense that it concerns a single individual.

Subsumptive and analogical inference

Even those who take deductive reasoning to go from the general to the particular should recognize that the reasoning from (1) all humans have fears and (2) all who have fears are vulnerable to (3) all humans are vulnerable is deductive (and valid). Perhaps they focus on cases in which we draw a conclusion about something or someone, say Socrates, by *subsuming* the person or thing under a generalization about similar entities, say people. If so, it is better to call such inference *subsumptive reasoning* (or *instantial reasoning*).

As for inductive reasoning, it has often been said to "go from" the particular to the general, as where one bases the conclusion that everyone has fears on the enumerative premises that Abe does, Beatrice does, Carl does, Donna does, and so on. This characterization is good so far as it goes, but it does not apply to reasoning from a premise stating the likeliest explanation of a noise to the conclusion that it is a backfire. Nor does it do justice to certain reasoning by *analogy*, such as my concluding that a plant probably has a property, say hardiness, because it is much like (highly analogous to) another plant that has that property.

It is better, then, to think of inductive reasoning as reasoning that, first, "aims" at providing good grounds for its conclusion, but not at validity, and, second, is best evaluated in terms of the degree of probability of its conclusion relative to its premises. This conception has the further advantage of applying to all three main kinds of inductive reasoning: generalizational, explanational, and analogical.

The inferential transmission of justification and knowledge

We are now in a position to explore the conditions for transmission of justification and knowledge. Clearly the success of transmission is partly a matter of the status of the underlying argument: the one whose premise or premises are one's basis for the belief in question. The natural thing to say initially is that justification and knowledge are transmitted in deductive inference *only* if the underlying argument is valid and, in inductive inference, *only* if the underlying argument is (inductively) good (I use 'inference' rather than 'reasoning' here because the former is preferable for the wide range of contexts we are exploring). But these principles, though probably correct, need clarification. Let us consider the cases of inductive and deductive transmission separately.

Suppose Luigi hastily infers from the propositions (1) all opera lovers appreciate *The Magic Flute* and (2) Wilhelm appreciates *The Magic Flute* that (3) Wilhelm is an opera lover. This is invalid deductive reasoning, and even with true premises it would not transmit either justification or knowledge from beliefs of them to a belief of its conclusion. Bad reasoning cannot realize the inferential potential of good premises.

Suppose Luigi then produces the better argument (1) all opera lovers appreciate *The Magic Flute* and (2) Wilhelm appreciates it in the way one would expect of an opera lover, to (3) Wilhelm is an opera lover. *If* we conceive his reasoning as deductive, say because Luigi's underlying principle – roughly, the one by which his reasoning is actually guided – is not the expected inductive one – that if all As are Bs and x is an A of a kind that might well be expected to be a B then *probably* x is a B – but the false principle that if all As are Bs, and x is an A of a kind that might be expected to be a B, then x *is* (definitely) a B, then we must also say that transmission is blocked because his reasoning is invalid. He employs a mistaken (deductive) logical standard.

Apparently, then, *deductive transmission requires validity*. Specifically, the argument underlying an inferential belief – i.e., the argument whose premise(s) constitute(s) what that belief is inferentially based on – must be valid if knowledge or justification is to be deductively transmitted to that belief from the premise belief(s) it is based on. To be sure, I could have independent grounds, such as testimony about Wilhelm, on which I know my conclusion. But if I do not have such grounds, then I cannot come to know it *through* deductive transmission of my knowledge from premises I have for it if those premises do not entail it, and hence the argument from them to it is invalid. We cannot build anything solid on weak supports, even if they themselves rest on a good foundation; the structure is still defective.

Inductive transmission

The case with inductive reasoning is more complicated. For one thing, the notion of good inductive reasoning is highly vague. It might seem that we could simply define it as reasoning with premises that render its conclusion more likely than not to be true. But this will not do, though such reasoning may be called *probable* to indicate that it has this specific merit. Two points are important here.

First, a probability of just over .50 (indicating just over a fifty–fifty chance of truth) allows that even given the truth of the premises, the falsehood of the conclusion is almost as likely as its truth (since probabilities range from 0 to 1, with .50 representing the same likelihood of truth as of falsehood on the part of the proposition in question). One would not want to describe reasoning as good when its premises give its conclusion a probability of truth of just over 50 percent.

Second, judging how good the reasoning is may require assessing the conclusion in relation to more than the premises. This certainly holds if we are viewing the reasoning as occurring in a context in which various kinds of information are accessible to the reasoner. Relative just to the premise that Dave has a certain kind of cancer, the probability of the conclusion that he will die of it may be .60, since 60 percent of its victims do; but relative to his youth, vigor, and treatment, the probability of his death from it may be .08. Thus, the inductive reasoning from the premise that he has the particular cancer to the conclusion that he will die of it ignores relevant evidence and is not good, even though the conclusion does have a probability of more than .50 relative to its premise.

Suppose we assume for a moment that good inductive reasoning has premises taking account of *all* the relevant evidence. May we then conclude that justification and knowledge are inductively transmitted only by inductive reasoning good in this comprehensive sense? This view is too strong. For it may often happen that some of the relevant evidence is not needed for such inductive justification of one's belief because one's premises already contain sufficient evidence. Evidence may be relevant to a belief without being *needed* for its justification, as where testimony from a tenth witness who agrees with the rest is unnecessary though perfectly relevant. The point is important; for even if we can understand the notion of all the relevant evidence, we at best rarely have *all* the evidence relevant to a belief and may need it all if we do.

Is good inductive reasoning simply the kind of inductive reasoning that is *sufficient* to transmit justification? This is a promising characterization for single pieces of inductive reasoning, those using a set of premises directly for one conclusion. But inductive reasoning can occur in chains, with the conclusion of the first piece of reasoning serving as a premise in the second piece, and the conclusion of that serving as a premise in the third, and so on. Unfortunately, in an inductive chain extended through many inferences, justification may not be transmitted from the conclusion of the first to the conclusion of the last, even if each piece of reasoning has premises giving high probability to *its* conclusion. To see why, notice first that the *degree* of justification inductively transmitted from one's premises to one's conclusion may drop, even if nothing new enters the picture, such as someone's challenging one's conclusion the moment one draws it.

If the degree of probability repeatedly drops, the degree of justification may drop drastically. To see this, notice that even if one starts with excellent justification for one's premises, if they give a probability of only, say, 0.75 to one's conclusion, one will have much weaker justification for the conclusion than for the premises, if they are one's *only* basis for it. (I am assuming, somewhat artificially, that justification admits of degrees in the way probability does.) Roughly, one should take the chance that the conclusion is true to be only 75 percent of the chance that the premises are true. Suppose that I know that Tom said that the weather forecaster predicted rain. If the chance that Tom (who is biased by optimism and may have misheard the forecast) is right is only 75 percent and the chance that the forecaster's prediction is right is, say, 60 percent, then my warrant for believing it will rain is presumably just 75 percent of 60, i.e., 45 percent. (The idea is that the probability that the forecast was even made is only 75 percent, and we would then have a 60 percent chance of rain; the multiplication takes account of both probabilities.) Such chains of inference can be indefinitely long, as where I must rely on still other people for my belief that Tom said the forecaster predicted rain. This allows for the occurrence of even more reduction of one's justification for believing one's conclusion.

These points should make it apparent how it is possible for good inductive reasoning, carried out through a series of inferences, to fail to transmit justification from its initial premises to its final conclusion. Even if the probability that the initial premises give to the first conclusion is 0.9, if one went on inferring further conclusions, each being a premise for the next conclusion, then even with the same degree of probability in each case, one could eventually infer a conclusion for which one has less justification than 0.5. With each case, the likelihood that one's conclusion is true would be 10 percent less than

(90 percent of) the likelihood of the truth of one's previous conclusion, which is serving as one's premise.

In some respects, *knowledge* differs from justification in relation to transmission conditions. Since knowledge does not admit of degrees (at least not in the way justification does), it might be transmitted across an inductive inference without diminution in degree even if such transmission does imply some reduction in one's justification (other things being equal). If, for instance, you know that the weather is bad and you inductively infer that Jane, who is driving, will be late, you could know the latter proposition on the basis of the former even though there is a very slight chance that she left early and compensated for the weather. Your *grounds* for your conclusion may not be as good as your grounds for your premise, which may render the conclusion only very probable, rather than entailing it; but you may still unqualifiedly know your conclusion. This knowledge may not be as good, say as securely grounded, as your knowledge of the premises; for instance, it might not be as nearly certain. But it *can* still be knowledge. Although there are kinds of knowledge, apparently a belief either constitutes knowledge or falls short of that, as opposed to constituting knowledge to a degree.

It may happen, however, that knowledge is not transmitted even across an inductive inference whose premises give its conclusion extremely high probability. For example, you might know that you hold just one out of a million coupons in a fair sweepstakes, which will have one winner. You may inductively infer, with very high probability, 0.999999, that you will lose, since 999,999 of the million coupons will lose. But you do not *know* you will lose. You might be lucky; and you have as good a chance to be lucky as any other holder of a single coupon – including the possessor of the winning one. Your knowledge of your premises, then, is not inductively transmitted to your conclusion. (If we change the example so that you *deduce* the qualified statement that the probability of your losing is 0.999999, you may know *that*. But that is a very different conclusion.)[9]

Some inferential transmission principles

We have seen some important points. Inference transmits justification and knowledge; it is not a basic source of them. It can generate them only derivatively, by transmission, from knowledge and justification already possessed. Inference can originate knowledge or justified belief in the sense that the beliefs in question are new to the believer, but not – as the basic sources of knowledge and justification can – from something other than belief, such as perception. Deductive transmission apparently requires validity; and inductive transmission apparently requires an inductive counterpart of validity, something like a strong relation of support between premises and conclusion. But even where the support is strong, the degree of justification may drop in a way that it need not drop in the deductive case.

As our examples show, to understand the transmission of justification and knowledge we must consider two sorts of conditions: those necessary for transmission of knowledge and justification, conditions such that transmission occurs *only* if they are met by an inference; and sufficient conditions, those such that *if* they are met by an inference, then transmission occurs.

It is by and large even harder to specify sufficient conditions than necessary ones. For a sufficient condition must "cover" all the necessary ones: if it does not imply that each of them holds, it leaves out something necessary, and so is not sufficient.[10] Let me simply suggest the sort of thing we must add to what we so far have in order to arrive at sufficient conditions for inferential transmission.

It will help to take inductive cases first. Might we say that if, by good inductive reasoning, one infers something from premises which take account of all the relevant evidence, then if one is justified in believing those premises, one is justified in believing the conclusion? Even in the sweepstakes case, where one holds only one of a million coupons, this condition is plausible for justification. For instance, one may be justified in believing one will lose. If justification is like knowledge in this respect, however, the answer is negative. For as the sweepstakes example shows, even when the probability is very high, the counterpart of this condition, with knowledge substituted for justification, does not hold.

Let us see what we can learn from a different example. Imagine that I enter my house and find evidence of a burglary, such as ransacked drawers. I infer that valuables have been stolen. From that I infer that the $20 in my daughter's piggy bank is missing. And from that in turn I infer that my daughter will be upset. At each point I am justified in believing my premise and, it would seem, make a good inductive inference from it.

In most such cases, my justification would carry right down the line from my initial premise to my final conclusion. But it need not. There is a chance that the bank was overlooked and a chance that my daughter will be calm, if only because she is so grateful that important things, like the teddy bears, are undisturbed. Could it not be that at each step my justification for my conclusion drops in such a way that, unlike my inference that I will lose the sweepstakes, my last inference fails to produce a justified conclusion?

The general point here is that as inference proceeds, the crucially relevant evidence, the evidence one must take into account, may mount up or at least change. For instance, by the time I get to the question of whether my daughter will be upset about the piggy bank, it becomes relevant to note that the teddy bears are unharmed before inferring that she will be upset, whereas this information would not have been relevant if the disappearance of the piggy bank were the only disturbance in the house.

But how should we decide what is relevant to drawing a conclusion? And how is one's justification for believing a conclusion affected by ignoring only some of what is relevant? These are hard questions, which I can only partially answer. One positive point is this: whether we are inferentially justified in holding a conclusion we draw depends on many factors, including some *not* expressed in our premises.

My believing the premises of an inference may be the origin of my belief and a source of my justification. But there are other relevant factors – such as what I know, or should know, about what will preoccupy the child upon discovering the burglary. My justification ultimately depends on complex relations among all the relevant factors. We might say that although justification may emerge from a straight inferential line, it will do so only if the line figures in the right kind of *pattern* of related beliefs and available relevant information. Some patterns contain obstacles on the would-be path to justification; others have clear, straight passageways.

Deductive transmission of justification and knowledge

Let us turn now to deductive transmission. One might think that valid deductive inference is sufficient as well as necessary for transmitting justification and knowledge. Certainly it commonly does transmit them, for instance when we learn theorems by validly deducing them in doing geometrical proofs.

I do not mean that whenever there is a valid inference, in the sense of 'a set of propositions constituting a valid argument', from something one believes to a conclusion, then one "implicitly" knows the conclusion, or even has situational justification for believing it. If that were so, then simply by knowing the axioms of Euclidean geometry (which, like the axiom that parallel lines never meet, are quite simple), one might implicitly know, and be justified in believing, all its theorems. (This assumes that these theorems are all within one's comprehension, since one cannot believe or, at the time, even be justified in believing, a theorem too complex for one to understand.) The main issue here is the transmission of justification and knowledge from justified beliefs, or from beliefs constituting knowledge, to other beliefs *arrived at* by inference, or to situational justification for propositions that we *could* infer from those we know or are justified in believing.

Even if we restrict our concern to transmission of knowledge across inference processes, it is at least not obvious that knowledge is always transmitted across valid deductive inferences.[11] Recall the backfire. Suppose I am sufficiently acquainted with the sound to *know* that it is a backfire. Then, from what I know, it follows that it is not the sound of a firecracker with a similar muffled sound. Suppose that, aware that this follows, I infer that it is not such a sound. Do I know that it is not? What if I have no evidence that there is no one around setting off such firecrackers? Perhaps I then do not know this. It may well be that from my general experience, the most I am justified in believing is that this alternative explanation of the sound is sufficiently improbable to be irrelevant. But it is still not clear that I know there is no one around setting off such firecrackers.[12]

Thus, it is not clear that, simply through validly inferring a proposition from an inferential ground that I know, I know this proposition, say that the sound is not that of a firecracker with a similar muffled quality. One might now say that this just shows that I did not know in the first place that a vehicle backfired. But I do not see that we must say that. It may be equally plausible to say that because one *now* realizes that one's basis for believing this might not have been decisive, one *no longer* knows it, yet did know it in the first place. *If* that is so, it shows something important: that sometimes reflection on our grounds can bring into our purview considerations that weaken them or at least weaken their power to support inferences.

Consider a different case. I add a column of fifteen figures, check my results twice, and thereby come to know, and to be justified in believing, that the sum is 10,952. As it happens, I sometimes make mistakes, and my wife (whom I justifiedly believe to be a better arithmetician) sometimes corrects me. Suppose that, feeling unusually confident this time, I now infer that if my wife says this is not the sum, she is wrong. From the truth that the sum is 10,952, it certainly follows that if she says it is not, she is wrong. If it is the sum, then if she denies that, she is wrong. But even though I know and am justified in believing that this is the sum, can I, on the basis of my grounds for this belief, *automatically* know or be justified in believing that if she says it is not the sum, she is wrong? That is far from self-evident, and I am assuming that I have no other basis for holding this belief, such as a calculator result that coincides with mine.

Suppose my checking just twice is enough to give me only the *minimum* basis for justified belief and knowledge here. Surely I would then not have sufficient grounds for believing that if she says the answer is wrong, she is wrong. Given my background justification for believing that she is the better arithmetician, the justification-threatening prospect this proposition puts before me seems to demand that I have more justification than the minimum I do have if am to be justified in believing that if she says the sum is not 10,952, she is wrong.

One way to interpret the example is this. To be justified in believing that if she says the sum is not 10,952, she is wrong, or to know or justifiedly believe this about her, I need grounds for believing it that are good enough not to be outweighed by the supposition that she (the better arithmetician) says that 10,952 is not the sum. In inferring that if she says this is not the sum, she is wrong, I *am* making the supposition that she says it. Of course, I need not *believe* she will say it; but because I am supposing she will, I am justified in believing that if she does, she is wrong, only if my justification for believing that the sum is 10,952 is good enough to withstand the supposition that she denies it is the sum. My making this supposition may also be regarded as implicit in my holding the belief that if she says this, she is wrong, whether I infer it or not. In either case, under the supposed conditions, her justification is good enough to reduce mine below the threshold which it just barely reaches.

One might now object that I really do not know or have justification in the first place for believing that the sum in 10,952. Depending on my arithmetic skills, that might be true if I have checked my sum only twice. But suppose that carefully checking three or four times is required to reach the threshold of justification and that I have done this. For *any* reasonable standard of justification or knowledge, there will be a point where I *just* meet, and do not exceed, that standard, and I (again assuming I justifiedly believe her to be the better arithmetician) will then not know or be justified in believing the further proposition that if she says the sum is wrong, then she is wrong. (This point concerns situational justification. It is also true that if I infer this further proposition without first getting *additional* grounds for my answer, I would not know it or justifiedly believe it, i.e., have a justified belief of it.)[13]

The example can be varied to make the same point in a different way. If the sum is 10,952, then even if there are two mistakes in the calculations I made to get it, it is *still* 10,952. This may sound strange, but the mistakes could cancel each other, say because one mistake yields a 9 instead of the correct 7, and the other yields a 6 instead of the correct 8 (so an excess of 2 is offset by a shortage of 2). Now imagine that in fact I again justifiedly believe that the sum is 10,952 and know this. I have been careful enough and have not actually made errors, but still I have checked only the minimum amount necessary for justification. Perhaps simply to test my intuitions about deductive transmission, I might infer that (even) if there are two errors in my calculation, the sum is 10,952. Surely I am not justified in believing this and – assuming that the same minimum of checking is sufficient for knowledge – I do not know it (if more checking is required, then the same point will hold for knowledge if we build in the assumption that I just reached the required minimum). My original, minimal justification does not give me situational justification for believing it or adequate grounds for knowledge. If I had done *extra* checking, say enough to be adequately justified in believing (or to know) that I made no mistakes, it might be otherwise; but that is not my case.

Still another way to conceive the example is this. One might think of (1) 'If she says the sum is not 10,952, then she is wrong' as equivalent to (2) 'Either she doesn't say this or she says it and is wrong'. Thus, if I am justified in believing (or know) (2), I am (arguably) justified in believing (and know) (1). It may seem that I would be justified in believing (1), since this can occur in any of these three ways: through my being justified in believing that (a) she will not say this, through my being justified in believing that (b) she says it and is wrong, *and* through my being justified in believing that (c) at least one of those two things is true.

Am I, however, justified in believing any of (a)–(c)? My justification for believing the sum is 10,952 is (chiefly) my reasonably careful calculations' indicating this. *That* justification does not extend to justifying my believing that (a) my wife will not say this is false, and it surely does not extend to my believing that (b) she (whom I justifiedly believe to be the better arithmetician) says it is false and is wrong. Thus, it seems at best unlikely that I should be justified in believing that (c) at least one of these two things is the case.

Indeed, in the imagined case I could have some reason to believe my wife *will* deny my results, say because she occasionally does. To be sure, I may also have *some* reason to believe that if she says the sum is not 10,952, she is wrong; but the point is that I would not have enough justification for this to know or have a justified belief of it, as I did know and have a justified belief that the sum is 10,952.[14]

Cases of this sort strongly argue for at least two points. First, justification and knowledge *need* not be transmitted through valid inference from known or justifiedly believed premises to belief of a conclusion inferred on the basis of them. Second, situational justification is not automatically transmitted even to propositions clearly entailed by those we are justified in believing.

These negative points should be balanced by another. *Some* degree of (situational) justification may automatically transmit – what we might call some *reason for believing*: it is not as though I have nothing in the way of reason to believe that if she says the sum is not 10,952, then she is wrong (for instance, I did check my sum with some care). Still, merely having some reason to believe does not imply being justified *in* believing, any more than one piece of evidence for a proposition is sufficient for knowledge of it.

The sort of failure of transmission I have noted is probably not common for inferences rational persons normally draw, and I stress it because it has often been denied (and is important in dealing with skepticism). Typically, transmission of both justification and knowledge does occur through valid reasoning. That qualified principle is of major importance in epistemology. It is difficult to say under just what conditions it does not, but one can see what some of them are from the points that have emerged here. The general conclusion to draw, however, is that whether one is justified in believing something, or knows it, depends not only on one's specific evidence for it but also on a pattern of factors including one's relation to the proposition itself and one's particular circumstances.

Memorial preservation of inferential justification and inferential knowledge

Let me conclude by introducing a further point that applies to both deductive and inductive inferential transmission. Imagine that you learn something, say a theorem, by validly inferring it from something you know, say a set of axioms. You may remember the axioms *as* your grounds; then your memory preserves both your premises and your conclusion. But eventually you may forget your grounds, for instance how you proved, and even how *to* prove, a theorem. Similarly, you may forget the testimony or book from which you learned (perhaps by inductive inference partly based on the premise that the book is reliable) that the Battle of Hastings was in 1066. Can you still know and justifiedly believe these now premise-less propositions?

The answer in both cases is surely that you can. Memory can retain beliefs *as* knowledge, and as justified beliefs, even if it does not retain the original grounds of the relevant beliefs. But because in these instances it does not retain the inferential grounds, and no new grounds need be added, it does not necessarily retain the beliefs *as* inferential. Moreover, where the grounds are not retained and none are added, one might find it at best difficult to indicate *how* one knows, beyond insisting that, say, one is sure one remembers, perhaps adding that one certainly did have grounds in the past. But so long as one did have adequate grounds and *does* remember the proposition, surely one can know that proposition. One can also justifiedly believe it, provided one has an appropriate memory of it.

This example is another illustration of the point that a belief which is inferential at one time may be non-inferential at another. This may happen repeatedly with the same belief. Long after a belief – for instance, of a theorem – has ceased to be inferential, one could acquire new grounds for it, such as that one has a clear recollection of a mathematical friend's affirming the theorem. One could later forget the new grounds also, and simply remember the theorem or indeed find an altogether new proof of it.

Suppose, however, that one's memory of the theorem is very weak and one has no confidence that one has it right. The result might be that one has merely a belief which not only does not constitute knowledge but also is only weakly justified, if justified at all. It will certainly not be justified if one acquires new evidence that clearly counts strongly against it and nothing happens, such as one's getting new information, to neutralize this hostile evidence. Often, however, the new beliefs, justification, and knowledge we acquire through inference may be retained even when their inferential grounds are long forgotten.

*

At any given moment in waking life, we have operative basic sources of belief, if only the stream of our own consciousness. As we experience the world around us and our own interactions with it, new beliefs arise, both from basic sources and inferentially. As rational beings, we are almost constantly forming beliefs on the basis of other beliefs, whether through a process of inference or only through acquiring structurally inferential beliefs: beliefs based on other beliefs but not arising from them by a process of inference. Both deductive and inductive inference are common. Both transmit justification and knowledge when they give rise to beliefs on the basis of inference which meets the appropriate deductive, inductive, and evidential standards.

Among the transmission principles that have emerged as plausible are these two broad ones. First, knowledge and justification are inferentially transmitted only if the underlying argument is good. If we start with false or unjustified premises or we unreasonably infer a conclusion from them (i.e., infer it invalidly or in an inductively inadmissible way), it is not to be expected that a belief we base on the argument in question consitutes knowledge or is even justified. (This does not, of course, prevent it from having an independent sound basis.) Second, at least normally, if the argument *is* good, (1) situational justification is transmitted and (2) belief justification and knowledge are transmitted provided the subject believes the proposition in question (the conclusion of the inference) on the basis of its premises (the underlying ones).

The kinds of transmission described in the second principle seem to occur quite often, and abnormal conditions such as those described in the column of figures case are surely not common. Given a normally retentive memory, we have not only a vast store of direct (non-inferential) knowledge and directly justified belief, but also a huge variety of indirect knowledge and indirectly justified beliefs. False and unwarranted beliefs arise from some inferences. But from many inferences we learn something new; and in making inferences to propositions that we think best explain something we takes ourselves to know already, we sometimes learn truths that are both new and important. Through inference, then, we often enlarge, strengthen, and develop our body of knowledge and justified beliefs.

Notes

1 Two points are appropriate here. (1) I am talking about beliefs *that* (propositional, not objectual, beliefs). (2) It is perhaps misleading to call propositions objects of beliefs, if only because they can express the *content* of beliefs – their primary role here – whether or not believing is a relation to a proposition – an object. It could instead be something like a "contentful" property of persons.

2 One might object that, from my recognition of the backfire, I *must* have inferred, hence reasoned to the conclusion, that someone drove by. Granted, this recognition is a ground of my belief that someone drove by. Still, I need not *do* anything that qualifies as drawing a

conclusion from the recognition. I did not even stop reading to think about the noise, whereas, in the case of the woodpecker, I focused on the question of whether someone was at the door and, when I heard the distinctive rapid knocking, inferred that it was that of a woodpecker.

3 Granted, the notion of a process of inference is not sharp; sometimes we cannot get enough information about how a belief was formed even to make an educated guess about whether or not it arose from an inference.

4 The distinction between episodically and structurally inferential beliefs and the notion of one belief's being based on another are discussed in detail in my 'Belief, Reason, and Inference', in my *The Structure of Justification* (Cambridge and New York: Cambridge University Press, 1993).

5 Bertrand Russell is among a number of philosophers who have at least implicitly denied this: "our knowledge of the physical world is not at first inferential, but that is because we take our percepts [roughly sense-data] to *be* the physical world . . . adults have got used to the idea that what is really there can only be *inferred* from what they see . . . " See *An Outline of Philosophy* (London: Allen & Unwin, 1927), chs. XII–XIII. This is the kind of view criticized by J. L. Austin in *Sense and Sensibilia* (Oxford: Oxford University Press, 1962), esp. ch. X. Austin subjects A. J. Ayer to criticism on similar counts.

6 There is no one way to arrive at a suitable premise, but a typical one would be to count the cats individually up to seventeen, checking to be sure of overlooking none, and thereby believe one has arrived at a total of seventeen cats. There may be ways, however, of passing non-inferentially from counting n things of a kind K to the belief that there are n Ks.

7 I say this appears to be so because it is controversial. The issue will be discussed in Chapter 7.

8 This is a permissive sense of 'valid' and 'entail', because both apply where the premise set is contradictory or the conclusion is a necessary truth (a truth whose falsity is impossible). For it is impossible that a contradiction be true, hence impossible for a contradictory premise set to be true *and* the conclusion false; and this is also impossible if the conclusion is a necessary truth. Usually, we deal with arguments valid in a narrower sense, their premises being both mutually consistent and relevant in subject matter to their conclusion. But nothing said in this book should turn on our using the wider notion of validity.

9 The point here is associated with what is called the *lottery paradox*, introduced into the literature by Henry E. Kyburg Jr and widely discussed. See his *Epistemology and Inference* (Minneapolis: University of Minnesota Press, 1983).

10 Since a sufficient condition implies *all* of the conditions that are minimally necessary, i.e., are *the* (possibly complex) conditions necessary and sufficient for the phenomenon to occur, some have wondered how a sufficient condition can fail to be a necessary one as well. The answer is that it can imply something more that is *not* necessary, as taking a letter to the postbox by car, although sufficient for getting it there, is not necessary for this, since it implies something not necessary for getting it there, namely driving it there.

11 I mean, of course, the non-trivial kind, having consistent premises none of which is equivalent to the conclusion. From inconsistent premises anything may be validly derived. If, for example, we start with a premise consisting of (1) some proposition, p, and its negation, not-p (with a contradiction), we may infer that (2) either p or q, for any proposition q we like (on the ground that if p holds, then *either* it or anything whatever holds). But we may now bring in (3) not-p, which, together with (2), entails q. Our arbitrarily chosen proposition, q, is thus validly derived.

12 On some views, a central feature of knowledge *is* that the belief in question is justified in a way that allows one to rule out, or itself in some way rules out, relevant alternatives. For a valuable discussion of this issue see Alvin I. Goldman, 'Discrimination and Perceptual

Knowledge', *Journal of Philosophy* 73 (1976), 771–91. The issue is addressed, sometimes indirectly, in Chapter 8.

13 This column of figures example has generated considerable discussion in the literature. For detailed critical discussion of my case see Catherine Canary and Douglas Odegard, 'Deductive Justification', *Dialogue* 28 (1989); Richard Feldman, 'In Defense of Closure' *Philosophical Quarterly* 45 (1995); and Peter D. Klein, 'Skepticism and Closure: Why the Evil Demon Argument Fails', *Philosophical Topics* 23, 1 (1995), 213–36. For my replies see 'Justification, Deductive Closure, and Skepticism', *Dialogue* 30 (1991), 77–84; and 'Deductive Closure, Defeasibility, and Skepticism: A Reply to Feldman', *Philosophical Quarterly* 45 (1995), 494–9. (This paper discussed the example construed as appealing to a subjunctive such as 'If she were to say the sum is not *n*, she would be wrong'.) For related treatments of the transmission problem see Fred Dretske, 'Epistemic Operators', *Journal of Philosophy* 67 (1970); Robert Nozick, *Philosophical Explanations* (Cambridge, Mass.: Harvard University Press, 1981), chapter 3; and Gilbert Harman, *Change in View* (Cambridge, Mass.: MIT Press, 1986), esp. chapters 1–4.

14 No precise notion of justified belief fits all the contexts in which we speak of it; but when we speak of it unqualifiedly we usually have in mind a kind and degree such that it is reasonable, overall, for the person to hold the belief. This is perhaps a kind and degree such that, if the proposition in question is true (and there are no special problems of the kind to be considered in Chapter 8), then the belief constitutes knowledge.

CHAPTER 7
The architecture of knowledge

Inferential chains and the structure of belief
Infinite inferential chains
Circular inferential chains

The epistemic regress problem
Infinite epistemic chains
Circular epistemic chains
Epistemic chains terminating in belief not constituting knowledge
Epistemic chains terminating in knowledge

The epistemic regress argument

Foundationalism and coherentism

Holistic coherentism
Patterns of justification
A coherentist response to the regress argument

The nature of coherence
Coherence and explanation
Coherence as an internal relation among cognitions

Coherence, reason, and experience
Coherence and the a priori
Coherence and the mutually explanatory
Epistemological versus conceptual coherentism
Coherence, incoherence, and defeasibility
Positive and negative epistemic dependence

Coherence and second-order justification
The process versus the property of justification
Beliefs, dispositions to believe, and grounds of belief
Justification, knowledge, and artificially created coherence

Moderate foundationalism
The role of coherence in moderate foundationalism
Moderate foundationalism and the charge of dogmatism

The architecture of knowledge

On the mountain in the distance before me, I see the huge oak and tulip trees swaying, with their leaves turned upward revealing the lighter green of their undersides. Waves of green seem to cross the surface of the upper region from west to east as the leaves show the different colors of their inner and outer sides. Parts of the hillside seem almost to breathe in and out as the trees bend away from me and back. It is a familiar sight and I quickly realize that there is a wind. My belief that there is a wind is based on my belief that the trees are swaying. It is also justified on the basis of that belief. And if I know that there is a wind, I know it on the basis of my belief that they are swaying. In each case, one belief is inferentially based on another.

My belief that there is a wind, then, is inferential; I hold it on the basis of a further belief, though I need not go through a process of drawing an inference in order to arrive at it. Surely I also know that there is a wind, and this knowledge is also inferential in the same way. Structurally, my perceptual belief and knowledge that the trees are swaying are *more basic* than my belief and knowledge that there is a wind. To what extent does this relation in which one belief is based on another represent the structure of our belief systems as a whole? The question is especially pertinent to epistemology as it concerns the common cases in which our beliefs constitute knowledge, as they so often seem to. Might perceptual beliefs, for instance, form a foundation on which others are inferentially built? Or are the former just a stopping place on the way to something yet more basic, or perhaps merely a place where we often stop pursuing further premises, though we might go on seeking them and find deeper grounds that support perceptual beliefs?

These questions represent perennial issues, and we shall see many versions of the foundations view – the classical position – and various opposing theories. The questions also take us, as often happens in epistemology, into questions about nature of mind as well as questions directly about justification and knowledge. This is certainly to be expected where the central topic is the structure of knowledge and justification; for knowledge is apparently constituted by belief, and, in epistemology, justification is important chiefly in connection with belief. It is appropriate, then, to begin an exploration of the structure of knowledge and justification with some major points about the structure of a person's body of beliefs.

Inferential chains and the structure of belief

As in discussing inference, it is useful to call the kind of inferential belief, justification, and knowledge just illustrated *indirect*. For one has such beliefs, justification, and knowledge only on the basis of, and thereby *through*, other beliefs, justification, or knowledge. By contrast, my belief that the trees are swaying is direct. I believe this simply because I see it, not on the basis of something else I believe.

Infinite inferential chains

Could *all* my beliefs be indirect? And could all justification of belief, and all our knowledge, be indirect? An adequate epistemology requires answers to these questions about the structure of a body of belief, justification, or knowledge. In exploring them, I want to talk above all about knowledge and justification, and especially about knowledge. But what we know (propositionally) we believe; and the kind of justification epistemology is chiefly concerned with is that of belief. The structure of my knowledge and justification, then, is chiefly that of a certain body of my beliefs.

I am not talking about knowledge in the abstract, as we sometimes do. We talk, for instance about the extent of "human knowledge." Some of this knowledge is solely in books, and not remembered by anyone. Thus, some scientific knowledge might be of propositions no one actually believes, propositions available to us should we need them, but not objects of actual belief. We *can* talk about the structure of such knowledge in the abstract, say about whether all the propositions of scientific knowledge can be systematized by certain basic laws of physics and chemistry, so that these basic laws are like the axioms of geometry and the other laws, like its theorems, are derivable from the basic laws. But that is not my topic. I am exploring how people's beliefs may actually be structured.

I want to start with a simple example. When I am being very cautious, my belief that the trees are swaying could be based on my belief that I have a visual impression of swaying. Could the latter belief also be based on another one? What might that be? Might I now believe that it *seems* to me that I have a visual impression of swaying, and base my belief that I have that impression on this new belief? This is doubtful. I cannot base one belief on another simply because I want to.

This example shows that the view that what we believe, and certain relations between our beliefs, are entirely under the direct control of our wills – a strong version of *voluntarism* – is a mistake. Suppose, for instance, that I want to believe someone's testimony. If it seems false to me, I cannot simply make myself believe it by willing to believe it; and if I already know first-hand that I am gravely ill, I cannot, simply by willing it, also *base* my belief of this on someone's testimony that it is so.[1]

Even if one cannot base one belief on another at will, it might still seem that a sequence of beliefs, each based on the next, could go on without limit. But could I, for instance, believe what seems the next proposition in the evidential series, the involuted proposition that it appears to me that it seems to me that I have a visual impression of swaying? I suppose I could (though not simply at will). Again, I do not see that I would now come to hold anything on the *basis* of believing this strange proposition.

Suppose, however, that I did come to hold, on the basis of this involuted proposition, that it seems to me that I have an impression of swaying. I cannot in this way manufacture an *inferential chain* of beliefs – a chain in which each belief is based on the next – running to infinity. Nor do I already have an infinite set of appropriate beliefs as raw material waiting to be brought to consciousness – if indeed I can have an *infinite* number of beliefs (particularly outside mathematics, where it may seem that I can have an infinite number corresponding to the series 2 is even, 4 is even, 6 is even, etc.).[2]

Circular inferential chains

So far, however, I have ignored another way in which it might be thought to be possible that every belief is indirect: by virtue of lying not at one end of an infinite chain, but instead in a circular chain. Imagine that I could hold one belief on the basis of a second and a second on the basis of a third, and so on, until we come full circle and get to a belief I hold on the basis of the first. Then all my beliefs would be indirect, yet I need not have infinitely many beliefs. To assess this, recall my belief that there is a swaying. Might there be a circle here? For instance, could my belief that it appears to me that it seems to me that I have a visual impression of swaying be based on my belief that there is a swaying? This is far from clearly possible.

Suppose for the sake of argument that I do have a circular chain of beliefs, each based on the next. This raises a problem. First, there is good reason to think that (a) one belief is based on a second only if the second is at least in part causally responsible for (one's holding) the first. For instance, if I believe there is a wind, on the basis of my believing that the trees are swaying, then I believe that there is a wind, at least in part *because* I believe that the trees are swaying. Second, there is good reason to think that (b) if one thing is in part causally responsible for a second and the second is in part causally responsible for a third, then the first is in part causally responsible for the third. But together these two points imply that (c) in a circular chain of beliefs, each based on the next, every belief is in part causally responsible for, and thus a partial cause of, itself. That seems impossible. To see this, let us explore how such a circle might go in a simple case.

Imagine a circle of three beliefs, each based on the next. (1) I believe there is a wind. I believe this on the basis of (2) my believing there is a swaying of the trees; I believe that there is this swaying, on the basis of (3) my believing I have an impression of such swaying; and I believe that I have this impression, on the basis of believing there is a wind. This case would be a *circular causal chain*, one whose last link is connected to its first in the same way that each is connected to its successor. For, given point (a), belief (1) is in part causally responsible for belief (3), and, given point (b), (3) is in part causally responsible for (1). This implies, however, given (b), that (1) is in part causally responsible for itself. That is apparently impossible. The belief would be pulling itself up by its bootstraps.

If circular causal chains of this kind are not possible, then there cannot be a circular chain of beliefs each based on the next; for on the highly plausible assumptions, (a) through (c), this would have to be a circular causal chain. (We have not assumed that the imagined chain implies that some belief must be *based* on itself, only that such chains imply a belief's being in part causally responsible for itself; this basis relation implies more than a causal connection.)

It may seem that a wheel is a model of a circular causal chain of the relevant kind and that something must therefore be wrong with the reasoning just noted. Consider a wheel standing on the ground in a line running east and west, and imagine the wheel having eight equal sections and an axle, each section consisting of a pie-slice segment with its apex at the axle. Does each section not support the next, so that each is "based on" or rests on the others and ultimately (in the eighth link) on itself?

If we distinguish between the relation of *being connected with* and that of *supporting*, the answer no longer seems clear. Granted that if one section is connected to a second, it *will* support the second if a force is applied to the second in the direction of the first. But a wheel can exist in empty space with no such forces acting on it. Mere connectedness between segments does not imply any actual support relations, only a readiness to enter them.

Consider, then, the realistic case in which the wheel is on the ground. Gravity exerts a downward force on the entire wheel. Here, however, the ground supports the entire wheel, and each segment of the wheel that has a segment above it supports that segment, with the two top sections (whose common seam, we may assume, runs from the center of the wheel to its highest point) being the only ones plausibly said to support each other directly. But notice that each of the top sections supports the other *with respect to* a different force. There is a westward force in the case of the western section's support of the eastern one (which would fall backwards to the east if disconnected from its western counterpart because all the seams become unfastened); and there is an eastward force in the case of the eastern section's support of the western one (which would fall backwards to the west if disconnected from its eastern counterpart because all the seams become unfastened). Each top section, then, pulls on the other in the opposite direction, with the result being a balance. In no case do we get a force in one direction that goes fully around the circle with the result that any section supports itself in that same direction. The forces on the two top sections are, as described in physics, equal and opposite.

Returning to the case of belief, here the support in question – the kind of cognitive support given by one belief to a second that is based on it – is also in one direction. It is, in good part, support with respect to three dimensions: conviction, explanation, and memory. Consider this cognitive force in relation to a common case, that of a conclusion belief being based on a belief of a premise for it, such as a point made by a respected friend in favor of the conclusion. My premise belief tends to increase or buttress my conviction in my conclusion belief, to explain (in part) why I hold that belief, and to help me remember my conclusion. This is not the kind of support relation that a belief may be plausibly thought to bear *to itself*.

One might think that a belief of a self-evident proposition can be in part causally responsible for itself and in that way support itself. But this seems at best an inaccurate way of saying that such a proposition is not believed because one believes *something else*. That is normally so; normally, one believes it because one grasps the appropriate conceptual relation(s). In any case, our concern is beliefs in general, not just beliefs of self-evident propositions. On balance, then, it is reasonable to conclude not only that we *have* direct beliefs, such as beliefs about colors before us and beliefs of self-evident propositions, but also that we could not have *only* indirect beliefs.

The epistemic
regress problem

Is knowledge like belief in this, so that some of it is direct, or could all our knowledge be indirect, that is, based on other knowledge we have? It may seem that this is possible, and that there can be an infinite *epistemic regress* – roughly, an infinite series of knowings each based on the next.

It is especially likely to appear that indirect knowledge need not always be based on direct knowledge, if one stresses that, very commonly, 'How do you know?' can be repeatedly answered, and one then supposes that we stop answering only for practical reasons having to do with our patience or ingenuity. Let us explore this issue by assuming for the sake of argument that there is indirect knowledge and seeing what this implies.

Assume that a belief constituting indirect knowledge is based on knowledge of something else, or at least on a further belief. The further knowledge or belief might be based on knowledge of, or belief about, something still further, and so on. Call this sequence an *epistemic chain*. It is simply a chain of beliefs with at least the first constituting knowledge, and each belief linked to the previous one by being based on it.

It is often held that there are just four possible kinds of epistemic chain, two kinds that are unanchored and do not end, and two kinds that are anchored and do end. First, an epistemic chain might be infinite, hence entirely unanchored. Second, it might be circular, hence also unanchored. Third, it might end with a belief that is not knowledge, and thus be anchored in sand. Fourth, it might end with a belief that constitutes direct knowledge, and thus be anchored in bedrock. Our task is to assess these chains as possible sources of knowledge or justification. This is a version of the epistemic regress problem.

Infinite epistemic chains

The first possibility is difficult to appreciate. Even if I could have an infinite number of beliefs, how would I ever know anything if knowledge required an infinite epistemic chain? To know, and thus to *learn*, the simplest kind of thing, such as that there is a green field before me, I would apparently have to know an infinite number of things.

It is doubtful that, given our psychological make-up, we can know, or even believe, infinitely many things. It might seem that we can have an infinite set of arithmetical beliefs, say that 2 is larger than 1, that 3 is larger than 2, and so forth. But surely for a finite mind there will be some point or other at which the relevant proposition cannot be grasped. Imagine the "largest" proposition a supercomputer could formulate after years of work. It could easily be too long to understand and so cumbersome that one could not even take in a formulation of it, being unable to remember enough about the first part of it when one gets to the end. What we cannot understand we cannot believe; and what we cannot believe we cannot know.[3]

Even if we could have infinite sets of beliefs, however, infinite epistemic chains apparently could not account for all, and probably not for any, of our knowledge. In the case of some beliefs, such as the belief that if some dogs are pets, some pets are dogs, I cannot even find *any* belief that yields another link (a belief this one seems to be based on). The proposition is luminously self-evident, and it is difficult even to imagine a further proposition on the basis of which I could believe it if I should think I needed a basis for it. Thus, it is not clear how this belief could be grounded, as knowledge, by any chain, much less by an infinite one.

Indeed, it is far from clear how, in any event, infinite epistemic chains would help to account for any other knowledge (or justified belief). Notice that many kinds of infinite chain are possible. No one has provided a plausible account of what kind might generate justification or knowledge. But some restrictions are badly needed. For any proposition, an infinite chain can be imagined (in outline) that may be claimed to provide support for the proposition. Thus, even for a proposition one believes to be obviously false, one would find it easy to form beliefs to back it up; and though one could not continue doing this to infinity, one could nonetheless claim that one *has* the infinite set required to support the original belief.

Take the obviously false proposition that I weigh at least 500 pounds. I could back up a belief of this by claiming that if I weigh at least 500.1 pounds, then I weigh at least 500 (which is self-evident), and that I *do* weigh at least 500.1 pounds. I could in turn "defend" this by appeal to the propositions that I weigh at least 500.2 pounds, and that if I do, then I weigh at least 500.1. And so forth, until the challenger is exhausted. A chain like this can be infinite; hence, no matter how ridiculous a proposition I claim to know, there is no way to catch me with a claim I cannot back up in the same way. Given such resources, anything goes. But nothing is accomplished.

Circular epistemic chains

The possibility of a circular epistemic chain as a basis of knowledge has been taken much more seriously. It might seem that if there cannot be a circular causal chain of indirect beliefs, each based on the next, then there cannot be a circular epistemic chain either. But perhaps knowledge can be based on premises in a way that differs from the way belief is based on them; perhaps, for instance, my *knowledge* that there is a wind could be somehow based on my belief that the leaves are swaying, even though my *belief* that there is a wind is not based on any further belief. We would then have a circle of knowledge, but not of belief, and no causal bootstraps problem. If this is possible, it may turn out to be important. But how realistic is it?

Does any of our knowledge really emerge from circular epistemic chains? Let us try to go full circle. I know there is a wind. I know this on the basis of the swaying of the trees. Now I think I know they are swaying because I *see* them do so. But it might be argued that my seeing this is only the causal basis of my *belief* that they are swaying, and I just do not notice that it is only on the basis of, say, my knowledge that I have a visual impression of swaying that I *know* they are swaying. Perhaps. But how far can this go?

I do not see how to go full circle, unless I *think up* propositions I do not originally believe, hence do not originally know. If I do not originally have any belief of them, then I (originally) have no *justified* belief or knowledge of the premise they express, and thus no belief appropriate to serve as a link in the epistemic chain or play any supporting role toward my original knowledge.

Suppose, however, that I do think up a suitable set of evidential propositions, come to know them, and make my way full circle. Suppose, for instance, that I get as far as knowledge that it seems to me that I have a visual impression of swaying. Might I know this on the basis of knowing that there is a wind (the first link)? It is doubtful. I apparently know introspectively, not perceptually or inferentially, that I have the impression of swaying. Other difficulties also beset the circular approach. But these problems alone cast sufficient doubt on it to suggest that we consider the remaining options.

Epistemic chains terminating in belief not constituting knowledge

The third possibility for the structure of epistemic chains, that an epistemic chain terminates in a belief which is not knowledge, can be best understood if we recall that in discussing the transmission of knowledge, we noted both source conditions and transmission conditions. If the third possibility can be realized, then knowledge can originate through a belief of a premise that is not known. On the basis of believing that there is a swaying, for example, I might know that there is a wind, even though I do not know that there is a swaying. The regress is thus stopped by grounding knowledge on something else, but not in the *way* it is normally grounded in experience or reason.

Is this possible? In one kind of case it is not. Suppose that (in foggy conditions) I simply guess that what I see is a swaying of trees, but happen to be right. Might I then know there is a wind anyway, provided there is? Surely not; knowledge cannot be grounded in such guesswork, even when the guess is correct.

Imagine, however, that although I do not know there is a swaying, I do hear some sounds that might indicate swaying, and I make an *educated* guess and am thereby justified, to *some* extent, in believing that there is. If, on the basis of this somewhat justified belief that there is a swaying, I now believe that there is a wind, and there is, do I know this?

The answer is not clear. But that would be no help to proponents of the third possibility, who claim that knowledge can arise from belief which does not constitute knowledge. For it is equally unclear, and for the same sort of reason, whether my guess that there is a swaying is *sufficiently* educated – say, in terms of how good my evidence is – to give me (a weak kind of) knowledge that there is a swaying. If it is clear that my guess is *not* sufficiently educated to yield this knowledge, then I also do not know there is a wind. If it is clear that the guess is educated enough, I apparently do know that there is a wind, but my knowledge would be based on other knowledge, hence would not realize the third possibility.

Notice something else. In the only cases in which the third kind of chain is at all likely to ground knowledge, there is a degree – perhaps a substantial degree – of justification. If there can be an epistemic chain which ends with belief that is not knowledge only because the chain ends, in this way, with justification, then it appears that we are at least in the general vicinity of knowledge. We are at most a few degrees of justification away. The sand has turned out to be rather firm; it is at least close to being firm enough to support knowledge.

Epistemic chains terminating in knowledge

The fourth possibility is the one apparently favored by common sense: epistemic chains end in direct knowledge – in the sense that they have direct knowledge as their last link. That knowledge, in turn, is apparently grounded (anchored, if you like) in experience or in reason, and this non-inferential grounding explains how it is (epistemically) direct: it arises, directly, from perception, memory, introspection, or reason (or indeed from testimony, provided this has an appropriate grounding in at least one of the first four). The ground-level knowledge could not be inferential; otherwise the chain would not end without a further link. To illustrate, normally I know that there is a swaying just because I see it. Hence, the chain grounding my knowledge that there is a wind is anchored in my perception.

Such experientially or rationally grounded epistemic chains may differ in many ways. They differ in composition, in the sorts of beliefs constituting them. They differ in the kind of transmission they exhibit; it may be deductive, inductive, or combine both deductive and inductive links. Epistemic chains also differ in their ultimate grounds, the anchors of the chains, which may be experiential or rational; and epistemic chains may vary in justificational strength, the degree of justification they give to the initial belief.

Different proponents of the fourth possibility have held various views about the character of the *foundational knowledge*, that is, of the beliefs constituting the knowledge that makes up the final link of the epistemic chain that is anchored in experience or reason. Some philosophers, for instance, have thought that the appropriate beliefs must be infallible, or at least indefeasibly justified. But this is not implied by anything said here. All that the fourth possibility requires is direct knowledge, knowledge not based on other knowledge (or other justified belief).

Direct knowledge need not be of self-evident propositions, or constituted by indefeasibly justified belief. The case of introspective beliefs shows this. The proposition that I am now thinking about knowledge is not self-evident; to most people it is not evident at all. It is not even self-evident to *me*: first, it is evident to me, not in itself, as is the proposition that if some dogs are pets then some pets are dogs, but on the basis of my conscious experience; second, since I realize that my reflections can sometimes merge into daydreaming, I do not even consider it rock-solidly true in the way I do self-evident propositions. But surely I do have direct knowledge of the proposition.

The epistemic
regress argument

What we have just seen suggests a version of the *epistemic regress argument*. It starts with the assumption that

(1) if one has any knowledge, it occurs in an epistemic chain.

Epistemic chains are understood to include the special case of a single link, such as a perceptual or a priori belief, which constitutes knowledge by virtue of being anchored directly (non-inferentially) in one's experience or reason).[4]
The argument then states that

(2) the only possible kinds of epistemic chain are the four
mutually exclusive kinds just discussed: the infinite, the
circular, those terminating in beliefs that are not knowledge,
and those terminating in direct knowledge.

Its third, also restrictive premise is that

(3) knowledge can occur only in the fourth kind of chain.

And the argument concludes that

(4) if one has any knowledge, one has some direct knowledge.[5]

A similar argument was advanced by Aristotle, and versions of this regress argument have been defended ever since.[6]
As proponents of the argument normally understand (1), it implies that any given instance of indirect knowledge depends on at least one epistemic chain for its status *as* knowledge. So understood, the argument clearly implies the further conclusion that any indirect knowledge a person has *epistemically depends on*, in the sense that it cannot be knowledge apart from, an appropriate inferential connection, via some epistemic chain, to some direct knowledge that the person has.
Given this dependence assumption, the regress argument would show not only that if there is indirect knowledge, there is direct knowledge, but also that

if there is indirect knowledge, that very knowledge is *traceable* to some direct knowledge as its foundation. One could trace an item of indirect knowledge to some premise for it, and, if there is a premise for that, to the next premise, and so on until the chain is anchored in a basic source of knowledge.

A similar argument applies to justification. We simply speak of *justificatory chains* and proceed in a parallel way, substituting justification for knowledge; and we arrive at the conclusion that if one has any justified beliefs, one has some directly justified beliefs. Similarly, if one has any indirectly justified belief, it exhibits *justificational dependence* on an epistemic chain appropriately linking it to some directly justified belief one has, that is, to a foundational belief.

Foundationalism and coherentism

These two sets of conclusions constitute the heart of the position called *epistemological foundationalism*. The first set, concerning knowledge, may be interpreted as the thesis that the structure of a body of knowledge, such as yours or mine, is foundational, and therefore that any indirect (hence non-foundational) knowledge there is depends on direct (and thus in a sense foundational) knowledge. The second set, regarding justification, may be interpreted as the thesis that the structure of a body of justified beliefs is foundational, and therefore that any indirectly (hence non-foundationally) justified beliefs there are depend on directly (thus in a sense foundationally) justified beliefs.

In both cases, different foundationalist theories may diverge in the kind and degree of dependence they assert. A strong foundationalist theory of justification might hold that indirectly justified beliefs derive *all* their justification from foundational beliefs; a moderate theory might maintain only that the former would not be justified apart from the latter, and the theory might grant that other factors, such as coherence of a belief with others one holds that are *not* in the chain can add to its justification.

None of the foundationalist theses I have stated says anything about the *content* of a body of knowledge or of justified belief, though proponents of foundationalism usually specify, as René Descartes does in his *Meditations on First Philosophy* (first published in 1641), what sorts of content they think appropriate. Foundationalism thus leaves open what, in particular, is believed by a given person who has knowledge or justified belief and what *sorts* of propositions are suitable material for the foundational beliefs. I want to talk mainly about foundationalism regarding knowledge, but much of what I say can be readily applied to justified belief.

Foundationalism has been criticized on a number of points. Let us focus in particular on the most important objections that stem from the best alternative theory of the structure of knowledge, *coherentism*. There are many versions of coherentism, including some that seem to be based mainly on the idea that if an epistemic circle is large enough and sufficiently rich, it can generate justification and account for knowledge. But we have seen serious difficulties besetting circular chains. I therefore want to formulate a more plausible version of coherentism.

The central idea underlying coherentism is that the justification (justifiedness) of a belief depends on its coherence with other beliefs one holds. The *unit of coherence* – roughly, the scope of the beliefs that must cohere in order for a belief among them to derive justification from their coherence – may be as large as one's entire set of beliefs (though of course some may figure more significantly in producing the coherence than others, say because of differing degrees of closeness to one another in their subject matter).

The variability of the unit of coherence would be accepted by a proponent of the circular view, but the thesis I want to explore differs from that view in not being *linear*: it does not construe justification or knowledge as emerging from an inferential line going from premises to that conclusion, and from other premises to the first set of premises, and so on, until we return to the original proposition as a premise.

In the circular coherentist view, no matter how wide the circle, there is a *line* from any one belief in a circular epistemic chain to any other. In practice one may never trace the entire line, as by inferring one thing one knows from a second, the second from a third, and so on, until one re-infers the first. Still, on this view, there is such a line for every belief that constitutes knowledge. Thus, the kinds of problems we encountered earlier regarding circular epistemic chains must be resolved (as I doubt they can be) if the view is to be sustained.

Holistic coherentism

Coherentism need not be linear. It may be holistic. To see how a holistic theory of knowledge (and justification) works, consider a question that evokes a justification. John wonders how I know, as I sit reading, that the wind is blowing. I say that the leaves are swaying. He then asks how I know that Sally is not just making this noise by walking in the high grass. I reply that the high grass is too far away. He now wonders whether I can distinguish swaying leaves from the sound of a quiet car on the pebbled driveway. I reply that what I hear is too much like a whisper to be the crunchy sound of pebbles under tires.

Patterns of justification

In giving this kind of justification, I apparently go only one step along the inferential line: just to my belief that the leaves are swaying. For my belief that there is a wind is based on this belief about the leaves. After that, I do not even mention anything that this belief, in turn, is based on. Rather, I defend my beliefs as appropriate, in terms of an entire pattern of mutually cohering beliefs I hold. And I may cite many different parts of the pattern. For instance, I might have said that walking through high grass sounds different from windblown leaves. On the coherentist view, then, beliefs representing knowledge do not lie at one end of a grounded chain; they fit a coherent pattern, and their justification emerges from their fitting that pattern in an appropriate way.

Consider a different sort of example. A gift is delivered to you with its card apparently missing. The only people you can think of who send you gifts at this time of year live in Washington and virtually never leave, but this is from Omaha. That origin does not cohere well with your hypothesis that it was sent by your Washington benefactors, the Smiths. Then you open it and discover that it is frozen steak. You realize that this can be ordered from anywhere. But it is not the sort of gift you would expect from the Smiths. A moment later you recall that you recently sent them cheese. You suppose that they are probably sending something in response. Suddenly you remember that they once asked if you had ever tried frozen gourmet steaks, and when you said you had not they replied that they would have to serve you some one of these days.

You now have a quite coherent pattern of beliefs and might be justified in believing that it was they who sent the package. If you come to believe this on the basis of the pattern, you presumably have a justified belief. When you at last find their card at the bottom of the box, then (normally) you would *know* that they sent the package.

The crucial things to notice in this example are how, initially, a kind of *incoherence* with your standing beliefs prevents your justifiedly believing your first hypothesis (that the box came from the Smiths) and how, as relevant pieces of the pattern developed, you became justified in believing, and (presumably) came to know, that the Smiths sent it. Arriving at a justified belief, on this view, is more like answering a question in the light of a whole battery of relevant information than like deducing a theorem by successive inferential steps from a set of luminous axioms.

A coherentist response to the regress argument

It is important to see how, using examples like those just given, holistic coherentism can respond to the regress argument. It need *not* embrace the possibility of an epistemic circle (though its proponents need not reject that either). Instead, it can deny that there are only the four kinds of possible epistemic chains so far specified. There is a fifth: one terminating with belief that is *psychologically direct*, yet *epistemically indirect* (or, if we are talking of coherentism about justification, *justificationally indirect*). The idea is that terminal belief is not psychologically based on any other, as where it is inferentially grounded on another, yet its justification *is* based on other beliefs. Hence, the last link is, as belief, direct, yet, as knowledge, indirect, not in the usual sense that it is inferential but in the broad sense that the belief constitutes knowledge only by virtue of receiving support from other knowledge or belief. This belief is psychologically foundational but epistemically dependent on a pattern of supporting beliefs.

To illustrate all this, consider again my belief that there is a swaying of the trees. It is psychologically direct because it is simply grounded, causally, in my vision and is not inferentially based on any other belief. Yet (the coherentist might argue) my *knowledge* that there is such a movement is not epistemically direct. It is epistemically, but not inferentially, based on the coherence of my belief that there is a swaying with my other beliefs, presumably including many that represent knowledge themselves. It is thus knowledge *through*, but not by inference from, other knowledge – or at least not through justified beliefs. The knowledge is therefore epistemically indirect. Hence, it is at best misleading to call the *knowledge*, as opposed to the belief expressing it, direct at all.

This coherentist view grants, then, that the belief element *in* my knowledge is non-inferentially grounded in perception and is in that sense direct. But this is just a kind of psychological directness: there is no belief through which I hold the one in question in the way that I hold a conclusion belief on the basis of premise beliefs. But there are beliefs through which the belief constitutes knowledge: those with which it coheres even though it is not based on them. The basis relation between beliefs and the counterpart premise–conclusion relation between propositions are simply not the only producers of coherence.

One could insist that if a non-inferential, thus psychologically direct, belief constitutes knowledge, this *must* be direct knowledge. But the coherentist would reply that in that case there will be two kinds of direct knowledge: the kind the foundationalist posits, which derives from grounding in a basic experiential or rational source, say perception or reflection, and the kind the coherentist posits, which derives from coherence with other beliefs and not from being based on those sources. Why not classify the directness of knowledge in terms of what it *evidentially* depends on and the directness of belief in terms of what it *psychologically* depends on? This is surely a plausible response.

Is the holistic coherentist trying to have it both ways? Not necessarily. Holistic coherentism can grant that a variant of the regress argument holds for belief, since the only kind of belief chain that it is psychologically realistic to attribute to us is the kind terminating in direct (non-inferential) belief. But even on the assumption that knowledge is constituted by (certain kinds of) beliefs, it does not follow that direct belief which is knowledge is also direct *knowledge*.

Thus, the coherentist is granting *psychological foundationalism*, which says (in part) that if we have any beliefs at all, we have some direct ones, yet denying epistemological foundationalism, which says that, assuming there is any knowledge at all, there is knowledge which is epistemically (and normally also psychologically) direct. Holistic coherentism may grant experience and reason the status of psychological foundations of our entire structure of beliefs. But it gives them no place, independently of coherence, in generating justification or knowledge.[7]

The nature of
coherence

If holistic coherentism is interpreted as I have described it, it avoids some of the major problems for linear coherentism. But there remain serious difficulties for it. First, what is coherence? Second, what reason is there to think that coherence *alone* counts toward the justification of a belief, or toward its truth, as it must in some way if it is to give us the basis of a good account of knowledge?

It turns out to be very difficult to explain what coherence is. It is not mere mutual consistency, though inconsistency is the clearest case of *in*coherence. Two propositions having nothing to do with each other, say that $7 + 5 = 12$ and that carrots are nourishing, are mutually consistent but do not exhibit coherence.

Coherence and explanation

Coherence is sometimes connected with *explanation*. Certainly, if the Smiths' sending the package explains why the card bears their names, then my belief of the first proposition coheres with my belief of the second (other things being equal). What explains something makes it understandable; and making understandable is a coherence-generating relation between propositions (as well as between other kinds of things).

Probability is also relevant to coherence. If the probability of the proposition that the Smiths sent the steaks is raised in the light of the proposition that I sent them cheese, this at least counts in favor of my belief of the first cohering with my belief of the second. But how are we to understand the notions of explanation and of probability? Let us consider these questions in turn.

Does one proposition (genuinely) explain another so long as, if the first is (or is assumed to be) true, then it is clear why the second is true? Apparently not; for if that were so, then the proposition that a benevolent genie delivered the box explains why it arrived. In any event, if that proposition did explain why the box arrived, would I be justified in believing it because my believing it coheres with my believing that I know not what other source the box might have come from? Surely not.

Even if we can say what notion of explanation is relevant to understanding coherence, it will remain very difficult to specify when an explanatory relation generates *enough* coherence to create justification. For one thing, consider cases in which a proposition, say that Jill hurt Jack's feelings, would, if true, very adequately explain something we believe, such as that Jack is upset. Believing Jill did this might cohere well with his being upset, but that would not, by itself, justify our believing it. There are too many possible competing explanations we might just as well accept.

Similar points hold for probability. Not just any proposition I believe which raises the probability of my hypothesis that the gift is from the Smiths will strengthen my justification for believing that it is. Consider, for example, the proposition that the Smiths send such gifts to all their friends. Suppose I have no justification for believing this, say because I have accepted it only on the basis of testimony which I should see to be unreliable. Then, although the proposition raises the probability of my hypothesis (since I am among their friends) and (let us assume) coheres with what I already believe, I am not entitled to believe it, and my believing it will not add to my justification for believing that the Smiths sent the box.

It might be replied that this belief about the Smiths' habits does not cohere well with *other* things I believe, such as that people do not generally behave like that. But suppose I believed nothing about the Smiths' or other people's habits of gift-giving that conflicts with the Smiths' being so generous, and I happened, without grounds, to believe the Smiths to be both generous and rich. Then there might be a significant degree of coherence between my belief that the Smiths send gifts to all their friends and my other beliefs; yet my forming the belief that they give gifts to all their friends still would not strengthen my justification for my hypothesis that the steak is from them.

Coherence as an internal relation among cognitions

These examples suggest the second problem. So far as we do understand coherence, what reason is there to think that by itself it generates any justification or truth at all? Whatever coherence among beliefs is, it is an *internal* relation, in the sense that whether it holds among beliefs is a matter of how those beliefs (including their propositional content, which is intrinsic to them) are related *to one another* and not to anything outside one's system of beliefs, such as one's perceptual experience. Now why could there not be a vast number of equally coherent systems of beliefs that are mutually incompatible, so that no two of them can be entirely true? If there can be, what enables my having one of these coherent systems to provide any reason to think my beliefs are justified or represent knowledge, rather than those of someone with one of the "opposing" systems?

This is part of what might be called the *isolation problem*: the problem of explaining why coherent systems of beliefs are not readily isolated from truth, and thus do not contain knowledge, which implies truth. There is also a problem of explaining why there is not a similar isolation from justification, which seems in some way to point toward truth. Why should coherence by itself imply that any of the cohering beliefs is justified or constitutes knowledge, when both justification and knowledge point toward truth as something external to the belief system? It is not as though coherentists could count on the implication's being guaranteed by God; and nothing else seems to assure us of it.

Consider a schizophrenic who thinks he is Napoleon. If he has a completely consistent story with enough interlocking details, his belief system may be superbly coherent. He may even be able to explain quite coherently why there are coherent belief systems that conflict with his, such as those of his psychiatrists. If coherence alone generates justification, however, we must say that each system is equally well justified – assuming their belief systems are *as* coherent as his. We need not attribute knowledge to any of the systems, since any of them might contain falsehood.

But is it plausible to say that a system of beliefs is highly justified even when there is no limit to the number of radically different yet equally justified belief systems – even on the part of other people with experience of or pertaining to many of the same things the beliefs are about – that are incompatible with it in this thoroughgoing way? The question is especially striking when we realize that two equally coherent systems, even on the part of the same person at different times, might differ not just on one point but on *every* point: each belief in one might be opposed by an incompatible belief in the other.

To appreciate the significance of the possibility of multiple coherent systems of belief that are mutually incompatible, recall the plausible assumption that a well-justified belief may reasonably be considered *true*. If, however, the degree of justification of a belief is entirely a matter of its support by considerations of coherence, no degree of justification by itself can carry any greater presumption of truth than is created by the same degree of support from coherence on the part of a belief of the contradictory proposition. Thus, if "Napoleon" (unlike his historical namesake) has a sufficiently coherent set of beliefs yielding justification of his belief that he fought in and won the Battle of Waterloo, this belief may be as well-justified as his psychiatrists' belief that he never fought it.

If this coherentist picture of justification is correct, is there any reason to suppose that a belief justified solely by considerations of coherence is true? And if Napoleon's and the psychiatrists' belief systems are equally coherent, how can we justify our apparently quite reasonable tendency to regard their belief systems as more likely to represent truths, and on that count more likely to contain knowledge, than his?

Granted, the psychiatrists' belief that he never fought the battle coheres with our beliefs. But why should our own beliefs be privileged over equally coherent conflicting sets? And why should agreement even with nearly every-one's beliefs, say about Napoleon's being dead, be a factor, unless we assume that some element other than coherence, such as perception or memory, confers justification without drawing on coherence? If coherence is the only source of justification, it is not clear how perception or memory or introspection contributes to justification. Moreover, even what seems the highest degree of justification, such as we have for simple introspective beliefs and beliefs of self-evident truths, provides us no presumption of truth or knowledge.

Coherence, reason, and experience

This brings us to a third major problem for coherentism: how can it explain the role of experience and reason as sources of justification and knowledge? Certainly experience and reason *seem* to be basic sources of justification and knowledge. Coherentists themselves commonly *use* beliefs from these sources to illustrate coherent bodies of beliefs that are good candidates for knowledge. How can holistic coherentism explain the role of these sources in relation to justification and knowledge?

Why is it, for instance, that when I have a vivid experience of the kind characteristic of seeing a green field, I am apparently justified (though prima facie rather than indefeasibly justified), simply by that experience, in believing that there is a green field before me? And why do I seem so very strongly justified, simply on the basis of my rational grasp of the proposition that if some dogs are pets then some pets are dogs, in believing this?

One thing a coherentist might say here is that in fact many of our beliefs are *causally* and non-inferentially based on perception or on the use of reason; and given these similarities of origin, it is to be expected that they often cohere with one another. Hence, although we do not, and do not need to, infer propositions like those just cited from any others that might provide justifying evidence for them, they *do* cohere with many other things we believe, and this coherence is what justifies them.

Coherence and the a priori

This response by way of associating the coherence of beliefs with their causal basis is more plausible for perceptual beliefs than for beliefs of simple a priori truths, at least if coherence is construed as more than consistency and as related to explanation, probability, and justification. For notice that, unlike the proposition that there is a green field before me, the proposition that if some dogs are pets, then some pets are dogs apparently need not explain, render probable, or justify anything else I believe; nor is it obvious that anything else I believe need explain, render probable, or justify my believing this proposition. Where is the need for coherence as a requirement for my justification? I may *have* other beliefs that cohere with this one, but my justification for it does not seem to *derive* from them. Yet my belief of this proposition is justified to about as high a degree as is any belief I have.

By contrast, the proposition that there is a green field before me perhaps does cohere, in a way that might serve coherentism, with other things I believe: that there is grass there, that I am on my front porch, and so on; and there appear to be some explanatory and probability relations among these propositions. For instance, the proposition that there is a green field before me adds to the probability that I am on my porch; and that I am on that porch partly explains why I see a green field.

A coherentist might respond to the difference just indicated by qualifying the coherence view, applying it only to beliefs of empirical, rather than a priori, propositions.[8] This move could be defended on the assumption that propositions known a priori are necessary and hence are not appropriately said to be made *probable* by other propositions, or to be explained by them in the same way empirical propositions are explained. In support of this it might be argued that although we can explain the *basis* of a necessary truth and thereby show *that* it holds, still, since it cannot fail to hold, there is no explaining *why* it, *as opposed to something else*, holds.

This is plausible but inconclusive reasoning. We may just as reasonably say that we can sometimes explain why a necessary truth holds and in doing so explain why a contrasting proposition is false. Imagine that someone mistakenly takes a certain false logical proposition to be a theorem and cannot see why a closely similar, true principle is a theorem. If we now prove the correct one step by step, with accompanying examples, we might thereby explain why this theorem, as opposed to the other proposition, is true.

So far as explanation is central to coherence, then, coherentism apparently owes us an account of knowledge of at least some necessary truths. But suppose that it can account for knowledge of *some* necessary truths. There remain others, such as simple, luminously self-evident ones, for which we cannot find anything plausibly said to explain why they hold, or at least no other way of accounting for knowledge of them as grounded in coherence. Consider how one might explain why, if it is true that Jane Austen wrote *Persuasion*, then it is not false that she did. If someone did not see this, it would probably not help to point out that no proposition is both true and false. For if one needs to have the truth of such a clear and simple instance of this general truth explained, one presumably cannot understand the general truth either. But suppose this is not so, and that one's grasp of the general truth is somehow the basis of one's seeing the particular truth that instantiates it. Then the same point would apply to the general truth: there would apparently be nothing plausibly said to explain why *it* is true.

Coherence and the mutually explanatory

It might now be objected that the general truth that no proposition is both true and false, and the instances of it, are *mutually explanatory*: its truth explains why they hold, and their truth explains why it holds; and this is the chief basis of their coherence with one another. But is it really possible for one proposition to explain another *and* the other to explain it? If what explains why the grass is wet is that there is dew on it, then the same proposition – that there is dew on it – is not explained by the proposition that the grass is wet (instead, condensation explains that).

Reflection on other purported examples of mutual explanation also suggests that two propositions cannot explain each other. It might seem that a man could say something because his wife did, and that she could say it because he did. But notice how this has to go to make good sense. One of them would have to say it first to cause the other to; but then we would have a case in which something like this occurs: her saying it explains why he says it, later (this could be so even if her saying it is explained by her believing he *thinks* it). His saying it earlier than she does might still explain her saying it. But then the fact that he says it at a given time does not both explain and get explained by her saying it at some particular time. When we carefully specify what explains something, we seem to find that the latter, carefully specified, does not explain the former. In the case where she says something because he did, earlier, and he says it because she did, earlier than he did, we would have a kind of *reciprocal* explanation but not a *mutual* explanation of the kind in question. The first may look like the second, but it is a different thing.[9]

Perhaps mutual explanation of the kind the coherentist needs – as opposed to reciprocal explanation and other kinds involving two-way relations – is somehow possible. But until a good argument for it is given, we should conclude that even if an explanatory relation between propositions is sufficient for a belief of one of the propositions to cohere with a belief of the other, coherentism does not in general provide a good account of knowledge of self-evident truths.

If coherentism applies only to empirical beliefs, however, and not to beliefs of a priori propositions, then it is not a *general* theory of justification or knowledge and leaves us in need of a different account of a priori justification (and knowledge). In any case, it would be premature to conclude that coherentism does account for empirical justification. Let us return to the perceptual case.

Epistemological versus conceptual coherentism

It might seem that we could decisively refute the coherence theory of justification by noting that one might have only a single belief, say that there is a green field before one, and that this lone belief might still be justified. For there would be a justified belief that coheres with no other beliefs one has. But could one have just a single belief? Could one, for instance, believe that there is a green field before one, yet not believe, say, that it has any vegetation? It is not clear that one could; and foundationalism does not assume this possibility, though the theory may easily be wrongly criticized for implying it.

Foundationalism is in fact consistent with *one* kind of coherentism, namely, a coherence theory of the acquisition and function of concepts – for short, the *coherence theory of concepts*. According to this theory, concepts are what they are partly in relation to one another, and a person acquires concepts, say of (physical) objects and shapes, and of music and sounds, only in relation to one another and must acquire an entire set of related concepts in order to acquire any concept. The concept of an object in some way includes that of shape (if only the notion of something bounded), as that of music includes the concept of sound. This may be why any object must have some shape or other, and why anything that makes music produces some sound. One cannot (fully) acquire object concepts without acquiring some shape concepts, or (fully) acquire the concept of music without acquiring that of sound.

If the coherence theory of concepts is sound, foundationalists must explain how it squares with their epistemology. The central point they may appeal to is a distinction between *grounding conditions* for belief and *possession conditions* for it. What grounds a belief in such a way as to justify it or render it an item of knowledge is largely independent of *what* other beliefs one must have, and what concepts one must have, to be able to *hold* the first belief. Perhaps I cannot believe that music is playing if I do not have a concept of sound; I may even have to believe sounds with a certain structure to be occurring. And perhaps I could not have acquired these and other relevant concepts one at a time. Indeed, it may be (as suggested in Chapter 5) that at least normally we cannot acquire concepts without acquiring some knowledge or justified belief. Still, what it is that justifies a belief can be a matter of how it is grounded; it need not be a matter of the coherence conditions required for *having* the belief.

If, however, coherence relations are essential for holding a belief at all, they are on that ground necessary for, and – in ways that will soon be apparent – important in understanding, the belief's being justified. The point here is simply that we cannot treat conditions for having a belief at all as doing the more specific job of grounding its justification – by and large beliefs can be possessed without being justified at all, and there is commonly a good distance between meeting the conditions for simply having beliefs and meeting the standards for justification in holding them.

Coherence, incoherence, and defeasibility

We must directly ask, then, whether my justification for believing that there is a green field out there *derives* from the coherence of the belief with others. Let us first grant an important point by focusing on a line of reasoning that seems to lead many philosophers to think it does derive from coherence. Suppose this visual belief turns out to be incoherent with a second belief, such as that one is standing where one seems to see the field around one yet *feels* no grass on the smooth ground beneath one's feet and can walk right across the area without feeling any. Then the first belief may *cease* to be justified. Incoherence, then, defeats my justification.

This defeating role of incoherence is important, but it shows only that my justification is *defeasible* – liable to being outweighed (overridden) or undermined – should sufficiently serious incoherence arise. It does not show that justification is produced by coherence in the first place, any more than a wooden cabin's being destroyed by fire shows that it was produced by the absence of fire. In the case in which I feel no grass beneath my feet, the justification of my visually grounded belief is outweighed: my better justified beliefs, including the conviction that a field must have a certain texture, make it more reasonable for me to believe that there is *not* a field here.

A major lesson that emerges here is that we cannot tell what the basis of something is simply from the range of things that outweigh it, much less conclude that this basis is the absence of the things that destroy it. Incoherence is absent where there are mutually irrelevant beliefs as well as where there are mutually coherent ones. Mutual irrelevance between beliefs certainly does not make one a justificational or epistemic basis for the other.

Two important questions arise here. First, could incoherence outweigh justification of a belief in the first place if we were not *independently* justified in believing something to the effect that a proposition incoherent with certain other ones is, or probably is, false? Second, are the other relevant propositions not precisely the kind for which, directly or inferentially, we have some degree of justification through the basic experiential and rational sources? Foundationalists are likely to answer the first negatively and the second affirmatively.

There is also a second case, in which one's justification is simply *undermined*: one ceases to be justified in believing the proposition in question, though one does not become justified in believing it false, as one does where counter-evidence demands a belief contrary to the initial one. Suppose I cease to see a bird on a branch when, without obscuring my line of sight to the bird, I move six feet to my left. This could justify my believing that I might be hallucinating. This belief is incoherent with, and thereby undermines the justification of, my visual belief that the bird is there, though it does not by itself justify my believing that there is *no* bird there. Again, however, I am apparently justified, independently of coherence, in believing that my seeing the bird there is incoherent with my merely hallucinating it there. It seems, then, that coherence has the role it does in justification only because *some* beliefs are justified independently of it.

Positive and negative epistemic dependence

Examples like these show that it is essential to distinguish *negative epistemic dependence* – which is simply a form of defeasibility – from *positive epistemic dependence* – the kind beliefs bear to the sources from which they *derive* any justification they have or, if they represent knowledge, derive their status as knowledge. The defeasibility of a belief's justification by incoherence does not imply, as coherentists have commonly held, that this justification positively depends on coherence. If my well is my source of water, I (positively) depend on it. The possibility that people could poison it does not make their non-malevolence part of my source of water, or imply a (positive) dependence on them, such as I have on the rainfall. Moreover, it is the rainfall that explains both my having the water and its level.

So it is with perceptual experience as a source of justification. Foundationalists need not claim that justification does not depend negatively on anything else, for as we have seen they need not claim that justification must be indefeasible. Its vulnerability to defeat can be construed as a kind of dependence. A belief's justification is, then, not *completely* independent of the justification of other beliefs, actual or hypothetical. But negative dependence does not imply positive dependence. Justification can be defeasible by incoherence, and thus outweighed or undermined should incoherence arise, without owing its existence to coherence in the first place.

Coherence and second-order justification

There is something further that should be granted to the coherentist, and in assessing it we can learn more about both coherentism and justification. *If* one should set out to *show* that one's belief is justified, one *would* have to cite propositions that cohere with the one in question, say the proposition that there is a green field before me. In some cases, these are not even propositions one already believes. Often, in defending the original belief, one forms new beliefs, such as the belief one acquires, in moving one's head, that one can vividly see the changes in perspective that go with seeing a physical object.

The process versus the property of justification

More importantly, these new, back-up beliefs are especially appropriate to the *process of justifying* one's belief; and the result of that process is (a kind of) *showing* that the original belief is justified, together (in typical cases) with one's forming the *second-order belief* – a belief about a belief (such as a perceptual one) which is not about any other belief – to the effect that this second belief is justified. Thus, coherence is important in showing that a belief is justified and is in *that* sense an element in a typical kind of process of justification.

The moment we reflect on this point, however, we may wonder why the beliefs appropriate to showing that a belief is justified have to be involved in its being justified in the first place. There is no good reason to think they need be. Indeed, why should one's simply having a justified belief imply even that one is (situationally) justified in holding beliefs appropriate to showing that it is justified? It would seem that just as one can be virtuous even if one does not know how to defend one's good character against attack or even show that one has good character, one can have a justified belief even if, in response to someone who doubts that one has it, one could not show that one does.

Justifying a second-order belief is a sophisticated process. The process is particularly sophisticated if the second-order belief concerns a special property like the justification of the original belief. Simply being justified in a belief about the color of an object is a much simpler matter.

Confusion is easy here because of the way we often speak of justification. Consider the question of how a simple perceptual belief "is justified." The very phrase is ambiguous. For all it tells us, the question could be 'By what process, say of reasoning, has the belief been (or might it be) justified?' or, on the other hand, 'In virtue of what is the belief justified (possessed of the property of justifiedness)?' These are two very different questions. But much of our talk about justification makes it easy to run them together. A belief said to be "justified" could be one that *has* justification or one that *has been* justified; and asking for someone's justification could be either a request for a list of justifying factors or an invitation to recount the process by which the person has in fact justified the belief.

Does coherentism have any plausible argument, not grounded in the mistakes just pointed out, for the (positive) dependence of perceptual justification on coherence? I do not see that it does, though given how hard it is to discern what precisely coherence is, we cannot be confident that no direct argument is forthcoming.

Granted, one could point to the oddity of saying things like, 'I am justified in believing that there is a green field before me, but I cannot justify the belief'. One might think this is odd because, if I have a justified belief, I can surely give a justification for it by appeal to beliefs that cohere with it. But look closely. Typically, in asserting something, I suggest that I *can* justify it in some way or other (particularly if the belief I express is not grounded in a basic source); yet here I deny that very suggestion. It seems, then, that it is apparently my *asserting* that my belief is justified, rather than its being so, that gives the appearance that I must be able to give a justification to the belief. I have not, or not merely, *expressed* a first-order justified belief, something a tiny child of three can do; I have *ascribed* first-order justification to my belief.

Beliefs, dispositions to believe, and grounds of belief

To be sure, when I say that there is a green field before me, I can give a justification: for instance, that I see it. But *before* the question of justification arises I need not *believe* that I see it. That question leads me to focus on my circumstances, in which I first had a belief solely about the *field*. I did also have a *disposition*, based on my visual experience, to form the belief that I *see* the field, and this is largely why, in the course of justifying that belief, I then form the further belief that I *do* see it. But a *disposition to believe* something does not imply one's already having a *dispositional belief* of it: here I tend to form the belief that I see the field if, as I view it, the question whether I see it arises; yet I need not have subliminally believed this already.

Thus, the justification I offer for my belief that there is a green field before me is not by appeal to coherence with other beliefs I already hold – such as that I saw the field and heard the swishing grass beneath my feet – but by reference to a basic source, perceptual experience. It is thus precisely the kind of justification that foundationalists are likely to consider appropriate for a non-inferential belief. Indeed, one consideration favoring foundationalism about both justification and knowledge, at least as an account of our justificational practices in everyday life (including much scientific practice) is that typically we cease offering justification or defending a knowledge claim precisely when we reach one or more of the basic sources.[10]

Suppose, however, that I would be dumbfounded if asked, in clear daylight, what justifies me in believing there is a green field before me. Would it follow that I am not justified? No, for I might be simply unable to marshal my quite ample justificatory resources. Coherentism offers no good argument to show that being justified requires being able to show that one is, any more than having good character entails being able to show that one has it.

Justification, knowledge, and artificially created coherence

There is one further point to be made here. If coherentism regards justification as deriving from coherence alone, then it accords *no* justificatory weight to experiential or rational grounding except insofar as they contribute to coherence. Our reflections about examples cast much doubt on this view.

Consider a related implication of coherentism: if I want to have the best-justified body of beliefs possible – which is surely a rational goal – then I am free to consider adopting, or somehow manipulating my brain to cause myself to form, an entirely new system of beliefs even if it contains few of the experiential and a priori beliefs I now have and perhaps eventually contains none of them at all. It might even run counter to my experience. If I see a square field of green grass before me, I might quite coherently believe that there is an oval field of brown shrubbery there, since my other beliefs might support this. I could, for instance, coherently believe that when I seem to see green grass I am having a hallucination caused by brown shrubbery. There is no limit to the number and kinds of beliefs for which one might be able thus to rationalize away the experiential information that it is natural to call the *evidence of the senses*.

We are apparently incapable of changing our belief systems in this way, but suppose that we could do so by properly setting a neurological machine to instill an optimally coherent set of beliefs and remove the rest. Would that be rational from the point of view of maximizing the justification of one's beliefs? I do not believe that it would, particularly if, in seeking justification, we aim, as we normally do, at discovering or retaining *truths*.

A coherentist might reply that if we are talking not only about justification but also about *knowledge*, then we must give some special role to beliefs (and perhaps dispositions to believe) grounded in experience and reason, for if we ignore these sources we cannot expect our justified beliefs to be true, hence cannot expect them to constitute knowledge.[11]

Now, however, we face what seems an artificial separation between what justifies a belief and what is plausibly taken to count towards its truth. If, because it implies truth, knowledge must in some way reflect experience or reason, should not justification, which seems in some way to count toward truth, also reflect them? Is it really reasonable to suppose that what justifies a belief may in no way count towards its truth?

It is not reasonable to separate justification and knowledge in this way (even though in some ways they are very different); nor have coherentists generally thought that it is (though some have held a justification-based coherence theory of truth of a kind to be discussed in Chapter 8). Often, what motivates asking for a justification of a belief is doubt that it is true; and if so, then the view that what justifies a belief has no tendency whatever to count toward its truth seems plainly mistaken. Moreover, if we can know a priori, as I believe may be possible, that perceptual and rational grounding of beliefs count, in some way, toward their truth, why may we not know equally well that they count toward justifying beliefs?

Moderate foundationalism

There is far more to say about both foundationalism and coherentism. But if what has emerged here is on the right track, then the problems confronting coherentism are worse than those confronting foundationalism. The most serious problems for foundationalism are widely taken to be the difficulties of specifying source conditions for justification and knowledge and, second, of accounting, on the basis of those sources and plausible transmission principles, for all that we seem to know. The first of these problems is addressed in Part One, which describes the basic sources and illustrates how they generate direct – though not indefeasible – knowledge, and direct (though again not generally indefeasible) justification. The second problem is treated in Chapter 6, which indicates many ways in which, even without actual inferences, knowledge and justification can be transmitted from beliefs which are justified, or represent knowledge, by virtue of being grounded in the basic sources, to other beliefs. Both problems are difficult, and they have not been completely solved here. But enough has been said to make clear along what lines they can be dealt with in a foundationalist framework.

The role of coherence in moderate foundationalism

Still another problem for foundationalism is the difficulty of accounting for the place of coherence in justification. But this is not a crippling difficulty for the kind of foundationalism I have been describing, which need not restrict the role of coherence any more than is required by the regress argument. Indeed, while (pure) coherentism grants nothing to foundationalism beyond perhaps its underlying psychological picture of how our belief systems are structured, foundationalism can account for some of the insights of coherentism, for instance the point that a coherence theory of the acquisition and function of concepts is plausible.

More positively, foundationalism can acknowledge a significant role for coherence in relation to justification and can thereby answer one traditional coherentist objection. I have in mind a kind of *moderate foundationalism*: a foundationalist view of knowledge or justification which (1) takes the justification of foundational beliefs to be at least typically defeasible; (2) is not *deductivist*, that is, does not demand that principles governing the inferential transmission of knowledge or justification be deductive; and (3) allows a significant role for coherence by requiring, not that inferentially justified beliefs derive *all* their justification from foundational ones, but only that they derive enough of it from the latter so that they would remain justified if any other justification they have were eliminated.[12] Some versions are more moderate than others, but the most plausible ones give coherence at least two roles.

The first role moderate foundationalism may give to coherence, or strictly speaking to incoherence, is negative: incoherence may defeat justification or knowledge, even of a directly justified (foundational) belief, as where my justification for believing I may be hallucinating prevents me from knowing, or even remaining justified in believing, that the green field is before me. (If this is not ultimately a role for coherence itself, it is a role crucial for explaining points stressed by coherentism.)

Second, moderate foundationalism can employ a principle commonly emphasized by coherentists, though foundationalists need not grant that the justification or truth of the principle is based on coherence and will tend to treat it as a transmission principle accounting for generation of inferential justification or as a combinatorial principle applying to the simultaneous testimony of sources of non-inferential justification. I refer to an *independence principle*: that the larger the number of independent mutually consistent factors one believes to support the truth of a proposition, the better one's justification for believing it (other things being equal). This principle can explain, for instance, why my justification for believing that the box of steaks is from the Smiths increases as I acquire new beliefs, each of which independently supports that conclusion.[13]

Similar principles consistent with foundationalism can accommodate other cases in which coherence enhances justification, say those in which a proposition's explaining, and thereby cohering with, something one justifiably believes tends to confer some degree of justification on that proposition.

Moderate foundationalism and the charge of dogmatism

Moderate foundationalism contrasts with *strong foundationalism*, which, in one form, is deductivist, takes foundational beliefs as indefeasibly justified, and allows coherence only a minimal role. To meet these conditions, strong foundationalists may reduce the basic sources of justification to reason and some form of introspection. The easiest way to do this is to take the skeptical view (considered in Chapter 10) that our only justified beliefs are either a priori or introspective.

Moreover, since strong foundationalists are committed to the indefeasibility of foundational justification, they would not grant that incoherence can defeat the justification of foundational beliefs. They would also refuse to concede to coherentism, and hence to any independence principle they recognize, any more than a minimal positive role, say by insisting that if a belief is supported by two or more independent cohering sources, its justification is increased only additively, that is, only by bringing together the justification transmitted separately from each relevant basic source.[14]

By contrast, what moderate foundationalism denies regarding coherence is only that it is a basic source of justification. Coherence by itself is not sufficient for justification. Thus, the independence principle does not apply to sources that have *no* justification; at most, it allows coherence to raise the level of justification originally drawn from other sources to a level *higher* than it would have if those sources were not mutually coherent.

Similarly, if inference is a basic source of coherence (as some coherentists seem to have believed), it is not a basic source of justification. It may enhance justification, as where one strengthens one's justification for believing someone's testimony by inferring the same point from someone else's. But inference *alone* does not generate justification: I might infer any number of propositions from several I already believe merely through wishful thinking; yet even if I thus arrive at a highly coherent set of beliefs, I have not thereby increased my justification for believing any of them. My premises, based in the way they are on desire, are ill-grounded.

At this point it might occur to one that the main problems faced by coherentism could be solved by taking *coherence with experience* to be required by coherentism as a condition for the coherence of a body of beliefs of the kind we normally have. This is, to be sure, not how coherence is characteristically understood by coherentists; they typically take it to be a relation among beliefs or their propositional contents or other items that may be said to be true or false, or some combination of these.[15] Might it be, however, that leading coherentists misrepresent the resources of their own theory?

If we think this, we must ask how a coherentist view that gives a crucial epistemological role to coherence of beliefs with experience differs from a moderate foundationalism. One would, after all, be insisting that in order to contain justified beliefs about the world, a person's belief system would in some sense have to be based on experience. This gives an essential role to foundations of justification (or knowledge) – grounds of belief that are not true or false and do not themselves admit of justification. It is true that the view would also require coherence as an essential element; but a moderate foundationalist could agree that coherence is necessary in a body of justified beliefs such as normal people have, yet insist that this coherence is not a basic source of justification rather than, chiefly, a product of the elements, such as grounding in experiential and rational sources, that *are* basic. If coherentists cannot show that coherence among beliefs is a basic source of justification – as it is far from clear they can – then requiring coherence with experience to make their theory plausible yields a view that is apparently at least compatible with a moderate foundationalism and may well be a version of that view. This may be a welcome conclusion for epistemologists uncommitted on the foundationalism–coherentism issue, but it would be unwelcome to philosophers in the coherentist tradition.[16]

Suppose, however, that moderate foundationalism is correct. We must not suppose that this theory leads easily to an adequate, detailed picture of a typical body of knowledge or justified belief. Moderate foundationalism as so far described – mainly structurally – tells us only what sort of structure a body of knowledge or of justified belief has. It says that if one has any knowledge or justified belief, then one has some direct knowledge or directly justified belief, and any other knowledge or justified belief one has is traceable to those foundations. A belief direct and foundational at one time may be indirect and non-foundational at another; it may gain or lose justification; it may have any kind of content; and some foundational beliefs may be false or unjustified or both.

By leaving this much open, however, moderate foundationalism avoids a narrow account of what it takes to have knowledge and justification and allows many routes to their acquisition. For similar reasons, it avoids *dogmatism*, in the sense of an attitude of self-assured certainty, especially concerning claims that are neither self-evident nor obvious. For moderate foundationalism allows alternative kinds of foundational beliefs for different people and under different circumstances; and, by acknowledging the fallibility of the experiential sources and of many inferences from the beliefs they generate, it also explains why it is so difficult to know that one has knowledge or justified belief, and hence important to be open to the possibility of mistakes.

Moderate foundationalism even allows that a person may not always be able to see the truth of a self-evident proposition; one might lack the conceptual resources for adequately understanding it. This should induce humility about how extensive our knowledge is even regarding what is in principle readily known. Ignorance can occur where one would least expect it. The position also treats reason as a fallible source of belief: we can easily take a false proposition to be true on the basis of a specious sense of its being a priori. This should induce humility about how confident we are entitled to be. Error can occur where it might seem impossible. Foundationalism is committed to unmoved movers; it is not committed to unmovable movers. It leaves open, moreover, just what knowledge is, and even whether there actually is any. These questions must still be faced.

Notes

1 I say 'simply' because clearly there could be devices or strategies by which one could manipulate one's beliefs; what I deny is that one can control belief "at will" (simply by willing it) the way one can normally raise one's arms at will. The point is not that the will has *no* power over belief. For a wide-ranging critical discussion of doxastic voluntarism see William P. Alston, 'The Deontological Conception of Epistemic Justification', *Philosophical Perspectives* 2 (1983), 257–99. Critical discussion of that paper is provided by Matthias Steup in 'Epistemic Obligation and Freedom to Believe Otherwise', forthcoming.

2 There is dispute about whether people can have infinite sets of beliefs. I have offered some reasons for doubting this (and cited some of the relevant literature) in 'Dispositional Beliefs and Dispositions to Believe', *Nous* 28 (1994), 419–34.

3 Granted, one could look at the formulation, say by tracing it along a mile-long print-out, and believe *that* it expresses a truth; but the point is that one could not grasp, and so could not believe, the *truth* that it expresses. Of course, if we are talking about infinity, the relevant formulations would approach an infinite number of miles in length.

4 An item of knowledge can occur in more than one epistemic chain, as where you have two entirely independent sets of premises showing the same conclusion. The argument requires one chain, but it allows more than one.

5 We may also draw the more general conclusion that if there is any knowledge, there is some direct knowledge. This more general conclusion follows only on the assumption that if there is any knowledge, then there is at least one knower who has it. This is self-evident for the main sense of 'knowledge'; but if we think of certain books as containing knowledge and then imagine the possibility that all knowers cease to exist while the books live on, it may then seem that there would be (residual) knowledge without there being any knowers (though even here there would *have been* knowers). Such *unpossessed knowledge* is discussed in some detail in Chapter 9.

6 See Aristotle's *Posterior Analytics*, Books I and II. His argument is importantly different in at least one respect: he spoke of the foundational items as "indemonstrable," which implies that there *cannot* be any deeper foundations. The regress argument as stated here implies only that one's foundational knowledge is of something that (at the time) one has not demonstrated. This leaves open that one might later demonstrate it by appeal to something "deeper."

7 The possibility of combining psychological foundationalism with epistemological coherentism seems quite open to Wilfrid Sellars, a leading coherentist. See, for example, his 'The Structure of Knowledge', in Hector-Neri Castañeda (ed.) *Action, Knowledge, and Reality: Essays in Honor of Wilfrid Sellars* (Indianapolis: Bobbs-Merrill, 1975).

8 This is the position taken by Laurence BonJour in *The Structure of Empirical Knowledge* (Cambridge, Mass.: Harvard University Press, 1985). (It should perhaps be noted that he has rejected the coherentist epistemology of this book in 'Back to Foundationalism', forthcoming.)

9 Does the fact that the topmost eastern section of the wheel is in place not explain why the topmost western section, which is contiguous with it, is in place, and isn't the converse not true? Only, I suspect, if this comes to saying that given these facts we can infer that each *is* in place. Why each is in place is explained by the same thing: the overall pattern of forces including the support provided by the ground. Each is in place because the gravitational force pulling it backward and downward is matched by a gravitational force pulling it forward and holding it up: both phenomena are indeed explained by the "same thing" – the qualitatively identical forces – but not by the same thing in the sense of the other, qualitatively identical phenomenon. Explanation by two phenomena that are "exactly alike" exhibits a kind of mutuality, but it is not the same as explanation of each of two exactly alike phenomena in terms of the other.

10 On the topic of practices of justification, Ludwig Wittgenstein's *On Certainty* (Oxford, 1969) is a valuable source. He is often cited as stressing that there comes a point at which one says "My spade is turned" (a foundationalist metaphor).

11 This line of thought is suggested by what Laurence BonJour, in *The Structure of Empirical Knowledge*, calls "the observation requirement." For extensive discussion of the theory he puts forth there and of coherentism in general, especially that of Keith Lehrer, see John W. Bender (ed.) *The Current Status of the Coherence Theory* (Dordrecht and Boston: Kluwer, 1989).

12 A slightly different formulation may be required if, for the sorts of reasons to be given in Chapter 8, knowledge does not entail justification; but the formulation given will serve here. Here and elsewhere the reference to foundational beliefs is to those that are justified; I also omit an other-things-equal clause appropriate after the 'if' in clause (3). For a highly detailed statement of a moderate foundationalism, see Paul K. Moser, *Knowledge and Evidence* (Cambridge and New York: Cambridge University Press, 1989).

13 The independence principle cited here is not the only one that seems sound. For instance, it is plausible to hold that one's justification for a proposition also rises (other things being equal) the larger the number of factors one is appropriately aware of that *do* support it, whether or not one believes them to do so.

14 It is a strong foundationalism, especially the kind found in Descartes' *Meditations*, that is influentially criticized by Richard Rorty in *Philosophy and the Mirror of Nature* (Princeton, NJ: Princeton University Press, 1979). Many of Rorty's criticisms do not hold for the moderate foundationalism developed in this chapter. His doubts about the very idea that the mind is a "mirror of nature," however, cuts against at least the majority of plausible epistemological theories. This book as a whole can be seen as a case for *some* kind of realist epistemology, and some aspects of Rorty's challenge are treated at least implicitly in Chapter 10 and in parts of other chapters, such as the sections on phenomenalism and truth.

15 Keith Lehrer provided an influential statement of this view in *Knowledge* (Oxford: The Clarendon Press, 1974): having said that "complete justification is a matter of coherence *within* a system of beliefs" (p. 17, emphasis added), he added, "There is no exit from the circle of ones [*sic*] own beliefs from which one can sally forth to find some exquisite tool to measure the merits of what lies within the circle of subjectivity" (pp. 17–18). Such sensory states as an impression of green grass are among the excluded tools. Further indications of why a coherentist view disallows appeal to experiential and other non-truth-valued states as justificatory are given by Wilfrid Sellars, 'The Structure of Knowledge', in Hector-Neri Castañeda (ed.) *Action, Knowledge, and Reality* (Indianapolis: Bobbs-Merrill, 1975); and Donald Davidson, 'A Coherence Theory of Truth and Knowledge', in Dieter Hendrich (ed.) *Kant oder Hegel* (Stuttgart: Klett-Cotta, 1983), 432–8.

16 The idea of enriching coherentism by making coherence with experience an essential element in coherentist justification is proposed and defended by Jonathan L. Kvanvig and Wayne

D. Rigg, 'Can a Coherence Theory Appeal to Appearance States?', *Philosophical Studies* 67 (1992), 197–217. This paper deserves study. Here I raise just one difficulty. Although they grant that "coherentism arises historically because of dissatisfaction with the foundationalists' picture" (p. 199), they characterize a foundationalist warranting relation in a way that does not distinguish it from the relation coherentists take to confer justification. "One such account could claim that a belief is foundationally warranting just in case the evidence for it is an appearance state involving the same content as that of the belief. For example, . . . perhaps my belief that something is red is intrinsically warranting because it appears to me that something is red" (p. 199). A foundationalist will not take an appearance state, such as a sensory impression of red, to have the same content as a belief: a propositional content in virtue of which the belief is true or false. Rather, the experiential content is qualitative and may be *appropriate to* certain propositions but is not itself truth-valued. Such a content might be *an appearance of red* but not the proposition that "it appears to me that something is red." The latter *is* a candidate to enter into a coherence relation with beliefs or their contents. Perhaps it is because Kvanvig and Rigg are thinking of experiential justification of belief as possibly working through beliefs or other states having propositional content and truth value that they find such justification available to coherentism. If, however, experiential justification could work that way, then one could *still* have a coherent system of beliefs that goes against experience. Beliefs *about* one's states – such as the (appearance) "belief that something is red" – would have to play a role, but those states would not be any kind of bedrock grounding these beliefs, even if the beliefs happened to be based on them. The problem, then, is that either the coherence-with-experience approach assimilates coherentism to a kind of foundationalism or it fails to capture the role of experience, which seems essential for a body of justified beliefs about the world.

PART THREE

The nature and scope of justification and knowledge

CHAPTER 8
The analysis of knowledge

Knowledge and justified true belief

Knowledge as the right kind of justified true belief

Dependence on falsehood as a defeater of justification
Knowledge and certainty
Knowing and knowing for certain
Knowing and making certain

Naturalistic accounts of the concept of knowledge

Knowledge as appropriately caused true belief
Knowledge as reliably grounded true belief

Problems for reliability theories

The specification problem
Reliability and defeat
Reliability, relevant alternatives, and luck

Knowledge and justification

The apparent possibility of clairvoyant knowledge
Natural knowledge

Internalism and externalism

Some varieties of internalism and externalism
Internalist and externalist versions of virtue epistemology
The internality of justification and the externality of knowledge

Justification and truth

The correspondence theory of truth
Minimalist and redundancy accounts of truth
The coherence theory of truth
The pragmatic theory of truth

Concluding proposals

The analysis of knowledge

Knowledge arises in experience. It emerges from reflection. It develops through inference. It exhibits a distinctive structure. The same holds for justified belief. But what exactly is knowledge? If it arises and develops in the way I have described, then knowing is at least believing. But clearly it is much more. A false belief is not knowledge. A belief based on a lucky guess is not knowledge either, even if it is true.

Can something be added to the notion of true belief to yield an analysis of what (propositional) knowledge is, that is, to provide a kind of account of what constitutes knowledge? Plato addressed a question significantly like this. He formulated an account of knowledge (though in the end he did not endorse it) which has sometimes been loosely interpreted as taking knowledge to be justified true belief.[1] For him, the term 'belief' would represent a grade of cognition lower than knowledge. But if we substitute, as most interpreters of Plato would – minimally – have us do, some related term for 'belief', say 'conviction', 'certainty', or 'understanding', then the account may be nearer to what Plato held and closer to some of the historically influential conceptions of knowledge. In any case, the notion of belief, as we have seen, is wide and subtle; and one or another form of the justified true belief account prevailed during much of this century until the 1960s.[2] What can be said for it?

Knowledge and justified true belief

What is not true is not known. To be sure, when we claim we know something and later discover that it is false, we sometimes say things like 'Well, I certainly believed it'; but we do not seriously maintain that we knew it. One might say 'I just *knew* it', but this is usually taken to exhibit an inverted commas use of 'know', a use in which 'know' stands in for something like 'was certain' or 'thought I knew'. If we seriously insisted we knew it, others would likely conclude that (for instance) we do not really believe that it is false, or perhaps that we are unaware that we are using 'I knew' to mean 'I felt great confidence', as in 'I just knew I'd win – I still can't really believe I lost'. In cases like the commonsense ones just described, when truth is subtracted from what appears to be knowledge, what remains is not knowledge but belief.

These points suggest that knowledge is at least true belief. Admittedly, people who feel certain of something, for instance that a friend is angry, may say that they do not believe it, but know it. This is best understood, however, to mean that they do not *merely* believe it, but know it.

Similarly, it may be misleading to say 'I believe he's angry' where I think I also know it – unless I intend, for instance, to indicate caution or perhaps polite disagreement with someone I think mistaken. But it is often misleading to say less than one is fully entitled to say; and my saying that I believe he is angry may be misleading precisely because I am expressing only part of what I am entitled to express, namely that I know he is. For I am thereby suggesting that I do *not* know, or perhaps doubt, that he is. If this point is what explains why my statement is misleading, that confirms that knowing implies believing.

Does knowing something also imply *justifiedly* believing it? If it does, that would explain why a true belief based on a lucky guess is not knowledge. If, from a distance, I see Jim walk hurriedly down the hall and simply guess that he is angry, I am not justified in believing that he is angry. If my belief turns out to be true, it still does not constitute knowledge. That fact seems explainable by its lack of justification. Now suppose I go into his office and see him briskly shuffling papers and angrily mumbling curses. At this point I might come to know that he is angry; and my acquiring knowledge that he is can be explained by my having acquired evidence which justifies my true belief that he is.

Still, could a true belief that is not justified constitute knowledge? Suppose I simply see Jim briskly shuffling papers as I pass his office, but do not hear any curses. A bit later, I see him walk hurriedly down the hall. Given that I know his fiery temperament, I might have just enough evidence so that I have some reason to believe he is angry, even though I am not quite justified in believing this. Might I now have a kind of low-grade knowledge that he is angry? This is doubtful. My evidence for believing this is not firm. But the case does show this much: that as our evidence for a truth we believe mounts up in a way that brings us closer to justification for believing it, we also tend to get closer to knowledge. These and similar points support the view that justified belief is an element in knowledge. This view is highly plausible, and for the time being I want to assume it.

We are, then, on the way toward an analysis of knowledge. For it looks as if we have a very substantive threefold necessary condition for (propositional) knowledge. Specifically, it seems that knowledge is at least justified true belief: that one knows something only if one believes it, it is true, and one's belief of it is justified. Still, a correct, illuminating analysis, one that provides a good account of the nature of what is being analyzed, must also provide sufficient conditions. It might be true that I know something *only if* I justifiedly and truly believe it, yet false that *if* I justifiedly and truly believe something, I know it.

It apparently *is* false that if one has a justified true belief, one (always) has knowledge. Suppose that when I first visit the Wallaces I have no idea that they have a photographic collection which includes very realistic, life-size pictures of themselves. When I approach the doorway to their living room down a long hallway, I see, just twelve feet before me, and constituting all I can see through the doorway, a life-size picture of Jane, standing facing me and smiling like the good hostess she is, with the background in the picture looking just like the living room's rear wall. I say 'hello' before I get close enough to realize that I see only a photograph of her taken against the background of that very wall. I discover that the picture is so lifelike that this happens to everyone who knows Jane and enters unaware of the photograph. I might thus be quite justified, for a moment, in my belief that Jane is opposite me. As it happens, however, Jane *is* standing opposite me – in the next room, right behind the wall on which the picture is hung. My belief that she is opposite me is thus true, as well as justified. But I do not know that she is opposite me.[3]

This example shows that if we analyze knowledge as justified true belief, our analysis is too broad. What can be done to improve it? If we think we are on the right track, we can restrict the kind or degree of justification involved. We might also suspect that justification is not so important after all, but only correlated with something that is important. We might then seek an account in which justification is not central to understanding knowledge. There are many approaches of both kinds. I want to consider two of each, starting with the "justificationist" accounts.

Knowledge as the right kind of justified true belief

In the photographic case, something seems wrong with the *kind* of justification I have. It is sometimes said to be defeated, where this is not to say that it is eliminated or overturned, as in the more common cases of defeated justification we have so far noted, but rather (in part) that it is prevented from playing what would seem to be its normal role in such a case, namely, rendering a true belief knowledge. Contrast this kind of defeat with the more common kind that eliminates or overturns justification – as where one discovers a witness one had believed was lying – call the former *epistemic defeat*: it eliminates the power of the justification to turn a true belief that has that justification into knowledge. In that sense, it vitiates the justification, eliminating its characteristic power to raise the status of a merely true belief to that of knowledge.

Perhaps, then, with epistemic as opposed to justificational defeat in mind, knowledge might be analyzed as *undefeatedly justified true belief*.[4] This idea is well worth exploring.

Dependence on falsehood as a defeater of justification

How is (epistemic) defeat to be characterized? One natural view is that the justification of a belief is defeated provided the belief depends on a falsehood. A dependence on falsehood is a bad thing from the point of view of the candidacy of a belief to constitute knowledge. This is in part because, even where a belief that depends on falsehood is true, that may be just by good luck. Furthermore, dependence on falsehood tends to lead one to believe further falsehoods, as a decay in a tree trunk tends to spread to some of its branches. A belief might depend on falsehood in either or both of the following ways.

First, a belief might depend on a falsehood in the sense that it would not be justified except on the basis of one's being (situationally) justified in believing a falsehood about the subject in question (say, Jane). This is a kind of justificational dependence (dependence for justification), which I will call *presuppositional dependence*. In the photographic case, my belief that Jane is opposite me depends presuppositionally on the falsehood that I am seeing her directly (or at least in a way that does not misrepresent her location). The point is not that in order to know she is opposite me I would have to believe the false proposition that I am seeing her directly; rather, my belief that she is opposite me epistemically depends (depends for its claim to be knowledge) on this proposition. Not only does it seem to be because this proposition is false that I do not know Jane is opposite me; it is also the kind of proposition whose truth is central for the grounding of my would-be knowledge and whose falsity I would tend to be surprised to discover.

The second case is *psychological dependence*: a belief might psychologically depend on a falsehood in the causal sense that one has the belief by virtue of holding it on the basis of believing a falsehood. In this kind of case my would-be knowledge is sustained by a false belief, which is a kind of rotten foundation. My belief about Jane would psychologically depend on falsehood if, say, I knew about the Wallaces' life-size photographs, yet trusted my vision and believed that Jane was opposite me on the basis of concluding that this time I was viewing her directly. I am not viewing her directly, so my underlying belief is false.

Unfortunately, the appeal to a false presupposition, or even to other kinds of dependence on falsehood, may not always explain why a justified true belief is epistemically defeated and fails to constitute knowledge. Recall the sweepstakes with a million coupons. You might have a justified true belief that you will lose, but you do not know that you will. You might win. What falsehood defeats your justification here? You are not making any mistake, but simply do not have the right *kind* of positive ground for knowledge.

It might seem that your belief that you will lose the sweepstakes depends on the false proposition that the outcome of a chance process can be known beforehand by merely calculating odds. But does your belief depend on this? You might reject this and still believe – even justifiedly – that you will lose, whereas I could not reject the false presupposition that I see Jane directly and still believe (justifiedly, at least) that she is in front of me.

We cannot plausibly say, then, that in the sweepstakes example either your belief or its justification depends on the falsehood about foreknowledge of chance outcomes. Points like these do not show that nothing can save the undefeatedly justified true belief analysis of knowledge. But it is at least not easy to make the analysis work, and I want to consider other accounts of knowledge.

Knowledge and certainty

The sweepstakes example suggests that knowledge requires one's having *conclusively justified true belief*: belief justified in such a way that what justifies it guarantees its truth. For it is plausible to claim that if the evidence guarantees that you will lose, say because it includes knowledge of the sweepstakes being fixed in favor of someone else, then you would know you will lose. Moreover, conclusive justification is precisely the kind not plausibly thought to be liable to defeat.

Different theories offer different accounts of a guarantee of truth (as will be apparent when we discuss skepticism in Chapter 10). The sweepstakes example supports the view that the right kind of guarantee is not simply a matter of high probability. After all, we can have as many coupons as we like and you would still not know yours will lose. Thus, no matter how probable it is that you will lose, your justification is not sufficient for knowledge.[5]

Another reason to think that knowledge requires conclusive justification is that knowing is closely associated with certainty. When I wonder if I know, I sometimes ask myself how I can be certain. I also sometimes wonder if what I believe *is* certain. Particularly in the latter case, I am thinking of the status of the proposition in question, not of *psychological certainty*, which is, roughly speaking, confidence of the truth of what one believes. If I am confident enough that something is so, I am certain that it is (and certain of it); and if I am certain of it, I am confident that it is so (and certain that it is so).

Even 'How can I be certain?' does not concern only psychological certainty. It typically means something like 'How may I justifiedly be (psychologically) certain?' And if I say that it is not certain that your coupon will lose, I am talking about *propositional certainty*, roughly, the certainty a proposition has when there are extremely strong grounds for it, grounds that guarantee its truth. I want to leave open how readily *available* the grounds must be, if readily available at all, for instance whether ordinary reflection on what evidence one has would reveal them. *Saying* something is certain surely implies that one thinks sufficient grounds are in some sense available, even if only by a careful study of the matter and perhaps consulting others about it. But for a proposition just to *be* certain, the kind of availability (if any) is more difficult to assess.

Given these connections between knowledge and certainty, one might hold that knowledge is constituted by conclusively justified true belief, meaning that (1) the believer may justifiedly be *psychologically* certain of the true proposition in question and (2) this proposition is so well-grounded as to be itself *propositionally* certain. Knowledge constituted by such belief may be (and has been) called *epistemic certainty*.[6]

This analysis of knowledge seems too narrow. It would, for instance, apparently rule out most knowledge based on testimony. If Jane tells me that she wants to meet to discuss something, and I know her well and have no good reason to doubt her word, may I not know that she wants to meet with me? Yet I do not have conclusive justification. Unlikely though it is, error is barely possible for me; she could act out of character and deceive me (or herself).

Knowing and knowing for certain

Does knowing imply, if not conclusive justification, then at least the certainty of what is known? In the case described, I doubt that it is propositionally certain that Jane wants to meet with me (but the notion of propositional certainty is vague, and it is often difficult to tell whether it applies). Thus, my knowledge here is apparently not knowledge of something that is certain. Indeed, we speak sometimes of knowing something *for certain*, implying a contrast with simply knowing. Imagine that Tom tells me that Jane is deceiving me, but I believe him to be mistaken. Someone probing my grounds for thinking Tom mistaken might ask if I know for certain. This might be asked not from doubt about whether I know, but to find out if the *proposition* that he is mistaken is certain, perhaps because much hangs on it, as in a criminal trial. The existence of such cases suggests that what is not known for certain still can be known.

Perhaps, however, what can be known at all can always be known for certain, as I might come to know for certain – provided I do enough checking into her motivation – that Jane wants to meet with me. But even if what is knowable *can* be known for certain, it is doubtful (as examples to be given will also suggest) that everything that is known *is* certain. Still, is it even true that whatever is known must at least be such that it *can* be certain? Our example suggests that knowledge need not meet this standard: I might know that Jane wanted to meet even if she has just died and the additional evidences – such as recollections by third parties, letters by her – on the basis of which this can be certain, do not exist.

One might reply that knowledge is always of the *sort* of proposition that can be certain. But consider propositions about the past, such as that a ship sank in a certain lonely region in the ocean. Perhaps these may be knowable, yet not even be the sort of thing that can (for human beings, at least) be certain (the evidence of its apparent traces at the bottom is good enough for knowledge, but no further evidence, such as eye-witness accounts, can be obtained regarding where it sank).

Knowing and making certain

Perhaps, however, these points show only that I cannot *make* certain that Jane wants to meet with me. There might still be a basis for this proposition which renders it (propositionally) certain. I will continue to leave open the question of whether what is known is the sort of thing that can be certain, since knowledge, not certainty, is my main concern here. But it will help, in that connection, to explore how an understanding of the notion of making certain may bear on the view that knowledge requires conclusive justification.

If we can make certain of something that we already know, then there is some reason to think that conclusive justification is not required for knowledge. Suppose I lock the back door and, as I get in my car, have a clear recollection of doing so. Still, if someone asks me if I am absolutely sure I did, I may truly believe I know I did, yet still check to make certain I did. Now where we need to (or even can) make certain of something we know, it would appear that it need not *be* either certain or conclusively justified: getting conclusive justification seems to be the main point of making certain, though on some views the latter may be weaker, in that there are cases in which we make certain of something but still lack utterly conclusive justification for it.

It might be replied that here 'make certain' means not 'make it certain' but, roughly, 'make sure that it is certain', and that if I really knew it, it was certain in the first place. Let us assume this for the sake of argument. Now suppose I do not make certain that I locked the door, because it begins to hail and I must leave before I can check the door. This does not show that I do not know the door was locked; and, on later finding that it was, I would be correct in saying that I was right all along to think I knew. Moreover, supposing I did know all along, that does not imply that it was certain all along. I had good reason, at least at the time when I could not check, to think it was not certain. Thus, the possibility of making certain of what we already know suggests that knowing a proposition does not entail its being certain. Moreover, if we can know something, yet make certain it is so, then apparently we can know it without being conclusively justified in believing it.

Notice that similar points apply to what we know from memory. Even on topics with respect to which our memory is highly reliable, the justification of our memory beliefs is generally not conclusive. Even if I can recite a stanza from memory, my justification for believing I have it right need not be conclusive. Yet I may well know that I have it right, and confirm that I do when I look it up to make certain I do and I find that it reads just as I thought.

Naturalistic accounts of the concept of knowledge

Perhaps we should consider a quite different approach. Must we appeal to the notion of justification to understand knowledge? Suppose we think of knowing as *registering truth*, somewhat as a thermometer registers temperature. Knowledge, so conceived, results from the successful functioning of our epistemic equipment, which consists above all of finely tuned perceptual, memorial, introspective, and rational instruments. The thermometer analogy holds for simple knowing – knowing (in an acquaintance sense) of persons and objects – and for objectual knowing – knowing something *to be* a certain way – as well as for propositional knowing. But propositional knowing is the main topic of this chapter; and, from a study of the chapter on perception, one could largely adapt to the other cases what emerges about propositional knowledge.[7]

This view goes well with the idea that we are biological creatures with sense receptors that gather information and with mental capacities that manipulate it. Indeed, perhaps we can analyze knowledge *naturalistically*, that is, using the kinds of concepts the natural sciences use in understanding things. This is not by appeal to plainly value-laden notions like that of justification, but (largely) in terms of physical, chemical, biological, and psychological properties, together with causal relations between these.

I want to consider two naturalistic approaches. The first emphasizes the role of causation in producing our knowledge, as in the case of perceptual beliefs caused by the perceived object. The second approach stresses the reliability of the processes, such as seeing, through which knowledge arises.

Knowledge as appropriately caused true belief

On the causal theory, knowledge is true belief caused by something connected with its truth in a way that makes it plausible to call the belief knowledge. Roughly, knowledge is appropriately caused true belief, where appropriate (causal) production of a belief is production of it in which the fact, object, event, or other thing in virtue of which the belief is true plays a certain role in generating or sustaining the belief. In the examples of knowledge that best support the view, the belief in question is apparently a case of knowledge because it is caused in a way that guarantees its truth. Thus, I know that there is a green field before me because the field itself plays a major part, through my vision, in causing me to believe there is a green field before me. I know that Jane wants to meet with me because her wanting to do so plays a major part in causing her to say she does, and thereby in causing me to believe that she does. I know that the stanza I recite from memory has four lines because its having them is a major causal factor, operating through my memory, in my believing that it does.

The causal view can even accommodate knowledge of the future. I know that I am going to continue thinking about knowledge for a long time. That truth (about the future) does not cause me to believe this; but that truth is causally connected with my belief, and in a way that suggests why the belief may be expected to be true. For what causally explains *both* why the proposition I believe about the future is true and why I believe it, is the same element: my intending to continue thinking about knowledge. Here my future-directed belief is knowledge, but not by virtue of being produced by the thing it is about – my future thinking – for that has not occurred.

Does this view of knowledge of the future show that since the relevant facts lie in the future, knowledge need not represent "the facts," as the commonsense view has it? The case need not be so interpreted. Representing facts does not require being caused by them. Recall my belief about the future. This belief constitutes knowledge, but not because what it is about is the way the belief represents it *and* causes the belief, as where the green field's being before me causes me to believe that it is before me; rather, such a future-directed belief correctly represents what it is about in part because *the belief itself* causes that state of affairs. Moreover, the causal theory is right about this much: my belief that I will continue thinking about knowledge is caused by something – my intention to continue thinking about it – of a kind that makes it at least likely that I will be as the belief represents me. Roughly, not only can knowledge be produced by what is known, as in perceptual cases; both knowledge of certain facts and the facts known can also be common effects of the same causes, as with knowledge of the future.

There are, however, serious troubles for the theory that knowledge is appropriately caused true belief. One problem is how to apply the basic idea – that what underlies the truth in question is a causal factor in the grounding of the belief of that truth – to a priori knowledge. How might what underlies the truth that if one tree is taller than another, then the second is shorter than the first be causally connected with my believing this truth? This truth is not (in general) perceptually known, nor is its status dependent on any particular object in the world, as is the case with the (empirical) knowledge to which the causal theory best applies.

It may be that the only way a truth can be causally connected with a belief so as to render it knowledge is through a connection with something in the world that does at least partly cause (or is at least partly an effect of) the belief. The truth that there is a green field before me is about an object that produces visual impressions in me. But the strictly a priori knowledge just cited does not depend on trees in that way. It does not even depend on there ever being any trees. It seems to be based simply on a grasp of the concepts involved, above all that of a tree and that of height. My having this grasp does not appear to imply causally interacting with those concepts (supposing it is even possible to inter-act causally with concepts).[8] This is not to say that the belief has no causal ground, such as the comprehending consideration (the understanding) of the relevant proposition. The problem is that the belief seems to lack the kind of ground the causal theory requires.

Knowledge as reliably grounded true belief

There is another serious problem concerning the causal account, this time in relation to empirical beliefs. When we understand it, we can see the rationale for a different way of understanding knowledge. As in many instances, the trouble arises from examples of justified true beliefs that are not knowledge.

Consider a case in which something causes me to have a true belief, yet that belief is not knowledge. Suppose Tom tells me, on the basis of his knowing it, that Jim is angry, and as a result of his testimony I believe this. My belief might be justified and true. But imagine that, although I have no reason what-ever to believe this about Tom, he is in general highly unreliable, and some-times lies, in what he says about Jim. The mere fact of Tom's unreliability prevents me from knowing through his testimony that Jim is angry. Even if Tom knows Jim is angry, and knows it because he observes Jim acting angrily, his knowledge is not transmitted to me. For he might well have said this even if Jim had merely acted, say, hurriedly, and was not angry.

It is important to see that although the causal connections here seem to be what they usually are in testimony cases, I do not acquire knowledge from Tom's testimony. Jim's anger causes Tom to believe him angry; Tom's belief (partly) causes his telling me that Jim is angry; his telling me this causes me to believe it. But, though I have a justified true belief that Jim is angry, I do not know it. For while Tom has it right this time, he is in general unreliable regarding Jim.

The testimony example brings out something very revealing. It suggests that the reason I do not know on the basis of Tom's testimony is that he is not reliable. By contrast, perception normally does seem reliable. Normally, at least, we may justifiedly count on the beliefs it typically produces to be true, and presumably perception is also reliable in the sense that the vast majority of beliefs it produces are in fact true. Where there is a photograph that we are unaware of, however, our perception through it is typically not reliable. Cases of these sorts suggest that we might plausibly analyze knowledge as *reliably grounded true belief.*[9]

Even a priori knowledge might perhaps be accommodated on this view. For it is at least normally produced by grasping concepts and their relations, or perhaps by certain simple valid inference on the basis of beliefs grounded in such a grasp; and these processes of producing belief seem reliable. In both the empirical and a priori cases, then, when we know, we have reliably *registered* the truth.

To see how this approach works, recall Tom's testimony about Jim. Suppose that Tom is only very occasionally mistaken about Jim. Then might I acquire knowledge on the basis of Tom's testimony? A crucial question is *how* reliable a belief-producing process, such as testimony, must be in order to yield knowledge. The theory gives us no precise way to answer this.

The theory can be defended on this point, however, by noting that the concept of knowledge is itself not precise. This means that there will be times when, no matter how much information we have, we cannot be sure whether someone knows or not, just as, because the term 'bald' is vague, we cannot always be sure whether it applies, no matter how much information we have (including the number of hairs on the person's head). It might be added that as the reliability of Jim's testimony goes up, so does our inclination to say that I know on the basis of it. This seems to confirm the reliability theory.

Problems for reliability theories

The reliability theory apparently does receive support from the kind of correlation illustrated here: the tendency to count my true belief about Jim as knowledge apparently varies with the tendency to regard the belief's testimonial basis as reliable. But perhaps our underlying thought in so speaking about the belief is that the more reliable Tom is, the better is my justification for believing what he says. If so, then the reliability theory might give the right results here because it draws on the role of justification as a constituent in knowledge.

To be sure, neither reliabilists nor their justificationist critics need hold that I must *believe* anything specific about Tom's reliability in order to acquire justified beliefs from his testimony. But it might be argued that my knowledge has a presuppositional dependence on the proposition that he is sufficiently reliable to justify my accepting his testimony, and that it is either because this presupposition is false or because I lack justification for believing it that my justification for believing his testimony in the first place is defeated. Thus, it might be argued that even if the reliability account is correct about the conditions a belief must meet to constitute knowledge, its success may be due to its tacit dependence on the justificationist concepts it seeks to abandon.

The specification problem

There is a different kind of problem that must also be faced by the reliability theory. This difficulty is deeper than the question of how reliable a process has to be in order to ground knowledge. It concerns how to specify what is reliable in the first place. It will not do to say, for instance, simply that the reliable processes we are talking about are mainly those by which the experiential and rational sources of knowledge produce belief. This is not obviously wrong, but it leaves too much undetermined.

Consider vision. Its reliability varies so much with *conditions of observation* that it would be wrong to say without qualification that it is a reliable belief-producing process. It might seem that we may say that it is reliable in producing beliefs in good light with the object of vision near enough relative to the visual powers of the perceiver. But this will not do either. It does not rule out external interferences like deceptive photographs, such as the one of Jane. It also fails to rule out internal interferences like hallucinogenic drugs. These interferences might produce false beliefs about objects which one clearly sees and concerning which one also has many true beliefs, as where, because of brain damage, one hallucinates a dark blight on a green tree which one otherwise sees plainly as it is.

There are, moreover, so many possible factors that affect reliability that it is not clear that we can list them all without using blanket terms such as 'too far away' as applied to the object, and 'insufficiently attentive' or 'not acute enough' as applied to the perceiver. These terms are not only quite vague; the more important point is that they may be argued to come to something like 'too far to be reliably (or justifiedly) judged', 'too inattentive to form reliable (or justified) beliefs', and 'not acute enough for reliable (or justified) judgment of the features of the object'. If so, their interpretation may well depend on our already having a good philosophical understanding of reliability (or justification), and they are thus unlikely to help us much in clarifying reliability, or if they do, it is because we are relying on a different theory.

Suppose we can devise a vocabulary that overcomes these problems. Another, related difficulty may persist. Belief-production might be reliable described in one way and unreliable described in another. Hence, even if we are able to specify what, in general, a reliable belief-producing process is, we need a way of deciding what reliable-process description to use in order to understand a particular case. Recall my seeing Jane in the photograph and thereby believing that she is opposite me. Suppose we say – what seems correct – that my belief arises from a process of seeing someone in a photograph that accurately shows the person's features and general location. Then my belief presumably should be knowledge. For the picture shows her to be where she is: opposite me.

Suppose, on the other hand, we say something else that is true about the grounding of my belief that Jane is opposite me: that the belief-producing process is one of seeing a person in a picture which gives the false impression that the person is directly in front of one. Then my belief arising from the process is not reliably produced – since often in such cases the person is not opposite one at all – and the belief should thus not be knowledge. The trouble is that both descriptions apply to the production of my belief. Using one description, the theory says I know; using the other, it says I do not.

How can the theory enable us to choose between the two correct reliable-process descriptions, or justify our choosing whatever kind of description it accepts? Call this the *specification problem* (or description problem). If we first have to decide whether I know that Jane is in front of me by relying on some quite different understanding of knowledge and only in that light can we frame a description, the theory would seem to give us very limited help in understanding knowledge. For the theory itself can apparently be put to work only insofar as we already understand knowledge in the light of some alternative view, at least well enough to be in a position to tell systematically, in a vast range of cases of true belief, whether or not the belief constitutes knowledge.[10]

This point, however, might be said to show no more than that to use the reliability view we need a good intuitive grasp of the concept of knowledge. Let us accept this for the sake of argument.

The deeper point is that if we seek to clarify knowledge (or justification) by appeal to reliable belief-grounding processes naturalistically understood, then we need a way of explaining what those processes are without inadmissibly appealing, in our explanation, to the concept of knowledge (or justification). A belief that is knowledge should be such because it is reliably grounded true belief; a reliable belief-grounding process should not be characterized as the kind that yields, say, perceptual knowledge.[11]

Similarly, if we have to find the right reliable-process description in terms of what I am *justified* in presupposing, say that I have direct visual access to what is before me, then the theory works only insofar as it can exploit some justificationist principles. In that case, it would be more accurately described as a reliabilistic justification theory.

Reliability and defeat

Even when the degree of reliability of a belief-grounding process or state seems very high and the process or state is normal, there can be a defeat of would-be knowledge. On this score, the sweepstakes example also challenges reliability theories of knowledge, as it does justificationist theories, and it, too, illustrates the specification problem. Granted, we can characterize the process grounding my belief that I will lose as one in which chance is crucial, and thus claim that the process is not reliable. But since I hold just one out of a million coupons, we might *also* truly describe it as a process that yields true beliefs virtually 100 percent of the time – and we can get as high a percentage as we like by increasing the number of coupons. Under this description, the process sounds very reliable indeed; yet it does not produce knowledge.

Moreover, if something like the former description of the belief-grounding process is what the theory would have us use, say, 'process in which chance plays a crucial role in determining the truth of the belief', why is that? A good answer cannot be that unless we call a process in which chance plays a role unreliable, we cannot account for knowledge; for that would just assume the reliabilist view that knowledge must be reliably grounded. In any event, even in perceptual knowledge chance may play a role. It might be by chance that I see you on a passing train: you just happened to be visible to me at the window as the train rushed past. This role of chance leaves untouched whatever it is by virtue of which my vision yields knowledge. So how are we to specify just what kind of role chance may play in the grounding of knowledge?

There could well be a way around these problems. For instance, one might point out that in the photographic case my belief about Jane's location does not causally *depend* on where she is, since I would believe she is before me even if she were not behind the picture. But this is only the beginning of a solution. For suppose I see her in a mirror, again without knowing that I am not seeing her directly, perhaps because I do not realize that there are trick mirrors at the yard party I am attending. Imagine that she happens to be opposite me, behind the mirror in which I see her, and is reflected into it by other mirrors I do not see (and have no reason to think are there). Here my belief about where she is would depend on where she is, since her movements would be reflected in the mirror in which I see her; yet I would still not know that she is opposite me.

The case of my belief that I will lose the sweepstakes is similar. It depends on my beliefs about, and in that way may indirectly depend on, the mechanisms that actually result in my losing; but still the belief is not knowledge. The dependency is of course not of the required kind. But now we have another specification problem: how to describe the right kind of dependency, often called a *functional dependency*. If there is a straightforward and illuminating way to specify the right kind of dependency, it is not obvious what it is.

Reliability, relevant alternatives, and luck

Even when the appropriate dependency is present, our would-be knowledge can be defeated. Recall the deceiving portrait case: my belief that Jane is before me, though justified and true, does not constitute knowledge. We can alter the example so that my belief that she is before me does have the normal kind of dependence on her location, yet I still do not know she is before me. Imagine that I *do* see her standing twelve feet before me and recognize her as I always have, but this time her identical twin, of whose existence I had no inkling, is a few feet to her right and walking toward the very spot where I see Jane. If I have not learned to tell them apart and would have taken Jane's sister to be Jane had I been ten seconds later, then I surely do not know that Jane is before me.

One way to see that I do not know it is Jane before me is to say that when one knows something, it cannot be just good luck that one is right in believing it, as it is here. But it is not easy to say what constitutes good luck without resorting to something like the notion that you do not have a true belief by mere good luck when your belief is reliably produced – or perhaps, sufficiently reliably produced, or undefeatedly justified. Any of these ways of solving the problem will take us back to problems not yet solved.

Some philosophers have dealt with such cases by arguing that the problem in the identical twin case is the existence of a "relevant alternative" to the situation that in fact renders one's belief true, an alternative such that one cannot discriminate between the truth of the proposition in question (here, that Jane is before me) and the alternative situation (her sister's being before me). What makes this non-discriminable alternative relevant is the twin's moving toward my field of vision when I first enter, so that I am about to be deceived. Knowledge is reliably grounded in roughly the sense that the knower can discriminate any relevant alternative from the situation known to be exist.

Now, however, we must have a way of deciding what alternatives are relevant; the mere possibility of Jane's having a twin in the indicated situation is apparently not – or we would never know our friends are before us (a skeptical view we shall consider in Chapter 10). But suppose Jane has a twin who never sees her, or is currently abroad, or on the way to the party? And does it matter if we realize there is such a person? These are difficult questions of a kind that a good reliability theory should adequately answer.[12]

I do not present any of these problems facing reliability theories of knowledge as insurmountable. But reliability theories do face serious difficulties, as do the other theories we have considered. One conclusion that might be drawn here is that knowledge is simply unanalyzable. But that certainly should not be inferred from the difficulties I have brought out. They may be resolvable;

and I have of course not discussed all the promising lines of analysis of knowledge there are.[13]

One might also conclude that the concept of knowledge is simply so vague that we should not hope for an account any more precise than, say, the view that knowledge is appropriately justified true belief or, if one prefers a naturalistic account, suitably produced true belief. But that conclusion would be premature, particularly so far as it favors a justificationist account of knowledge. Indeed, it is time to consider some very special cases that raise the question of whether justification is even strictly necessary for knowledge.

Knowledge and justification

So far, I have spoken as if, although not all justified true belief constitutes knowledge, all knowledge is at least justified true belief. But if the reliability view is correct in any of its plausible forms, it should be possible for a belief to be reliably grounded *without* the subject's having grounds of the right kind to yield justification. Let us explore some cases in which knowledge without justification seems possible.

The apparent possibility of clairvoyant knowledge

Imagine a man who foretells the results of horse races. He always gets them right, even though he never inspects the horses or their records, but merely looks at them closely as they line up. He has no idea why he believes what he does about the results; and after the races he does not even check his accuracy. He does not bet nor especially care who wins. He does, however, have definite conviction, and we can suppose that it seems natural to him to believe what he does and that there is nothing in his state of mind that would lead him to mistrust himself or think he is guilty of wishful thinking or "crazy." It is not clear just how such a thing is possible; but it clearly is possible. There could be a way, for instance, in which both his belief that a horse will win and its actually winning are common effects of the same causes, so that his getting the right answers is not lucky accident, but prophetic in a way, or perhaps sixth-sensory.[14]

Now it appears that this man knows who will win the races. But he surely does not have justified beliefs as to who will win. He *would* have them if he kept track of his record and noted how well his forecasts turn out. But he does not bother to check on his predictions regularly and has no idea that he is constantly getting the results right. Perhaps we may also assume that (as may be thought to be essential in the case) he also has no good justification for thinking he is *not* reliable or not justified.[15]

One might protest that he has a kind of foresight which generates directly justified beliefs on the basis of certain experiences, somewhat in the way perception does. But is there any reason to say this, other than to preserve the view that knowledge implies justified belief? There is no candidate for a sense organ, nor need he have sense impressions representing the victorious horse crossing the finish line; and although we assume that there is some causal process by which he receives the crucial information, we have no idea what it is and cannot plausibly regard it as conferring justification, particularly since the man is puzzled by his having the predictive beliefs at all and has no good reason to think they are justified.

Natural knowledge

Another kind of case argues for the same point. In some of the literature of psychology we read of the *idiot savant*. Such people are considered mentally deficient, yet they have some extraordinary abilities. We may assume that they understand enough to count and to use elementary mathematical concepts. Some of them can apparently just reel off the answers to arithmetical problems that normally require calculation in writing. Let us assume that they regularly get the answers right, yet can give no account of how they do so: it is not, for instance, by rapidly doing in their head what we would laboriously do in our heads if our memories enabled us to solve the problem mentally. Nor is it by rational insight into the truths in question, such as one has for certain simple logical or arithmetic propositions. It is not known how they do it, and they need have (we may assume) no sense of why they believe the answers in question.

Now consider the first time one of these people – Pip, let us say – reels off the answer to a multiplication problem involving two three-digit numbers. There is no time for him to realize he has a built-in ability or to note a series of successes. (We may make a similar assumption about the horse race predictor's initial success.) But he believes the answer and might also know it. For one thing, the belief is a manifestation of an arithmetic ability that is stable and reliable. Again, one can say that there is a mathematical sense that yields directly justified beliefs. But this seems an *ad hoc* move, designed only to save the view which the example counters: the view that knowing entails justifiedly believing.

If we all turned out to have this mathematical ability under certain conditions, such as an impression of the proposition as true (if only in the form of an image of it written in boldface), then we might come to believe that there is an arithmetic sense which generates such directly justified beliefs. Perhaps that shows that our concept of justification might evolve; but it does not show that the arithmetic beliefs now in question are justified. If, as seems likely, these beliefs and those of the horse race predictor are knowledge, they are special cases. We might call them *natural knowledge*, since they seem rooted in the nature of their possessors and do not depend on their having learned anything (beyond acquiring the concepts needed to hold the beliefs in question) or on their using either their senses or, so far as we can tell, their powers of reason. But even if natural knowledge is rare, its possibility would show that justified belief is not necessarily a constituent in knowledge.

If there can be natural knowledge, that possibility may show something important about both knowledge and justification. What inclines us to grant that Pip knows the answer is chiefly the regularity of correct results and apparent stability of the mechanism yielding them. The accuracy of the results cannot, we suppose, be accidental; it must be rooted in some inner arithmetic process which regularly – and reliably – yields the right results. On being presented with the problem, he registers the truth. There need be no sense of calculating or even an appearance of truth or self-evidence, such as one may have where one directly grasps an a priori proposition.[16]

There is, then, no mental process of arithmetic calculation of which the person is aware, or anything else that seems of the right sort to ground justification, as visual impressions can ground it even when one is (unknowingly) having a vivid hallucination. The calculator cannot point to anything to justify the sum, even in the elementary way we can cite how things look to us to justify believing there is a green field before us. This contrast suggests that there may be a major difference between knowledge and justification that explains why the former seems possible without the latter. Let us explore this.

Internalism and externalism

Could it be that justification and knowledge are grounded in quite different ways? Perhaps there is a difference between them connected with the basic contrast between them in relation to truth. Apart from self-knowledge, knowledge is at least true belief about the external world (or external matters, such as those of logic). Insofar as it is true belief about the external world, one might expect its grounds to be essentially in that world. The justifiedness of a belief, by contrast, does not entail its truth and seems to many philosophers to rest on a source "inside" the mind.

Some of our examples suggest that justification is grounded entirely in what is internal to the mind, in a sense implying that it is accessible to introspection or reflection by the subject – a view we might call *internalism about justification*. Some of the same examples, such as those of the predictor and the calculator, suggest that knowledge is grounded entirely in what is external to the mind, and hence not internally accessible to the subject in that way – a view we might call *externalism about knowledge*.

The plausible counterparts of these views are not (I believe) pure (or unrestricted) externalism about justification and pure (or unrestricted) internalism about knowledge. For one thing, if knowledge entails truth it cannot be understood entirely in terms of internal variables, since no combination of these, however well it may justify a belief about the external world, entails the truth of that belief. And there appears to be *some* respect in which justification is internally grounded, even if it must also imply (say) some objective probability that a justified belief is true.[17] I propose to say, then that internalism about knowledge is the restricted internalist view that knowledge is at least in part grounded in elements internal to the mind; and externalism about justification is the restricted externalist view that justification is at least in part grounded in elements external to the mind.

Consider beliefs based on sense-experience as plausible support for internalism about justification. My justification for believing that there is a green field before me is grounded in my sense impressions, and I can become directly aware of them (so have access to them) by simply "looking within" or by appropriate reflection on my experience. By contrast, the grounds of my knowledge of something through Lizzie's testimony are not thus accessible. I cannot become aware of her reliability – which is a crucial ground of my knowing anything through her testimony – without doing more than considering the contents of my mind. To become aware of the grounds for my knowledge of the truth of what she says, I need evidence of her reliability, say through checking her testimony by making observations over time.

Justificationist views of knowledge (roughly those that construe it as essentially embodying justification of a kind that is not analyzable in terms of reliability) typically embody an internalist conception of justification. Reliability views of knowledge typically embody an externalist conception of knowledge and (if they appeal to the notion) of justification, take both to be grounded in ways to which we do not necessarily have access by introspection or reflection. (Reflection need not be introspection and is important for the internalist account of our internal access to the grounds of a priori justification: above all to our understanding of concepts and their relations.)

The internalist view of justification becomes internalism about knowledge if one adds the requirement that the belief be true and one appropriately strengthens the standards of justification, for instance by requiring that the justification essential for knowledge be undefeated. The externalist view of knowledge becomes externalism about justification if one subtracts the requirement that the belief be true and appropriately weakens the epistemic standards, such as the required degree of reliability. If, as this view says, a justified belief must be reliably grounded, for instance in a reliable perceptual process, the reliability need not be such as to guarantee its truth. Justified belief, unlike belief constituting knowledge, need not be true.

Some varieties of internalism and externalism

Internalism about justification and externalism about knowledge are, in their qualified forms, compatible, whereas pure internalist and externalist views cannot both hold, either for justification or for knowledge. There are many versions of internalism and externalism, whether they are restricted as I have suggested or meant to apply unrestrictedly to both justification and knowledge. An important respect in which internalist views differ among themselves concerns how readily the justifiers are accessible to introspection or reflection. An important and parallel way in which externalist views differ among themselves is in the kind of non-introspective knowledge or justified belief they take to be possible regarding the grounds of knowledge: one might, for instance, think that commonsense observation is enough to ascertain how reliable perception is, or one might take scientific evidence to be necessary for determining this.

Many points underlie the contrast between internalism and externalism. My concern is chiefly with what seem the most plausible internalist and externalist views: internalism about justification and externalism about knowledge. To simplify matters, let us consider these views mainly in relation to the nature of the grounds of justification and knowledge, not as applied to *how*, or how strongly, those sources justify. This is, however, a further respect in which internalist and externalist views differ among themselves as well as from one another, and I will note some points about it below.

The imagined internalist about justification holds only that the grounds of one's justified beliefs are internal, for instance sensory states of the kind present in perception. The view does not say that *how*, or how strongly, those grounds justify beliefs based on them must (say, by guaranteeing their truth) be an internal matter and thereby, in principle, accessible to introspection. Similarly, the imagined externalist holds that what grounds knowledge – reliable grounding of the constituent true belief – is not wholly internal, and so not wholly accessible to introspection, even if part of the ground, say sensory experience, is. If what grounds knowledge is not wholly internal, then how it does so is not either.

It is of course natural to think (as reliabilists tend to) that how such belief production grounds knowledge is *less* likely to be accessible to introspection or reflection than what elements ground knowledge; the former is, for one thing, more complex. Similarly, internalists may hold (plausibly, I think) that our access by introspection or reflection to what grounds our justification is better than our access to how it grounds that justification.

If these internalist views about justification and externalist views about knowledge are roughly correct, then the main point of contrast between knowledge and justification is this. Apart from self-knowledge, whose object is in some sense mental and thus in some way internal, what one knows is known on the basis of one's meeting conditions that are not (at least not entirely) internally accessible, as states or processes in one's consciousness are. By contrast, what one justifiedly believes, or is simply justified in believing, is determined by mental states and processes to which one has internal (introspective or reflectional) access: one's visual experiences, for instance, or one's memory impressions, or one's reasoning processes. All of these are paradigms of the sorts of things about which we can have much introspective knowledge.

It is significant that for the externalist about knowledge, even introspective knowledge is based partly on what is not accessible to introspection, namely on the appropriate kind of functional relation between the thing known, say my imaging, and the beliefs about it that constitute self-knowledge, in this case my believing that I am imaging. Roughly, because my imaging process reliably grounds my believing that I am imaging, I know I am; but I have no internal access (and ordinarily none at all) to the reliability of this process. Even if I can be aware of some of the presumably causal connections between imaging and believing I am imaging, I would apparently need inductive, partly external evidence to become aware of the reliability of the process grounding such belief.

What is central for knowledge, in the externalist view, is that the beliefs constituting it register truth, and this objective connection between the grounds of a belief and its truth is understood in a way implying that the belief-grounding factors are not internal in the crucial way: they are not necessarily accessible to introspection or reflection. Perhaps I can become directly aware of my imaging, in a way that even externalists grant gives me a kind of internal access to the imaging; but I have no such access to how reliably imaging produces true beliefs that one is doing it. I can become aware of that reliability only through a study of how well imaging works in producing true introspective beliefs. This requires at least making observations, some of which are external, and relying on memory of one's results; nor would this awareness be introspective or reflectional.

On the other hand, what is central for internalism about justification is that justified beliefs be those that one is in some sense in the right in holding, given the sensory impressions, rational intuitions, and other internal materials introspectively accessible to one. In very broad terms, the strongest contrast may be this. Insofar as we may appropriately use the language of rights, we might say that the internalist regarding justification tends to conceive justification, in accordance with certain justificational standards, as a matter of having a *right to believe*, and of knowledge as occurring when justification is combined with truth in a certain way; the externalist about knowledge tends to conceive knowledge, in accordance with certain epistemic standards, as a matter of *being right* and of justification as occurring when one's belief is, in a certain way, likely to be right.[18]

This terminology can be misleading if one thinks of having a right as always applicable to actions; for beliefs are not actions, nor can we in general (if ever) bring it about at will that we believe something, the way we can move our limbs at will. But there are rights to property, and that is not action either. The central internalist idea about justification is that of meeting a certain justificational standard that one can conform to on the basis of a kind of response to accessible elements. Internalists strongly associate having justification for belief and a readiness to *justify* it: roughly, to give one's ground(s) for it. This readiness presupposes that the grounds are accessible. This contrasts with the reliabilist notion of justification as having, on the right kind of ground, a true or probably true belief. The contrast might be described as roughly between a kind of permissible belief and a kind of successful belief. Moving further from the language associated with rights (as I think wise), we might say that the contrast is between belief that is *internally and justificationally well-grounded* and belief that is externally (in an objective way) *truth-conducively grounded*. One appeal of this conception of justification is that it links grounds of justification closely with grounds of knowledge, which in some sense seem to be clearly truth-conducive.

Internalist and externalist versions of virtue epistemology

Internalist and externalist approaches in epistemology represent a basic division. The contrast between them can help in understanding any comprehensive epistemological theory, and applying them to a sample theory can also help in understanding them. Consider, for instance, *virtue epistemology*, which is roughly the position that knowledge and justified belief are to be understood as expressions of epistemic virtue, taken roughly as a capacity, such as observational acuity, apt for arriving at truth.

Virtue epistemology is modeled on virtue ethics, which takes the concept of moral virtue to be the basic moral concept and construes moral actions as the kinds that express that capacity, say by being grounded in the virtuous character traits of honesty or justice. For instance, Aristotle said of the virtues of justice and self-control, "acts are called just and self-controlled when they are the kind of acts which a just or self-controlled man would perform; but a just or self-controlled man is not [defined as] he who performs these acts."[19]

Different theories analyze and divide epistemic virtue in different ways, say into observational and a priori virtues and further into perceptual versus introspective virtues and (on the a priori side) into logical and mathematical ones. On an internalist virtue theory, justified belief would (roughly) be belief based on internally accessible grounds understood in terms of, and connected in the person with, an epistemic virtue. For instance, a justified belief might be based on sensory experiences taken as the kind of thing an epistemically responsible person relies on for the kind of proposition in question. On an externalist virtue theory, justified belief would be roughly belief based on processes that are connected with a virtue and reliably lead to truth. Accurate observations producing perceptual belief would be an example of such a process, and making them is a typical manifestation of epistemic virtue.[20]

For either kind of virtue theory, knowledge would imply truth; but whereas the internalist would *also* require its resting on accessible grounds, the externalist would not. To see the contrast better, recall Macbeth's hallucination of the dagger. For an internalist virtue theorist, if his sensory experience is normal enough and he has no accessible reason to doubt his acuity, his belief that there is a dagger before him may be justified: it is the kind of belief a person with virtuous intellectual character would form in the circumstances. For a reliabilist (hence externalist) virtue theorist, the relevant process grounding his belief is presumably not reliable and his belief is not an expression of epistemic virtue.[21] (On neither view would he know there is a dagger, since there is none before him.) Similarly, the *idiot savant* would lack epistemic virtue on the internalist account but might, on the externalist account, have it – in the form of a specific arithmetic virtue.

The chief difference is that virtue is defined in terms of internal standards in the first case and external ones in the second. Both views, however, are virtue approaches to justification because they construe it as an expression of epistemic virtue, as opposed to defining epistemic virtue (as most epistemologists would) as the sort of character feature that tends to produce justified belief.

This contrast between externalist and internalist virtue theories can be developed in many ways. For instance, on externalist lines, the crucial feature of the relevant epistemic virtue would be producing a favorable ratio of true to false beliefs; on internalist lines, the crucial feature would be either producing such a ratio on the basis of internally accessible grounds or – if justification rather than knowledge is the epistemic target – producing a suitable ratio of beliefs that are internally justified.

At this point, we can discern a general problem confronting epistemic virtue theories. Precisely how can we specify the kind of character feature we wish to call an epistemic virtue without *already* having at least a rough account of justified belief and knowledge? For most theorists, the natural approach is first to understand justified belief and knowledge in some non-virtue-theoretic way and then to explicate epistemic virtue as the kind of character trait suited to producing them, a kind, indeed, that can be cultivated by internalizing the more basic standards for appraising belief. Roughly, the idea is that an epistemic virtue is to be analyzed as a trait apt for producing knowledge or justified belief; knowledge is not to be analyzed as, say, true belief reliably produced by an exercise of an epistemic virtue, or justified belief as the kind grounded in an epistemic virtue.

There are various approaches to solving this kind of problem. Quite apart from whether they succeed, the notion of epistemic virtue provides a distinctive perspective on both knowledge and justification. Moreover, knowledge and justified belief could usefully be understood as equivalent to notions rooted in virtue theory, even if the best way to analyze the former is along the kinds of internalist or externalist lines we have been exploring.

The internality of justification and the externality of knowledge

Quite apart from whether we focus on virtue theories or on the more common epistemological positions we have been considering – individual belief accounts of justification and knowledge as opposed to intellectual character accounts – the idea that knowledge is externally grounded and justification internally grounded would help to explain why reliability theories are, in the ways I have indicated, as plausible as they are for knowledge, yet less plausible for justification.

It is true that the sources of justification of belief seem generally to be sources of true belief. But must they be? Could not my apparently normal visual experience in hallucinating a green field where there is none sometimes justify me in believing there is one quite as strongly as an ordinary seeing of it? Surely it could. Moreover, though I would not know that there is a green field before me, the internalist would hold that my justification for believing there is could be quite as good as it would be if I did know it.

To be sure, if I justifiedly believe I may be hallucinating, then I am unlikely to be justified in believing there is a green field there. But my beliefs, including beliefs about possible hallucinations, are themselves internal; we thus have one internal factor affecting the way another bears on justification, not an external factor preventing the generation of justification by a basic source of it. Here, then, internalism can do justice to the phenomenon of defeat of justification.

Moreover, notice how the clear cases of highly reliable belief production illustrated by the predictor and the lightning calculator do not appear to generate justification, though they do appear to generate knowledge. Furthermore, no matter how reliable my perceptual processes are, say in giving me impressions of birds flying by, and thereby true beliefs that they are flying by, if I confidently and reflectively believe that my vision is unreliable, and especially if I also justifiedly believe this, then it is doubtful that I am justified in believing that birds are flying by. The more confident and reflective my justified belief that my vision is unreliable, the less the justification, if any, of my belief that birds are flying by. Thus, in addition to reliable grounding alone not producing justification, its apparent capacity to produce justification in common circumstances is vulnerable to justified beliefs that the beliefs it produces are unjustified or their underpinnings unreliable.

If knowledge and justification do contrast in the suggested way, why is justification important to knowledge at all, as it certainly seems to be? Part of the answer may be that first, the sources of justified belief – experience and reason – are generally (if in a different way) sources of knowledge, and second, virtually the only knowledge we can conceive of for beings like ourselves is apparently grounded, at least indirectly, in those sources. If these points are correct, then we can at least understand how knowledge typically arises if we think of it as (in part) justified belief. If, moreover, we think of it as *appropriately* justified true belief, then, conceiving knowledge under that description, we can at least pick out the vast majority of its instances.

Justification
and truth

There may be a further, perhaps deeper, point implicit in what has been said about justification and knowledge. Justification by its very nature has some kind of connection with truth. One can see this by noting that there is something fundamentally wrong with supposing that a belief's being justified has nothing whatever to do with its truth. This in turn can be seen by noting how the *process* of justifying a belief, conceived as showing that the belief has the *property* of being justified, is always taken to provide grounds for considering the belief true. Justification of our beliefs is by its nature the sort of thing we do when their truth is challenged; justifiedness of those beliefs – which entails justification for taking them to be *true* – is what this process of justification shows when it succeeds.

The connection between justification and truth is perhaps most readily seen in the case of a priori justification. In the paradigm cases, as with beliefs of self-evident propositions and with what self-evidently follows from them as do some very simple theorems of logic, one's having a priori justification apparently entails the truth of the beliefs so justified.[22] These cases are unlike perceptual ones in that if a belief claimed to be so justified turns out to be false, there is at least normally a defect in the purported justification, say a misunderstanding or a careless error in reasoning.

Justification of empirical beliefs also seems connected with truth. If, for instance, I am justified in believing there is a field before me by a clear visual impression, it in some sense follows that I may take it to be true that there is one. If, on the other hand, we discovered that the sense of smell almost never yielded beliefs that corresponded to the facts (thus to truth) as determined by other sources of belief, we would have good reason to cease to regard olfactory impressions as a source of direct justification, or at least to consider them a far weaker source than we now take them to be.

These points about the relation of justification to truth suggest that even if it is an internal matter whether a belief is justified, the standards we use for determining justification are responsive to our considered judgments about which internal sources tend to produce true beliefs. The way we conceive justification, then, makes it well suited to help us understand knowledge, in at least this respect: when a belief is justified, it has the sort of property which, by its very nature as apparently grounding the belief in the real world, we take to count toward the truth of the belief, hence (other things being equal) toward its being knowledge.

Justified true belief need not be knowledge, and knowledge apparently need not be justified belief. But normally knowledge arises from the same sources as justification: normally, the internal states and processes that justify our beliefs also connect our beliefs with the external facts in virtue of which those beliefs are true.

The correspondence theory of truth

This way of speaking of the truth of beliefs suggests that (except in the case of propositions about oneself, say that I am thinking about knowledge and truth) it too is external. That is indeed the view I am taking. Whether there is a green field before me is not a matter of states of my mind. It seems to be an objective matter independent of anyone's mind and the green seems to be present or not regardless of whether we believe it is. Indeed, whether my belief is true is determined by whether the field is actually there; the truth of such obser-vational beliefs depends on external reality, which does not in turn depend on what we believe.

Sometimes this is put by saying that in general the truth of our beliefs is not *mind-dependent*. If truth is not mind-dependent and is at least in that sense objective, then we have a version of *realism*, roughly the view that (external) things are as they are independently of how we take them to be. I am thinking of true propositions, whether believed or not, along the lines of a version of the correspondence theory of truth, whose central thesis is that true propositions "correspond" with reality. It is usually added that they are true in virtue of that correspondence. Thus, the proposition that there is a green field before me is true provided that in reality there is a green field before me; and it might also be said that it is true in virtue of there really being such a field before me.[23]

An expression apparently equivalent to the first, modest formulation of the correspondence view would be this: to say that the proposition is true is to say that it represents reality. This, in turn, is usually taken to mean that it is, or at least expresses, a *fact*. How else could we even think of truth, one might wonder? What else could it mean to say that a proposition is true than that things (or the facts) really are as the proposition has it?

Minimalist and redundancy accounts of truth

One answer to the question of how to conceive truth makes use of the schematic idea that 'p' is true if and only if p; for instance, 'Grass is green' is true if, and only if, grass is green.[24] One might now argue that to say something is true is equivalent to asserting it, in the way illustrated here, and go on to hold that this equivalence is at least the main thing we need to understand about truth. This approach is associated with a *minimalist account* of truth; the idea is roughly that there is no more to understanding truth than understanding this equivalence. For instance, we know what it is for people to assert propositions; we normally know what kinds of considerations confirm or disconfirm the propositions; and we know, in very general terms, under what sorts of conditions to agree or disagree.

If the minimalist account is correct, then either asserting the correspondence of true propositions with "reality" or with "the facts" is nothing more than an equivalent of asserting the schema, or it goes too far. One might think that to give such a minimalist reading of the correspondence view is to abandon it altogether. Perhaps that is so, but at least the schema expresses a *kind* of correspondence: an equivalence between calling a proposition true and asserting it.

One might go even further than the minimalist account and say that, for instance, '"Grass is green" is true' is not just equivalent to 'Grass is green' but essentially the same in *meaning*. This would make the phrase 'is true' redundant: predicating it of a proposition adds nothing to the meaning of the simple assertion of that proposition. On that basis, one might speak of a *redundancy account* of truth. On this view, saying 'That is true' is another way, perhaps sometimes more emphatic, of saying the thing in question. But it has exactly the same content.[25]

The coherence theory of truth

There are other alternatives to the correspondence view. The most widely known is perhaps the coherence theory of truth. Though it takes many forms, its central idea, expressed very broadly, is that a true proposition is one that coheres appropriately with certain other propositions. (The theory may also be expressed in terms of what it is for beliefs to be true, but that formulation invites confusion of the coherence theory of truth with the coherence theory of knowledge, which, though knowledge is constituted by belief, is a quite different theory and does not depend on the coherence theory of truth.)

I cannot discuss truth in detail here, but let me indicate how a coherence theory of truth might go if justification is its central concept. In outline, the theory might say that a true proposition is one which is fully justified by virtue of coherence with every other relevant justified proposition, where a justified proposition is, minimally, one that at least someone is (or anyway might be) justified in believing.[26]

There are serious difficulties in determining what justified propositions are relevant to the truth of another proposition which is true in virtue of coherence with them. A plausible example of how truth can be based on coherence might be a proposition I am perceptually justified in believing, say that there is a maple tree before me, which coheres with what I justifiedly believe on the basis of memory, introspection, inference, and so on, as well as with what I or others would be justified in believing in these ways. This proposition would be true in virtue of coherence with others, such as that I seem to remember a maple there. To say that it is false, by contrast, would be to call it incoherent with certain others, such as the proposition that I fail to have a visual impression of a tree in the relevant place.

The propositions for which I now have justification are not the only ones that matter. If they were, then if I visually hallucinated a maple tree systematically enough, say with accompanying tactual hallucinations and supporting memory impressions, it would be true that there is one before me. By making the set of relevant propositions indefinitely large, the theory seeks to prevent such embarrassing results. Thus, if I am hallucinating, there is surely some proposition I could come to be justified in believing, say that the "tree" will not burn – something I might discover by trying to ignite it – which is not coherent with the proposition that there is a maple there.

Suppose, however, that owing to some quirk of nature – or to some evil genius of the kind Descartes imagined in describing the power of skepticism – there is no proposition I could come to be justified in believing that is incoherent with there being a tree before me. If, for instance, I take a torch to the "foliage," I hallucinate flames. If the deceiving genius undetectably ensures that every such test is positive, the coherence theorist seems forced to conclude that in this case it is true after all that there is a tree before me. But surely it is still possible I am merely hallucinating and that it is false that there is a tree there, despite the unending series of justified beliefs I have or can have confirming that there is one.

This kind of possibility has led critics of the coherence theory to say that the truth of a proposition is simply not exhausted by our coherent beliefs or potential beliefs supporting that proposition, even when they are justified.

Another way to put it is to say that truth is not a construct out of evidence, even excellent evidence that produces a coherent body of beliefs. We can better understand this point if we consider a related theory of truth.

The pragmatic theory of truth

There is also a negative motivation for the coherence theory of truth. When we try to understand what correspondence means, we seem thrown back on some kind of coherence. To say that the proposition that the tree is green corresponds with reality seems to come to little more than saying that in testing this proposition, say by examining the tree in good light, one will always get (or will at least in the main get) confirming results, that is (one might argue), discover propositions that cohere well with the original one. For instance, boiling its leaves will produce a green broth.

This kind of point has led some thinkers to go further and hold a pragmatic theory of truth, on which true propositions are simply those that "work," in the sense that they are successful in practice (pragmatically). What this comes to is chiefly that believing them, acting on them, and otherwise confirming them, leads (at least in the long run) to positive results, such as spectrographic confirmation of the tree's color.[27]

Certainly we do not expect a genuine truth to fail us. If, for instance, there really is a maple there, then I can find shade under it, cut wood from it, and expect others to verify its presence. And we do expect falsehoods to fail us eventually. With enough testing, we tend to think, there will (in principle) be disconfirmation. What more is there to truth as correspondence or, for that matter, truth as coherence, than such pragmatic success?

Correspondence theorists have replied that points made by proponents of coherence (and pragmatic) theories of truth confuse the *criteria* of truth, roughly, the standards for determining whether a proposition is true, with the *nature* of truth, what it is. Turning blue litmus paper red is a criterion of acidity, but it is not what acidity is; that must be characterized in theoretical terms. In support of this, they often argue that a false proposition could cohere with all propositions that are ever justified, including those discovered in attempted confirmation of it. We might, after all, be permanently unlucky in testing it – or permanently foiled by an evil genius (a possibility pursued in Chapter 10) – so that we never discover its falsity; or an ingenious demon might always prevent us from discovering our mistake.

These points parallel some made against phenomenalism, which may (though it need not) be held by a proponent of a coherence theory of truth. In general, a sufficiently powerful evil genius might prevent one from discovering that a stable, recurring set of sense-data which coheres with one's other sense-data derives from hallucination and does not represent a concrete object.

If it is possible for coherence to be systematically misleading in this way, then neither coherence with justified propositions nor any other kind of pure coherence can be what truth is.

I cannot pursue this issue, but it should be plain that it is crucial to assessing the pragmatic and coherence theories of truth. I want to add only that despite the similarities between the coherence theory of truth and the coherence theory of justification, neither theory entails the other. The analysis of knowledge, moreover, can be discussed within either framework for conceiving truth.

It appears, however, that particularly if one favors a reliability theory of knowledge, the correspondence view of truth, even if given a minimalist interpretation, seems most appropriate. This is in part because the notion of reliable production is at least not readily analyzed along coherentist or pragmatic lines, especially if the notion of justification is central in that of truth as the coherence and pragmatic theories of truth conceive truth. For then the apparently value-laden notion of justification would be required for understanding reliability, which is characteristically conceived by reliabilists in naturalistic terms, in part as a property belonging to processes that produce true beliefs. None of this implies that what has been said here refutes coherence or pragmatic theories in every form, but perhaps enough has been said to create a presumption in favor of *some* version of the correspondence theory.

Concluding proposals

Is there no analysis of knowledge that we may tentatively accept as correct and illuminating? There certainly may be; the ones I have discussed are only a representative sample of the available analyses, and even they can be refined in response to problems of the kind I have raised. But there may be no simple and straightforward analysis of knowledge which is *both* illuminating and clearly correct. Much depends on how detailed an account must be to count as an analysis.

We may be able to formulate what is at least a sound *conception* of knowledge, and this should help in seeking a full-dress account. We might say that knowledge is *true belief based in the right way on the right kind of ground*. This conception leaves a great deal open, but what we have seen in this chapter and earlier ones indicates many ways in which one might develop the conception into a detailed account. The conception leaves open that it may, but need not, turn out that the right kind of basis is in part causal. It may, but need not, turn out that the right kind of ground always justifies the belief. It may, but need not, turn out that the right kind of ground is accessible to introspection or reflection, or is a reliable producer of true beliefs, or is an epistemic virtue. And it may, but need not, turn out that ultimately epistemic chains terminate in experience or reason, or in some other kind of ground of knowledge, that is direct in the way foundationalism maintains it is.

In a similar vein, we might conceive justified belief as *well-grounded belief*. Like knowledge, it must be based in the right way on the right kind of ground. We have seen what at least some of the appropriate kinds of grounds are: most basically, perceptual, memorial, introspective, and rational, but also testimonial and inferential. However, the conception leaves open the same kinds of things as the conception of knowledge: whether the right kind of ground is in part causal, whether it is accessible to introspection or reflection or is instead a reliable producer of true beliefs, whether it is an epistemic virtue, and whether, ultimately, justificational chains terminate in experience or reason, or in some other kind of ground of knowledge, that is direct in the way foundationalism maintains it is. In exploring justification and knowledge, I have made a case for some of these options being preferable to others, but here my point is simply that there are conceptions of knowledge and justification that provide a good focus for inquiry regardless of what position one takes on these options.

Quite apart from how these broad questions about knowledge and justification are resolved, then, the conceptions just sketched indicate where a great deal of the work in understanding knowledge and justification must be done. We need an account of how knowledge and justification are based on whatever it is in virtue of which it they count as knowledge or justification, for instance perception, introspection, and reason; and this will require an account of the inferential transmission of knowledge and justification as well as of their non-inferential grounding. Here I have suggested a partly causal account of non-inferential grounds and a holistic account of inductive and deductive transmission of justification and knowledge. We need an understanding of whether the appropriate bases of knowledge must ground it through generating justified belief, or may yield knowledge independently of justification. Here I have suggested that an internalist account seems preferable for justification and a qualifiedly externalist one seems preferable for knowledge. We also need a general understanding of what it is for a belief constituting knowledge to be true. And we need an account of whether the ultimate grounding of knowledge and justification is some kind of coherence among one's beliefs or, as seems more likely on the basis of what has emerged in this book, anchoring in experiential and rational foundations.[28]

Notes

1 The most important passages are probably those in Plato's *Theaetetus*, 201c–210b.

2 The defeat of this account, which set a spate of detailed critiques in motion, was due to Edmund L. Gettier's now famous 'Is Justified True Belief Knowledge?' *Analysis* 23 (1963), 231–3.

3 If I had believed that she is *directly* opposite me, in the sense that there is no obstacle between us, my belief would have been false; but I would not normally have believed that here, where I have no reason even to imagine obstacles.

4 The idea that we can learn much, and perhaps the most important things, about the nature of knowledge by determining what renders a true belief knowledge is also used by Alvin Plantinga. In place of undefeated justification he puts a different concept – warrant – which he characterizes functionally as whatever it is that renders true belief knowledge. See esp. *Warrant and Proper Function* (Oxford and New York: Oxford University Press, 1993), particularly chs. 1–3. Extensive critical discussion of this book, and his replies to it, are found in Jonathan L. Kvanvig (ed.) *Warrant in Contemporary Epistemology: Essays in Honor of Plantinga's Epistemology* (Lanham, Md: Rowman and Littlefield, 1996).

5 This of course assumes that we rule out a probability of 1, which is commonly reserved for necessary truths. For a brief and plausible statement of the view that only beliefs based on conclusive (truth-guaranteeing) grounds constitute knowledge, see Fred Dretske, 'Conclusive Reasons', *Australasian Journal of Philosophy* 49 (1971), 1–22.

6 For a valuable treatment of certainty particularly relevant to the one given here see G. E. Moore, 'Certainty', in his *Philosophical Papers* (London: George Allen & Unwin, 1959).

7 The thermometer analogy, and some of the impetus for naturalism in recent epistemology, comes from D. M. Armstrong. See esp. his *Belief, Truth and Knowledge* (Cambridge: Cambridge University Press, 1973), though some of the relevant ideas are suggested in his (and others') earlier work.

8 The idea that abstract objects, like concepts and propositions as standardly construed, are altogether causally inert should not be taken uncritically. For discussion of this issue and a case that no plausible causal requirement undermines the possibility of a priori knowledge, see Alvin Plantinga, *Warrant and Proper Function (op. cit.)*, pp. 113–17.

9 It seems better to call it reliably *grounded* than reliably *produced* (as many call it), since I could have a belief that is not knowledge until I get appropriate evidence (such as testimony from someone who *is* reliable), and here the belief is not produced by what makes it knowledge, but rather becomes grounded therein. Some writers speak of knowledge as true belief that is reliably produced or *sustained* to capture what I am calling reliable grounding. A further advantage of the wider terminology I use is that it covers both *process reliabilism*, which takes the reliability of process of belief production or sustenance to be crucial for knowledge, and *indicator reliabilism*, which simply requires that the belief be suitably connected with something that indicates it is true.

10 Plantinga's recently developed approach would suggest that the crucial factor in deciding what description to use is how the faculty in question, say vision, is *designed* (whether by God of by evolution or in some other way) to function, for example, in judging the identity of persons directly or despite the presence of impervious objects. Since our visual faculties are not designed to judge in the latter way, the relevant process is not one in which believing someone is in a given place results from seeing the person in a photograph that accurately indicates her whereabouts. One difficulty here is how to determine the design of a faculty. For a detailed presentation of this view see Plantinga, *op. cit.*

11 1For an approach to solving this specification problem, see William P. Alston, 'How To Think about Reliability', *Philosophical Topics* 23, 1 (1995), 1–29. This paper is in part a response to

Richard Feldman's presentation of the problem – under the description 'The Generality Problem' – in 'Reliability and Justification', *The Monist* 68 (1985), 159–74.

12 For a detailed and plausible approach to such questions see Alvin I. Goldman, 'Discrimination and Perceptual Knowledge' *Journal of Philosophy* 73 (1976), 269–82.

13 On Plantinga's notable theory referred to earlier, knowledge is roughly a true belief that results from our cognitive faculties functioning properly in the relevant situation, which is a matter of their functioning as they were designed to function in such a situation. This idea can be adapted to a naturalistic view by construing proper function in biological and psychological terms drawn from a theory of human design, but it is also consonant with a theistic view of our design as determined by divine plan. Plantinga's approach provides a different way of dealing with a number of the problems posed in this chapter (though they remain significant problems), but there is not space to discuss it or other recent theories separately.

14 This example is a variant of the central case described in D. H. Lawrence's story, 'The Rocking Horse Winner'.

15 One might argue that it is obvious that such a belief must be unjustified. I can see a case for its being so, but I do not find it compelling. I also doubt that his having justification for believing his predictive belief unjustified must prevent its constituting knowledge.

16 As this description suggests, I am not thinking of the relevant knowledge as a priori even in the loose sense, but perhaps a case can be made that a kind of understanding of the relevant proposition, as opposed to, say, a subliminal calculation, grounds the knowledge.

17 For two quite different externalist compromises with internalism see Alvin I. Goldman, 'Strong and Weak Justification', *Philosophical Perspectives* 2 (1988) 51–69, and William P. Alston, 'An Internalist Externalism', in his *Epistemic Justification* (Ithaca, NY and London: Cornell University Press, 1989).

18 A. J. Ayer is widely known for having taken knowledge (and I think the kind of justification appropriate for it as well) to entail a "right to be sure." See *The Problem of Knowledge* (Harmondsworth, Middlesex: Penguin Books, 1956), esp. ch. 1. For further discussion see R. M. Chisholm, *Theory of Knowledge*, 2nd edn. (Englewood Cliffs, NJ: Prentice-Hall, 1977), and Carl Ginet, *Knowledge, Perception, and Memory* (Dordrecht: D. Reidel, 1978), esp. ch. 3.

19 *Nicomachean Ethics* 1105b6–9 (trans. by Terence Irwin).

20 Virtue epistemology, despite its roots in ancient Greek philosophy, has received attention in epistemology only in recent years. See esp. Ernest Sosa, 'Knowledge and Intellectual Virtue', in his *Knowledge in Perspective* (Cambridge and New York: Cambridge University Press, 1991); Jonathan L. Kvanvig, *The Intellectual Virtues and the Life of the Mind* (Lanham, Md.: Rowman and Littlefield, 1992); James Montmarquet, *Epistemic Virtue and Doxastic Responsibility* (Lanham, Md.: Rowman and Littlefield, 1993); John Greco, 'Virtues and Vices of Virtue Epistemology,' *Canadian Journal of Philosophy* 23 (1993); and Linda Zagzebski, *Virtues of the Mind* (Cambridge and New York: Cambridge University Press, 1996).

21 I say 'presumably' because it might be that sensory experience *is* a reliable ground, owing to how rarely it misleads, say because hallucinations are either uncommon or (because they do not feel normal) do not produce belief.

22 This entailment thesis is obvious if we adopt the conceptions of the self-evident and of strict a priori justification proposed in Chapter 4. But simply working with the intuitive notions of the self-evident and the a priori, the entailment claim has some plausibility.

23 A classical statement of the correspondence theory of truth is found in Aristotle's *Metaphysics*. For a study of the correspondence view and a defense of realism concerning truth in general, see William P. Alston, *A Realist Conception of Truth* (Ithaca, NY and London: Cornell University Press, 1996).

24 The schema is question is commonly called (Alfred) Tarski's T schema or the *disquotation principle*, since in the way illustrated it provides for eliminating quotation marks. For

minimally technical discussions of its bearing on our understanding of truth see W. V. Quine, *Pursuit of Truth*, revised edn. (Cambridge, Mass.: Harvard University Press, 1992), ch. V, and Mark Sainsbury, 'Philosophical Logic', in A. C. Grayling (ed.) *Philosophy: A Guide Through the Subject* (Oxford: Oxford University Press, 1995).

25 The literature on truth, even on any one account of it, is immense. For a brief defense of the redundancy view see Quine, *op. cit.* and for brief criticism of it see Alston, *A Realist Conception of Truth*. One might, like Quine in many places, speak of (declarative) sentences as true or false, and the minimalist and redundancy approaches have been taken to apply primarily to sentences. For reasons I cannot detail, this may have advantages over the standard terminology in the text, but it also raises problems.

26 Although G. W. F. Hegel (1770–1831) is often regarded as the leading historical proponent of the coherence theory of truth, a clearer statement is probably to be found in Brand Blanshard, *The Nature of Thought* vol. 2 (London: Allen & Unwin, 1940). Cf. Donald Davidson, 'A Coherence Theory of Truth and Knowledge', in Dieter Hendrich (ed.) *Kant Oder Hegel* (Stuttgart: Klett-Cotta, 1983), 423–38.

27 William James argued that truth is what works. See esp. his *Pragmatism: A New Name for Some Old Ways of Thinking* (New York: Longman, Green, 1907). Cf. John Dewey, 'Propositions, Warranted Assertibility, and Truth', *Journal of Philosophy* 38 (1941).

28 I have not presented these conceptions of knowledge and justification as analyses, in part because of how much they leave unspecified. But it may be argued that they do constitute analyses and indeed say as much as an analysis, as opposed to a full-blown theory meant to foreclose options an analysis should leave open, ought to say. For a case to this effect regarding the proposed conception of knowledge, see James E. Taylor, 'Conceptual Analysis and the Essence of Knowledge', *American Philosophical Quarterly* 30 (1993).

CHAPTER 9
Scientific, moral, and religious knowledge

Scientific knowledge

The focus and grounding of scientific knowledge
Scientific imagination and inference to the best explanation
The role of deduction in scientific practice
Fallibilism and approximation in science
Scientific knowledge and social epistemology
Social knowledge and the idea of a scientific community

Moral knowledge

Relativism and noncognitivism
Preliminary appraisal of relativist and noncognitivist views
Moral versus "factual" beliefs
Ethical intuitionism
Kantian rationalism in moral epistemology
Utilitarian empiricism in moral epistemology
Kantianism and utilitarianism compared

Religious knowledge

Evidentialism versus experientialism
The perceptual analogy and the possibility of direct theistic knowledge
Problems confronting the experientialist approach
Justification and rationality, faith and reason
Acceptance, presumption, and faith

Scientific, moral, and religious knowledge

In perceiving the world around us we constantly acquire knowledge: of colors and shapes, objects and events, people and their doings. We also acquire knowledge as we look into our own consciousness. By thinking about things we already know and by drawing inferences from those proposi- tions, we extend some of our knowledge. And through memory, we retain much of our knowledge. Justification is acquired, extended, and retained in much the same way.

But how far does our knowledge extend? We have explored how knowledge is transmitted once we have some, but not the range of subjects and questions to which it extends. There are three important domains in which we are widely thought to have knowledge of truths that are central in guiding our lives: the scientific, the moral, and the religious. We should consider how both know- ledge and justification may occur in these domains. The task is immense; here I simply want to show how the framework laid out so far might help us to understand knowledge and justification in relation to some important aspects of science, ethics, and religion. The focus will be more on knowledge than on justification. But much of what comes to light regarding knowledge will apply to justification, and some of it may hold in other domains, such as that of art or history or literature.

Scientific knowledge

If we knew nothing through perception, we would have no scientific know- ledge or even everyday observational knowledge. And however much scientific knowledge one can acquire by instruction and testimony from someone else, the discoveries which that knowledge represents must be made partly on the basis of perceptual experience: if not through someone's laboratory work or observations of nature, then by somebody on whose perceptions the discoveries depend, directly or indirectly.[1]

The focus and grounding of scientific knowledge

How does scientific discovery fit into the framework I have developed? If we start with the idea that perception is basic for scientific knowledge, the picture which readily comes to mind is that one makes observations, inductively generalizes from them, and, through the inductive transmission of knowledge from one's premises to one's conclusion, comes to know the truth of a generalization. Imagine Galileo rolling balls down his famous inclined plane. He measures their acceleration, collects the individual items of knowledge he thereby acquires, arrays them as premises, and generalizes (in a special way) to his formula (Galileo's Law), which gives the rate of acceleration for such balls in general. What does a case like this show?

First, the example rightly suggests that scientists tend to be interested in the nature and the behavior of *kinds* of things, such as accelerating objects, and that what is typically considered scientific knowledge is of generalizations: for instance, propositions about all freely falling bodies, not about any particular one. Knowledge of particulars is needed to obtain such general knowledge, but the former may be just ordinary perceptual knowledge. Granted, knowledge which is of a particular thing, but derived from a scientific generalization, say knowledge that a parachutist will land at a specific time, is scientific in the sense that it is scientifically *based*. Still, it is not the sort of knowledge regarded as paradigmatically scientific, or the kind scientists directly seek in trying to understand nature.

The second point suggested by the example is that scientific knowledge is inductively, not deductively, grounded. For instance, the generalization Galileo discovered concerning acceleration does not *follow* from the premises he formulated in expressing his data, say that ball 1 accelerated at a certain rate, that ball 2 accelerated at that rate, and so on. The generalization is strongly confirmed by such premises, but not entailed by them. For this reason, such premises, regardless of how well they justify it, do not prove it. Proof of a proposition requires either a premise that entails it, or at least an event whose occurrence establishes it, as where one proves that someone is in town by introducing him.

The same point holds for premises of other scientific reasoning that yields, from knowledge of data, knowledge of a generalization. Thus, it is best to avoid calling the reasoning that supports a scientific generalization "scientific proof," as some people do. It is not even deductively valid, much less the kind of reasoning illustrated by a geometrical proof of a theorem from axioms.

A third aspect of the example, however, may mislead. The example portrays Galileo simply observing and then generalizing, yet says nothing about *why* he is observing. But he made his observations for a reason. This is to be expected; scientific knowledge typically does not arise simply from haphazard observations. Normally there is a question, such as whether falling objects speed up, that leads to observing a particular kind of thing.

Moreover, there is normally a tentative answer to such a question – a *hypothesis* – which both guides observation and sets the epistemic goal of the observations or the experiments that lead to scientific discovery. For instance, one might hypothesize that the balls speed up 100 percent in a given time interval and thus observe their speed at each such interval to see whether the initial speed doubles, quadruples, and so on. One's goal in this is to show that the hypothesis is true and thereby come to know it, or, if it is not true, to find a hypothesis that does account for the behavior of the balls.[2]

The central point here is that scientific knowledge does not automatically arise as we observe our surroundings. Normally, we must first raise questions about the world; they direct our inquiry. Only in the light of such questions are we in a good position to formulate hypotheses. These, in turn, are the raw material of scientific knowledge. Some are rejected, some are confirmed, and some that are confirmed become knowledge.

Scientific imagination and inference to the best explanation

Scientific knowledge does not develop, then, simply by inferential extension of what we already know. Normally, it emerges only after we use some imagination, both in formulating questions and in framing hypotheses to answer them. This is one place where scientific *invention* occurs. It is not only machines and devices that are invented but also hypotheses and theories. Invention and discovery may, however, coincide: if you invent a theory that is true, you may be said to discover the truth it states.

The essential place of imagination in developing scientific knowledge is also illustrated by discoveries that result not from coming to know a generalization, but from apparent refutations of a proposition thought to be already known. The planet Neptune was discovered because the observed orbit of Uranus (then the farthest known planet) was not as expected according to the laws of planetary motion, the principles astronomers use in describing the motions and paths of the planets. Partly in order to avoid having to revise well-confirmed laws, it was hypothesized that the deviation of Uranus from its expected orbit was caused by the gravitational effect of a more distant planet. The observations made to test this hypothesis revealed Neptune.

If the Neptune hypothesis was considered the best available explanation of the data, we could speak here of an *inference to the best explanation*: roughly, an inference to a hypothesis on the ground that it best explains one or more other propositions taken to be known or justifiedly believed – or at least taken to need explanation and to be candidates for justified belief or knowledge if the hypothesis turns out to be true. (If two or more hypotheses are equally good explanations, we may justifiably choose between them as we see fit.)[3]

Once again, through the use of imagination, a hypothesis is formulated, and through testing it, a discovery is made and new knowledge acquired. And again, the basis of the new knowledge is inductive, though unlike Galileo's knowledge about freely falling bodies, it is not a result of generalization. The pattern here is a successful case of inference to the best explanation. One imaginatively hypothesizes a gravitational influence by another planet as best explaining the deviation, tentatively infers that there is such a planet, tests the hypothesis, and, through positive results of the test, comes to know that the hypothesis is true.

We have already seen, in discussing the structure of knowledge and justification, that a proposition's explaining one or more others can count toward its justification, and that this point can be accounted for in either of two ways. First, one might note the role of explanation in increasing the coherence of the patterns to which the explaining and explained propositions belong. Second, we might take, as a principle of the transmission of justification from justified premises to a conclusion drawn from them, that if we are justified in believing the premise that a proposition explains one or more others, then we tend to have some justification for believing the proposition itself. The point here, however, is not mainly about justification but about discovery. We discover a great deal by seeking explanations and positing one or another hypothesis to explain the puzzling data.

The role of deduction in scientific practice

These examples do not imply that deduction has no substantial role in the development of scientific knowledge. Far from it. Once we have a hypothesis, we typically need deduction to determine how to test it. For instance, one needs deductive mathematical reasoning to predict where to look for an as yet undiscovered planet, given a certain deviation in the orbit of Uranus.

Moreover, from very general laws, such as Newton's laws of motion, one may deduce less general laws, for instance the laws of planetary motion and Galileo's law of acceleration. (Actually, the best that one may be able to do is deduce generalizations which these laws only approximate; for instance, Galileo's law, which represents increase in acceleration as uniform, does not take account of slight changes in acceleration due to minute increases in gravitational attraction as the falling object nears the Earth. But this deduction still helps to explain why we should get approximately the results we do in testing or applying that law.) Deduction may, then, not only take one both from a hypothesis and auxiliary assumptions (such as propositions about conditions of observation and the power of one's telescope) to a proposition about a single event, say the sighting of a planet; deduction may also take one from general laws or wide-ranging theoretical principles to less general laws or narrower principles.

Deductions of the second kind help to unify scientific knowledge. For example, they enable us to exhibit all the special laws of motion – for planets, for falling bodies, for projectiles, and so on – as instances of the general laws of motion. Even the behavior of gases, conceived as collections of molecular particles, can be explained by appeal to the general laws of motion. Their pressure in a container of air, for instance, is explainable in terms of how hard the particles hit its walls. This pressure, in turn, is connected with their temperature viewed as explainable by their average speed of movement. Thus, the laws of motion provide an understanding of what determines both pressure and temperature. They also give us, by appropriate deductive inferences, a subsidiary law (Boyle's Law) correlating temperature with pressure at a constant volume.

Can we, then, have scientific proof after all, where we validly deduce a special law of, say, motion, from more general ones? No; for even if we might prove the special law *relative to* the more general ones, our knowledge of the more general laws is ultimately inductive. That knowledge is based on inference to the best explanation or on generalization from observed data or, more likely, on a combination of these procedures. If our scientific premises are not proved, and if indeed they stand to be revised as new discoveries are made, which is a common fate of generalizations in science, then what we know only through deduction from those premises is not proved either. These premises are indeed exposed to possible disconfirmation through the discovery of counter-evidence to what we deduce from them. If what is deducible from a set of propositions turns out to be false, then the premises that entail it are false as well: as presumptive guarantors of its truth, they must share in its falsification.

Fallibilism and approximation in science

So far, I have sketched some of the ways in which what we call scientific knowledge develops, and I have criticized certain stereotypes of science. It is not, for instance, a domain in which hypotheses are proved conclusively. Nor are they typically discovered by simply generalizing from observations we happen to collect. These points, however, imply nothing about whether scientific generalizations are true, or can be known.

If a common fate of generalizations in science is their eventual revision, one might now wonder whether we should not also reject the idea that there is scientific knowledge at all. Even the incomparable Sir Isaac Newton, as he was called, turned out to be mistaken on some important points; and even if discovering this took more than centuries, is there good reason to believe that any other scientific generalizations are, strictly speaking, true, in the sense that they describe the world both correctly and timelessly, and apply to its past, present, and future? If some are true, that may not be typical. Very commonly, what we call scientific knowledge is regarded by scientists as needing refinement and as possibly mistaken. Quite properly, their attitude is fallibilistic.

If scientists accept *fallibilism* regarding scientific beliefs – the view that these beliefs may be mistaken – they also tend to hold a kind of *objectivism*: the position that there is an objective method for ascertaining whether beliefs about the world are true, that is (roughly speaking), a method which can be used by any competent investigator and tends to yield the same results when properly applied by different competent investigators to the same problem. Scientific method is widely taken by scientists and philosophers alike to be a paradigm of an objective method.

Since we cannot know propositions that are not true, one might conclude that we should really not speak of scientific knowledge at all, but only of relatively well-confirmed scientific hypotheses. This is a defensible position. We may prefer, however, to account for the apparent facts in a way that allows us to maintain that there is scientific knowledge. One possibility is that in speaking of scientific knowledge we are often speaking a bit loosely of what might be called *approximate knowledge*: well-grounded belief which holds true up to a certain level of precision in measurement – apart from "minor inaccuracies," one might say. Newton's laws have not, after all, been found to be completely inaccurate. In building bridges, as opposed to dealing with astronomical distances or elementary particles, they seem to be an adequate guide, and their being only approximately true need cause no trouble.

One can insist that what is not precisely true is simply not known. But we could also say that what is approximately true may be an object of approximate knowledge, and that beliefs of such propositions are both fallible and typically held with an openness to their revision in the light of new discoveries. I prefer the latter way of speaking.

There is, however, a second way to account for the apparent falsity of certain scientific generalizations. It seems that often their formulations are not properly taken to be absolutely precise, and that, rightly interpreted, they are true within the appropriate limits. Consider the general law that metals are conductors of electricity. Perhaps this should be interpreted with the understanding that certain abnormal (or for practical purposes impossible) conditions do not obtain. If metals should fail to conduct electricity at absolute zero, would this show the generalization false or simply that its appropriate *scope of application* is limited? The latter view seems more plausible.

These points in defense of scientific generalizations against the charge of wholesale falsity do not imply that none of those generalizations can be shown to be simply false. The point is that in some cases, instead of saying that scientific generalizations are not really true and hence do not represent genuine knowledge, it is preferable to speak either of approximate knowledge of a precisely formulated, but only approximately true, generalization or, as in this case, of unqualified knowledge of an imprecisely formulated truth. The difference is roughly that between *approximate knowledge* and *knowledge of an approximation*. In practice, however, there may be no easy way to decide which, if either, of these cases one is confronted with, or which indicates the better way to represent the state of one's knowledge in a given scientific area.

Scientific knowledge and social epistemology

I have so far spoken mainly about knowledge as individual belief. There is, however, scientific knowledge in journals no one entirely remembers. This can be called *virtual knowledge* since no one has it, but many of us can easily acquire it. It is as accessible as our connections to our libraries; and a day could come when much information of that kind is more readily accessible by computer than are items of information we must carefully draw from long-term memory.

A natural assumption, however, even for such knowledge in the public domain, is that individuals have generated it and that only one or more individuals can acquire it. This is not an uncontroversial assumption. Science is often said to be a social enterprise, and some thinkers, including some proponents of *feminist epistemology*, consider it unreasonably "individualistic" and even atomistic.[4]

The bearing of the social character of science on the justification and knowledge it generates is a major focus of *social epistemology*. If individual epistemology is roughly the theory of knowledge and justification as applied to individual persons – the enterprise we have been engaged in – social epistemology is roughly the theory of knowledge and justification as applied to groups of people.[5] The field of epistemology has traditionally been concerned with individuals taken one at a time, apart from the notable exception of the status of testimony as a source of grounds for belief. Why should there be this individual emphasis, if indeed there should be?

It seems quite possible that a single individual could have both knowledge and justification even if no group does, whereas it is not possible that there be a group that has actual knowledge or justification when no individual member of that group has knowledge of or justification for the proposition in question. *We* cannot know anything unless you or I or some other individual knows it – though there are things we cannot *learn* by ourselves. Thus, in the case of a map of the world, knowledge by many people is needed to build the resulting social representation of geographical knowledge. Nonetheless, one of us could survive the rest and retain knowledge, or an omnipotent God could have created just one finite person with the capacity for knowledge and an environment in which it is exercised. In this respect, individual knowledge and justification are apparently *logically prior* to their social counterparts: the former is possible without the latter, but not conversely.

Virtual knowledge is an exception: "we" can have it in our libraries, though no one in particular has it. There is still another case in which we can have virtual knowledge of something that no individual literally knows. You and I might each know one of two things that obviously imply a third, and, if we work together, we might thus be said to "know" the third but to have not quite have articulated it. Perhaps I know that the assailant wore a full-length cape and you know that only one person near the crime scene did so; between us we have a solution to the crime.

Social knowledge and the idea of a scientific community

Both examples of virtual knowledge are instances of what might be called *social knowledge*. But the first kind of virtual knowledge (illustrated by the library case), though *socially accessible,* is *individually realizable,* whereas the second kind of virtual knowledge (illustrated by the detective case) is in a sense *socially constituted.* Any competent individual can get the former; only cooperating individuals can get the latter.

The priority of individual over social knowledge by no means implies that given an adequate understanding of individual epistemology, one can easily construct a social epistemology. That is not so. It is an interesting and difficult question what relation must hold between a group and its members in order for *its* knowledge or justification regarding a proposition to reside in one or more of those members. This brings us to a related kind of priority of the individual over the social.

As the metaphor of residing suggests, what a group knows or justifiedly believes is constituted by what one or more members knows or justifiedly believes. If *we* (human beings) know that wet grass is slippery, for instance, then some of us must have appropriately grounded true beliefs of that proposition. Not all of us have to; but if only a few of us do, then it would be wrong to say that *we* know, as opposed to, for instance, 'It is known', referring to the group as the context in which the knowledge occurs.

Where a subgroup is intended by 'we', the situation may be different. If the 'we' designates the scientific community, then it is permissible that only a few members know in order for the group to know. It can be true that "we" now know the mass of a proton even if only a very few have the appropriate information. This may be precisely because scientific knowledge is social in the sense of *socially sharable* (in a way introspective knowledge of one's own sensations is not sharable). It is also both *publicly accessible,* at least in the sense that it is normally open to public testing and proper use by any competent investigator, and, typically *cooperatively generated*, in that most of it arises from team efforts.

These three points about the social character of scientific knowledge in part explain what it is to say that there is a *scientific community*. It is arguable, moreover, that some kinds of knowledge are (empirically) impossible without cooperation, as in the case of knowledge of a theory whose development and confirmation requires a team effort.[6] Indeed, a measure of scientific cooperation is commonly required even to *maintain* scientific knowledge once it is acquired. For given the problems and challenges facing scientific hypotheses and theories as new information is acquired, the grounds on which they are maintained will often be eroded unless new evidences or arguments are found to explain away new data found by opposing theorists or new investigations.

What the relevant examples of social knowledge seem to suggest is, on the one hand, the *genetic priority* of the social over the individual in the development of our scientific knowledge – with testimony as well as scientific cooperation playing a crucial role in producing that knowledge – and the *constitutive priority* of the individual over the social in epistemological matters: social knowledge, justification, and indeed belief, are constituted by individual knowledge, justification, and belief, respectively. The constitutive priority in question applies both to actual knowledge and justification, as I have illustrated, and (with such qualifications as are indicated by the detective case) to virtual knowledge (and virtual justification).

The notion of virtual knowledge is implicit in the idea of "scientific knowledge" as the scientifically grounded "knowledge" accessible to us within a certain degree of readiness – for instance in journals that are widely available – but not residing in any person's belief. It is because there is no belief of the relevant propositions that there are scare quotes around 'knowledge'. What is not believed (or in any way stored in someone's mind) is not literally known. Nonetheless, the constitutive priority of the individual clearly applies to virtual knowledge: plainly, we would not have access to the relevant knowledge unless some individual(s) among us did, at least in the sense of having access to crucial premises, as in the detective case.

Even if we do not take individual knowledge to be prior to social knowledge, we still have the question of the status of apparent scientific knowledge (and any other social knowledge). If we consider science in historical perspective and do not idealize it, it turns out that there is no unqualified answer to the question of whether what is called scientific knowledge is knowledge as I have been conceiving it in this book. If we assume that there are some scientific propositions which are strictly true – and I see no cogent reason to doubt that there are some – then we apparently have no good ground for thinking that they cannot be known (or at least justifiedly believed). But the history of science indicates much change and extensive, apparently ceaseless correction of previously accepted hypotheses. For all the progress it exhibits, it also gives us cause to wonder whether even at this advanced stage in scientific development we grasp many scientific truths about the world that future investigation will never show to be inaccurate.

I am inclined to say that in spite of both scientific error and the fallibility of scientific attitudes, we do have much scientific knowledge, even if it is all only approximate knowledge, or knowledge of approximations. But even if we have a great deal of scientific knowledge, if much of it is approximate or is knowledge of approximations, we are quite some distance from the artificial picture one might have of scientific knowledge as a set of beliefs of precisely formulated and strictly true generalizations, arrived at by inductive transmission of knowledge from its basic sources in experience and reason. Those sources remain basic, and scientific method provides an objective way of building on them. But there is no straightforward transmission, or, when transmission occurs, any clearly final destination toward which it proceeds.

Moral knowledge

The possibility of moral knowledge raises rather different sorts of questions from those just explored. Moreover, whereas there is a widespread tendency to take for granted that there is much scientific knowledge, there is a widespread inclination to take moral judgments to be at best cultural assumptions with no claim to genuine truth.

Consider the judgment that cruelty to children is wrong. A clear example would be the judgment that it is wrong to thrash a three-year-old for accidentally spilling milk.[7] We accept this, but do we know it? Suppose someone denies it or simply asks us to justify it. It does not appear that we can establish it scientifically. It is apparently not a scientific judgment in the first place. Furthermore, it is not in any obvious way a judgment grounded in perception, nor is it clearly grounded in reason, at least in the way the a priori truths discussed in Chapter 4 apparently are. Many people find it natural to consider this judgment to be grounded in our culture and to be accepted simply as part of the social fabric that holds our lives together.

Relativism and noncognitivism

There are at least two major variants of the view that moral judgments are somehow grounded in our culture. One of them allows that they are true, but only in a qualified sense that reflects their being anchored in the culture in which they occur. The other takes them not to belong to truth-stating discourse at all. Let us take these views in turn.

The first view – *a kind of relativism* – says roughly that moral judgments are true relative to our culture (or even some subculture), but not unqualifiedly true, as judgments of fact, such as that a green field lies before me, may be. This is not to say merely that moral judgments are *relativized* – true in relation to certain circumstances, as where 'We should not kill' is said to be true relative to non-self-defensive conditions. This relativization view does little more than restrict moral judgments, often uncontroversially, to the cases in which they properly apply. Relativism of the kind in question is the thesis that there are, say, American moral truths, British moral truths, Chinese moral truths, and so on, but no *universally valid* moral truths – even if some moral principles are *universally held*.

The second view that (in a way) takes moral truths to be culturally grounded – *the attitudinal view* – says roughly that such judgments are not literally true at all; rather, they are expressions of moral attitudes, not assertions of a proposition. Normally, these are attitudes rooted in the culture of the person judging, but a noncognitivist might allow a subgroup or even a single individual alone to qualify as having a morality in the sense relevant to providing the basis of moral judgment. On one version of the attitudinal view, to say that cruelty to children is wrong is like uttering 'Cruelty to children!' in a tone expressing revulsion and adding, 'I condemn it!'. The attitude is moral both because of what it concerns and because it represents a certain kind of cultural stance. Such attitudes may be reasonable or unreasonable and may be defended with reference to what is true or false; but attitudes are not themselves true or false.

On both views, there is no moral knowledge, since either there are no moral propositions at all (the negative claim of the attitudinal view), or there are at least none that are true or false unqualifiedly (the negative claim of the relativist view in question), whereas propositions expressing empirical or a priori truths are unqualifiedly true or false. The attitudinal view is thus committed to (ethical) *noncognitivism*, which is roughly the claim that there are no moral propositions to be known, or otherwise "cognized." The (ethical) relativist position in question need not endorse noncognitivism; but doing so can clarify a relativist view, since, as will be evident in some examples, it is not clear precisely how propositions can be true in a way other than the sense in which empirical and a priori truths are, and it is clear (at least in outline) how moral attitudes can be rooted in a culture.

The attitudinal interpretation of moral judgments is on the surface the more radical view. It implies that there simply are no moral truths – or moral falsehoods either. There are no moral propositions to be known, or to be justifiedly or even mistakenly believed in the first place. What makes this view plausible?

Suppose one is very impressed with the basic sources of knowledge as our only routes to knowledge, and one notes that apparently no propositions known on the basis of sense experience seem to entail the truth of any moral judgment, for instance that cruelty to children causes them pain does not entail that it is wrong. Needed surgery, after all, may cause them pain yet not be wrong.

When we judge something to be wrong we apparently go beyond the evidence of the senses, and indeed beyond scientific evidence. For example, suppose that (as is surely possible) we know scientifically that in fact cruelty to children commonly breeds brutality in its victims. Unless we already know or are justified in believing that breeding brutality is wrong, the fact that cruelty to children breeds brutality does not justify us in believing that cruelty to children is wrong.

It seems to noncognitivists, then, that we cannot know that cruelty to children is wrong just on the basis of the fact that it causes brutality; this fact would (deductively) ground that knowledge for us only if we already knew that brutality is wrong. Now suppose we also assume that nothing known a priori entails that cruelty to children is wrong: no logical truth surely, and not even a synthetic proposition like the truth that nothing is red and green all over at once. These points serve as premises for the negative conclusion that there is no moral knowledge. For if knowledge is grounded in the basic sources and moral judgments are not grounded in them, then moral judgments do not constitute knowledge.

There is also a positive thesis held by the attitudinal theory: that (even though moral judgments do not express propositions) moral judgments do express significant attitudes. A main reason for saying they express attitudes is that we are not neutral in making moral judgments; we are (normally) pro or con regarding the things we morally judge. Normally, we at least indirectly commend or condemn when we make a positive or negative moral judgment.

Now suppose we combine the positive view that moral judgments express attitudes with the negative view that there are no moral propositions, which itself implies that there is no moral knowledge. It is now plausible to conclude that the *point* of making a moral judgment is not to assert an unknowable proposition, but to express a positive or negative attitude and thereby to influence human conduct, if only by endorsing or condemning one or another kind of behavior. Many noncognitivists hold this third position.

Noncognitivism does not imply that in moral matters "anything goes"; for it is still possible to hold an unreasonable moral attitude, say one based on misinformation or prejudice. The view can thus allow that there are even moral mistakes. But mistakes that are specifically moral are mistakes in attitude, not about what is true.

The relativistic view that moral judgments are culturally grounded endorses the first argument just set out, based on the premise that those judgments are not rooted in the basic sources of knowledge, but not the second, attitudinal argument. On this relativist view, although moral judgments are not rooted in those basic sources, they are learned as we absorb (or react against) our culture, and they may thus share with judgments that do represent knowledge a wide social acceptability. Still, we are at best entitled to assert them within our society (or one that morally agrees with it), and they are at best true for one or another society. They are not unqualifiedly true, hence not genuinely known in the sense that implies cross-culturally valid standards of evidence. If they express propositions, those propositions are assertable in our culture, but not unqualifiedly true.

Preliminary appraisal of relativist and noncognitivist views

To assess the relativist and noncognitivist views, consider first the part of each position not shared with the other one. Let us start with the attitudinal aspect of noncognitivism and proceed to the cultural groundedness thesis of relativism.

Is there an alternative explanation of the attitudinal aspect of moral judgments? Might they be true or false and still have, for instance, the commendatory or condemnatory force they do? Take the utterance, 'The curtains are on fire!' Sincerely uttered by any normal person, this would commonly express alarm and be meant to evoke action. But it is clearly factual and can be unqualifiedly true.

Moreover, it seems to be because of its factual content that the judgment that the curtains are on fire expresses the kind of alarm it does. Perhaps certain statements of those facts that are significantly and obviously linked to human concerns are no more attitudinally neutral than are typical moral judgments. For this reason (among others), one might resist the idea that either the distinctive or the main function of moral judgments is to express attitudes, as opposed to asserting propositions. It might just be that the facts relevant to moral judgments are socially important in a certain way, as is the curtains' being on fire.

Similarly, one might explain the fact that moral judgments are, in some cases, culturally tinged and differ from one culture to another, by arguing that the *beliefs* they express may be learned through absorbing a culture, even if what *justifies* those beliefs or renders them knowledge does not depend on a particular culture, for example on its customs or prejudices. Clearly, the origin of a belief need not be what justifies it, nor need it reflect the truth of the proposition believed, if it is true. Thus, we might learn a moral principle through something characteristic of our culture (such as our moral education), even though what justifies it is not grounded in our culture but, perhaps, something pertaining to human life as such. Our moral education might reflect this universality; but one could first learn a moral truth from an unreliable source – say, someone who deceitfully calls another person unfair – and later get a good justification for it.

Suppose that our moral beliefs do arise from our education and culture, and are in this sense culturally and historically "conditioned," as it is sometimes put by theorists working in the *sociology of knowledge*, a field that overlaps both social epistemology and feminist epistemology. There is good reason to say that at least many of our scientific beliefs are also culturally and historically conditioned. If we need not thereby regard the relevant scientific beliefs as culturally relative, why should we so regard moral beliefs?

One might think that unless they are scientifically justified, moral judgments are merely true for those who hold them. But both moral and scientific judgments, moreover, are "true for" the social groups that hold them, at least in the sense that the people in question believe them. Does that not indicate a kind of relativity in both cases? That is doubtful: *anything* we believe is in that sense true for us. If this is how moral judgments are relative to those who make them, their "relativity" is shared with simple self-evident truths, such as that if the spruce is taller than the maple, then the maple is shorter than the spruce.

Is there some other sense of 'true for' that discriminates between the sense in which anything we believe is true for us and the elusive sense in which moral judgments are, according to some relativists, true for some people and not others? One might try taking 'true for' as equivalent to 'true from the (cultural) point of view'; but what does this come to beyond saying that 'It is true for my culture' means 'My culture believes it'?

Another possibility is that 'true for' means something like 'successfully works for'; this would be illustrated by 'One ought to drive on the left side of the road' is true for the British but not (many) others. But this does not yield a general relativism or at least not one that sets ethics apart from science. It is equivalent to something like '*In Britain* one ought to drive on the left', and that simply specifies circumstances in which the judgment applies, just as 'at sea level' specifies when the air pressure on Earth is 14.7 pounds per square inch. This *circumstantial relativism* – as we might call it – is simply the plausible view that what we ought to do depends on circumstances. It says nothing about the status or nature of the truth of moral principles once they are stated in relation to – relativized to – the circumstances they apply to. It leaves open that they might then be seen to be true of false in the usual sense appropriate to propositions about the empirical world.

There are certainly different kinds of circumstances in different cultures, and there may be important moral principles true for one society and not another, in the sense that in one of the societies, but not the other, people generally *believe* them. But, as the analogy to scientific disagreement indicates, that would show nothing about whether moral principles or judgments are relative in any sense implying that they cannot be known or justifiedly believed.

Moral versus "factual" beliefs

We are now getting close to the heart of the issue concerning the possibility of moral knowledge. For it will be objected that we can use experience and reason, say perceptual facts and deductive logic, to test scientific beliefs, but not to test moral judgments, which are still relative in a way scientific judgments are not. We are back to the argument which the relativist and attitudinal views commonly share: that since experience and reason do not ground moral judgments, those judgments cannot express knowledge. This argument must be squarely met.

The first thing to be stressed is that from the premise that moral judgments are not formally deducible – derivable by the rules of deductive logic – from facts, it simply does not follow that they are not justifiable by appeal to facts. That this conclusion does not follow seems evident from our discussion of scientific knowledge, which (assuming that there is some such knowledge) illustrates that knowledge can arise through inductive transmission from evidential premises. Scientific generalizations, for example, are inductively known (if known at all) on the basis of the facts, such as observational data, which we use to confirm them. If there can be scientific knowledge on this basis, then there can be knowledge based on inductive grounds, grounds that do not entail the proposition we know on the basis of them. Thus, there might be inductively grounded moral knowledge even if no moral knowledge is deductively grounded.[8]

The obvious reply to this argument is that moral generalizations are not even inductively supported by the facts. But is that true? We certainly appeal to facts to justify moral judgments. I might justify my judgment that I must meet with Jane by citing the simple fact that I promised to. This does not prove that I must meet with her, but it surely provides a good reason for the judgment that I must. There is, moreover, a third possibility we should examine: that even if such a fact does not imply a moral judgment by the rules of logic, it implies it in a different kind of a priori way.

Ethical intuitionism

This brings us to a major account of moral knowledge, one quite different from the deductive and inductive ones so far specified. Suppose someone asks why I should keep my promises in the first place. I could perhaps explain why I believe this. But suppose that I cannot justify it by appeal to anything more basic. This would not show that I do not know or justifiably believe it. At some point or other in defending a factual judgment I may be equally incapable of giving a further justification. It would not follow that the judgment I am defending does not express knowledge or justified belief.

The issue before us should be explicitly considered in the light of what we saw concerning the structure of knowledge. A foundationalist may say that (with some special exceptions) the principle that one should keep one's promises, or at least some more general principle, such as that people should be treated with respect, is self-evident, knowable a priori, and needs no defense by derivation from prior principles. This *intuitionism* does not claim that everyone who considers the relevant principle will find it obvious immediately; but that same point will hold for certain truths of logic which, when they are finally understood, are comfortably accepted as self-evident. The crucial thing is that the principle can be seen to be true through intuitive reflection.[9]

Foundationalists will tend to argue that such a response is legitimate when we get to certain stages in a process of justification, because some beliefs (including many that are not self-evident) are foundational in a way that entitles us to hold them without doing so on the basis of prior premises. If that were not true, then we could not be justified in holding anything. A coherentist may be willing to go on arguing, perhaps pointing out that if we do not keep our promises life will be unbearable, and then, for each thesis attacked, defending it with respect to one or more others. The objector may not be pacified by this approach either. But neither approach can simply be rejected out of hand. To be warranted in rejecting either approach, one must have a plausible alternative conception of knowledge and justification. What would it be? That is far from evident, as we shall soon see in exploring skepticism.

These responses in support of the possibility of moral knowledge do not go as far as one might like. They rest on limited analogies and on simply showing that the case against moral knowledge is inconclusive. But there are two other important responses we should consider. One, defended perhaps most powerfully by Kant and later Kantians, as well as by intuitionists, construes knowledge of moral principles as a priori. The other, defended perhaps most powerfully by Mill and later utilitarians, represents moral principles as empirical. In either case, moral knowledge and moral justification are grounded in the basic experiential and rational sources I have been discussing.

Kantian rationalism in moral epistemology

To understand the first, broadly Kantian, response, consider another application of the principle that cruelty to children is wrong: the proposition that flogging infants for pleasure is wrong. There is some plausibility in saying that we know this. Intuitionists would tend to say we know it non-inferentially; Kantians would likely hold that we know it as an obvious application of the categorical imperative, which, in one form, says that we are to act only on principles that we can (rationally) will to be universal laws of nature obeyed by us all.[10] The proposition that flogging infants for pleasure is wrong seems plausible on even brief reflection about what it is to flog infants. It is difficult to conceive exceptions, and it is certainly difficult to conceive circumstances that would lead rational persons not to endorse it provided they are taking either the point of view of universalizability or the equally Kantian point of view of commitment to treating people as ends and never merely as means. To be sure, perhaps such cruelty as flogging an infant might be excusable. Terrorists might electrically manipulate my brain so that I change in personality and am somehow brought to flog an infant; but even then I would be doing something wrong, though doing it in an excusable *way*.[11]

Consider another example, a modest version of something more powerful: we ought to treat people equally in matters of life and death, say in regard to wartime military service, unless they differ in some relevant way (and not merely in being different people). This is a kind of principle of consistency, not logical consistency, but something like consistency in roughly the sense of using a principled policy or procedure in deciding important matters. It says that such prima facie inconsistent treatment is wrong and that differential treatment in these mortal matters must be justifiable by a difference. It does not specify what kind of difference is relevant, for example that the health of candidates for organ transplant is relevant and their skin color is irrelevant. Specifying relevant differences is a further step. But the principle is still a moral one, and it implies the important requirement that a reason be given to justify the indicated differences in treatment. Particularly since it is a kind of consistency principle, there is some reason to believe that if it is true, it is knowable a priori, though defending this idea would be a major task.

As this perspective on the principle of equal treatment suggests, it is natural to take the Kantian view to be internalist in its moral epistemology: it is by the use of reason, and hence through grounds accessible to reflection, that we know and can justifiedly believe sound moral principles. We may need much experience to understand moral concepts; but once we understand them, sufficient reflection on them provides justification for basic principles of action and thereby for moral principles.

Utilitarian empiricism in moral epistemology

The second response to relativist and noncognitivist views in moral epistemology, the response of Mill's utilitarianism, is very different. It says that (1) our moral judgments are knowable on the basis of factual knowledge of how our acting in accordance with them would contribute to something that is intrinsically good: good in itself, independently of what it leads to. Mill maintained that (2) only pleasure and freedom from pain are good in themselves. He apparently believed that if these two premises can themselves be known (as he thought they could be), they justify holding, as one's fundamental principle of moral action, something like this: that precisely those acts are right which contribute at least as much to pleasure (and freedom from pain) in the world as any alternative available to the agent in question. (I ignore the points Mill raises later about qualities of pleasure.[12])

Since, on Mill's view, we can determine what these optimal acts are, that is, what acts have the most utility, by a combination of common sense and scientific procedures, moral judgments are knowable in the same way as common sense and scientific statements. By contrast with Kant's moral epistemology, Mill's (and that of at least the majority of utilitarians) is externalist: we have access to grounds of moral truths only through considerations about the consequences of actions for pleasure and pain, and those considerations require observational or other kinds of inductive evidence.

A question that now arises is how we know that pleasure or anything else is intrinsically good. Mill argued that (for one thing) we can know this by determining what people by nature actually desire for its own sake. But the utilitarian approach is by no means committed to that view (which many commentators on Mill find implausible). For instance, it might be argued instead that what is intrinsically good is what people want or would want for its own sake provided their wants are adequately rational, say held in the light of reflection that is logically and scientifically rational, vivid, and appropriately focused on the nature of the thing wanted.[13]

Kantianism and utilitarianism compared

The Kantian and Millian utilitarian responses to challenges to moral knowledge are nicely parallel to Kant's and Mill's views of the truths of reason. On Kant's rationalistic view (only part of which has been introduced), moral principles are (synthetic) a priori. On Mill's empiricist view (only part of which I have stated), moral principles are empirical.

There is a further epistemologically interesting contrast here. On Kant's approach, or at least in some approaches of the same rationalistic kind, such as intuitionism, there can be direct (non-inferential) moral knowledge. For on these views at least one moral principle is so basic that knowledge of it need not be inferentially grounded in knowledge of any other propositions. On the utilitarian approach, there cannot be direct moral knowledge except in special cases. The main and perhaps only cases seem to be these. First, some direct moral knowledge is only *memorially direct*, that is, direct (non-inferential) as preserved in memory but originally indirect and now direct just by virtue of one's forgetting one's evidential grounds for it, as one forgets the steps in proving a theorem and remembers only the theorem. Second, some moral knowledge is *testimonially direct*, that is, non-inferentially grounded in testimony, where (for the utilitarian) this requires that at some time *someone* (say, the attester) knew the truth inferentially.

Both of these memorial and testimonial cases would be *secondary knowledge*, since the knowledge depends on other knowledge of the same proposition and is not primary in the way that, say, perceptual knowledge is. Secondary knowledge need not, however, be inferential, since it need not at the time in question be based on other knowledge. For Mill, knowledge that, say, keeping one's promises is obligatory would ultimately depend on someone's knowing a good deal about the effects of promise-keeping on happiness. One could know the principle through parental teaching given in the course of one's moral education, and one could establish it for oneself by studying human behavior and then retain one's knowledge of it after forgetting one's grounds. But no one could know it directly unless someone knew it inferentially, through evidence.

This difference between Kant and Mill – the former providing, as do intuitionists, for direct moral knowledge and the latter not – is no accident. According to Mill's utilitarianism, moral properties, such as being obligatory, are unlike sensory properties in not being directly experienced. As an empiricistic, and thus experience-based, moral theory, it must treat knowledge of moral truths as ultimately indirect (unless, as has occasionally been done, it posits moral experience as a source of knowledge that grounds knowledge rather in the way perception does). Thus, even if, by memory, I have some direct moral knowledge, no moral knowledge is *independently basic*, in the sense that it need not at *any* time be grounded in another kind of knowledge. If I know that cruelty to children is wrong, it is by virtue of my (or someone's) knowing that it does not contribute optimally to happiness in the world.

For a broadly Kantian view, on the other hand, we can rationally grasp this principle, at least as a consequence of a more general principle; and for intuitionism, we can sometimes even *directly* grasp a moral principle, for instance that arbitrarily unequal treatment of persons in matters of life and death is wrong. On both these views, then, we can have moral knowledge which is direct and independently basic. But even if Kant is best interpreted as construing the most general moral knowledge as depending on non-moral premises, he took all general moral knowledge to be deductively derivable from (and only from) a priori premises and thus itself a priori (at least in the loose sense).

Should Kantian or utilitarian or intuitionist views convince us that there is moral knowledge? From what I have said about them, it is not obvious that they should. But, when carefully developed, they are each plausible, and each may be held with the attitude of objectivistic fallibilism that is also appropriate to scientific views. Each view certainly seems to warrant the conclusion that there *can* be moral knowledge; and apparently there is some, despite the sorts of relativistic and attitudinal arguments I raised to indicate why some thinkers deny its possibility.

There are, of course, other issues that should be explored in deciding whether moral principles or judgments can be known, or even justifiably believed. There may, for instance, be sources of moral knowledge, such as a special moral faculty analogous to perception, which are not in the end rooted in experience or reason as conceived in Part One. But I see no reason to believe there are. Suppose, however, that we have a special moral faculty. Presumably, it is a kind of rational capacity whose insights are rational ones capable of being known or at least justifiedly believed. Whatever the problems that remain, perhaps enough has been said to connect those problems with the epistemological framework developed in this book. Certainly, locating moral judgments in that framework is at least a good way to approach the question of whether they can constitute knowledge.

Religious knowledge

The case of possible religious knowledge is different in many ways from that of possible moral knowledge, but it can still be clarified in the light of some of the concepts and principles introduced in this book. Again, I want to be brief and to start with the negative view, in this case that religious propositions are simply beyond the scope of human knowledge. I have in mind propositions about God, such as that God exists, brought order out of chaos, and loves us: propositions that do not merely have a religious subject matter but also imply that God (or some other spiritual reality worthy of a central place in a religion) *exists*.

Why would it be thought that no religious propositions are known? The most common ground for holding this view is probably much like the most common reason for holding that there is no moral knowledge, namely, that religious propositions, such as that God exists, cannot be known either a priori or on the basis of experience, say by inferring God's existence from the premise that God's designing the universe is the best explanation of the order we find in it.

Both aspects of this negative claim have been discussed by philosophers and theologians at great length, and there are well-known arguments for the existence of God meant to provide knowledge that God exists. Some of these make use only of a priori premises; others use only empirical propositions as premises. For instance, the ontological argument, in one form, proceeds from the a priori premises that God is supremely perfect (has all perfections in the highest degree), and that existence is a perfection, to the conclusion that God exists. By contrast, the argument from first cause (in one form) uses the empirical premise that there is motion, together with the general premise that there cannot be an infinite chain of causes of motion, and concludes that God, as an unmoved first mover, exists.

There is a vast literature about these and all the other historically important arguments for the existence of God.[14] I am not concerned here with arguments for God's existence. All I want to say about those arguments is that nothing in the framework I have developed implies either that there can or that there cannot be cogent arguments for God's existence. For instance, nothing said about the basic sources of knowledge or about its transmission implies that those sources could not in some way lead to arguments yielding knowledge of God or of some other spiritual reality. The same point applies to justification of beliefs about God or some spiritual reality, and both points hold within either a foundationalist or a coherentist epistemology.

Evidentialism versus experientialism

But what about the possibility – less often discussed than arguments for God's existence – of direct (non-inferential) knowledge of God? Does the framework of this book rule out that possibility? General epistemological considerations have sometimes been thought to do so, but they do not. Indeed, if there can be what I have called natural knowledge, as in the case of direct knowledge of arithmetical results ordinarily knowable only through lengthy calculation, then there is some reason to think that knowledge can be built into a person in such a way that the person could have direct knowledge of God. To be sure there may be less mystery about how a mere calculational mechanism could be built into the brain than about how knowledge of an external, spiritual reality could be. But a mystery is not an impossibility.

If, however, it is even possible that there is an omnipotent God, then that God could create such direct theistic knowledge. If there can be such knowledge, then one form of what is called *evidentialism* is mistaken, namely, *evidentialism about theistic knowledge*, the view that knowledge of God is impossible except on the basis of adequate evidence. (The kind of evidence intended is not the non-inferential "evidence of the senses," such as we have for there being a printed page before us, but the sort one would have in the form of premises from which one may infer theistic conclusions).[15]

How might evidentialism apply to justification? Recall the prima facie cases of direct knowledge of something that is ordinarily knowable only through evidence or inference, such as the results of multiplying two three-digit numbers. If there is direct knowledge here, it need not be a case of justified belief. So we cannot use such examples to refute *evidentialism about theistic justification*: the view that justified beliefs about God are impossible except on the basis of evidence.

Could one be directly justified in believing such religious propositions as that God exists? Would this require one's having a sixth sense, or some kind of mystical faculty? And even if there should be such a thing, would it generate justification directly, or only through one's discovering adequately strong *correlations* between its deliverances and what is believed through reason and ordinary experience, for instance through one's religious views enabling one to predict publicly observable events? In the latter case, the mystical faculty would not be a basic source of justification. Before it could justify the beliefs it produces, it would have to earn its justificational credentials through a sufficient proportion of those beliefs receiving confirmation from other sources, such as perception and introspection.

There is, however, a way to resist evidentialism and argue for the possibility of direct justification of certain religious beliefs without assuming that there are any sources of justification beyond reason and normal experience. In particular, this approach need not posit either mystical apprehensions, such as overpowering, ineffable, otherworldly experiences, or special divine revelations, whether in those experiences or in the presence of apparently miraculous changes in the external world.

I call the position I have in mind *experientialism*, since it grounds the justification of some very important religious beliefs in experience rather than in evidential beliefs or direct rational apprehension. Religious people sometimes say that, in perfectly ordinary life, God speaks to them, they are aware of God in the beauty of nature, and they can feel God's presence. Descriptions of these sorts might be considered metaphorical. But if God is, as many think, properly conceived as a (divine) person, these avowals might have a literal meaning.

It is natural to object that all one directly hears in such experiences is a special kind of voice (presumably in one's mind's ear), that all one directly sees is the natural beauty which one takes to manifest God, and that one simply feels a spiritual tone in one's experience. From these moves it is easy to conclude that one is at best indirectly justified in believing one is experiencing God. After all, one believes it inferentially; for instance, on the basis of one's belief that the voice one hears is God's, one might believe that the beauty one sees is a manifestation of divine creation, and so forth.

The perceptual analogy and the possibility of direct theistic knowledge

To assess the case just made to show that theistic beliefs are inferential and so not candidates to be directly justified (or direct knowledge), compare perception. Suppose it is argued that one is only indirectly justified in believing there is a green field before one, since one believes it on the basis of believing that there is grass, a green textured surface, and so on. Must we accept this? I think not. I do not normally even have these beliefs when I believe there is a green field before me, even if I do see it by seeing its grassy surface.

The matter is far more complicated than this, however. It may be argued that since God is both infinite and non-physical, one *cannot* be acquainted with God through experience. But this argument will not do. Even if a stream were infinitely long, I could still see it by seeing part of it. Seeing an infinite thing is not seeing its infinity. On the other hand, if seeing the stream is not seeing its infinity, then how can seeing it be a basis for knowing that the stream is infinite?

Similarly, if God is experienced, how can the experience reveal that it is God who is experienced? The problem is not that God is non-physical. The non-physical can be quite readily experienced, and indeed in a direct way. Thus, my introspective experience presumably *need* not be of something physical, even if in fact it is of something physical, say a brain process; and even if it must be (because of some necessary connection that might hold between the mental and the physical), it is not experience of, say, my thoughts *as* physical.

The problem, then, is not that there cannot *be* experience, even quite unmystical experience, of God. It is (in part) that if experiencing, say, God's speaking to one, is possible, it is not clear how one could know (or justifiedly believe) that it is *God* speaking. How would one know that one was not having a merely internal experience, such as talking to oneself in a voice one thinks is God's, or even hallucinating a divine voice? (Some of these are skeptical questions of a kind to be discussed in the next chapter.) In part, the question is how one might *recognize* God. Plainly, this requires having a concept of God. But that is acquirable without already having knowledge of God. One also needs a concept of, for instance, an aircraft carrier to recognize one. These concepts are very different, but either one can be acquired without actually knowing of the existence of (or experiencing) what it represents.

Here it is important to recall the perceptual analogy. Why would it be less likely that my experience of looking toward the green field is hallucinatory? It is true that there is a difference: we can, with all the other senses, verify that we see a grassy field, whereas God seems perceptually accessible at most to sight and hearing – presumably indirectly, since God is seen in appropriate things and heard through hearing voices that are not literally God's (at least if a being's voice must be physically grounded in a physical embodiment, though even in that case, some would argue that God's voice was physically embodied in Christ). But even if God is accessible to sight and hearing only indirectly, it does not follow that knowledge and belief about God are indirect. As we saw in exploring the sense-datum theory, we can know one thing through another without inferring facts about the first from facts about the second. The force of this difference between the possible perceptual accessibility of God and that of physical objects can be exaggerated. Surely it is not true that sense experience can be trusted only when verification by all the other senses is possible. If that were so, we could not justifiably believe we see a beam of light that is perceptually accessible only to our vision.

Problems confronting the experientialist approach

There are many other relevant questions. Take first a psychological one of the kind relevant to epistemology. Do people ever really believe directly that, say, God is speaking to them, or is such a belief based – though not self-consciously – on believing that the voice in question has certain characteristics, where one takes these to indicate God's speaking? Second, how is the possibility of corroboration by other people – what we might call *social justification* – relevant? Does it, for instance, matter crucially, for experiential justification for believing in God, that not just any normal person can be expected to see God in the beauty of nature, whereas any normal person can be expected to see a green field? Or is this contrast blunted by the marked differences in perceptual acuity we find between clearly normal people, particularly in complicated matters such as aesthetic perception in music and painting, where what is directly heard or seen nevertheless cannot be seen or heard without both practice and sensitivity?

A related question is the possible role of testimony as a social source of direct justification. If it is true that (as argued in Chapter 5) beliefs based on testimony are commonly direct, then perhaps certain theistic testimony by some provides knowledge of God to others. Even if one supposed that very few people have theistic knowledge or justified theistic belief, one might argue that the relevant testimonial chains can extend to many people – either during a given period of time or, where there is a community of believers, across time extending as long as thousands of years. To be sure, justification seems different from knowledge here, at least insofar as one must have justification for believing someone in order to acquire justification for what is attested. But perhaps religious believers often have this justification; it is at least not obvious, for instance, that they must as rational persons have a kind of justification that is out of their reach.

Whatever the place of testimony in providing theistic knowledge or justification, one might expand the possibilities for direct experience of God. Might God be seen, not necessarily in the ethereally direct way mystics have sometimes imagined, but in a more ordinary, if no less direct, fashion? If so, there is more ground to testify *from* as well as less need for testimony as a source of theistic knowledge or justification. Might God be seen, for instance, in nature, rather than so to speak inferred from it? Here is one of Gerard Manley Hopkins's poetic expressions of that idea:

> The world is charged with the grandeur of God.
> It will flame out, like shining from shook foil;
> It gathers to a greatness, like the ooze of oil
> Crushed . . .
> And for all this, nature is never spent;
> There lives the dearest freshness deep down things . . .[16]

After all, if nature is God's work – perhaps God's ongoing work – there might be a sense in which God is seen in it by those with the appropriate sensitivity – a condition also required for seeing the beauty in a painting.

This is not to say that nature is partly constitutive of God, at least not in the way that the color and shape by which I see a spruce tree are in part constitutive of it. Still, could nature, as some views apparently have it, be partly constitutive of God? If it is, then directly perceiving God may in a way be too easy, or at least quite easy to do without directly perceiving the divinity in what one sees. One could not see a beautiful landscape without seeing God, though one could see it without seeing it as manifesting God.[17]

The dimensions of these questions quickly widen, and even the many points that have come to light do not put us in a position to say whether there can be directly justified religious beliefs. It has so often been taken to be obvious that there cannot be, however, that it is important to see why it is really not obvious. It is at best very difficult to establish absolute restrictions on what sorts of beliefs can be directly justified. This holds even if the only way in which beliefs can be directly justified is by virtue of their grounding in the basic sources of justification.

A parallel point holds for absolute restrictions on what we can justifiedly believe (or know) on the basis of one or more arguments. It is particularly difficult to determine what can be justifiedly believed (or known) through a combination of plausible but individually inconclusive arguments for the same conclusion. As both coherentists and moderate foundationalists are at pains to show, there are times when a belief is justified not by grounding in one or more conclusive arguments, but by its support from – which implies some degree of coherence with – many sets of independent premises none of which, alone, would suffice to justify it.[18]

Furthermore, it is often hard in practice to distinguish, even in our own case, between beliefs that are grounded directly in one of the basic sources and beliefs that are grounded in those sources through other beliefs of which we may not even be aware, or through inferences we do not realize we are making from propositions which we are aware we believe. This means that what we take to be direct belief may really be based on at least one other belief and may depend for its justification on the evidence or grounds which some other belief expresses. If there cannot be directly justified religious beliefs of the kind we have been discussing, however, it might still be true that there can be direct

knowledge of such propositions; and for some religious people, even knowledge without justification might be considered very precious in this case. It
would, perhaps, be one kind of faith.

Justification and rationality, faith and reason

Our topic in these passages about theistic justification is sometimes called the
question of faith and reason. In discussing that question, reason – above all
rationality in holding religious beliefs – is commonly thought to be roughly
equivalent to justification. I take it, however, that although a justified belief
must be rational, a rational belief, while it perhaps cannot be patently unjustified, need not be positively justified.[19] Consider a belief that someone likes
you. It can be rational on the basis of a vague "intuitive" sense before it is
justified by evidence.

Moreover, justification seems tied more to specific justifiers than rationality
is to any analogue of a justifier. If I justifiedly believe there is a cold glass in my
hand, my justification is (chiefly) my tactual sensations; if I rationally believe
that a painting is beautiful, there need be nothing comparable. I must have
color sensations, but there is no sensation specifically of beauty as there is of
the cold glass.

Perhaps rationality belongs for the most part to beliefs that are broadly
consonant with reason and hence contrast with those that are irrational,[20]
whereas justification not only contrasts with irrationality but seems always to
trace to some kind of specific, adequate ground. Mere absence of conditions
that would make a belief *un*justified do not imply that it is justified, but at
most that one may suspend judgment on its negation as opposed to being
justified in disbelieving the proposition in question (believing it false). But *in* a
rational person, absence of conditions that would make it irrational to hold a
belief, together, at least, with certain experiential or social patterns favoring it,
do tend to imply that it is rational. I may rationally believe a painting is
beautiful if it seems so to me and I can find no reason to the contrary; I cannot
justifiedly believe this without some ground (though the ground may be only
a sense that it is like others widely considered beautiful by competent
observers).

If rationality is a weaker – i.e., more permissive – notion than justification,
then in the theistic case as in the scientific and moral cases, it provides a
positive status that a belief can have short of being justified. This is an important point. For if rationality is possible without justification yet implied by it, a
plausible conclusion is that the experiential and rational grounds that, when
sufficiently weighty, produce justification may, even when not quite weighty
enough to yield justification, still render a belief based on them rational. A
theistic belief might then be rational even if not justified. There might, to be

sure, have to be *some* consideration weighing in the direction of justification, and one could speak here of some degree of justification; but as examples we explored earlier show, one can have some degree of justification for a proposition without being (unqualifiedly) justified in believing it.

These points about the difference between justification and rationality do not show that anyone *does* hold rational theistic beliefs, or even that scientific or moral beliefs are ever rationally held. But if rationality is a weaker notion than justification, there would at least be better reason to think that this is so than there would be if the requirements for rationality were as strong as those for justification. In particular, whatever the weight of the considerations we have seen favoring the possibility of justification for scientific, moral, and theistic beliefs – and I think the weight is substantial – those considerations weigh more heavily in favor of the possibility of rational scientific, moral, and theistic beliefs.

Acceptance, presumption, and faith

One further line of thinking should be introduced here. We need not explore either justification or rationality in these three domains only in terms of belief. There are attitudes weaker than belief in the degree of conviction they imply, yet strong enough in that psychological dimension to guide thought and action. Some philosophers have taken *acceptance* in this way. Accepting a scientific hypothesis, in this terminology, does not imply believing it, but it can commit one to using the hypothesis – say, that a certain disease is caused by a particular chemical – as a premise in (tentative) reasoning and in guiding one's day-to-day actions. Similarly, in ethics one might *presume* the truth of a moral proposition, say that a certain job would involve one in a conflict of interest – without believing it. And in theology, one might have faith that, for instance, God is sovereign in the universe, without unqualifiedly believing this. In all three cases, one cannot have extremely strong doubts about the proposition; but one can have or entertain some degree of doubt, in a way one cannot if one genuinely believes it.[21]

It seems clear that the weight of evidence or grounding required for *either* justification or rationality will be less for these non-belief-implying attitudes than for belief. For instance, faith that a friend will recover from a disease can be rational when the situation is too bleak for justified (or even rational) *belief* that the recovery will occur. I might be perfectly reasonable, so far as the evidence goes, in having faith where I would be unreasonably underplaying the facts if I *believed* the recovery will occur. And I can accept a hypothesis, at least for purposes of determining how to think and act in an urgent matter, when it would be premature to believe it. To be sure, religious faith differs in significant ways from the kind just described, but the main point still applies:

whatever the grounds needed for justified theistic belief, weaker grounds will suffice for theistic faith with the same content, say that God is sovereign.

It turns out, then, that epistemology broadly conceived may consider not just the scope of our knowledge and justified belief but also the scope of our rational belief and even of other rational attitudes toward propositions, such as certain kinds of acceptance, presumption, and faith. This extension of epistemological appraisal to other, weaker attitudes provides more scope for rationality that there would be if it applied only to belief: the same level of evidence or grounding may take us further in the domain of attitudes like acceptance, presumption, and faith than in that of belief.

The question of how far our knowledge and justification extend beyond our beliefs grounded directly in experience or reason turns out to be complicated. We at least have warrant for rejecting the stereotypic view that whereas there obviously exists scientific knowledge as an upshot of proof, it is at best doubtful that there is any moral knowledge, or even can be religious knowledge. It seems a mistake to talk of scientific proof at all if that means (deductive) proof of scientific hypotheses or theories from observational or other scientific evidence. Moreover, scientific knowledge does not often represent uncontroversial beliefs of precise generalizations, but is typically either approximate knowledge, often known to need refinement, or knowledge of approximations, formulated with the appropriate restrictions left unspecified.

There is good reason to think that we also have, and certainly have not been shown not to have, moral knowledge. And there is apparently no cogent reason to deny the possibility of religious knowledge. The same holds for moral and religious justification; and in all three instances, the scientific, the moral, and the religious, the case for the possibility of rational beliefs seems undefeated and, beyond that, stronger than the case for justification. Both cases appear stronger still as applied not to beliefs but to attitudes like acceptance, presumption, and faith conceived as in a certain way weaker than belief. There are, of course, important skeptical arguments we have not considered, arguments that attempt to undermine all these positive conclusions and many views about the scope of knowledge, justification, and rationality. It is time to examine some of those arguments.

Notes

1 Cf. W. V. Quine's point that "Observation sentences [such as 'Rain' (for 'It is raining') and 'Milk' (for 'That is milk')] are . . . the vehicle of scientific evidence . . . But they are also the entering wedge in the learning of language." See *Pursuit of Truth*, revised edn. (Cambridge, Mass.: Harvard University Press, 1992), p. 5.

2 For a good non-technical discussion of scientific inquiry and confirmation, see Carl G. Hempel, *Philosophy of Natural Science* (Englewood Cliffs, NJ: Prentice-Hall, 1966).

3 My characterization of inference to the best explanation quite properly does not require that the inferred hypothesis be true. If, however, we make the plausible assumption that only true propositions are (genuine) explanations, then the term 'inference to the best explanation' is misleading: the idea is roughly that of inference to what seems the (or a) best explanation.

4 Feminist epistemologists have emphasized the social and cultural "situatedness" of knowers and their interdependence. They have also challenged the claims to scientific objectivity that many philosophers have made for scientific work properly carried out. For wide-ranging essays in and about feminist epistemology, see Kathleen Lennon and Margaret Whitford (eds) *Knowing the Difference: Feminist Perspectives in Epistemology* (London and New York: Routledge, 1994); and *Feminist Epistemology: For and Against*, The Monist 77, 4 (1994).

5 For a representative collection of essays in this field, see Frederick Schmitt (ed.) *Socializing Epistemology* (Lanham, Md.: Rowman and Littlefield, 1994). The field is interdisciplinary, particularly in raising issues for philosophers, sociologists, psychologists, and others. For a wide-ranging study see Steve Fuller, 'Recent Work in Social Epistemology', *American Philosophical Quarterly* 33, 2 (1996).

6 The paper by Hardwig cited in Chapter 5 notes an example of a scientific article with scores of co-authors, each of whom may be presumed essential for some item of knowledge important to the overall knowledge the article presents.

7 The wrongness is prima facie, not absolute, but this need not be made explicit, since it is ordinarily presupposed – and is certainly presupposed here.

8 That there is such moral knowledge is a major thrust of what is sometimes called 'Cornell Realism', since so many philosophers at or associated with Cornell University have defended it. For some of the seminal papers and other relevant studies see Geoffrey Sayre-McCord (ed.) *Essays in Moral Realism* (Ithaca, NY and London: Cornell University Press, 1988); and for a wider treatment of these issues see Walter Sinnott-Armstrong and Mark C. Timmons (eds.) *Moral Knowledge?* (Oxford and New York: Oxford University Press, 1996).

9 This is the kind of thing W. D. Ross and other intuitionists have said about basic moral principles: they are intuitively knowable and self-evident, though seeing their truth may take a good deal of reflection. See, for example, Ross's *The Right and the Good* (Oxford: Oxford University Press, 1930), esp. ch. 2.

10 See esp. Immanuel Kant, *Foundations of the Metaphysics of Morals*, trans. by Lewis White Beck (New York: Liberal Arts Press, 1959), section 2. Kant offered other formulations of the imperative, but nothing will turn on that here.

11 The wrongness in question is prima facie: this allows that excuses are possible but is compatible with the prohibition being very strong, so that, for example, inexcusable violation is a grave moral offense.

12 In ch. 2, shortly after introducing his utilitarian principle, Mill contends that some pleasures are preferable to others, offers an empirical way to determine which of two pleasures is better (paragraph 5), and attempts to provide a similar way to weight quality of pleasure against quantity (paragraph 8). All this complicates his moral epistemology but does not alter the basic features in question here. A further complication is the possibility that he is best read as holding that the maximization of happiness standard applies to rules rather than individual acts. No major epistemological point made here turns on these issues of interpretation.

13 Mill's attempted proof that pleasure is good is given in ch. 4 of his *Utilitarianism*; for an account of the view that goodness is to be determined by seeing what one would desire given adequate information and suitable reflection, see Richard B. Brandt, *A Theory of the Good and the Right* (Oxford: Oxford University Press, 1979).

14 For an assessment of some of the most important arguments and an indication of the relevant literature see Keith Yandell's introduction to the philosophy of religion, forthcoming from Routledge.

15 A more modest form of evidentialism, holding only that there is in fact no actual direct knowledge of God, would be unaffected by the bare possibility of the existence of an omnipotent God, but that evidentialist view is not our focus here.

16 From Gerard Manley Hopkins's 'God's Grandeur', in A. J. M. Smith (ed.) *Seven Centuries of Verse*, 2nd edn. (New York: Scribner's, 1957) p. 529.

17 For an extensive treatment of the possible ways in which God may be perceived, with much general epistemology as context for demonstrating this possibility, see William P. Alston, *Perceiving God: The Epistemology of Religious Experience* (Ithaca, NY and London: Cornell University Press, 1991).

18 It should be noted that noncognitivism can be applied to the philosophy of religion as to ethics. For many contemporary theological views, religious language is construed noncognitively, say as expressing reverent attitudes about people and their world, rather than as asserting metaphysical propositions about the ultimate origin and nature of the universe.

19 I have compared and contrasted justification and rationality in 'Rationality and the Practice Conception of Justification', in Thomas D. Senor (ed.) *The Rationality of Belief and the Plurality of Faith* (Ithaca, NY and London: Cornell University Press, 1995).

20 Bernard Gert has defended in detail the wider view that rationality is simply the contradictory of irrationality, which he takes as the prior notion. He might not accept, however, the use I make of a similar view here. See esp. *Morality* (Oxford and New York: Oxford University Press, 1988).

21 A detailed discussion of one of these non-belief cognitive attitudes is provided in my 'The Dimensions of Faith and the Demands of Reason', in Eleonore Stump (ed.) *Reasoned Faith* (Ithaca, NY and London: Cornell University Press, 1993).

CHAPTER 10
Skepticism

The possibility of pervasive error

Perfectly realistic hallucination
Two competing epistemic ideals: believing truth and avoiding falsehood
Some dimensions and varieties of skepticism

Skepticism generalized

Skepticism about direct knowledge and justification
Inferential knowledge and justification: the problem of induction
The problem of other minds

The egocentric predicament

Fallibility

Three kinds of epistemic infallibility
Knowledge and fallibility

Uncertainty

Knowing, knowing for certain, and telling for certain
Entailment as a requirement for inferential justification
Knowing and showing
Negative versus positive defenses of common sense

Deducibility, evidential transmission, and induction

Epistemic and logical possibility
Entailment, certainty, and fallibility

The authority of knowledge and the cogency of its grounds

Epistemic authority and cogent grounds
Grounds of knowledge as conferring epistemic authority
Exhibiting knowledge versus dogmatically claiming it

Refutation and rebuttal

Prospects for a positive defense of common sense

A case for justified belief
The regress of demonstration
A case for knowledge
A circularity problem

Skepticism and common sense

Skepticism

I think that we all know many things. I believe I know many facts about my immediate surroundings, much about myself, something about the past, and a little about the future. I believe that we also have scientific knowledge, that we know some general moral truths, and that it is certainly possible that we know some religious truths. But there are reasons to doubt all of this. There are reasons to think that at best we know very little, perhaps just self-evident truths, such as that if no vixens are males then no males are vixens, and a few propositions about our present consciousness, such as that I am now thinking about the scope of human knowledge.

The possibility of pervasive error

As I consider these matters, I look back at the green field before me. I reassure myself that I see it vividly. I certainly cannot help believing that it is there. But an inescapable belief need not be knowledge, or even justified. Suppose I am hallucinating. Then I would not know (through vision, at least) that the field is there.

Perfectly realistic hallucination

I find it impossible to believe that I am hallucinating. But I might find that impossible even if I were, provided the hallucination was as vivid and steady as my present visual experience. I begin to wonder, then, whether I really know that I am not hallucinating. If I do not know this, then even if I am in fact not hallucinating, can I know that there is a green field before me? Similarly, if I do not know that I am not simply having a vivid dream in which it seems to me that there is a green field before me, can I know that there is one there?[1]

Remembering that one can justifiedly believe something even if one does not know it, I think that at least I may justifiedly believe that there is a green field before me, even if I do not know that I am not hallucinating one (or merely "seeing" one in a dream). Moreover, if I justifiedly believe that there is a green field before me, how much does it matter whether I also know this? It matters whether the belief is true. But the likelihood that it is true, so far as that likelihood is something I can discern, depends on how probable the presence of the field is, given the sensory experience on which my belief is based; and in my attentiveness and caution as an observer, I have contributed all I can to that probability. My belief remains justified and is as likely to be true as I can make it by any steps in my power, such as more carefully observing its texture. Internally, in my own consciousness, I am being perfectly reasonable in continuing to believe that there is a green field there. So far as justification is concerned, I am beyond reproach.

These points about justification are plausible, but they give false comfort. Doubtless, I may have a belief which, though it does not constitute knowledge, is justified, and one can have such a belief even if its basis is hallucinatory. But it is now not merely possible that I am hallucinating: I am also quite *aware* that I could be. Given this awareness, am I still justified in believing that there is a green field there? Should I not regard this belief as unjustified, suspend judgment on whether the field is there, and merely hope that it is?

Two competing epistemic ideals: believing truth and avoiding falsehood

These questions produce a tension. I want to believe that the field is there if it truly is, for I have a deep-seated desire to believe as many significant truths as I can. But I also want to avoid believing that it is there if it is not, for I have a deep-seated desire to avoid believing falsehoods. For most of us, these two desires are important, and they represent ideals that govern much of our thinking. But the two ideals pull against each other: the former inclines us to believe readily, since we may otherwise miss believing a truth; the latter inclines us to suspend judgment, lest we fall into error by believing a falsehood. The former ideal pushes us in the direction of credulity: believing on grounds that evidentially are too thin – or without grounds at all – and thereby believing too much. The latter ideal pushes us toward a kind of skepticism: believing only on absolutely conclusive grounds, and thereby – if common sense is right about the matter – believing too little.

How can one balance these ideals with each other? So far in this book, I have spoken more about how we fulfill the former, the ideal of believing as many significant truths as we can, than about how we might fulfill the latter, the ideal of avoiding belief of falsehoods. Clearly, the easiest way to fulfill the latter would be to suspend judgment on every proposition one entertains, or at least on all those which, unlike certain self-evident truths, do not tend to compel assent by virtue of their luminous certainty. This is the kind of response characteristic of *Pyrrhonian skepticism*, an ancient variety tracing to Pyrrho of Ellis (*c.* 360–275 BC). On this view, we should suspend judgment at least on all propositions concerning which there is conflicting evidence (or none), and Pyrrhonians took this to include at least all empirical propositions.

These reflections about possible error through hallucination, about the apparent vulnerability of justification in the face of such possibilities, and about the ideal of avoiding error suggest why philosophers have been so concerned with *skepticism*. In very broad terms, skepticism is most commonly conceived by philosophers roughly as the view that there is little if any knowledge. Call this *knowledge skepticism*.

There is related sense of 'skepticism' in which the term designates an attitude or feature of temperament, such as a disapproval of believing without conclusive grounds. This is not our direct concern; but if philosophical skepticism is not justified, then some common skeptical attitudes are not either, and some people who go through life with a skeptical attitude are lacking the kind of intellectual and psychological balance that go with epistemic virtue. One reason, then, for studying skepticism is to approach a mean between excessive credulity – a disposition to doubt or withhold belief too little – and excessive skepticism, a disposition to doubt or withhold belief too much.

Skepticism may also concern justification. Typically, skeptics do not take our justified beliefs to be of a significantly larger number than our beliefs constituting knowledge. Call the view that we have little if any justification for belief *justification skepticism*. How far-reaching might a plausible skepticism of either kind be, and how is skepticism to be assessed? I want to pursue these questions in that order and at some length.

It may seem that skepticism offends so blatantly against common sense, and so lopsidedly prefers the ideal of avoiding falsehood over that of believing truths, that it should be dismissed as ridiculous. But it will soon become evident that skepticism is a serious, perhaps even irrefutable challenge to common sense. Moreover, even if skepticism turns out, as phenomenalism apparently does, to be quite unreasonable, we learn a great deal about knowledge and justification from studying it.

A serious exploration of skepticism, whether or not we finally accept some form of it, also tends to help us to avoid dogmatism about our own personal views and a self-satisfied assurance that our collective outlook as rational observers of the world embodies knowledge of the sorts of things we think it does: facts about ourselves, our surroundings, and the ways of nature.

Some dimensions and varieties of skepticism

To understand a skeptical view we should locate it in relation to at least four dimensions: subject matter, say the past or the future or physical objects or other minds; epistemic attitude, such as knowledge, justified belief, or rational belief; modality, above all contingency or necessity, or the empirical versus the a priori; and the kind of being it purports to limit, say human, subhuman, or superhuman. Regarding subject matter, my concern is wide-ranging. As to the other three categories, my concern is with human beings and mainly with knowledge and justification regarding contingent empirical propositions.

Much skepticism, whether about knowledge or about justification, is restricted to a given kind of subject, for instance to propositions about the world outside oneself, or about the past, or about the future, or about ethics, religion, or science. Skeptical views also differ markedly in the status of the knowledge, and in the degree of the justification, they concern. A strong skepticism regarding propositions about the past, for instance, might hold that there is no knowledge, or even partially justified belief, about the past. A weaker skepticism might hold that although some beliefs about the past are justified to some degree, there is neither certain knowledge of the past nor any beliefs about it that are *sufficiently* justified to make it more reasonable to hold them than to suspend judgment on them.

Still another difference between skeptical views concerns their order. The usual skepticism is first-order, in the sense that it concerns the sorts of beliefs we have discussed as typical of those grounded in experience or reason, and not beliefs *about* such beliefs, say beliefs that ordinary perceptual beliefs often do constitute knowledge. First-order skepticism might deny, then, that I know there is a cold glass in my hand, even when I have the seemingly familiar experience I would describe as smelling the mint in my iced tea, tasting it, and feeling the cold glass in my hand.

It is natural, however, for a first-order skeptic also to maintain second-order skepticism, holding, for instance, that there is no second-order knowledge to the effect that there is (first-order) knowledge, for example that no one knows that there is knowledge of people, places, and things. This second-order skepticism is obviously true if there is in fact no first-order knowledge – since then no one could know there is. But a second-order skeptic could hold that even if there is first-order knowledge, no one knows this.

It is, moreover, natural for skeptics to hold their main views as necessary truths, since, for one thing, they commonly believe that for fallible creatures like us there *cannot* be knowledge or justification of certain kinds. I do not intend to discuss skepticism in detail in each of the many forms described, but what follows will apply to a huge range of cases.

Skepticism
generalized

The skeptical challenges I have brought forward can be directed against all our beliefs about the external world, all our memory beliefs, all our beliefs about the future, and indeed all our beliefs about any subject provided they depend on our memory for their justification or for their status as knowledge. Memory is, after all, at least as fallible as vision.

Skepticism about direct knowledge and justification

Plainly, if all of the senses can deceive through hallucination, then beliefs grounded in any of the senses may be justificationally or epistemically undermined in the same way my belief that there is a green field before me may be undermined by a realization that I might have been hallucinating. Quite apart from whether perceptual beliefs are true, skeptics tend to claim that either the possibility of such hallucinations prevents them from being justified or, even if they are justified, it precludes their constituting knowledge.

Suppose, for instance, that I might be having an auditory hallucination of bird songs. Then my present experience of (apparently) hearing them may not justify my believing that there are birds nearby and is certainly not a sufficient basis for my knowing there are, even if it is true that there are. Similarly, there is a counterpart of hallucination for memory beliefs: *memorial hallucination*, we might call it. I may have the memorial impression that when I was four I saw my parents kissing under the mistletoe, but this could be just a romantic fantasy masquerading as a memory.

Beliefs about the future are rather different from memory beliefs, in that the former are not grounded in experiential states that we think of as in some way causally deriving from the object about which we have knowledge. But even if there is no counterpart of memorial hallucination, there are equally undermining possibilities. For instance, a confident belief that I will talk with Jane could be a product of wishful thinking, even when in fact it is grounded in remembering my long-standing intention to talk with her. Perhaps the belief could be an anticipatory delusion. Even my belief that I will live to discuss skepticism could be mistaken owing to many sorts of reasons, including dangers to me of which I am now unaware.

Now consider what we take to be our general knowledge, whether a priori or scientific, say of arithmetic truths or scientific laws. Since it is possible to misremember propositions, or to seem to remember them when one does not, or to have a kind of memorial hallucination that gives rise to a completely groundless belief, it would seem that the only secure beliefs of general propositions are of the relatively few that we can know directly without ever having needed any evidence. This apparently leaves none of our general scientific beliefs, and only our a priori knowledge of self-evident propositions, epistemically unscathed.

Inferential knowledge and justification: the problem of induction

Even if we leave aside problems about perceptual and memory beliefs, there is a difficulty for the commonsense view that justification or knowledge grounded (directly or indirectly) in a basic source can be transmitted inductively. The classical statement of this *problem of induction* – the problem of how to justify such inductive inferences – comes from David Hume.[2] Hume showed that one cannot know a priori that if the premises of a specific piece of inductive reasoning are true, then its conclusion is also true. One can clearly conceive the former being true while the latter is false, whereas one cannot conceive its being true that (1) all human beings are mortal and Socrates is one of them, and yet false that (2) Socrates is mortal. Thus, no matter how good the inductive reasoning is, it is always (deductively) invalid.

Consider the inductive reasoning from the premise that the sun has always risen each twenty-four hours to the conclusion that it will rise tomorrow. Of all such reasoning – reasoning "concerning matter of fact and existence" – Hume says "That there are no demonstrative [roughly, valid, evidentially conclusive] arguments in the case seems evident, since it implies no contradiction that the course of nature may change and that an object, seemingly like those which we have experienced, may be attended with different or contrary effects." Hence, even if I do know that the sun has risen every day since time immemorial, and even allowing that on such an extensive basis I believe that it will rise tomorrow, I *could* be mistaken in believing this, and it seems questionable whether I am justified in believing it.

More generally, Hume's arguments lead us to ask whether, if our premises could be true yet our conclusion false, we have any reason at all, on the basis of the premises, for believing the conclusion. And how can we ever *know* the conclusion on the basis of such premises? Indeed, how can we even be minimally justified in believing the conclusion on the basis of such premises? The problem of induction, as most often understood, is largely the difficulty of adequately answering these questions.

The problem can also be put in terms of probability. We normally operate on the commonsense presumption that when one thing is associated with another, say a sunrise with the passage of twenty-four hours, and the two have never failed to be associated in the same way, then the greater the number of cases of association, the greater the probability that the association will occur in a new case – for instance that the sun will rise tomorrow.[3] We also operate on the related commonsense presumption that for natural phenomena, such an association can occur sufficiently often to yield justification for believing, and even knowledge, that the association will occur in a new case.

From a Humean perspective, it will not do to argue as follows: I am justified in believing my conclusion on the basis of inductive support for it, such as the past regular behavior of the sun, since past experience has shown that reasoning like this, which has had true premises, has also had true conclusions. For this way of defending an inductively based conclusion simply presents yet another inductive conclusion – it gives a kind of inductive reasoning to support the view that certain kinds of inductive arguments justify one in believing their conclusions. It just inductively generalizes about inductive arguments themselves, using as a guide past experience in which we seem to have found out that by and large their conclusions turned out true when their premises were true.

That reasoning, then, apparently *begs the question* against Hume: it assumes, without independent evidence, part of what he contends is false, namely, that inductive inference constitutes reasoning that either can ground *knowledge* of its conclusion, or can at least *justify* its conclusion, in the sense of providing good reason for it. We have taken the battle to a different field – that of inductive argumentation rather than sunrises – but we have added no new weapons nor enhanced our forces.

The problem of other minds

One of the major points that Hume so powerfully defended – roughly that non-deductive inferences are fallible – is by no means restricted to beliefs about the future. Such beliefs are, however, so prominent in his discussion of inductive inference that sometimes the problem of induction is narrowly conceived as that of how we can show that we have any reason to believe the future will be like the past. This conception is unduly narrow. Recall my observing Jim briskly shuffling papers and angrily mumbling curses. I cannot help believing, on this basis, that he is angry. But this reasoning leaves my belief clearly fallible: even if I know my premises (through perception), it does not follow that he is angry. He could be pretending.

The case of Jim's anger is alarmingly representative. Everything I believe about what is occurring in the inner lives of others seems to rest on grounds that are inductive in this way: what I observe – above all, their behavior – does not entail anything about their minds. There could still be pretending, or psychological abnormality, or some other source of error. So if I cannot have knowledge of people's inner lives from their behavior, apparently I can never have it.

Worse still, if I cannot know anything about the inner lives of others, can I even know that there *are* others, as opposed to mere bodies controlled externally or by hidden microscopic machinery, rather than directed through beliefs and intentions of the kind that animate me? There is, then, a *problem of other minds*. Can we know, or even justifiedly believe, that there are any? If our experiences would be just as they are if the human bodies we interact with are controlled from outer space and have no inner life of their own, how can we know that those bodies are, as most of us cannot help thinking, animated by minds like ours?[4]

The problem is compounded when we realize that we cannot directly verify, as we introspectively can in our own case, what is occurring in someone else's consciousness. Thus, all I can do to check on my inductively grounded beliefs about the inner lives of others is obtain further inductive evidence, for instance by observing whether they behave as one would expect if I am right in thinking them to be, say, angry. I cannot, as in my own case, introspectively focus on the events in their consciousness. How can I know anything about the mental and emotional life of others if I am in principle debarred from decisively verifying my beliefs about the contents and events of their consciousness? Even if I am sometimes right, I can never tell when.

It may be replied that by far my best explanation of why other bodies behave as if they were animated by a mind is that they *are* so animated. The other hypotheses, such as control from outer space or by a machine, are far-fetched. The suggested reasoning sounds plausible, but notice that it is still a kind of induction: inference to the best explanation.

The indicated inference to propositions about other minds as best explaining observed behavior is, however, supported by a strong *argument from analogy*: again and again when my body behaves in a certain way I am in a certain mental state, say in pain when I am burned and cry out; so (surely) the same behavioral pattern in another body is accompanied by a similar mental state. Other bodies are so much like mine in structure and behavior that they are very probably animated by minds like mine.

There is no need to deny either that positing other minds best explains what we seem to know about other bodies or that the analogical argument just sketched is strong. Still, from one proposition's best explaining another it does not follow that the first is true; and the analogies between my body and others at most render probable, rather than entailing, that some other body is associated with mental states as mine is with my mental states. For one thing, there are other possible explanations (such as the hypothesis of control of other bodies from outer space, or by a powerful and clever evil genius); these explanatory alternatives, if true, would leave my experience exactly as it is. For another thing, some of these alternative hypotheses can well explain the analogies that otherwise seem compelling.

Another way to see the power of these skeptical hypotheses is to note that our experience does not *discriminate* between the skeptical scenario and the commonsense one. Our experience would be just what it is if we were steadfastly hallucinating the external world, including even the human bodies we seem to see. The same holds if we were not hallucinating but the human bodies were externally controlled. How, then, can our experience justify us in believing that there is an external world or that there are other minds?

Putting the problem somewhat differently, if our experience *underdetermines* the truth of propositions we commonly believe about the external world, roughly in the sense that it does not decisively indicate their truth as opposed to the truth of skeptical (or other) alternative hypotheses that can explain our experience, how can our experience justify our believing such commonsense propositions? If it cannot, and if, as Hume plausibly argued, we also cannot know that proposition, how can we be justified in believing anything at all about the external world?[5]

It is only a short step from this full-scale attack on inductive inference to *a problem of the body*. If, as a skeptic might well hold, my apparent knowledge of my own body is inductively grounded, being based on perceptions and bodily sensations somewhat as beliefs about external objects are, then can I know, or even justifiedly believe, that I have a body? Could I not be steadily hallucinating even my own flesh?

It might be replied that thoughts, including my reflections on skepticism, necessarily require an embodied thinker. But that point would only imply that I *have* some kind of body, not that I can know anything about it. The point is also far from self-evident and is indeed denied by philosophers in the powerful tradition of Descartes, who hold that we (persons) are essentially mental (or spiritual), hence non-physical, substances. In any case, even if the point should be true, the only embodiment necessary might be a brain. Hence, on the skeptical view imagined, the most one could know is that one is embodied in some way, say in a brain. Whether that brain is itself embodied, or ever interacts with anything else, would be beyond one's knowledge. Why, then, could I not be alone in the world, and perhaps even a "brain in a vat," a brain kept alive in a nurturing liquid and subjected to hallucinations that falsely convey the impression of a normal life?[6]

The egocentric predicament

In this way, skepticism can drive us into an *egocentric predicament*: a position that makes it seem clear that all we can (empirically) know about the world, perhaps all we can justifiedly believe about it as well, concerns our own present experience. For all I know, I am a lone conscious ego vividly hallucinating a physical world that has no external reality.

Most skeptics have tended to push no further, or at least not to express very much doubt about our capacity to know propositions of two kinds: those about what is currently going on in our minds and at least those a priori propositions that are luminously self-evident. But skeptics can push further, and Descartes, in the first of his *Meditations*, raised the possibility that there was nothing of which he could (justifiedly) be certain. Recall introspectively grounded beliefs, such as that I am thinking about skepticism. It seems possible that this belief is mistaken. If that is possible, how can I know that I am thinking about skepticism? If I know, I cannot be wrong. But here error is possible. Perhaps I do not even have knowledge of my own conscious states.

To make this sort of argument work with beliefs of self-evident propositions we must, I think, strain. Descartes may perhaps be read as seriously entertaining the question of whether it is possible that God, being omnipotent, could have brought it about that even propositions of the sort I am calling self-evident might be false. Could an omnipotent being bring it about that while some dogs are pets, no pets are dogs? I see no reason to think so. As St Thomas Aquinas and many other philosophers have maintained, omnipotence is simply not the power to "do" things that are absolutely impossible.[7] Power is exercised within the realm of the possible: impossible "deeds" are not candidates for any being to do.

If one accepts this point, one might argue that there is no act of bringing it about that while some dogs are pets, no pets are dogs. Calling this an act misuses the vocabulary of action. Hence, the impossibility that an omnipotent being can bring it about does not imply that there is any act which that being cannot perform. This point, in turn, deprives the skeptic of a way to argue that beliefs of necessary truths could be false.

This reasoning may not settle the matter, but it is sufficiently plausible to warrant leaving aside skepticism concerning beliefs of luminously self-evident necessary propositions, particularly since these propositions seem not only incapable of falsehood, but also incapable of even being unjustifiably believed, at least when carefully and comprehendingly considered. Leaving such skepticism aside takes little from the skeptic in any case. If these are the only propositions we can know, then we can know nothing about our world, not even anything about our innermost consciousness. We are at best in an egocentric predicament.

Fallibility

In appraising skepticism, I want to formulate some of the main principles that underlie it in what seem its most plausible forms. If they can be shown to be unreasonable, then the skeptical threat to the commonsense view that we have a great deal of knowledge and justification can at least be blunted. In formulating and assessing these principles, it is well to distinguish skeptical threats to the generation of knowledge (or of justification) from skeptical threats to its transmission. It is natural to start with questions about its generation. If no knowledge is generated, there is none to be transmitted.

Three kinds of epistemic infallibility

Is there really any reason to doubt that, normally, introspectively grounded beliefs constitute knowledge? It may be true that such beliefs could be mistaken, but what is a skeptic entitled to make of this? The skeptical argument that comes to mind here is based on what I will call *the infallibility formulation*: *if you know, you cannot be wrong*. If we simply add the premise that you can be wrong in holding a given introspective belief, say that you are thinking about skepticism, it would seem to follow that such beliefs do not represent knowledge. This kind of *argument from fallibility*, as we might call it, can be applied to just about every sort of proposition we tend to think we know..

If, however, we look closely, we find that the infallibility formulation is multiply ambiguous. There are at least three quite different things that formulation might mean, and hence really three different infallibility principles.

The claim, 'If you know, you can't be wrong', might have the meaning of

(1) It must be the case that if you know that something is true,
then it is true (you cannot know something that is false).

Call (1) the *verity principle*, since it says simply that knowledge must be of truths. Knowledge can never have a falsehood as its object. The claim might, on the other hand, have the meaning of

(2) If you know that something is true, then it must be true, that
is, the proposition you know is necessarily true (you can
know only necessary truths).

Call (2) the *necessity principle*, since it says simply that knowledge is of necessary truths. It never has among its objects any propositions that could possibly fail to hold.[8] The claim 'If you know, you can't be wrong' might also have the meaning of

(3) If you know that something is true, then your *belief* of it
must be true, in the sense that your believing it entails or
guarantees its truth (only beliefs that cannot be false
constitute knowledge).

Call (3) the *infallibility principle proper*, since in saying that only infallible beliefs constitute knowledge it connects with skepticism more closely than (1) or (2). Knowledge, it says, is never constituted by beliefs that can have falsehoods among their objects.

Unlike (2), (3) implies nothing about the propositional or other objects of knowledge; instead, it restricts the kind of *belief* that can constitute knowledge.

And by contrast with (2), (3) also allows for knowledge of contingent (non-necessary) truths, such as that I exist. This proposition can be false (that I exist is not a necessary truth), but my *belief* of it is infallible and therefore cannot be false. If I now believe that I exist, it follows that I do exist.

Knowledge and fallibility

We can now assess the skeptical reasoning that employs the infallibility formulation in one or another interpretation. I will be quite brief in discussing the first two; the third is the most controversial and most important for skepticism.

The verity principle, (1), is plainly true: one cannot know something that is false. In *this* sense, knowledge is infallible. If it is false that the maple is taller than the spruce, then I do not know it is. But if this is all the infallibility formulation comes to, it provides no reason to conclude that I do not know that I am thinking (or that anything else I believe is not genuine knowledge). Granted, it must be true that *if* I know I am thinking, then I am. But that tells us nothing about whether I *do* know I am.

The necessity principle, on the other hand, principle (2), seems quite mistaken. Surely I know some propositions that are not necessary, such as that I exist (as noted earlier, it is not a necessary truth that I exist, as it is that vixens are female). Even the skeptic would grant that I cannot falsely believe this, since my believing it entails that I exist (non-existent things cannot have beliefs at all, true *or* false). It may indeed be impossible for me even to be unjustified in believing the proposition that I exist when I comprehendingly consider it (Descartes seems to maintain in *Meditation II* that this case is impossible). The same holds, of course, for you in relation to your belief that you exist.

Even if the necessity principle were true, however, a skeptic could not reasonably *use* it, without first defending it by adequate argument, against the commonsense view that introspective or even perceptual beliefs normally constitute knowledge. For clearly they are not beliefs of necessary truths, and defenders of common sense do not take them to be; hence, invoking the necessity principle against common sense, without first arguing for the principle, would be in effect a flat denial that such beliefs constitute knowledge. That would beg the question against the commonsense view.

Suppose, for instance, that a skeptic says that if you know, you cannot be wrong, where this means (2), then notes that introspective and perceptual beliefs (which are of propositions that are not necessary) can be false, and concludes that such beliefs do not constitute knowledge. This would not be presenting a good reason to believe the conclusion, but just asserting, disguisedly given (2), that the commonsense view that we have introspective and perceptual knowledge is mistaken. There may seem to be a good argument here, because it is so easy to take 'If you know, you can't be wrong' as asserting the verity principle. But that principle is acceptable to common sense, whereas the necessity principle is not. To argue for the latter by allowing the plausibility of the former to serve as support for it is to trade on an ambiguity and masks poor reasoning – or the absence of any argument or support at all.

The infallibility principle proper, (3), in effect says that only infallible beliefs can be knowledge. Now some beliefs of contingent propositions are infallible, for instance my belief that I now exist, and my more specific belief that I have a belief. Just as my believing I exist entails that I do exist, if I *believe* I have a belief, it follows that I have one: I have at least that very belief even if I have no other beliefs.

The infallibility of these two contingently true beliefs shows that despite appearances, (3) is not equivalent to (2), since (3), the infallibility principle, but not, (2), the necessity principle, allows knowledge of propositions that are not necessary (contingent propositions). But why should we accept (3)? What reason can the skeptic give for it? Not that if you know, you cannot be wrong; for when we look closely, we find that when plausibly interpreted as meaning (1), that is no help to the skeptic, and when interpreted as (2) or (3) it just asserts the skeptical position against common sense.

What makes the infallibility formulation seem to give the skeptic an argument against common sense is the way skepticism can trade on the ambiguity of that formulation: one finds the argument from fallibility attractive because its main premise, conceived as equivalent to (1), is so plausible; yet the argument succeeds against common sense only if (2) or (3) are legitimate premises, and I think we shall see that it is doubtful that the skeptic has a cogent argument for either of them. It will help to consider first the bearing of the concept of uncertainty, one closely related to the notion of infallibility.

Uncertainty

Like fallibility, uncertainty has seemed to many skeptics to leave us with little, if any, knowledge. Recall the possibility that I am hallucinating a green field before me when there is none there. Can it possibly be certain, then, that there is one there? And can I ever *tell* for certain whether or not I am hallucinating a field? Skeptics tend to answer these questions negatively and to contend that if we cannot tell for certain whether we are hallucinating, we do not know we are not hallucinating. They also tend to argue that if one does not know that one is not hallucinating, surely one does not know that there is a field there.

Moreover, in a way uncertainty cuts deeper than fallibility: for even if I believe a theorem of logic that cannot be false and so have an infallible belief,

I may not be warranted in my proof and cannot be justifiedly certain. Uncertainty arises where one's grounds are not conclusive, and it can arise even when one's belief is infallible. Thus, even the infallibility of a belief is not enough to render it knowledge. At least two important principles are suggested here.

One principle suggested by reflection on these questions about possible error is *the certainty principle*: if one cannot tell for certain whether something is so, then one does not know it is so. This principle is plausible in part because, typically, 'How can you tell?' and 'How can you be certain?' are appropriate challenges to a claim to know something. Moreover, 'I know, but I am not certain' sounds self-defeating, in a way that might encourage a skeptic to consider it contradictory. Further support for the certainty principle can be derived from the idea that if our grounds for a belief underdetermine its truth – as where a skeptical possibility such as the Cartesian demon hypothesis can also explain our having those grounds – then one cannot tell for certain that the belief is true.

Another principle suggested by our questions about the possibility of hallucination is *the back-up principle*: if one believes something, say that there is a field before one, which is inconsistent with a further proposition – such as that one is merely hallucinating a field where none exists – then one's belief constitutes knowledge only if it is backed up by one's knowing, or at least being in a position to know, that the further (undermining) proposition is false. This principle is plausible in part because one is in a sense responsible for the implications of what one claims to know. If, for instance, I claim to know that there is a green field before me, and that proposition implies that the field is not a pavement textured to look just like a green field, it would seem that I had better know that it is not such a pavement. This, in turn, is commonly taken to imply that I must at least be justified in rejecting that strange possibility.

The upshot of this skeptical reasoning is that if I know that there is a green field before me, I apparently must be prepared to back that up by justifiedly rejecting exactly the sorts of possibilities that the skeptic reminds us are always there, in abundance. But must I be thus prepared? Let us consider the certainty and back-up principles in turn.

Knowing, knowing for certain, and telling for certain

Chapter 8 argued that knowing does not imply knowing for certain. This conclusion suggests that the kind of certainty in question, epistemic certainty, is not required for knowledge, and that having such certainty may be something quite different from simply knowing. Still, from the point that knowing need not be knowing for certain, it does not follow that one can know without being *able* to *tell* for certain. Thus, the skeptic may still maintain that the certainty principle undermines the commonsense view that we have perceptual knowledge.

Let us first ask what it is to tell for certain. A skeptic may mean by this acquiring knowledge, in the form of an infallible belief, of a proposition that entails the truth of what one can tell is so. Thus, to tell (for certain) that one is not hallucinating a green field one might, like Descartes in the *Meditations*, prove that there is a God of such goodness and power that – since it would be evil for God to allow it – one could not be mistaken in a belief properly based on such a vivid and steadfast perception as one now has of a green field. We can tell for certain that there is an object before us because we can prove that God would not allow us to believe this under the present conditions unless it were true.

Some people might embrace Descartes' theistic solution here. But one might also reject the skeptical principle in question, the infallibility principle. To require that a belief can be knowledge only if – whether in Descartes's way or a similar fashion – it can be conclusively shown to be true would again beg the question against the commonsense view that a belief can constitute knowledge without being infallible (a belief that can be absolutely conclusively shown to be true is also infallible). Thus, if skeptics have no good argument for the principle of infallibility proper, they should not assume that principle in defending the view that we can know only what we can "tell for certain" in this strong sense of the phrase.

Perhaps, on the other hand, telling for certain is simply a matter of ascertaining the truth in question by some means that justifies one in being (psychologically) certain of what one can tell. If so, perhaps we normally *can* tell for certain that we are not hallucinating, for instance by seeing whether the senses of touch and smell confirm our visual impression. To be sure, the confirming experiences do not *entail* that there is a green field before me. But we still have no good argument that certainty (or knowledge) may arise only from entailing grounds (another controversial view, shortly to be discussed). Thus, this point does not establish that confirming experiences cannot enable us to tell for certain that we are not hallucinating.

Moreover, suppose that we interpret telling for certain in the modest way just suggested, and that we can tell for certain in this sense that what we know is true. In that case, perhaps there is a weak sense in which beliefs constituting knowledge are infallible. They need not be such that it is absolutely impossible that they be false, as in the case of my belief that I exist. There need only be something about our grounds for them in virtue of which they (empirically) cannot be false. Water cannot flow (as opposed to being pumped) uphill, but this is not absolutely impossible, as it is impossible for some pets to be dogs without any dogs being pets.

If grounds of what is commonly considered to be knowledge are such that the belief constituting that knowledge cannot be false, it will be arguable that many of our beliefs grounded in experience, such as my belief that there is a green field before me, cannot be mistaken. There surely might be causal laws which guarantee that if one is situated before a field in good light, as I am, and has visual experiences like mine caused by the field as mine are, then one sees it, and hence cannot falsely believe that it is there. (That there are such laws is one view that leads to the idea that knowledge is conclusively justified true belief.) The skeptic gives us no good argument to show that there are no such laws.[9]

Entailment as a requirement for inferential justification

The back-up principle fares no better than the infallibility principle proper. For one thing, it depends on the assumption, which defenders of common sense stoutly reject, that in order to know that something is true, one must have grounds that entail its truth. To see that the back-up principle depends on this, consider first a very simple case. Take the proposition that it is false that there is a green field before me. This is inconsistent with what I believe, namely, that there *is* one before me. Hence, the backup principle requires that I at least be in a position to know that this is false. Otherwise I cannot properly back up what I believe. But the falsity of this negative proposition entails that there *is* a green field before me; for if it is false that it is false that there is one, then it is true that there is one. Thus, if, by virtue of how I must be able to back up my original claim, I do know that this negative proposition is false, then I thereby have (and know) an entailing ground for the truth of what I originally believed – that there is a green field before me.

Now take a case in which backing up what I think I know is more complicated. Consider also the proposition that what I take to be a green field is really a pavement with such a realistic-seeming grassy green texture that I cannot tell (perceptually) that it is really not a field. Must I be in a position to know that this is false in order to know that there is a green field before me? The very description of the case suggests that I cannot know, at least by using the senses unaided by experimentation or specialized knowledge, that the field is not a textured pavement. But why must I be able to tell this at all? Is there any reason to think that the field might actually be dyed? Must I, in order to know, not only have a well-grounded true belief but also the further capacity to know, for every possible explanation of how my belief could be false, that this explanation is incorrect? I do not see that I must.

One might object that in order to know a proposition I must be in a position to know whatever follows from it (or at least obviously follows from it). After all, if something does follow from what I know, I could infer it by valid steps from what I initially know, and thereby come to know it, too.

This is an important objection. But in discussing the transmission of knowledge and justification, we considered cases that apparently refute the objection. I can apparently know the sum of a column of figures even if I cannot, without further checking, know something which obviously follows from it: that if my wife (whom I justifiedly believe to be a better arithmetician) says this is not the sum, then she is wrong. Neither knowledge nor justification is automatically transmitted across valid deductive inference.

It will not do, then, to say that knowledge can always be counted on to be transmissible from propositions we know or justifiedly believe to those they entail, even when the entailment is, as in our example, obvious. Thus, even though my seeing a green field plainly entails (for instance) that I am not seeing a pavement with a textured grassy-looking surface, I presumably do not have to be in a position to know or justifiedly believe (by inferring it) that this proposition is false.

Even if this view is mistaken and knowledge and justification *are* always transmitted across valid deductive inference, it may be plausibly argued that I *do* have enough justification to warrant rejecting the hypothesis that there is a pavement before me textured to look just like a green field. It is not just that it appears to me that there is a green field before me; I also have no reason to think there is anything abnormal in the situation, and some reason to think that, in cases like this, large, nearby familiar kinds of things are as they appear to me in such vivid and careful observation. Thus, I do know or justifiedly believe that there is a green field before me.[10]

There are other factors one might cite, indeed, too many to discuss here. My point is simply this. Since the skeptic has not provided good reasons for the principles I have already rejected (or for comparably strong principles), even if knowledge and justification are always transmitted across valid inference, there may be good reason to say that skeptical hypotheses, such as that the "field" is a cleverly painted and textured pavement, may be justifiedly rejected.[11]

Knowing and showing

There is something we may grant to the skeptic that will help to justify my rejection of the certainty and back-up principles. Admittedly, in order to *show* the skeptic that my original belief is knowledge, in the face of the *suggestion* that one of those explanations of its falsity holds, I may have to know that, and perhaps why, this explanation does not hold. Showing something, after all, commonly requires invoking premises for it, and one must presumably know or justifiedly believe those premises.[12] The question 'Do you know?' tends to move discussion to a second-order context in which one seeks not simply to offer grounds for what one takes oneself to know but grounds for the second-order proposition that one knows it. After all, a direct answer to, for instance, 'Do you know that she missed the train?' is something like, 'Yes, I know because I just checked the station', rather than 'I just checked the station'. The latter reply provides a *ground* on which one may know that she missed the train and only indirectly implies that I do know it. A skeptic would not grant this evidential power to such a ground, however, and would indeed not take my reply to answer this question at all.

Still, we may ask, why, in the absence of the need to show that I know, must I, in order simply to have knowledge, have the capacity to show that I have it, as the back-up principle would require? Surely I need not. I can know that if some dogs are pets then some pets are dogs, even if I cannot show this self-evident truth – perhaps simply because I can think of nothing more obvious to use as a reasonable premise from which to show it. And if my wife raises no question of whether my arithmetic answer is correct, I can know that answer even if I cannot show – without obtaining further grounds for the answer – that I do know it. (If I could show that if she says the sum is wrong, then she is wrong, perhaps I would be able to know that if she says this, she is wrong.)

Moreover, suppose I can show that if she says the sum is wrong, she is mistaken, by doing a more careful calculation twice over; does it follow that I know this proposition for certain? I do not see that it does, at least if knowing for certain implies having absolutely conclusive grounds. It would violate no law of nature if I turned out to have made a mistake even in calculations of a kind sufficiently careful to count, normally, as showing their result. Not all instances of showing proceed from absolutely conclusive grounds. On balance, then, it appears that the certainty principle is also mistaken.

Negative versus positive defenses of common sense

In the context of thinking about skepticism, it is easy to forget that knowing something does not require being able to show that one knows it. For in thinking about skepticism we are likely to be trying to defend, against a skeptical onslaught, the commonsense view that there is much knowledge, and we easily think of defending this view as requiring us to show that there is knowledge. There is, however, more than one kind of defense. The two kinds I have in mind are analogous to standing firm as opposed to attacking.

A *negative defense of common sense*, one that seeks to show that skeptical arguments do not justify the skeptic's conclusion, does not require accomplishing the second-order task of showing that there is knowledge or justified belief. That achievement is required by a *positive defense of common sense*, one that seeks to show that we have the kinds of knowledge and justified beliefs common sense takes us to have. A negative defense requires only contending that skepticism provides no good argument against common sense.

Thus, it does not appear that skepticism as so far examined provides a good argument against common sense. Why, for instance, should the skeptic's merely suggesting a possible explanation of how there could be no green field before me, without giving any reason for thinking the explanation is correct, require me to know, or be in a position to know, that it is not correct? All things considered, then, I reject the skeptical case as so far described.

Deducibility, evidential transmission, and induction

When we come to the problem of induction, it seems clear that one assumption the skeptic is making is that if we believe something on the basis of one or more premises, then we can know it on the basis of those premises only if it follows from them, in the sense that they entail it. Call this *the entailment principle*. It says in effect that *knowledge can be transmitted only deductively*.

Why should we accept this principle? Not simply because inductive reasoning is "invalid"; for that term may be held to be improperly applied to it: inductive reasoning is strong or weak, probable or otherwise, but it does not even "aim" at (deductive) validity. Even if it may be properly said to be (deductively) invalid, however, that may be considered an uncontroversial technical point about its logical classification. It is a point of logic, not of epistemology. So conceived, the point does not imply either that knowledge of the premises of inductive reasoning cannot ground knowledge of its conclusions, or that justified beliefs of those premises cannot ground justified beliefs of their conclusions.

One might, on the other hand, accept the entailment principle and argue that when properly spelled out inductive reasoning can be replaced by valid deductive reasoning. For instance, suppose we add, as an overarching premise in inductive reasoning, *the uniformity of nature principle*, which says that nature is a domain of regular patterns, in the sense of patterns that do not change over time. From this together with the premise that the sun has always risen each day it apparently does follow that it will rise tomorrow.[13]

But what entitles us to the premise that nature is uniform? Hume would reply that it is not knowable a priori, and that to say that we know it through experience – which would require our depending on inductive reasoning – would beg the question against him. (On the Humean view, if our belief of the uniformity principle is grounded wholly in premises that only inductively support it, we do not know it.) I believe that this Humean response is highly plausible. The problem of induction must be approached differently.

Epistemic and logical possibility

What perhaps above all makes the entailment principle plausible is the thought that if our premises could be true and yet our conclusion *might* be false, then we cannot know (or even justifiedly believe) the conclusion on the basis of those premises. At first, this thought may sound like just another formulation of the entailment principle. It is not; it is different and considerably more plausible. That is partly why, when it is conflated with the entailment principle, it seems to support that principle. The 'might' in question is epistemic; it is like a farmer's in 'That wood dust might mean carpenter ants' or a physician's in 'Those abdominal pains might mean appendicitis'. This 'might' suggests not only that for all we know the pains do mean appendicitis, but also that there is reason for at least some degree of suspicion that there is appendicitis and perhaps some need to rule it out.

The statement that certain abdominal pains might mean appendicitis is not merely an expression of a bare logical possibility of appendicitis – a statement that appendicitis is possible without contradiction – based, say, on no one's being absolutely immune to it. If that very weak and general statement represents all we know about the case, we are not entitled to say that the pains might mean appendicitis. Similarly, it is not a logical impossibility that the Tower of London levitate above the City; but we would be quite unjustified in saying that it might.

This distinction between *epistemic possibility* – what is expressed by the epistemic 'might' just illustrated – and mere *logical possibility* – what can be the case without contradiction or some other kind of necessary falsehood[14] – bears importantly on the problem of induction. It is true that if, no matter how good inductive reasoning is, its premises could be true and yet its conclusion might, in the *epistemic* sense, be false, perhaps we cannot know the conclusion on the basis of them. But is this generally the case with inductive reasoning? I cannot see that it is.

Moreover, suppose it could be true that, relative to its premises, the conclusion of inductive reasoning might, in the epistemic sense, be false, what reason is there to think that this really is true? Skeptics cannot justifiably argue for this claim as they sometimes do, maintaining, simply on the ground that the premises do not entail the conclusion, that the conclusion might be false. Arguing in this way is rather like saying, of just any stomach ache a child gets after eating too much Hallowe'en candy, that it might mean appendicitis.

It is barely possible that, relative to all we know or are justified in believing about the child, the stomach ache means appendicitis. But from that bare possibility we may not automatically conclude that appendicitis is *epistemically possible* – roughly, that relative to all we know or are justified in believing, we are unjustified in disbelieving that the stomach ache might mean appendicitis. Nor does this bare possibility rule out our knowing, on inductive grounds, that overeating is the cause.

Entailment, certainty, and fallibility

There are other reasons for the attractiveness of the entailment principle, at least from a skeptical point of view. If one embraces the infallibility principle, one is in fact committed to the entailment principle. For suppose that, from known – and hence on this view infallibly believed – premises, one inductively derives a belief which is not itself infallible, as (empirical) beliefs which are inferentially grounded normally are not. Since inductive transmission allows inference of a false conclusion from true premises, the belief one derives could, as far as sheer logic goes, be false despite the truth of its inductive premises and one's infallibly believing them. True premises, even if infallibly believed, simply do not absolutely guarantee the truth of a conclusion inductively inferred from them. Hence, this conclusion would be fallible. But then, being fallible, the belief of the conclusion would be capable of falsehood and hence would not constitute knowledge. Thus, knowledge can be inferentially transmitted only by deductive inference. *Only valid deduction inferentially preserves infallibility.*[15]

If one thinks of knowledge as entailing absolute certainty, one might again be drawn to the entailment principle. For even if a fallible belief can be absolutely certain, a belief that is only inductively based on it will presumably be at least a bit less certain and thus not absolutely certain. For the proposition believed – the conclusion belief – is supported by the original belief only with some (perhaps high) degree of probability, rather than with absolute certainty, as where the conclusion is entailed by the premises. This would allow that the premise belief be certain and the conclusion belief less so, since it would not inherit from the premise belief the same degree of protection against falsehood.

To see this, suppose that the premise belief only minimally meets the standard for absolute certainty. Then a belief inductively grounded on it can fall below that standard and thereby fail to be knowledge. Putting the point in terms of probability, we might imagine a case in which our premise meets the bare minimum conditions for absolute certainty, which we might represent by a probability of 1. Then, any conclusion that follows only inductively from this premise will thereby inherit from it only some lower probability and hence fall below the minimum level for absolute certainty. Thus, again the skeptic will argue that only deduction is sufficient to transmit knowledge.

But we have already seen reason to doubt both the infallibility principle and the view that a belief constitutes knowledge only if it is absolutely certain. Indeed, I do not see that skeptics give us good reason to believe either these principles or the entailment principle. It does not follow that the principles are, as they appear to be, false; but if there is no good reason to believe them, even skeptics would approve of our refusing to accept them. Absolute certainty is a high, and in some ways beautiful, ideal; but it is neither adequate to the concept of knowledge nor appropriate to the human condition.

The authority of knowledge and the cogency of its grounds

There is one further principle we should consider, one rather different from those examined so far and apparently more modest. It derives in part from the idea that if you know something, you have a certain authority regarding it, an authority presumably due to your being in a position to see the truth which you know. This authority is in part what accounts for the possibility of knowledge through testimony: if you know something, you have an authority about it such that normally I can come to know it, as well as to acquire justification for believing it, from your testimony.

Epistemic authority and cogent grounds

Indeed, if you tell someone that you know something – especially where you are asked whether you *really* know it – you put yourself on the line. It is as if you gave your firmest assurance – an epistemic promise, as it were – that it is true; and if it turns out to be false, your position is somewhat like that of a person who has broken a promise. You are open to a kind of criticism and may have to make amends. A good theory of knowledge should account for this *epistemic authority*.

A stronger, but closely associated view is that if you know that a proposition is true, then you must be able to say something on behalf of it. After all, the question how one knows is always intelligible, at least for beliefs that are not of self-evident truths or propositions about one's current consciousness (two kinds not in question for the most important kinds of skepticism); and if one really does know, one should be able to give more than a dogmatic answer, such as 'I can just see that it is true'.

The associated principle might be expressed in what I shall call *the cogency principle*: with the possible exception of beliefs of certain self-evident propositions and propositions about one's current consciousness, one knows that something is so only if one has grounds for it from which one can (in principle) argue cogently for it on the basis of those grounds.

Since the cogency principle requires only that one *can* argue cogently for what one knows, temporary inability to mount an argument would not prevent one's knowing. Even little children might have knowledge, for perhaps if they could just find a way to express their grounds they could provide cogent arguments. And since self-evident propositions and propositions about one's current consciousness are knowable even according to most skeptics, and may be objects of directly justified belief, there is a stopping place in epistemic chains and no regress need result when one produces a series of arguments to support a claim. What is known must simply be either traceable to those secure foundations or otherwise defensible by appeal to adequate grounds.

If the cogency principle is combined with the entailment principle, it will immediately preclude anyone's having knowledge on inductive grounds; for the entailment principle implies that inductive grounds are never cogent. But it need not be combined with the entailment principle. If it is not, it can allow for inductive reasoning of certain kinds to be cogent and thereby to transmit knowledge.

Granted, even a moderate skeptic is likely to accept at most a restricted kind of induction, a kind whose premises make its conclusion at least close to certain. The point, however, is that the cogency principle is separable from the entailment principle. Still, even if the cogency principle is not combined with the entailment principle, the cogency principle can be very hostile to the commonsense view that we can know the sorts of things I have been suggesting we can know, at least if this view is understood in a foundationalist framework. For this principle strikes at some of the main sources of knowledge as they are plausibly understood, and it threatens to undermine our claim to knowledge of the past, the future, and the external world. Let us pursue this.

It is true that some of our beliefs that constitute direct knowledge (and are directly justified) can be supported by apparently more secure premises. For instance, my belief that I see a green field before me can be supported by premises about how things appear to me, which concern only my present consciousness. After all, that this is so seems to be the best explanation of why my visual field contains a green field. But this supportability by premises need not hold for everything it seems reasonable to regard as directly known. It may not hold in the case of apparently memorial knowledge. As we saw in Chapter 2, one might know something through the success of one's sheer retentive powers even when the only premises one knows or is justified in using to support it fail to justify it.

A proponent of the cogency principle would certainly tend to deny that my memory can be trusted as a source of direct knowledge or direct justification, in part because memory seems far more subject to error than perception. Moreover, I might be unable to provide good inductive reasoning to support the reliability of memory even in cases where it is very vivid, if only because such an argument would require my depending on my memory for my justification in believing its premises, say premises about how often my past memory beliefs have been confirmed. To summarize their track record, I must remember how things turned out in the past – or at least remember that I wrote the results down as they occurred. I would thus be relying on memory in order to vindicate it. Still, even if I could give no cogent argument to justify my memorial beliefs, it does not follow that they are not justified, or that they do not constitute knowledge.

Grounds of knowledge as conferring epistemic authority

Must we accept even this apparently modest skeptical principle? I do not see why. Certainly one can have a kind of authority without being able to defend it by premises or exhibit it in argumentation. Consider, for instance, someone who can always tell "identical" twins apart but cannot say how. Moreover, saying 'I see it' need not be a dogmatic answer to 'How do you know?' It may simply specify one's grounds, as where one says, 'I see it' in answer to 'How do you know there is still ice on the road?' It says *how* one knows; it need not (though it may) *show* that one does, particularly if showing this requires more than exhibiting an appropriate source of the challenged belief.

There is a general lesson here. When skeptics ask how we know something, this is a challenge to show it. I have already argued that knowing something does not require being able to show it, so this challenge is not always appropriate. What I now want to stress is that the skeptical emphasis on 'How do you know?' as a request for a demonstration must not be allowed to obscure the possibility of taking it as a request to specify a ground of one's knowledge and of fulfilling that request simply by giving an adequate ground. In doing this successfully, one shows how one knows.

In saying how I know something by citing my ground I may also be doing something further: *exhibiting* my knowledge of what the ground supports and perhaps even of the fact that it does so. But even exhibiting knowledge need not be showing that one has it; and even if I know that, say, seeing ice on the roads shows that they are icy, I may not know how to use this connection to show that I know they are. Still, if my knowledge that they are carries an authority that can be confirmed by my citing my ground, why need I be able to go on to the sophisticated task of showing that I have knowledge? Again the analogy to virtue is pertinent: having it requires being able to manifest it in appropriate circumstances, but not to be able to show – in any further way – that one has it.

Exhibiting knowledge versus dogmatically claiming it

One might think this approach licenses dogmatism. Granted, saying 'I see it' would be dogmatic if intended to show conclusively that I know, for instance by proving that there is green grass before me. But indicating the basis for my knowledge is different from flatly claiming that I have knowledge; indeed, it exhibits a ground for my belief which, if sound, suggests that I am not being dogmatic in taking myself to know. Perhaps it is precisely because the skeptic's 'How do you know?' is commonly meant as a challenge to be shown conclusively that one knows, and not as a request to specify a source of the knowledge, that 'I see it' seems dogmatic in the context of discussing skepticism even when its function is mainly explanatory.

If the issue raised by skepticism is whether we can show that we have knowledge, the point that an appeal to visual experience does not conclusively establish visual knowledge is an important concession. But the issue here is whether the skeptic succeeds in showing that we do not have perceptual knowledge. In that context, the point is not a concession. Once again, we can see how skepticism can gain credibility because skeptics make it sound as if their case against the existence of one or another kind of knowledge succeeds if we cannot show that there is such knowledge. In fact, we need not be able to show that there is knowledge in order to have it; and the skeptic must give us good reason not to believe that there is knowledge.

Refutation
and rebuttal

Have I, then, refuted skepticism, even in the few forms considered here? I have not tried to. *Refutation* would require showing that those forms of skepticism are false, which in turn would entail showing that there is knowledge (and justified belief). What I have tried to do is to *rebut* skepticism in certain plausible forms, to show that the arguments for those skeptical views do not establish that we do not have knowledge (and justified belief). Now suppose I have succeeded. Where do we stand? May we believe that we have knowledge, or may we only suspend judgment both on this and on skeptical claims that we do not?

I have already argued, by implication, that one can know something without knowing that one knows it. For instance, in arguing that much of our knowledge is not self-conscious, I indicated how I can know that there is a green field before me without even believing that I know this. I do not even form such self-conscious beliefs in most everyday situations. Moreover, toddlers, who do not understand what knowledge is – and so are not in a position to believe they know anything – can apparently know such simple things as that Mama is before them.

Even if I did have the second-order knowledge that I know the field is there, I surely would not possess – if it is even possible for me to possess – the infinite series of beliefs required by the view that knowing entails knowing that one knows: the series that continues with my knowing that I know that I know; knowing that I know, that I know that I know; and so forth. There is no plausibility in thinking that if I know that (for example) the field is there, I must know that I know that I know . . . this, up to the limit of my capacity. I never have such a repetitive thought; I do not think that I believe (or disbelieve) the proposition in question (I have not tested my memory here): and I cannot imagine a good use for it.[16] Given these points (among others), it would be a mistake to think, as some skeptics might like us to, that if we do not know that we have knowledge, then we do not.

For similar reasons, it seems possible that we might be justified in believing that we have knowledge even if we are properly unwilling to claim that we know we do, and perhaps even if we are properly unwilling to claim justification for believing that we do. Let us explore these possibilities.

If foundationalism is correct, then if one can know anything, one can know at least something directly. Moreover, some of the sorts of things a plausible foundationalism says we know directly – for instance, self-evident truths and some propositions about our present consciousness – are the kinds of things which, simply on the basis of reflection on the examples involved, it is plausible to think we know. Perhaps, of course, this reflection, even if it does not involve arguing from premises, shows that we have knowledge. In any case, I think that we are justified in believing that we have some knowledge even if we cannot show that we do; and I am aware of no good argument against the view that we have some knowledge.

Might there be a way, however, to give a cogent, positive defense of common sense: to show that we have knowledge, even of the external world? And could we establish this second-order thesis even to the satisfaction of some skeptics? There is no satisfying a *radical skeptic*, one who denies that there can be *any* knowledge or justified belief (including justification of that very claim, which the skeptic simply asserts as a challenge). For such a skeptic, nothing one presents as a reason for asserting something will count as justifying it.

Could anything be said, however, to show that there is knowledge that might be plausible to a *moderate skeptic*: one who holds, say, that although transmission of justification and knowledge must be deductive, we may justifiedly believe, and perhaps know, at least self-evident propositions and propositions about our present consciousness? Even if the answer is negative, perhaps one can show that there is knowledge, or at least justified belief, whether any skeptics would find one's argument plausible or not.

Prospects for a positive defense of common sense

How might an argument for a positive defense of common sense go? Let us consider justified belief first, since showing that certain of our beliefs are justified, unlike showing that some of them constitute knowledge, does not require showing that the beliefs in question are true.

A case for justified belief

One might view the issue this way: if we are to show that there are justified beliefs, then one result of our argument will itself be producing justification, specifically justification for the second-order belief that there are justified beliefs. For to show something by argument is at least to produce justification for believing it.

If we are to provide such second-order justification, we apparently need at least two things: a general premise expressing a sufficient condition for justification, and one or more specific premises saying that a particular belief meets that condition. For instance, the general premise might be the justification principle that

(1)   An attentive belief to the effect that one is now in an
       occurrent mental state, such as thinking, is justified,

where an attentive belief is one based on careful attention to the matter in question, and where the justification is not absolute but simply strong enough to make it appropriate for a rational person to hold the belief.[17] The particular premise might be that

(2)   I have an attentive belief I am now in such a state, namely
       thinking.

If I am justified in believing these premises, I would surely be justified in inferring deductively from them, and thereby in believing on the basis of them, what they self-evidently entail, namely, that

(3)   My belief that I am thinking is justified.

Here I would be inferentially justified in believing (3), at least if I can hold all three propositions before my mind in a way that avoids dependence on memory of my premises; and this seems possible for me. Premises (1) and (2) self-evidently entail (3), and a moderate skeptic will grant that if, from premises that I am justified in believing, I infer (without dependence on memory) a conclusion that self-evidently follows from them, I am justified in believing that too.

But how am I now justified in believing premises (1) and (2), if I am? There is some plausibility in holding that the general principle, (1), is justifiable directly (non-inferentially) by reflection, and so my belief of it might itself be directly justified. This is not to deny that it *could* be justified by prior premises; the point is only that it is arguably justified by reflection not dependent on one's appealing to such premises. As for the particular premise, (2), I might be directly justified in holding it by virtue of a justification principle similar to the general one, but applying to beliefs, a principle to the effect that if, on careful introspection, one believes that one attentively believes something, then one is justified in believing one does (presumably directly justified, if one has introspected carefully).

Now if my belief of my general premise is justified, and if I may justifiedly hold the particular premise, then surely I may justifiedly conclude that I am justified in my belief that I am thinking. I may justifiedly conclude this even if my justification in believing my premises is not direct, as I am tentatively assuming it is. Moreover, if my beliefs of (1) to (3) are true, they may also constitute knowledge: my justification for each seems strong enough, and apart from this matter of degree there appears to be no other kind of bar to knowledge.[18]

Given the plausibility of the premises just used to try to show that I am justified in holding a belief about my own mental life, I am inclined to think that it can be shown that there are some justified beliefs. But even if the line of argument I have used is successful, one might question whether it extends to any beliefs about the external world. What would be our general principle for, say, visual perceptual beliefs?

In answer, perhaps we might first say that

(a)   If one believes, on the basis of a vivid and steady visual
      experience in which one has the impression of something
      green before one, that there is something green before one,
      then one is justified in so believing.

Surely we may say this, particularly since the justification in question is admittedly defeasible. (It could, for instance, be undermined by my knowing that I have frequently been hallucinating greens lately.) Suppose this premise may be believed with direct justification, and we may also believe (possibly with direct justification) that

(b)   I have a belief (that there is something green before me)
      grounded in the way the premise – principle (a) – requires.

Then I may, much as before, justifiedly conclude that

(c)   I am justified in believing that there is something green
         before me.

Suppose, moreover, that principle (a) provides the basis for only prima facie justification; I might conclude that my perceptual belief is *prima facie justified* – roughly, justified in the absence of defeating factors. This would be a significant conclusion, even if (as seems possible) I could not, by reflection alone, rule out all of those defeaters.

The regress of demonstration

Supposing this line of argument against the skeptic is sound, have I shown anything? If showing something is producing a good argument for it from true premises that one is justified in believing, presumably I have. It is easy, however, to think that the skeptic would be correct in denying that I have shown anything. For there is a subtlety here that is easily missed. Even if I have shown my conclusion, I might not be justified in *saying*, to the skeptic or anyone else, that I have shown it, or even in believing I have shown it. For justification for asserting or believing that second-order proposition about my beliefs would ordinarily require holding (or at least having justification for holding) *third-order* beliefs, such as the belief that my second-order belief that I believe I am thinking is justified and true (since this second-order belief has been shown by good argument). And what in my situation would give me that still higher-order justification?

The general point is that whatever one's justificational or epistemic achievement, justifiedly saying or even justifiedly believing that one has succeeded in it requires justification or knowledge at the *next* higher level. This higher-order justification or knowledge may or may not be forthcoming. Initially, this point may seem to doom my original attempt to show that I have a justified belief. But I do not think it does; it brings out only that one can show this without automatically showing the higher-order proposition that one has shown it. Plainly, we can achieve something even if we are in no way entitled to credit ourselves with it.

What we have encountered here is a counterpart of the regress of justification, a *regress of demonstration*: if one shows anything at all, there will be some unshown shower (premise). In a sense, there will always be some point at which self-congratulation – or a final dismissal of the skeptical challenges – is inappropriate. This is another reason why a moderate foundationalist perspective should not be thought to lead to dogmatism.

Still, even if I do not know that I have shown that my belief that I am thinking is justified, I may yet *have* shown this; and if I have, then I may well know the proposition that I have shown: that my belief that I am thinking is justified. Perhaps, moreover, a similar procedure may be repeated, with equal success, at each higher level to which one can ascend without losing track of the progressively more complex issue. Then, with sufficient patience, one could show any given justification-ascribing proposition in the hierarchy – that one has shown that one has a justified belief, that one has shown that one has shown this, and so on, to the limit of one's comprehension.

A case for knowledge

The reasoning we have been exploring in connection with justification also bears on skepticism about knowledge. If the premise beliefs, (a) and (b), are true, they may constitute knowledge. I may, then, not only be showing that I am justified in holding a belief about the external world but also may, as a result of my reasoning, know that I am justified in holding it. There would then be at least justificational knowledge: self-knowledge to the effect that one has justification for some beliefs.

In reasoning from (a) and (b) to (c), however, I do not automatically know that I am showing that I am justified in believing something about the external world. Suppose I do not know this. Perhaps I only hope that I am showing it. Then, even if I do have second-order knowledge that I have a justified belief about the external world, I may not be justified in holding the *third*-order belief that I have (second-order) knowledge that I have this (first-order) justified belief, the belief that there is something green before me. I have as yet no principle that would justify me in concluding that I know or justifiedly believe that I have a justified first-order belief. I lack a principle stating conditions that generate second-order knowledge or second-order justified belief.

It seems, however, that the sort of justification I apparently have for all the relevant beliefs, including the belief that I have a justified belief about the external world, is the kind whose possession by *true* beliefs is sufficient for their constituting knowledge. Thus, through reasoning using premises like (a) and (b) I may well know that I have justified beliefs about the external world. Certainly I have reason to think that the skeptic does not know, or justifiedly believe, that I *lack* justified beliefs about the external world.

One assumption of this strategy against skepticism deserves emphasis: the assumption that the crucial principles of justification are a priori, and believing them is justified by reflection (directly, or at least on the basis of self-evident steps from directly justified beliefs of a priori premises). Suppose the principles are empirical. Then our justification for believing them would presumably be broadly inductive. A skeptic could plausibly deny that, on an inductive basis, we can justifiedly believe them. Let us pursue this possibility.

A circularity problem

There would apparently be a circularity problem if we had to justify our crucial principles inductively. For justifying them by inductive reasoning would seem to presuppose using just such principles, principles that specify, for instance, under what conditions inductive inference can transmit justification or knowledge. We would have to use induction to develop a track record for such inferences, say by determining, observationally, how often their premises are found true and their conclusions determined to be false. We would need to rely on perception and memory to do this – in addition to using induction to infer from a good track record on the part of a source to its general reliability. To acquire justified beliefs about the reliability of perception, moreover, we would need to use perception, for instance in looking at objects again to see if our initial color perceptions were accurate.

Are the kinds of principles of justification I have been using a priori? That is certainly arguable; but it is also controversial. On a reliability theory of justification, for instance, a belief is justified by virtue of being grounded in reliable belief-producing processes such as perceptual ones; and it is apparently not an a priori matter what processes are *reliable*, that is, actually produce a suitably large proportion of true beliefs. This is the sort of thing that must be determined largely by observation.

Thus, for reliabilism, in order to know what principles account for justification, one must know what processes tend to generate true beliefs. One could determine that only through considerable experience. Hence, if these principles are empirical, the circularity problem just mentioned would beset the attempt, within a reliabilist framework, to justify them.

On the other hand, I argued above that reliability theories are less plausible for justification than for knowledge, and I believe that it is more reasonable, though by no means obviously correct, to suppose that at least some principles about the conditions for justification are a priori. I would include various principles expressing ways in which – as described by Chapters 1 through 4 – justification is produced by its basic sources.

Skepticism and common sense

Where, then, does this chapter leave us with respect to appraising skepticism? To begin with, there are forms of skepticism I have not mentioned, and I have also not discussed every plausible argument for the skeptical principles I have addressed: chiefly the infallibility, certainty, back-up, entailment, and cogency principles. But these principles are in some important ways representative of those on which even moderate skepticism rests. I have offered reasons for rejecting them, and on that basis I have maintained that skepticism, at least insofar as it depends on these and similar principles, can be rebutted. It can be shown to be rationally resistible.

We are, then, warranted in refusing to accept skepticism concerning justification and knowledge of propositions other than those that are self-evident or attribute to the believer a present occurrent mental property. If it is not false, it is at least not justified by what seem the main arguments for it. It is not clear, however, that anything said above refutes the kinds of skepticism we have considered. For refuting those views entails showing them to be false, and it is not altogether clear what that requires.

Positively, I have suggested that on one plausible notion of showing something, namely, validly and justifiably deducing it from true premises which one justifiedly believes and are good grounds for it, we can show that there are some beliefs we are justified in holding, probably even some justified beliefs about the external world (possibly including some about the inner lives of others).[19] I am less inclined to say that we can – by this strategy – show that there is knowledge, particularly knowledge of the external world. Much depends on the kind of grounding required for such premises as that I see a green field before me, which, because simple seeing *entails* the existence of the object seen, in turn entails that there is something external. Much also depends on how rigorous a standard of showing is appropriate.

I have argued, however, for the commonsense view that we can know that there is both justified belief and knowledge about the external world, and can know this even if we cannot show that there is. I also maintain that there is certainly justified belief and knowledge about one's own consciousness and about certain a priori matters. Skeptics certainly do not seem to have shown that we do not know this. I believe that we do know it, and that we also know that we know some a priori propositions.

Moreover, if, as argued in Chapter 9, it is true that rationality is a more permissive notion than justification, then whatever the anti-skeptical case for our having justification, it will count more strongly for the counterpart views concerning the rationality of our beliefs and other epistemic attitudes. Even if rationality, as applied to beliefs, is significantly weaker than justification, it is still the kind of status skeptics tend to deny is ever achieved by our beliefs about the external world, the past, and many other things.

Perhaps viewing knowledge, justification, and rationality in the way I have might be thought to be an article of epistemological faith. I do not think it is; but the difficulty of determining whether it is partly an article of unverifiable faith, or can be established by cogent argument, or is more than the former yet less than the latter, is some testimony to the depth and complexity of skeptical problems.

Notes

1 Some writers on skepticism prefer to raise skeptical possibilities using the dream case rather than the hallucination one, perhaps in part because Descartes so famously used a dream argument in his *Meditations on First Philosophy*. For relevant discussion, esp. of the dream argument, see, for example, Barry Stroud, *The Significance of Philosophical Scepticism* (Oxford: Oxford University Press, 1984); Michael Williams, *Unnatural Doubts* (Oxford: Basil Blackwell, 1991); and Robert Fogelin, *Pyrrhonian Reflections on Knowledge and Justification* (Oxford and New York: Oxford University Press, 1994). Another way to raise skeptical possibilities is to imagine that one is a "brain in a vat," i.e., that one's brain is kept alive artificially in a liquid and given just the sorts of stimulation it now has, so that one would presumably experience things just as one now does.

2 See, for instance, Section IV of his *Inquiry Concerning Human Understanding* (first published in 1748).

3 This formulation is roughly the one given by Bertrand Russell in *The Problems of Philosophy* (Oxford: Oxford University Press, 1912). The formulation should be understood to apply only to phenomena of a certain kind, such as we explore in scientific inquiry and much everyday investigation; it will not hold for certain special cases. For instance, with an increase in the number of cases in which I lose a fair sweepstakes in which I hold one of a million coupons, there is *no* change in the probability that I will lose. To think my good day is now more likely to come is to commit the *gambler's fallacy*.

4 A remark attributed to Bertrand Russell introduces (humorously) the possibility that we may, perhaps haphazardly, be sometimes right and sometimes wrong about other minds: "There may be other minds, but there certainly aren't many of them." In this spirit I might note another twist to the problem of other minds. As usually conceived, it concerns whether, in effect, there are as *many* minds as there seem to be. But reflection on skepticism can also lead us to a converse worry. How do I know that when I am asleep my body is not taken over by another mind, one connected, perhaps, with a part of the same brain as goes with my mind? And why might there not be several others who control this body when I do not? Granted there could be a conflict with another mind over, say, the movements of my right arm; but I could be built (or programmed) so as never to be conscious when another mind takes over this body. Call this the *problem of too many minds*.

5 There is much recent literature on the extent to which skeptical hypotheses undermine commonsense views about the extent of our knowledge. See, for instance, Moser's *Philosophy after Objectivity* and the books by Fogelin, Klein, Nozick, Rescher, Stroud, and Williams cited in the bibliography. For a helpful discussion of skepticism focusing on the underdetermination problem, see Jonathan Vogel, 'Dismissing Skeptical Possibilities', *Philosophical Studies* 70 (1993), 235–50.

6 This is the term widely used in recent literature in connection with a debate between, on the non-skeptical side, Hilary Putnam, who denies that one really could be both a brain in a vat *and* have the mastery of language needed to raise the question of skepticism, and, closer to the skeptical side in interpreting such examples, a number of other philosophers, including Anthony Brueckner, 'Trying to Get Outside Your Own Skin', *Philosophical Topics* 23, 1 (1995), 79–111, which contains references to Putnam's original discussions of the brain-in-a-vat problem and a number of more recent discussions.

7 See, for example, Thomas Aquinas's *Summa Theologica* (written in the thirteenth century), Ia, question 25, a.3.

8 As an epistemic principle, (2) – and indeed (1) and (3) as well – would commonly be taken by proponents to be necessarily true. Thus (2) would rule out even the *possibility* of

knowledge of falsehoods, as opposed to the mere occurrence of it. But for our purposes the formulations as more simply stated will serve.

9 If there are such laws, then there is empirical grounding that is conclusive in the sense that it implies the proposition it grounds with "natural necessity," the kind appropriate to causal laws. Since those are not absolutely necessary, as are logical laws and necessary truths as described in Chapter 4, it would not follow that the implication is an entailment.

10 This is the kind of strategy taken by Peter D. Klein in *Certainty: A Refutation of Scepticism* (Minneapolis: University of Minnesota Press, 1981), and it is extended by him in the paper cited in Chapter 6. In part, the issue concerns whether we may simply take it as obvious that we do know certain things before we have a *criterion* of knowledge, e.g. an account that tells us both what knowledge is and whether beliefs constituting it must be infallible. For detailed discussion of this *problem of the criterion* – the problem of whether cases of knowledge are prior to accounts or vice versa – see R. M. Chisholm, 'The Problem of the Criterion', in his *The Foundations of Knowing* (Minneapolis: University of Minnesota Press, 1982); and Robert Amico, *The Problem of the Criterion* (Lanham, Md.: Rowman and Littlefield, 1994).

11 There is a sophisticated and plausible compromise with skepticism that deserves note here. One could argue that knowledge must be understood not unqualifiedly but in terms of relativization to "contrast classes." Thus, relative to the contrast class of near perfect imitations, I do not know that there is a green field before me; relative to the contrast class of ordinary green things encountered in the same visual way, such as green ponds and green canvas laid out for picnicking, I do. For a detailed statement of this view see Walter Sinnott-Armstrong's chapter on moral skepticism in Walter Sinnott-Armstrong and Mark Timmons (eds) *Moral Knowledge?* (New York: Oxford University Press, 1996). One reply is that knowledge may be understood without relativization provided we at least (1) recognize that knowledge *attributions* occur in a context and are in some way relative to it, and (2) distinguish between the following kinds of things: (a) knowing there is a green field before one and (b) knowing that there is a green field before one *as opposed to* a pavement textured to look just like one. Knowing the former does not entail knowing the latter, contrastive proposition, but it is easily taken to require that because (i) the latter proposition apparently follows from the former and (ii) *noting* the possibility of ignorance of the latter is an intelligible challenge to a *claim* to know the former.

12 The 'presumably' is meant to allow that there is a sense of 'show' in which one need not have justification for one's premises: if they are true and are cogent grounds for what one wants to show, then invoking them may serve to show it. Here, however, one might not be justified in believing the very thing one shows. This objective, externalist way of showing – call it *de facto showing* – something is not the one of interest here, which might be called *dialectical showing*, since it figures crucially in philosophical disputation.

13 It does not strictly follow unless we define regularity to preclude the following kind of thing: the sun rises every day except every trillionth after the Earth came to be, where tomorrow *is* the trillionth.

14 As noted in Chapter 4, the synthetic a priori might be necessary without being logically necessary in the strict sense; similarly, something can be a synthetically necessary falsehood (thus impossible, as is a round square), but not strictly logically impossible.

15 This should be taken to apply to non-formal validity: infallibility would be preserved by the inference from something's being round to its not being square, but this is a case of synthetic a priori, as opposed to formal, entailment.

16 Reasons for doubting that we should posit such beliefs are given in my 'Dispositional Beliefs and Dispositions to Believe', *Nous* 28, 4, 1994, 419–34.

17 We might perhaps think of this as the kind of justification that is sufficient to render a true

belief knowledge, in the absence of the kinds of cases discussed in Chapter 8 showing that justified true belief need not constitute knowledge.

18 I ignore here the point that I might have only situational justification for my conclusion if my believing it is not *based* on my believing my premises. See note 19 for a comment on this problem.

19 I have not directly argued that there are *justified beliefs*. For I have not argued for the premise, apparently needed for this conclusion, that we are non-inferentially justified in believing that the relevant beliefs, such as that there is something green before me, are *based* on the visual impressions constituting my grounds for it. This basing is partly causal, and skeptics are likely to argue that justification for attributing causal propositions requires inductive, hence inferential, grounds. This is not self-evident, and I have challenged it in 'Causalist Internalism', *American Philosophical Quarterly* 26 (1989), reprinted in my *The Structure of Justification* (Cambridge and New York: Cambridge University Press, 1993). In any case, even if I am not justified in believing that my external world belief is based on a sense impression, but only that I *have* the relevant impression, I am justified in believing that I *have* this justification for the external world belief: we might say that I am entitled to hold it even though I may not hold it on the basis of my entitlement.

Conclusion

Once again, I look at the grassy green field before me. A haze has obscured it, but the afternoon sun now streaming down on it puts it in clear view. Its shape and its shades of color are plainly in my sight. The birds are still singing. The arm of my chair remains hard and smooth. As I look at the spruce tree, I remember cutting the poison ivy vine from it. I recall its furry stem, and the recollection is so vivid that as the scene fills my consciousness, I become almost unaware of what I see in the field before me.

I cannot help having these experiences of color and shape and sound unless I deaden my senses to the world; and I cannot help forming beliefs as I perceive the world or look into my consciousness. I can walk away and change the external sources of my belief. But as we saw in Chapter 1, in exploring perception, I cannot entirely resist those sources. If my senses are open to my surroundings, I perceive them; if I perceive them, I tend to form beliefs about them: about their colors and shapes, their sounds and scents and textures, and, if they have found a place in my memory, sometimes about their history.

These beliefs seem to arise directly from perceptions and through the recollections that surface from memory; they do not emerge by a process of inference from anything else I believe. I realize that such beliefs are fallible, and I understand the profound inclination toward skepticism which one experiences as one reflects on the significance of that fallibility. Still, I find no reason to think these everyday beliefs doubtful, and I am convinced that for the most part they are justified and constitute knowledge.

Our beliefs are countless and varied. A vast proportion of them are stored in memory, though beliefs do not originate there. As Chapter 2 brought out, memory preserves, but does not by itself normally produce, belief. It also preserves, but does not create, knowledge. Once I come to know through perception that the spruce is taller than the maple, I may know this from memory even when I have forgotten my evidence for it. By contrast, memory *is* a basic source of justification. It can be the only present source of justification for many beliefs stored therein, beliefs whose original grounds are long forgotten. It can also produce justification of certain new beliefs which, in a suitable way, seem to represent what I remember, even if I later discover that despite their apparent memorial authenticity they arose from wishful thinking.

Our justification for believing what is, so far as we can tell, grounded in memory, is defeasible, but it is significantly strong. If we had good reason to believe it lacked a certain minimal strength, we would not be justified in trusting our memories without external evidence of their reliability; and it is doubtful that we could get enough such evidence if we could not trust our memory directly in at least some cases. To test my memory of the texture of the maple by going closer to it, for instance, I must retain the belief whose truth I am trying to confirm. If memory were not a basic source of justification, we could never have a large enough store of justified beliefs to yield premises adequate for significant deductive and inductive extension of our justification. The scope of our justified belief would be drastically narrowed; and at least a great deal, and perhaps all, of our knowledge of the past, the future, and general empirical propositions would also be undermined.

If Chapter 1 concerns what might be called outer perception, Chapter 3 explores what is sometimes called inner perception. When we look into our own consciousness, we find beliefs also arising in the same natural, seemingly irresistible way in which they arise from outer perception. We have, however, far more control over the scenes and events that we experience only inwardly. I can blot out my sensations of color and shape only by closing my eyes, but I can dismiss my image of the vine at will and, just as directly, call up an image of the friend who helped me to pull it down. In this respect beliefs are more like perceptions: I cannot help believing that the image of the tree (or at least my imaging of the tree) itself represents something with a greenish cast, nor could I have come to believe this at will. The inner world, like the outer world, produces certain beliefs directly and irresistibly. And these beliefs tend to be both justified and to constitute knowledge.

If our only sources of knowledge and justification were perception, whether inner or outer, and memory, we would be at best impoverished. We can also turn our attention to abstract matters, even while our senses bombard us with impressions. Looking at the spruce and the maple and then further to the right where there is an ash tree at the side of the field, I realize that they are so far apart that I cannot see by direct comparison whether the spruce is taller than the ash. But I can see that it is taller than the maple and that the maple is taller than the ash. Clearly, then, the spruce is taller than the ash. As stressed in Chapter 4, reason makes it obvious that if the spruce is taller than the maple and the maple is taller than the ash, then the spruce is taller than the ash. This belief is as natural, and would be at least as difficult to resist when I vividly consider its propositional content, as my belief that there is something blue before me when I squarely see the spruce. Clearly, this a priori belief is also justified, and it constitutes knowledge.

The experiences and reflections of individuals, even when well-preserved in their memories, are limited. There is a great deal we cannot know about the world without relying on others. Much of what we justifiedly believe and know is, in a sense, socially grounded: based on what others have said to us, whether in person or impersonally in their writings. Testimony, the central concern of Chapter 5, is a special source of justification and knowledge: it often yields direct belief; yet unlike perception, perhaps its closest analogue among basic sources of knowledge, it is not a basic source of belief. It does not yield belief apart from perception, since it must be received through sensory stimulation, as in listening or reading. Testimony is, however, like memory and unlike perception in being unlimited in the scope and subject matter of the propositions we can learn from it. To be sure, we might gain no justification from testimony if we had none deriving from a basic source; but we would have, at best, far less justification than we do if our only knowledge and justification came from basic sources, or even from basic sources and inferences from their deliverances.

Once we have beliefs directly grounded in one of the five sources of non-inferential knowledge and justification – perception, memory, consciousness, reason, and, secondarily but indispensably, testimony – we are in a position to extend whatever justification and knowledge we then have. To take a simple case, on the basis of my beliefs that the spruce is taller than the maple and that the maple is taller than the ash, together with my belief that if those things are so, then the spruce is taller than the ash, I infer that the spruce is indeed taller than the ash. I began with non-inferential beliefs grounded directly in basic sources of knowledge: perception and reason. By a simple, spontaneous deductive inference, I extended both my knowledge and my justification. And when, on another occasion, I heard rapid knocking, believed it to sound like that of a woodpecker, and inferred that there was a woodpecker nearby, I extended my knowledge by inductive inference. Chapter 6 indicates how knowledge and justification can grow indefinitely in these ways. Inference has a virtually unlimited capacity to extend our outlook.

A picture has emerged. We are in almost constant interaction with the world, external and internal. We are regularly bombarded by sensation, often immersed in the stream of our consciousness, and sometimes occupied with reflection on abstract matters, such as questions of mathematics, philosophy, or science. Beliefs are a natural product of these engagements. They arise in perception, introspection, and reflection; they are preserved in memory; they are multiplied by inference and testimony. Many beliefs are grounded in the basic sources, or preserved, as non-inferential beliefs, in memory; many others are inferentially grounded in these direct beliefs, in the ways detailed in Chapter 7. This picture portrays two interconnected structures: foundational beliefs anchored in the bedrock of experience and reason, whether directly or through testimony that ultimately rests on it as well, and a superstructure of vast complexity erected from it by the building blocks of inference. The theory associated with this picture of our beliefs in relation to the world is psychological foundationalism. The picture is natural; and there is much to be said for the theory.

Once our psychology is understood in this way, another natural picture, similar to the first, emerges. The theory associated with it is epistemological foundationalism. I know that the spruce is taller than the ash. I know this on the basis of knowing that the spruce is taller than the maple and the maple is taller than the ash, together with the proposition that if this is so, then the spruce is taller than the ash. And I know that proposition directly, through rationally comprehending it, and I know the other premises by sight.

I do not readily see how to go any further in grounding my knowledge here; and even if I can go on, it is not clear how I could have knowledge at all if there were not some point or other at which my belief is connected with the reality in virtue of which it is true: the trees with their woody skeletons and colorful foliage; the unchanging abstract relations grasped by reason.

Metaphorically, this picture portrays both knowledge and justification as grounded in looking and thereby in seeing. Perception looks outward, and through it we see the physical world. Memory looks backward, and through it we see the past, or at least some of our own past. Introspection looks inward, and through it we see the stream of our own consciousness. Reason looks beyond experience of the world of space and time, and through it we see concepts and their relations. Testimony draws on all of these sources. It enables others to see – though at one remove, through the attester's eyes – virtually anything that an accurate and credible person attests to. By attending to testimony we can look through any of the basic sources of knowledge and justification, as they have informed others, upon any subject matter they can accurately describe to us.

The foundational pictures, both in epistemology and in psychology, have their appeal; yet one can imagine going further in the process of justification than they suggest we should. It may be natural to think that, at any given time, a chain of justification or knowledge will be anchored in the bedrock of experience or reason, just as its constituent beliefs apparently are – though, to be sure, the chains may be interconnected and, as where one of them puts stress on another, broken or torn from their moorings. Coherentism challenges this picture. Its proponents may grant that a foundational picture fits our psychological make-up. But their view of the structure of our knowledge and justified belief is different.

Coherentists see the structure of our knowledge and justified belief as something like a vast fabric of interlocking fibers. Some of these may be connected to experience, but those are not privileged in generating knowledge or justification. True beliefs constitute knowledge when they are suitably woven into the whole fabric, which, in turn, must hold together in a systematic way. Justification is also a matter of how beliefs are connected with the rest of the fabric. A belief that is a largely isolated strand, for instance one that is not inferentially based on any other or even significantly connected with any other in subject matter, would not be justified.

This and other coherentist pictures can also have profound appeal, particularly in understanding the process of justification, in which we commonly try to show that a belief is justified by connecting it with others that support it and thereby cohere with it. But the process of justification should not dominate our understanding of what it is for a belief simply to *be* justified – to have the property of being justified. Moreover, when it comes to knowledge, which entails truth, the coherence picture is less plausible. For indefinitely many fabrics can have internally coherent patterns; and coherentism – unless alloyed with foundationalist elements – does not require that any of the strands be anchored to the world, whether in perception or introspection or in any other way. Why, then, should we expect a coherent set of beliefs to contain truths that represent the world, and thereby to embody knowledge?

Indeed, if a belief's being justified counts in some way towards its truth, then why should coherence alone be the basis of justification given that coherence by itself implies nothing about truth? Furthermore, self-evident propositions, say that if no vixens are males, then no males are vixens, seem such that we need only understand them to be able to know or justifiably believe them. How does this knowledge or justification derive from coherence at all? There are certainly plausible attempts to provide such answers, but I am not aware of any clear success in doing so.

Whether the structure of my knowledge is foundational or not, I may know such things as that there is a cold glass in my hand and that there is rapid knocking nearby. Coherentists and foundationalists alike agree that I know this only if it is true, and they tend to agree that at least this sort of knowledge requires justified belief. But what is knowledge? This dauntingly simple question is the focus of Chapter 8. My knowing that, say, there is rapid knocking may seem to be simply my justifiably and truly believing this. But it is not. Through some remarkable coincidence, I could be hallucinating such a knocking while my ears, quite unbeknownst to me, are temporarily blocked. I could then have a justified true belief which is not knowledge. The suggested account of knowledge as justified true belief is, then, too broad. It also seems too narrow. For there might be knowledge without justification, as with someone who, by virtue of a stable cognitive capacity, unerringly computes difficult arithmetic results with lightning speed but is unaware of the success and is not (at first) justified in believing the answers.

We can strengthen our requirements on justification to deal with the true belief based on hallucination, and we can weaken them to deal with the lightning calculator. But it is not evident that this strategy will yield a correct and illuminating account of knowledge. We can abandon the concept of justification as a central element in understanding knowledge and try to account for knowledge by appeal to the notion of reliably grounded true belief. But it is not clear that this approach will fully succeed either, and it certainly leaves us with the problem of explaining why justification, which need not figure in the approach, has the close connection to knowledge which it apparently does have.

Moreover, justification is epistemologically important in its own right, and reliability theories seem less likely to succeed in accounting for justification than for knowledge. This is at least in part because the grounds of justification seem internal in a way the grounds of knowledge, or at least some of them, do not. We may say at least this, however: that knowledge is true belief based in the right way on the right kind of ground. Justification or reliability or both may be essential to adequately filling out this idea; and although it is not clear just how it is to be filled out, many of the important elements can be gathered from what we have seen in this book concerning the sources, development, structure, and analysis of knowledge.

However we analyze what knowledge is, there remains the question of how much of it, if any, we have. The question is particularly important as it bears on the major domains that concern Chapter 9: the scientific, the ethical, and the religious. It is sometimes thought that we have a wealth of scientific knowledge, as well as knowledge of certain moral principles and some knowledge of religious truths. But if what passes for scientific knowledge is often not, strictly speaking, true – or might be utterly rejected in the future – may we really say that there is scientific knowledge? If moral principles should turn out to be neither clearly grounded in experience nor plausibly regarded as a priori, on what basis might they be known? And if, as many philosophers think, there are no cogent arguments for God's existence and, in addition, God is not directly knowable through the experiential or rational sources that ground knowledge, how can there be knowledge of God?

These questions are very difficult. But we are warranted in giving some partial answers to them. Consider the scientific, moral, and religious domains in turn.

First, although some of what is termed scientific knowledge is no doubt mistakenly so called because it is far from the truth, there may be some precisely true propositions that are scientifically known, and in any case we may speak of approximate scientific knowledge where the proposition in view is inaccurate, but not grossly so. Moreover, perhaps we may sometimes speak unqualifiedly of scientific knowledge, even if this knowledge is only of approximations, when the truth known is not precisely formulated but is correct within the limits of its application. The degree of inaccuracy within which we may speak in these ways is not sharply specifiable. But particularly where a scientific proposition yields true predictions, helps to explain other apparently true propositions, and approximates a more accurate, true proposition, we may be justified in thinking we know it and correct in calling it approximate knowledge.

Second, although even our most plausible moral principles are neither obviously knowable a priori nor obviously knowable empirically, these rationalist and empiricist conceptions are each defensible for some moral principles. Indeed, neither conception has been refuted despite sustained ingenious attempts to discredit them. Moreover, once we cast aside the common stereotype of scientific knowledge as representing chiefly a body of facts and laws discoverable by simple inductive generalization, or rigorously provable by observations, the contrast between well-confirmed scientific beliefs and reflectively grounded moral beliefs appears at best less sharp. It now becomes far more difficult to discredit the view that there is moral knowledge by unfavorably contrasting moral beliefs with scientific ones, as if scientific generalizations were straightforwardly hard and moral principles unalterably soft. We should not conclude, then, that there is no moral knowledge. And if it is not obvious that there are some basic moral principles that are intuitively knowable, it is far from clear that we should adopt the noncognitivist view that there are no moral propositions to be known or justifiedly believed in the first place.

Third, in the religious domain the possibility of knowledge and justification may also be defended. Even if it is true that no argument for a theistic view of the world is decisive, it should be remembered that a diverse group of independent but individually inconclusive arguments may, if they are mutually supporting and each provides some degree of justification for a conclusion, together justify that conclusion even if none by itself does. It has not been established that this point could not apply in the case of arguments for the existence of God. In any event, discussions of the question of justified religious belief and possible religious knowledge should not simply assume the evidentialist view that such propositions can be known or justifiedly believed only inferentially, on the basis of further beliefs expressing evidence for the theistic propositions in question. One or another kind of religious experience might provide non-inferential grounds of justification, or of knowledge, or of both, somewhat in the way perception does.

There are, to be sure, many important differences between the religious and perceptual cases, and what we have seen does not show either that there is or that there is not direct justification or direct knowledge of theistic propositions. But apparently, even if there cannot be directly justified beliefs of them, there could be direct knowledge of them. Even supposing, however, that there could be neither theistic knowledge nor justified theistic beliefs, there might be rational theistic beliefs: beliefs a rational person with a certain range of experience may hold, even without having the kinds of specific grounds needed for justification. The case for the possibility of rational theistic beliefs seems stronger than the case for the possibility of their justification.

Powerful skeptical arguments threaten the view that our knowledge might have such wide scope, and even the commonsense view that we have any knowledge of the external world, the past, the future, or the inner lives of others. Chapter 10 is devoted to appraising some major skeptical arguments. When we realize that our beliefs concerning these domains are clearly fallible, we can begin to appreciate skeptical views. Even our sense that, whether or not we have knowledge, we do have justified beliefs weakens if we take seriously the possibility that what we accept as justification is no final guarantee of truth. But the common skeptical commitment to the ideal of infallible belief as central to knowledge is not warranted by careful inquiry into the nature of knowledge.

Infallibility may be a reasonable ideal for *proof*, conceived as decisively demonstrating a conclusion from rock-solid premises, such as self-evident truths or, on the empirical side, propositions about the believer's immediate consciousness. For one cannot decisively demonstrate from insecure premises, or by making merely inductive and hence fallible steps from even the most trustworthy premises. But why should proof be our standard of the kind of justification (or perhaps certainty) appropriate to knowledge? We are not talking about what is required to show conclusively that there is knowledge, but about whether there in fact is any.

If, however, we think that there is knowledge, and the skeptic challenges us, we want to show that there is. But we must not confuse – or allow skeptics to confuse – the requirements for showing that there is knowledge with the requirements for the existence of it. Perhaps it can be shown that there is knowledge. Certainly, if we want to argue for this, we need not accept the idea that showing something to be true is equivalent to proving it. But even if it cannot be shown that there is knowledge or justified belief, it does not follow that there is none. It also does not follow that we do not have something less difficult to achieve than justified belief, though significant in most of the same ways: belief that is rational.

But there surely is knowledge and justified belief. I justifiedly believe, indeed I know, that that green field lies before me. Those bird songs are not fantasy. My stream of thoughts is in unmistakably clear focus. Even my recollection that I cut a vine from the spruce tree is clear and steadfast. I am justified in believing that I did, and surely I know this. I have a huge store of beliefs of these and other kinds, including countless beliefs originally formed through testimony. These beliefs form a structure of great complexity, with innumerable changing elements that reflect my continuing experience and thought, my actions and emotions, my learning and forgetting, my inferring and accepting, my revising and rejecting, my speaking and listening. That structure is grounded in me: in my memory, my habits of thought, my mental and perceptual capacities, my rational nature. Knowledge of the truths of reason arises within the structure itself, once we have the needed concepts. Through our consciousness of what is inside of us, and our perceptual engagement with what is outside of us, with the social world as well as our physical environment, this structure is anchored, both internally and externally, to the world. That vast and various reality is at once the ultimate source and the object of our empirical knowledge.

Short annotated bibliography of books in epistemology

Alston, William P., *Epistemic Justification*, Ithaca, NY and London, 1989.
A collection of papers centering on justification and knowledge in a way that unites internalist and externalist elements. Especially relevant to Chapters 1, 3, and 7–10.

Alston, William P., *Perceiving God*, Ithaca, NY and London, 1991.
A major study in religious epistemology, also containing much general epistemology, particularly in the theory of perception. Highly relevant to Chapters 1, 8, and 9.

Aristotle, *Posterior Analytics*, trans. by G. R. G. Mure, Oxford, 1928.
A major text of immense influence. Especially relevant to Chapter 7.

Armstrong, D. M., *Belief Truth and Knowledge*, Cambridge, 1973.
A wide-ranging epistemological essay influential in the reliabilist tradition. Especially pertinent to Chapters 1, 3, and 6 through 9.

Audi, Robert, *The Structure of Justification*, Cambridge and New York, 1993.
A collection of recent papers covering most of the topics in Chapters 4, 6–8, and 10.

Aune, Bruce, *Knowledge of the External World*, London and New York, 1991.
A historically oriented, integrated treatment of empirical knowledge. Bears particularly on Chapters 1, 7, and 10.

Austin, J. L., *Sense and Sensibilia*, Oxford, 1979 (reprint).
A study of perception particularly pertinent to the appraisal of sense-datum theory and of relevance to understanding foundationalism. Especially relevant to Chapters 1 and 7.

Ayer, A. J., *The Problem of Knowledge*, Harmondsworth, Middlesex, 1956.
An epistemological survey in the empiricist tradition. Especially relevant to Chapters 1, 2, 8, and 10.

Baergen, Ralph, *Contemporary Epistemology*, Fort Worth, 1995.
    A textbook addressing most of the topics treated here, with something of relevance
    to each chapter.

Berkeley, George, *A Treatise Concerning the Principles of Human Knowledge*, New York, 1929
    (originally published in 1710).
    Perhaps the most important statement of phenomenalism, and of an idealist
    worldview in general, in the empiricist tradition. Bears particularly on Chapters 1,
    3, 9, and 10.

Bogdan, Radu, *Belief: Form, Function, and Content*, Oxford, 1985.
    A collection of papers on the notion of belief. Mainly pertinent to the areas where
    epistemology overlaps philosophy of mind, esp. to Chapters 1 and 6.

BonJour, Laurence, *The Structure of Empirical Knowledge*, Cambridge, Mass., 1985.
    A detailed statement and defense of coherentism regarding empirical knowledge.
    Especially pertinent to Chapters 1, 4, 7, 8, and 10.

Brandt, R. B., and Ernest Nagel (eds), *Meaning and Knowledge*, New York, 1965.
    A large, historically informed assembly of classical and recent readings in epis-
    temology. Bears on all the chapters.

Butchvarov, Panayot, *The Concept of Knowledge*, Evanston, 1970.
    A metaphysically oriented, foundationalist inquiry into the nature of knowledge.
    Especially pertinent to Chapters 1, 4, 7, 8, and 10.

Butchvarov, Panayot, *Skepticism in Ethics*, Bloomington, 1989.
    A detailed study of the possibility and possible extent of justification and know-
    ledge in ethics. Particularly relevant to Chapters 9 and 10.

Chisholm, R. M., *The Foundations of Knowing*, Minneapolis, 1982.
    A collection of essays, on topics relevant to each chapter, by one of the major
    epistemologists of this century.

Chisholm, R. M., *Theory of Knowledge*, 2nd and 3rd edns, Englewood Cliffs, NJ, 1977 and 1989.
    A rigorous treatment of many basic topics in the field, and an introduction to
    Chisholm's own epistemological views. Relevant to each chapter.

Chisholm, R. M., and Robert Swartz (eds), *Empirical Knowledge*, Englewood Cliffs, NJ, 1973.
    A large collection of recent writings. Especially pertinent to Chapters 1, 2, 3, and 7–10.

Coady, C. A. J., *Testimony*, Oxford, 1992.
    A comprehensive, historically wide-ranging treatment of testimony that links it at
    many points with the philosophy of language and the views of Wittgenstein.
    Pertinent above all to Chapter 5.

Craig, Edward, *Knowledge and the State of Nature*, Oxford, 1990.
    A sophisticated but lucid and concrete treatment of the problem of analyzing

knowledge, with considerable attention to skepticism and far more on testimony than most general books on epistemology. Particularly relevant to Chapters 5, 8, and 10.

Dancy, Jonathan, *Contemporary Epistemology*, Oxford, 1985.
A general introduction to contemporary epistemological literature. Bears on each chapter.

Dancy, Jonathan, and Ernest Sosa (eds), *A Companion to Epistemology*, Oxford, 1992.
A comprehensive reference work highly pertinent to every chapter.

Danto, Arthur C., *Analytical Philosophy of Knowledge*, Cambridge, 1968.
A broad epistemological essay with special focus on the structure of knowledge. Especially relevant to Chapters 6–10.

Descartes, René, *Meditations on First Philosophy*, in vol. 2 of *The Philosophical Writings of Descartes*, trans. by John Cottingham, Robert Stoohof, and Duglad Murdock, Cambridge, 1984 (originally published in 1641).
One of the greatest and most influential works in modern epistemology, and a powerful statement of both rationalism and foundationalism. Bears on every chapter.

Dretske, Fred I., *Knowledge and the Flow of Information*, Cambridge, Mass., 1981.
A major statement of a reliabilist, information-theoretic account of knowledge. Particularly pertinent to Chapters 1, 8, and 10.

Dretske, Fred I., *Seeing and Knowing*, London, 1969.
An intensive study of perception and its relation to empirical knowledge, with an influential defense of the notion of non-epistemic seeing. Especially relevant to Chapters 1, 3, 8, and 10.

Everitt, Nicholas, and Alec Fisher, *Modern Epistemology*, New York, 1995.
A high-level introductory textbook with special attention to mathematical and logical knowledge and detailed discussions of Quine (a major influence on the authors) and Rorty. Pertinent to most chapters, but especially 4 and 8.

Fales, Evan, *A Defense of the Given*, Lanham, M., 1966.
A defense of the view that justification is conferred by what is given in immediate experience, with detailed applications to the foundationalism conceived as a plausible theory that makes use of the given.

Fogelin, Robert, *Pyrrhonian Reflections on Knowledge and Justification*, Oxford and New York, 1994.
An intensive and sympathetic inquiry into skepticism, from a distinctively Pyrrhonian point of view. Relevant above all to Chapter 10.

Foley, Richard, *The Theory of Epistemic Rationality*, Cambridge, Mass., 1987.
A detailed development of a subjectivistic theory of justification. Pertinent to every chapter.

Foley, Richard, *Working without a Net*, Cambridge, Mass., 1993.
  A development and generalization of his theory of epistemic rationality. Especially relevant to Chapters 7–10.

Fumerton, Richard A., *Metaphysical and Epistemological Problems of Perception*, Lincoln, Neb., 1985.
  A study of both the nature of the objects of perception and the way perception yields justification and knowledge. Especially pertinent to Chapters 1, 3, and 7.

Fumerton, Richard A. *Metaepistemology and Skepticism*, Lanham, Md., 1996.
  A systematic treatment of skepticism with special reference to the controversies between internalism and eternalism and foundationalism and coherentism. Highly relevant to Chapters 7, 8, and 10.

Ginet, Carl, *Knowledge, Perception, and Memory*, Dordrecht and Boston, 1975.
  A rigorous high-level study of these three notions in relation to each other. Particularly relevant to Chapters 1–3, 7, 8, and 10.

Goldman, Alan H., *Empirical Knowledge*, Berkeley, Calif., 1988.
  A detailed presentation of a theory of knowledge and evidence with special emphasis on inference to the best explanation. Pertinent above all to Chapters 1, 6, and 8–10.

Goldman, Alvin I., *Epistemology and Cognition*, Cambridge, Mass., 1986.
  A presentation of reliabilism for justification and knowledge, with much discussion of related developments in cognitive psychology. Particularly relevant to Chapters 1, 2, 6, and 8.

Haack, Susan, *Evidence and Inquiry*, Oxford, 1993.
  An attempt to combine the best elements in foundationalism and coherentism, with special attention to the connections between epistemology and philosophy of science. Bears especially on Chapters 7, 9, and 10.

Harman, Gilbert, *Thought*, Princeton, NJ, 1975.
  A broad study of the nature of knowledge, with much attention to defeasibility conditions. Bears especially on Chapters 1, 2, 6, 8, and 10.

Harman, Gilbert, *Change in View*, Cambridge, Mass., 1986.
  A detailed study of evidence and justification as bearing on changing, as opposed to simply holding, a position. Especially relevant to Chapters 6–9.

Heatherington, Stephen Cade, *Knowledge Puzzles*, Boulder, Colo., 1966.
  A comprehensive introduction to epistemology with emphasis on the puzzles generated by many of its central questions. One or another section bears on any given chapter.

Heil, John, *Perception and Cognition*, Berkeley, Calif., 1983.
> A study of perception in relation to belief, with discussions linking epistemology to philosophy of mind. Especially pertinent to Chapters 1, 3, and 8.

Hintikka, Jaakko, *Knowledge and Belief*, Ithaca, NY, 1962.
> A rigorous, advanced study in epistemic logic. Particularly relevant to Chapters 6 and 8.

Hume, David, *An Enquiry Concerning Human Understanding*, Indianapolis, 1977 (first published in 1748).
> A major work in modern epistemology, particularly for the topics of causation, induction, and skepticism. Especially relevant to Chapters 1, 4, 6, and 10.

Hume, David, *A Treatise of Human Nature*, Oxford, 1888 (originally published in 1739).
> One of the greatest and most influential works in modern philosophy, and a powerful statement of empiricism. It bears on every chapter.

Kant, Immanuel, *Prolegomena to Any Future Metaphysics*, trans. by Lewis White Beck, New York, 1950 (originally published in 1783).
> A short presentation of the ideas in Kant's monumental *Critique of Pure Reason*, one of the greatest texts in modern philosophy. The *Prolegomena* bears particularly on Chapters 1, 4, 8, and 9.

Kitcher, Philip, *The Nature of Mathematical Knowledge*, New York and Oxford, 1984.
> A wide-ranging, historically informed treatment of mathematical knowledge, with a sustained critique of various apriorist conceptions of it and a positive account of a "defensible empiricism." Particularly relevant to Chapter 4.

Klein, Peter, *Certainty: A Refutation of Scepticism*, Minneapolis, 1981.
> A rigorous treatment of the nature of knowledge, certainty, and skepticism. Especially pertinent to Chapters 5, 8, and 10.

Kvanvig, Jonathan L., *The Intellectual Virtues and the Life of the Mind*, Lanham, Md, 1992.
> A statement and appraisal of a virtue epistemology, relevant mainly to Chapters 1 and 7–10.

Kyburg, Henry E., Jr., *Epistemology and Inference*, Minneapolis, 1983.
> A collection of advanced papers, of which several are especially pertinent to Chapters 6–9.

Landesman, Charles, *Epistemology: An Introduction*, Oxford, 1996.
> A nearly comprehensive introduction, with historically informed discussions making it particularly relevant to Chapters 1–4, and 8–10.

Lehrer, Keith, *Knowledge*, Oxford, 1974.
> A critique of foundationalism and development of the author's own coherentist theory of knowledge, with a detailed, non-causal account of justification. Particularly relevant to Chapters 1, 3, and 7–10.

Lehrer, Keith, *Theory of Knowledge*, Boulder, Col., 1990.
  A sucessor to his *Knowledge* that presents a revised theory and is also relevant to Chapters 1, 3, and 7–10.

Lewis, C. I., *An Analysis of Knowledge and Valuation*, La Salle, 1946.
  A systematic study, in the foundationalist tradition, of many major epistemological and metaphysical questions. Especially relevant to Chapters 1–4 and 6, 7, and 9.

Locke, Don, *Memory*, New York, 1971.
  A concise but wide-ranging treatment of memory and memorial knowledge. Bears mainly on Chapter 2.

Locke, John, *An Essay Concerning Human Understanding*, New York, 1928 (originally published in 1689).
  A major text in modern epistemology, and a powerful statement of a commonsense empiricism. Bears on each chapter.

Lycan, William, *Judgment and Justification*, New York, 1988.
  An account of justification and of aspects of knowledge, with emphasis on their connection with the notion of explanation and with selected topics in the philosophy of mind. Especially relevant to Chapters 1 and 6–10.

Malcolm, Norman, *Knowledge and Certainty*, Ithaca, NY, 1975.
  A collection of epistemological essays by a leading proponent of the philosophy of Wittgenstein. Especially relevant to Chapters 1, 2, 3, 8, and 10.

McGrew, Timothy J., *The Foundations of Knowledge*, Lanham, Md., 1995.
  A systematic defense of foundationalism (strong as opposed to moderate) relevant to Chapters 1, 4, 7, and 8.

Mill, John Stuart, *A System of Logic*, London, 1843.
  The leading nineteenth-century statement of radical empiricism. Especially relevant to Chapters 4 and 6–9.

Montmarquet, James A., *Epistemic Virtue and Doxastic Responsibility*, Lanham, Md., 1993.
  A statement and appraisal of a virtue epistemology with special emphasis on the relation between justification and intellectual responsibility. Especially relevant to Chapters 1 and 7–10.

Morton, Adam, *A Guide Through the Theory of Knowledge*, 2nd edn, Oxford, 1996.
  A brief but moderately comprehensive introduction, with more on probability and induction than many short books of the same range. Pertinent to nearly every chapter.

Moser, Paul K., *Knowledge and Evidence*, New York, 1993.
  A rigorous and detailed presentation of an account of knowledge and the nature and scope of its supporting grounds. Especially pertinent to Chapters 1, 4, and 7–10.

Moser, Paul K., *Philosophy after Objectivity*, Oxford and New York, 1993.
A rigorous treatment of the relation of realism to skepticism and of both to semantic questions about meaning and epistemological questions about evidence, reasons, and justification. Especially pertinent to Chapters 4, and 7 to 10.

Moser, Paul K., and Arnold van der Nat (eds), *Human Knowledge*, 2nd edn, New York, 1995.
An extensive set of classical and contemporary readings, with editors' introductions to each section. Pertinent to every chapter.

Nozick, Robert, *Philosophical Explanations*, Cambridge, Mass., 1981.
Contains a book-length epistemology section bearing on Chapters 6–8 and 10.

O'Connor, D. J., and Brian Carr, *Introduction to the Theory of Knowledge*, Minneapolis, 1982.
A general introduction bearing on each chapter.

Pappas, George S., and Marshall Swain, *Essays on Knowledge and Justification*, Ithaca, NY, 1978.
A collection of papers, many influential, mainly from professional journals. Especially relevant to Chapters 1 and 6–10.

Plantinga, Alvin, *Warrant and Proper Function*, New York, 1993.
A systematic development of a theory of warrant as to what renders true belief knowledge and of key epistemic concepts related to warrant. Particularly relevant to Chapters 1, 4, and 7–10.

Plantinga, Alvin, *Warrant: The Current Debate*, New York, 1993.
A critical study of many major epistemological theories. Highly relevant to Chapters 7–10.

Plato, *Theaetetus*, trans. by F. M. Cornford, Cambridge, 1934.
A major text in the history of epistemology. Especially relevant to Chapter 8.

Pojman, Louis P., *The Theory of Knowledge*, Belmont, Calif., 1993.
A collection of classical and comtemporary readings relevant to every chapter.

Pojman, Louis P., *What Can We Know?*, Belmont, Calif., 1995.
A wide-ranging, highly readable, historically informed introduction with attention both to basic issues and to classical and contemporary literature. Pertinent to every chapter.

Pollock, John L., *Contemporary Theories of Knowledge*, Totowa, NJ, 1986.
A treatment of some leading current theories in epistemology that also presents the author's own account of some key concepts. Bears especially on Chapters 1, 4, 7, 8, and 10.

Pollock, John L., *Knowledge and Justification*, Princeton, NJ, 1974.
A systematic, wide-ranging treatment of these notions which develops a foundationalist account of both. It bears on all the chapters.

Price, H. H., *Perception*, Oxford, 1932.
    A detailed major study of the topic, with important discussions of sense-data. Especially relevant to Chapters 1 and 10.

Quine, W. V., *The Pursuit of Truth*, Revised edn, Cambridge, Mass., 1992.
    A short statement of many of Quine's epistemological views, with valuable discussions connecting epistemology with the philosophy of science. The chapters devoted to evidence, meaning, perception, and truth (respectively) make it especially pertinent to Chapters 1, 4, 5, 6, 8, and 9.

Quine, W. V., and Joseph Ullian, *The Web of Belief*, 2nd edn, New York, 1978.
    An introductory treatment of the development of common sense and scientific knowledge. Bears particularly on Chapters 1, 4, and 8–10.

Quinton, Anthony, *The Nature of Things*, London, 1973.
    A survey of problems in metaphysics and epistemology, with much discussion of the foundationalism–coherentism controversy. Especially relevant to Chapters 1, 7, and 8.

Reid, Thomas, *Essays on the Intellectual Powers of Man*, London, 1869 (originally published in 1785).
    An important critique of other modern philosophers, rationalist and empiricist, and an original development of a commonsense epistemology. Especially relevant to Chapters 1–4, 7, 8, and 10.

Rescher, Nicholas, *Skepticism*, Oxford, 1980.
    A detailed critical survey of many of the arguments for skepticism. Especially relevant to Chapters 8 and 10.

Robinson, Howard, *Perception*, London and New York, 1994.
    A historically detailed defense of the sense-datum theory in the philosophy of perception. Bears on Chapters 1–3.

Rorty, Richard, *Philosophy and the Mirror of Nature*, Princeton, NJ, 1979.
    A widely discussed critique of the foundationalist tradition in epistemology (and indeed of aspects of epistemology itself), with special attention to strong foundationalism as deriving from Descartes. Pertinent especially to Chapters 1, 7, and 10.

Russell, Bertrand, *An Inquiry into Meaning and Truth*, London, 1940.
    An articulation of an overall epistemological position by one of the twentieth century's major epistemologists. Especially relevant to Chapters 1 and 7–9.

Russell, Bertrand, *The Problems of Philosophy*, London, 1912.
    An introductory and highly readable survey of epistemology and metaphysics. Particularly pertinent to Chapters 1, 3, 4, and 8–10.

Sellars, Wilfrid, *Science, Perception, and Reality*, London, 1963.
    A collection of advanced epistemological papers by a major contemporary philosopher. Especially pertinent to Chapters 1, 3, 4, and 7–9.

Shope, Robert, *The Analysis of Knowing*, Princeton, NJ, 1983.
> A highly detailed study of major kinds of analysis of knowledge. Especially relevant to Chapter 8.

Sosa, Ernest, *Knowledge in Perspective*, Cambridge and New York, 1991.
> A wide-ranging collection of papers intensively exploring most of the topics treated in Chapters 1, 4, and 7–10.

Steup, Matthias, *An Introduction to Contemporary Epistemology*, Englewood Cliffs, NJ, 1966.
> A comprehensive and systematic introduction to epistemology, with close attention both to theoretical and conceptual issues and to major statements in the literature. Pertinent to every chapter, but above all to Chapters 1, 4, 6–8, and 10.

Stroud, Barry, *The Significance of Philosophical Scepticism*, Oxford, 1984.
> An intensive study of skepticism, particularly as set out by Descartes. Particularly relevant to Chapters 1, 8, and 10.

Swain, Marshall, *Reasons and Knowledge*, Ithaca, NY, 1981.
> A rigorous statement of an account of knowledge that unites justificationist and reliabilist elements. Especially relevant to Chapters 1, 6, and 8.

Will, Frederick L., *Induction and Justification*, Ithaca, NY, 1974.
> A critical study of a foundationalist approach to justification, with much attention to the problem of induction. Especially relevant to Chapters 7–10.

Williams, Michael, *Unnatural Doubts*, Oxford, 1991.
> A detailed diagnostic account of skepticism and some major issues concerning the possibility of foundations of knowledge. Pertinent especially to Chapters 1, 7, 8, and 10.

Wittgenstein, Ludwig, *On Certainty*, trans. by Dennis Paul and G. E. M. Anscombe, Oxford, 1969.
> An important discussion of the topic by one of the major twentieth-century philosophers. Especially relevant to Chapters 8 and 10.

Wittgenstein, Ludwig, *Philosophical Investigations*, trans. by G. E. M. Anscombe, Oxford, 1953.
> Wittgenstein's most wide-ranging work, spanning topics in epistemology, metaphysics, and other philosophical areas. Its remarks and examples bear on every chapter.

Zagzebski, Linda, *Virtues of the Mind*, Cambridge and New York, 1996.
> A new statement of virtue epistemology distinctive for its background account of virtue ethics as the counterpart on which virtue epistemology should be based. Pertinent above all to Chapter 8.

Index

Page numbers in **bold** show where a term is defined